T0342106

HARVARD HISTORICAL STUDIES ◆ 192

Published under the auspices of the Department of History
from the income of the

Paul Revere Frothingham Bequest

Robert Louis Stroock Fund

Henry Warren Torrey Fund

The World That Latin America Created

The United Nations Economic Commission
for Latin America in the Development Era

MARGARITA FAJARDO

HARVARD UNIVERSITY PRESS
Cambridge, Massachusetts
London, England
2022

First printing

Cataloging-in-Publication Data is available from the Library of Congress

ISBN: 978-0-674-26049-8 (alk. paper)

Por mis papás, Edgar y Aura Cecilia

To my husband, Ollie

Contents

The World That Latin America Created

Introduction

In early 1964 Raúl Prebisch left Chile to tour the world and export the revolution he had fueled in Latin America. Traveling from Niamey to Tehran, Prebisch hoped to rally the forces of what almost two decades earlier he had termed the world's "periphery" to fundamentally transform the global system of trade and finance. As Prebisch spread the gospel of the unequal exchange between the world's industrial *centers* and the raw material-producing *peripheries,* his old companions in Santiago and a few newcomers who had joined the fold were tearing these ideas apart in an effort to breathe new life into what seemed a depleted theoretical framework. Frustrated with its results, they questioned the core assumptions behind the development project that together they had launched and that put their institution, the United Nations Economic Commission for Latin America (CEPAL for its acronym in Spanish and Portuguese), on the regional and global map.[1] Even as Prebisch was gaining international traction, his ideas clashed with the revolutionary ferment in the region. Those ideas were increasingly intellectually challenged and politically discredited for hindering more than fostering the region's desired autonomy from global economic forces. In this moment of political upheaval and intellectual turmoil, "dependency theory," a new paradigm, was born.

From center-periphery to dependency ideas, *The World That Latin America Created* recovers a vision and project for the transformation of Latin America and the world economy that both inspired and repelled *dependentistas* and that eventually transformed how statesmen, activists, and experts understood the global economic order.[2] Primarily working under the aegis of CEPAL, these Latin American economists—even more so than their more famous US counterparts—made the global institution their own and economic development a worldmaking project in the post–World War II era.[3] In words and concepts that echoed old categories of imperialist theories but departed dramatically from them, these economists, known as *cepalinos*, squared the problem of economic development with that of international trade. Using the global concept of center and periphery, they argued that the existing pattern of production and trade placed Latin America and the world's periphery at an extreme disadvantage. Given that the prices of primary products, mostly produced by the periphery, relative to those of manufactured goods, produced at the center, fell over the long term and were also much more volatile in the short term, the trade pattern hindered national accumulation and widened the global gap between the center and periphery. To transform this pattern and make the global economy work for the periphery, *cepalinos* spearheaded an internationalist development agenda that gave them regional and global influence even as they insisted on the importance of national industrialization and the expansion of domestic markets as the path to autonomy. Pushing for more, not less, international trade; more, not less, foreign aid; and more regionalism and less nationalism, *cepalinos* sought to transform Latin America, and through it, the global economy.

In an era of competing global projects, especially those forcefully emanating from the North, *cepalinos* held regional and global sway. Bearers of a momentous transformation of their own, *cepalinos* made their ideas the main economic paradigm in the region, in fact exercising their own form of hegemony. By recruiting local allies, making partnerships with key governments, training bureaucrats, spearheading cooperation policies, and themselves occupying positions of power, *cepalinos* gained a prominent space in the region. In the global battle of economic ideas unfolding in Latin America, *cepalinos* were not the underdogs, trying to defend a narrowing territory. More than a reaction or a refraction of the theories emanating from the North, Latin American economists imagined and created an intellectual world for Latin America. Furthermore, as *cepalinos* set the terms of the debate in the region, it was the Northern agencies and institutions, with their competing economic agendas, that tried to catch up with *cepalinos* and unseat them from their privileged position. When the position of *cepalinos* was threatened in Latin America, their ideas found new homes in the international arena. On the one hand, they provided the rationale for the demand for a new international economic order based on more equitable integration of the countries of the Third World into the global economy. On the other hand, recast by the *dependentistas,* who stormed the global social sciences, they paved the road for other theories of world systems.

Like the *cepalinos'* own project, this book is centered on Latin America, more specifically on Chile and Brazil. Like their work, this book has a global scope and significance beyond recovering an intellectual counterpoint to modernization theory from the global South.[4] It demonstrates the influence of *cepalinos* and *dependentistas* in the global development field and the global social sciences, respectively. The book also traces the emergence and transformation of a regionally grounded global vision that became the dominant explanatory framework for economic development and stability despite the existence of more powerful economic agendas that continued to emanate from the North. Through the story of *cepalinos* and *dependentistas,* this book stands not only as a contribution to writing more inclusive or "wider and deeper" global histories but also as a challenge to narratives of the universal triumph of the global North's economic ideas and institution.[5] Simultaneously, it explains how theories, conceptualized from particular local vantage points and drawing from global networks, become "Latin American." The book journeys the worlds that *cepalinos* and *dependentistas* created.

In an effort to make the world anew after the end of the Second World War, multiple projects with global aspirations emerged. Anticolonial movements crafted paths to self-determination and transformed the arena of world politics. In Western Europe, as countries struggled with devastation and reconstruction, integrationists brought together old rivals and paved the road for unprecedented political experiments of supranational sovereignty. In mainland China, old nationalists were defeated and new Marxists spearheaded a peasant-led revolution that transformed the global prospects of Communist revolution. And as the United States and the Soviet Union emerged victorious from the war, these global superpowers also sought to remake the world in their image.

In remaking the global economic order after the war, Latin Americans clung to internationalism.[6] In the early twentieth century, Latin Americans saw in the League of Nations an opportunity to strengthen their position in the international arena. Even if European affairs dominated the agenda and Latin America's role was eventually marginal in the League of Nations, Latin American jurists were influential in devising mechanisms of international governance in other contexts such as the Pan-American organization, itself conceived since the nineteenth century as a counterpoint to European influence in the Americas.[7] In midcentury, as Latin American lawyers fostered new discourses about human rights in the United Nations, regional economists began to take a much more decisive role. Their ideas shaped the early United States's wartime plans for the post-1945 economic order, and they were active participants in the Bretton Woods conference that led to establishment of the International Monetary Fund (IMF) and the International Bank for Reconstruction and Development (IBRD), also known as the World Bank.[8] At Bretton Woods and in the Havana conference for the aborted International Trade Organization, both of which were under the command of old and new global powers, Latin American economists insisted on the limits that the international system of trade imposed on development. They championed and obtained special provisions for developing countries and the cooperation of the developed world.[9] Even if old and new global powers held the upper hand, Latin Americans capitalized on these international organizations to upend existing power structures, resulting in the creation of CEPAL, a new institution whose very existence symbolized this vision[10] (figures I.1–I.3).

Established in 1948 in Santiago, Chile, the UN CEPAL became the dominant economic institution of the region's postwar era. In the hands of a group of mostly Argentinean, Brazilian, and Chilean economists, CEPAL swiftly became the institutional fulcrum for an intellectual project that delved into the problem of development and capitalism in and from the margins of the global economy. A foundational tenet of their project was that Latin America's place in the *periphery* of the global economy as producer of primary products and raw materials in exchange for manufactured goods from the world's industrial *centers* constituted an obstacle for economic development. Through regional economic surveys and in-depth country studies, international forums and training courses, international cooperation initiatives and national advisory missions, *cepalinos* made the worldmaking notion of center and periphery the central economic paradigm in Latin America.[11] Founded upon this global vision, *cepalinos* formulated a development agenda to transform Latin America, and through it, the global economy. Since their project emerged from the global South and expanded to the rest of the world, *cepalinos* effectively inverted the traditional directionality of worldmaking.

The economists brought together at CEPAL under the leadership of Argentine economist Raúl Prebisch became an influential cohort. Coming from across the region, these economists had taken on a distinct identity as *cepalinos* within a few years. At their helm was Prebisch, a university professor, Director of the Central Bank of Argentina during the Great Depression, and a banking advisor for regional governments.[12] His seniority and experience, combined with the prospects of UN-backed internationalism,

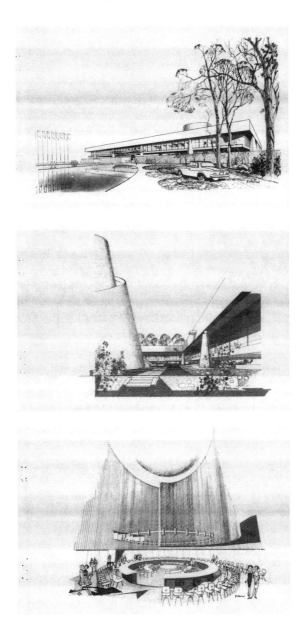

FIGURES I.I–I.3   Three sketches of the United Nations building in Santiago de Chile. Designed by a team of local architects led by Emilio Duharte and completed in 1966, the building is an example of Latin American modernist architecture and has been the headquarters of CEPAL since then. The first sketch shows the front of the building; the other two show exterior and interior views of the assembly hall known as the "snail." The assembly hall echoes and dialogues with the Andes mountains behind the building that dominate the Santiago landscape. (© United Nations. All rights reserved.)

attracted a group of economists whose careers had barely started. Given the incipient stages of economics as an academic discipline in Latin America, most of the members of this first group of *cepalinos* were initially trained as lawyers or engineers; some had graduate education in economics abroad. Brazilian economist Celso Furtado, who arrived at the institution even before Prebisch and was an enormously influential figure among *cepalinos,* studied at the University of Paris. Others, like Cuban Regino Boti and Chilean Jorge Ahumada, graduated from Harvard; many others, including Venezuelan José Antonio Mayobre, Mexican Víctor Urquidi, and Chileans Aníbal Pinto and Osvaldo Sunkel, attended the London School of Economics (LSE). While Ahumada and Noyola got their start at the IMF and Urquidi at the World Bank, many others began their careers at CEPAL. Decades later, Pinto summarized what was perhaps the experience of many of these *cepalinos:* "I considered myself a Marxist and a Keynesian but then I became a *cepalino.*"[13]

Although the term evoked Marxism and early theories of imperialism, the concept of center and periphery was a product of *cepalinos* and the development worldmaking project of the postwar era. In the early twentieth century, some intellectuals familiar with Marxism and other Marxist-influenced intellectuals in the European "periphery" began to transfer the concept of "exploited classes" into "exploited peoples" and to develop ideas of nations that were "peripheral" to capitalist centers.[14] Meanwhile, Marxist intellectuals in Latin America were more interested in the feudal trappings of the region's agriculture and economic structures than in the relations between the region and the world. It was in the wartime context that Prebisch, a central banker and public servant heavily influenced by Keynes, began to use the terms "center" and "periphery" to describe the inequality embedded in the gold standard system of trade and finance. Born to describe the inflows and outflows of gold between Great Britain at the center and Argentina in the periphery, the meaning of the terms center and periphery broadened in the following years to encompass the United States, the new economic center, and the international division of labor between global industrial centers and primary-producing peripheries. In the process, the concept became the cornerstone of the *cepalino* project. Eventually, with *dependentistas,* the definition of the notion of center and periphery expanded and came to represent the world economic system as a whole and at times was cast in Marxist terms of exploitation, subimperialism, and socialism. Nonetheless, since its earliest iterations in the pen of Prebisch, the term "center-periphery" implied a novel idea in the conceptualization of global capitalism. Although Lenin had prefigured similar ideas from the point of view of the capitalist center, the *cepalino* center-periphery foregrounded the existence of a single unified economic system that was "hegemonically organized" seen from the point of view of the periphery.[15] By doing so, the *cepalino* project broke from the linear notion of "progress" and "backwardness" that prevailed in comparisons of the "wealth of nations" in both Marxist and non-Marxist, North and South traditions. The notion, if not necessarily the term, would become crucial for the field of international development.

Throughout the postwar era, *cepalinos* created a world for Latin America centered on trade and development. Like most development experts North and South, East and West, *cepalinos* championed industrialization as the means to development. They provided a new rationale for an ongoing process that went beyond infant-industry arguments of "late" industrializers like Germany or Japan or even the "late, late industrializers" of the postcolonial world.[16] The new rationale stemmed from a particular interpretation of Latin America's past that continues to shape the main historical narratives about the region.[17] From coffee in Brazil to guano in Peru, from nitrates and copper in Chile to beef and wheat in Argentina, Latin American countries found in the specialization of the production of commodities for the global economy the solution to the economic turmoil and social disarray left by fall of empires, the age of revolutions, and the civil wars that ensued, both of which had disrupted colonial regional economies and imperial global trade.

Yet, in the early twentieth century and especially after the Great Depression, this privileging of global markets and export-orientation gave pause to many Latin Americans, including *cepalinos*. As a result of that orientation, peasants had been pushed off the land and a handful of families amassed land and power, key natural resources were concentrated in foreign hands, and national governments were increasingly dependent on the good graces of local elites, foreign companies, and the tax revenues produced by those exports, themselves vulnerable to global economic downturns. The collapse of global markets with the Great Depression and the imperative of domestically producing previously imported goods accelerated the process of industrialization that had begun in some cases as early as the late nineteenth century and became known as import-substitution industrialization (ISI).[18] For *cepalinos*, the promotion and growth of new industries promised a transformation of both national and global power structures that required turning what had been a series of ad-hoc, Depression-era emergency measures into a rational and organized process of state planning and economic expertise for industrialization and development as well as new terms of integration to global markets.

With the acceleration of industrialization during the war, the greatest policy challenge for *cepalinos* was how to help Latin America continue that process in a new postwar world. Protected by tariffs and closed markets

FIGURE I.4   The image depicts Joseph Stalin and Uncle Sam seated at the dinner table. They are offering meat to the plump Daxon dog labeled "Germany." Next to "Germany" is the emaciated little dog, "Latin America," who says, "It's a dog's life!: the best morsels are for this animal, who almost ate them both, and I who helped them, get nothing!" (*Revista Topaze*, November 25, 1949. Colección Biblioteca Nacional de Chile, available in Memoria Chilena.)

during the Depression and fueled by US wartime credits, many industries had flourished and vested interests had been created. As the United States turned to the reconstruction of Western Europe and Asia, including its former foes, in an effort to contain Soviet-led industrial socialism, the prospect of more credits for its Latin American allies waned (see figure I.4).

Since the export of commodities had taken a big hit during the Depression and the long-term prospects were dire, Latin Americans feared that export proceeds would not be enough to pay for the import of capital goods, machinery, and spare parts. Based on the notion of unequal exchange between center and peripheries, *cepalinos* became champions of industrialization and development planning in the postwar era. Thus "industrialization was fact before it was policy and policy before it was theory" in the hands of *cepalinos,* as historian Joseph Love succinctly captured.[19] Yet the *cepalino* project began but did not end with the promotion of industrialization.[20]

The world *cepalinos* created was based on the economic cooperation between centers and peripheries. Formulated gradually in the 1950s, their development agenda included trade, aid, and market integration. Even though international trade had been detrimental for the global periphery, *cepalinos* believed it did not need to be and, in fact, it was necessary to obtain the exchange resources to buy the capital and machinery necessary for industrialization. More than severing the ties with the global economy, *cepalinos* advocated for better terms of integration that included the commitment of the global center to open its markets for the periphery and stabilize the prices of those goods through commodity price agreements. Especially sensitive to the foreign exchange limitations and import-substitution needs dictated by the falling terms of trade for the periphery, *cepalinos* developed concepts and measures to capture the periphery's development paradox: the need for more trade and aid to withstand the long-term dependence on trade and aid. Since this problem was not unique to Latin America, it became the foundation not only of the *cepalino* development agenda but also of the international cooperation initiatives of the so-called Third World that had so far lacked a coherent plan for economic reform.[21] As such, they became part of the global repertoire of state-builders and policymakers at the United Nations Conference for Trade and Development (UNCTAD) and other forums where leaders from the global South demanded a new international economic order.

Though controversial for both donors and recipients, international aid was fundamental in the development agenda of *cepalinos.* With the bulk of an already constrained pool of resources directed toward Europe and Asia in the early cold war years, Latin Americans took it upon themselves to demand more than technical assistance to compensate for the loss of markets and export gains.[22] In the early 1950s *cepalinos* imagined foreign aid as something far removed from the tool of impoverishment and oppression of the periphery that critics proclaimed it to be.[23] To them aid could be the mechanism to offset the trade and financial imbalance in international trade between centers and peripheries. Unlike Great Britain, the old global center, the United States, the new one, had a continental-wide market that made it inward-looking and hindered the circulation of currency via trade. Thus, for Prebisch, development aid was a mechanism to promote the global circulation of dollars by the new hegemonic power. For *cepalinos*, aid and multilateral loans were also the mechanism to avoid financial dilemmas between economic development and monetary stability. The trade off between development and stability that *cepalinos* helped conceptualize raised their influence. It led to bitter policy disputes whose consequences in terms of inflation and debt accompanied the fall of many reformist governments and the rise of radically different alternatives. Staunch defenders of large-scale financial initiatives and foreign aid such as the "Not-a Marshall Plan for Latin America" proposal, *cepalinos* found themselves divided when push came to shove. The failure of the foreign-aid program known as the Alliance for Progress raised their influence and left them compromised and assessing the cost of aid.[24]

The third pillar of the world of *cepalinos* was regionalism. While recently decolonized countries in Asia and Africa turned to each other to escape the imperative of alignment to global superpowers, Latin Americans turned to Europe for new experiments in internationalism. While European integration promised to resolve deep-seated rivalries through interdependence, Latin American economic integration promised to surpass the limits to growth created by isolated and small national markets and redirect the region's export orientation toward itself. While Asian and African countries as well as Europeans distanced themselves from the United Nations and created parallel organizations in their pursuit of political or economic cooperation, Latin Americans cemented the commitment to the global body. Like the European experiment, the Latin American program of regional integration hinged on the cooperation of the economic center. Spearheading the creation of the Central American and the Latin American common market, *cepalinos* cemented their influence in the region while discovering that many of the tensions and limits toward cooperation that surfaced at the global level were reproduced within Latin America.

Their global vision and internationalist agenda catapulted the influence of *cepalinos* in Latin America. As they formulated planning techniques in partnership with national governments and spearheaded such ambitious development strategies as the regional common market, *cepalinos* located themselves at the forefront of Latin America's development agenda. Through the exchanges with government bureaucrats in the course of making regional surveys and country studies, the establishment of CEPAL offices first in Mexico and later in Rio de Janeiro, and the training courses in Santiago as well as in other capital cities, *cepalinos* established a physical presence in a vast continent. *Cepalinos* and their allies additionally served on the editorial boards of the leading professional economic journals, such as *El Trimestre Económico* and *Desarrollo Económico,* providing them a venue through which to disseminate their ideas and positioning them at the center of a network of expertise. In Chile and Brazil, *cepalinos* themselves were notorious public intellectuals, writing political manifestos for the non-Marxist left and making frequent appearances in both mainstream and more specialized press. While *cepalinos* themselves occupied high-level government positions in Cuba, Venezuela, Brazil, and Chile, among others, they cultivated political allies who in the 1960s and early 1970s became presidents of their respective countries. As a result, the *cepalino* framework of center and periphery and the development paradox became common parlance for economists, political leaders, and diplomats. From Colombian Minister and President Carlos Lleras Restrepo to the Chilean statesman Salvador Allende, regional leaders and lower-ranking officials relied on *cepalino* reports and concepts and used CEPAL forums to position their own agendas. In effect, *cepalinos* created an autonomous and regionally driven conversation about development and global capitalism in Latin America founded upon the vocabulary of center and periphery and the attempt to overcome the development paradox.

This book tells the story of *cepalinos'* rise to hegemony in Latin America, often obscured by the overbearing focus on and presence of Northern institutions in the region. The World Bank and the IMF turned their gaze to the world's periphery after the Marshall Plan undermined their efforts in Europe in the early Cold War years. These Northern institutions were and are considered proxies of the United States, a superpower waging an ideological cold war or extensions of imperial power of old. Yet, despite the financial clout and the power of the major shareholders of their institution, the staff at the IMF, initially committed to the success of CEPAL, found themselves outcompeted by *cepalinos*.[25] As the relations between the IMF and Latin America became more contested and controversial, the IMF, not *cepalinos*, were often behind the curve of economic policy initiatives and playing catch up to the new ideas about inflation that emerged within the *cepalino* milieu. The turf wars that unfolded between CEPAL and the IMF and the debate over what would eventually be called the IMF's "monetarism" engaged world-class North American and European economists in a debate over Latin American ideas, forcing IMF officials to recognize they had lost the battle over influence in Latin America. In fact, the IMF's "monetarism," one of the central concepts that symbolize late twentieth-century capitalism and neoliberalism, emerged *avant la lettre,* before Milton Friedman and his allies burst onto the scene. Far from an innate outgrowth of (neo)liberal orthodoxy emanating from the North, the term "monetarism" arose as response to *cepalino* and Latin American "structuralism." Like the IMF, philanthropic organizations such as the Rockefeller and Ford Foundations, credited for disseminating a US-centered vision of development and economic expertise, were on the defensive, not the offensive, when it came to Latin America and the realm of economic expertise.[26] Sponsored by the Ford Foundation, the infamous Chicago Boys, who dominate our narrative of the battle of economic ideas in Latin America, struggled to unseat *cepalinos* on their home turf and were only successful after a sweeping realignment of political forces in Chile and the use of coercion and violence. Neither of these economic agendas emanating from the North defined the arena of economic expertise in Latin America.

This book is not a story about how the developed world imposed its global vision and projects on peripheral areas of the world. Paradoxically, these studies are more informative about the assumptions and interests of the developed rather than the developing world.[27] Instead of focusing on the failures of the global North's development agenda and the unrivaled power of the underlying ideas, this book centers on the victories of Latin American economists to formulate a policy agenda that gained them influence in the region and the world by situating the discussion of development in the world system of trade. Rather than from Washington, London, or Moscow, *The World That Latin America Created* looks at the construction of a worldview of development from the intersection of Santiago and Rio de Janeiro, Mexico and Havana.

Development initiatives were numerous and diverse, but *cepalinos* brought a unique and powerful perspective. Whereas the global superpower struggle organized the world between East and West camps or First, Second, and Third Worlds, *cepalinos* produced and later *dependentistas* adopted a vocabulary of center and peripheries. Those categories also bespoke of a world order that was different from that of empires and colonies of the old theories of imperialism, on the one hand, and from the progress and backwardness axis or modernity and tradition dyad of contemporary theories of social change, on the other hand. Instead, the vocabulary of *cepalinos* aimed at describing and transforming a world system and the function and position of Latin America and the periphery within it. While some development experts focused on massive projects like dams, irrigation systems to increase agricultural yield, or new seed varieties that could result in high-yield crops to feed hungry populations, *cepalinos* envisioned an overhaul of the global economy. While others considered community building and literacy programs, *cepalinos* dreamed, for better or worse, of transforming the global economy through large-scale multilateral aid, regional integration, and better terms of international trade.[28] Through their global vision, *cepalinos* created a Latin American–centered conversation about development.

Paradoxically, *cepalinos* and their ideas increasingly lost influence just at the moment that Latin America reached the peak of its global influence in the international development agenda. By the early 1960s, when Third Worldism picked up pace globally and the prospects of US cooperation increased in Latin America, a new intellectual vanguard saw the work of the *cepalinos* as the orthodoxy of development. With overlapping but often conflicting ideas grouped under the term "dependency theory," a new generation of Latin American intellectuals, or *dependentistas*, contested the premises and promises of the *cepalino* development project while capitalizing on some of its most important intuitions. *Dependentistas* rejected the idea that the gap between the developed and the underdeveloped worlds could be closed by a combination of national industrialization and international economic cooperation. Instead, based on the Latin American experience, perhaps the longest of the postcolonial world, *dependentistas* insisted that such enterprise resulted in economic dependence between the world's industrial centers and the underdeveloped periphery. Politically influential, *dependentistas* mobilized their ideas in a wide variety of projects that attracted the world's attention: from Cuban revolutionary Third Worldism to the Chilean democratic transition to socialism. The arrival of dependency theory unified many *cepalinos,* now retrained as *dependentistas,* while creating a new rupture between those who claimed that "development led to underdevelopment" such as German-born but American trained economist Andre Gunder Frank and those who affirmed the coexistence of "dependency and development," such as Brazilian sociologist Fernando Henrique Cardoso and Chilean sociologist Enzo Faletto.

Soon enough, the *dependentistas,* too, encountered a political backlash. The subsequent waves of exile and worldwide solidarity movements catapulted *dependentistas* further onto the world stage, even as the space for their political and intellectual endeavors narrowed in Latin America. As their work became foundational for Latin American studies in the global North and highly influential in the English-speaking global social sciences, *dependentistas* established intellectual bridges between Europe and Africa and North America and paved the way for new transnational intellectual projects, such as world-system theory. As dependency theory stormed and reformed the global social sciences, the worldview it represented came to encompass the project of both *cepalinos* and *dependentistas.*[29] Politically positioning *cepalinos* and *dependentistas* in local power struggles, this book traces the origins and consolidation of a "Latin American dependency theory" that existed only in contrast to an also stylized "modernization theory" of the global North.

The World That Latin America Created centers on Chile and Brazil. As Brazilian and *cepalino* economist Celso Furtado explained, *cepalino* ideas attracted the most attention in Chile and Brazil; it was perhaps also where they generated the most opposition.[30] It was from these two countries, two of the most "developed" countries in the region, that *cepalinos* observed the region and the world. While Chile, flanked by the Pacific Ocean on the West and the Andes mountain range on the East, was an agriculturally oriented frontier of the Spanish empire, Brazil, clenching the Atlantic coast yet a continental giant, was the jewel of the Portuguese crown. Profoundly shaped by the persistence of slavery and monarchy until the end of the nineteenth century, the empire of Brazil contrasted with the Chilean republic that despite civil wars at the onset and dawn of the century emerged as a model of political stability and formal democracy in the region. By the early twentieth century, Chile and Brazil reorganized their national economies around foreign-owned, mining enclaves and nationally owned coffee plantations, respectively. Whereas mining camps led to increasing labor mobilization and the opening for nonelite political participation very early on in Chile, Brazil remained politically organized under vertical structures of patronage.[31] After the Great Depression, when the global markets crashed, deeply affecting the world-oriented economies of Chile and Brazil, significant economic and political transformations occurred. Like in other parts of the world, the Chilean and Brazilian states mobilized their resources to foster economic recovery, part of which entailed the promotion of industrialization and the inauguration or deepening of welfare and labor policies. In the interwar years Brazil saw the rise of an authoritarian, corporatist, and by the end, a populist regime whose legacy organized and divided political life in the postwar era. Meanwhile, a popular front coalition emerged in Chile whose end gave rise to a fierce competition between ideologically oriented parties along the whole political spectrum, mobilizing wide sectors of society in the following two decades. Whereas Brazil aspired to bring about "50 years of progress in 5" and colonize the interior with the futuristic new capital of Brasilia, Chileans engaged in fierce political debates over land redistribution and nationalization of the copper mining industry.[32] The inflationary and financial pressures as well as the deepening political polarization that shook these postwar democracies led to a developmentalist military regime in Brazil in the mid-1960s and a neoliberal one in Chile a decade later.

As *cepalinos* observed and traveled between these two landscapes, Chile and Brazil shaped the *cepalino* intellectual world.[33] While Prebisch's experience made the Argentine case foundational, this book contends that the experience of Chile and Brazil shaped the transformation and evolution of their ideas. It was Chile that spearheaded the establishment of the institution, but it was Brazil that provided the stepping-stone in the *cepalinos'* pursuit of policy influence in the region. While Chileans were fixated on the problem of stagnation, Brazilians were driven by the challenges of accelerated development. The contrast of these two images and the journey of the *cepalino* ideas about inflation from Chile to Brazil transformed a lukewarm synthesis into a radical perspective that positioned CEPAL as "the International Monetary Fund of the left."[34] The widespread political spectrum in Chile contrasted with the overbearing presence of populism in Brazil, giving rise to different and decisive political conundrums that reoriented *cepalino* positions and transformed their ideas. It was the migration of dependency ideas from Brazil to Chile, at a moment in which the military forces ousted the president in the former and the forces of the left envisioned a transition to socialism in the latter, that turned "dependency theory" into a radical political movement in Latin America and the world. Given *cepalinos'* critiques of generalizing from the experience of developed countries to the rest of the world, it is ironic that their economic-based notion of Latin America was itself the product of a generalization about the experience of Argentina and two of the most developed countries in the region—Chile and Brazil—to the rest.[35]

Despite the importance of Chile and Brazil to this story, *cepalinos* made claims about the region as a whole. Even though *cepalinos* were part of the global UN network and drew inspiration from many of these resources, they set themselves against the "money doctors" and foreign experts whose ideas, disconnected from regional realities, had hindered more than helped the region's economic development. Against the universalizing pretensions of the foreign experts, *cepalinos* insisted in their ability to speak for and from Latin America.[36] They strove to produce local, or rather regional, social scientific expertise and garnered support for the institution as a regional, homegrown product and by so doing, created different and equally contested claims to knowledge.[37] Their influence over policymaking varied by country and over time.[38] Yet they reclaimed the category of Latin America as a region at moment in which the division of the world into regions was an exercise of geopolitical and intellectual domination. This phenomenon was especially visible in the rise of area studies in the United States and Europe and what has been called the "internationalization" or the "Americanization" of the global social sciences, especially in economics.[39]

Yet, defining Latin America as a region created important constraints for *cepalinos* and their ideas, given the enormous differences in levels of development across the countries involved and the singularity of the proposed strategy.

This book portrays the political world *cepalinos* inhabited and the intellectual world that *cepalinos* created. Given his seminal contribution, decades-long leadership of the institution, charismatic personality, and seniority, the influence of Prebisch is undeniable. Yet *cepalinos* were never a unified group. Many crucial intellectual transformations in their collective project occurred despite rather than because of Prebisch. Representing neither the archetype of the militant intellectual nor of the cosmopolitan technocrat, *cepalinos* found a space in a rapidly changing political landscape.[40] They found different routes and political projects to carry their ideas forward. Beyond their institutional membership, *cepalinos* inaugurated or collaborated with wildly different and deeply opposed governments and parties. From the military junta that deposed Juan Domingo Perón in Argentina to the regime of Fidel Castro in Cuba, *cepalinos* occupied advisory or ministerial positions at the heart of government. Some disdained populism and feared the consequences of veering too far from long-term planning for the short-termism of politics. While some feared demagogues, others abhorred conservatives and their defense of privilege at the cost of the impoverishment of the masses. While some *cepalinos* remained convinced of the promise of cooperation between centers and peripheries, others embraced anti-imperialist and revolutionary projects. Their different political alignments and their interventions in different national policy debates created divisions within the group that moved the collective intellectual project forward until the tensions reached a turning point in the early 1960s and both *cepalinos* and *dependentistas* imagined a different paradigm.

The World That Latin America Created, like the enterprise of its actors, is transnational and comparative, crossing the implicit boundaries between Portuguese- and Spanish-speaking Americas. Since CEPAL became an important forum for regional intellectual change, most of the participants cited their experience with the institution as the moment that they "discovered Latin America."[41] The book follows *cepalinos* as they observe Latin America from the vantage point of Chile and Brazil and as they construct a system of both local alliances and vocal opponents, locating themselves at the center of a wide network of expertise. It was against *cepalinos* that both *dependentistas* and the radical left, on the one hand, and the Chicago Boys and the new liberal economists, on the other, set their projects. Drawing on a multiplicity of private and public, personal and institutional archives across Latin America, Europe, and the United States, the book re-covers the story of *cepalinos* themselves, and not just their ideas, from the outside in.[42] It uncovers the fertile yet fracturing tensions between them as well as the impact of their individual policy interventions on the ideas of the *cepalino* collective. A story of victories and defeats, the book follows *cepalinos* in their pursuit of influence over Latin America and the world.

Chapter 1 examines the origins of CEPAL and its place in the global insti-tutional landscape as well as the birth of the *cepalino* worldmaking project, whose foundation was the notion of center and periphery. Chapter 2 ex-plores the *cepalino* effort to move from theory to practice and, through trade, aid, and integration, resolve Latin America's development paradox. The middle two chapters of the book overlap chronologically, attesting to both the expanding scope of the development project and the accelerating pace of expectations for change at the end of the 1950s. Those chapters also show the different axes along which the *cepalino* and the regional con-sensus about development began to fracture. Chapter 3 examines the ori-gins and impact of the *cepalino* or "structural approach to inflation" and the intertwined birth of two contending global projects: "structuralism" and "monetarism." Tracing the *cepalino* intervention in the Cuban revolu-tionary experiment, on the one hand, and the rise and fall of the Alliance for Progress, on the other, Chapter 4 shows a new but definitive fracture of the *cepalino* project that paved the way for "dependency theory." As the global enterprise of development picked up momentum in the 1960s, Latin America confronted a development impasse. *Cepalinos* and their ideas en-countered more challenges, especially from the intellectual left. Chapters 5 and 6 together show how the intellectual projects of nascent *dependentistas* in "pre-revolutionary" Brazil gave rise to "dependency theory" as their ideas circulated in Santiago and radiated from a Chile in transition to socialism. The epilogue shows the impact of "dependency theory" writ-large in the world and its paradoxical afterlife in Latin America, while summarizing some of the main arguments of the book and offering some concluding remarks.

Latin America and the Postwar Global Order

The world that Latin America and *cepalinos* created began to take shape as the Second World War came to an end. In Latin America and across the world, visions of a postwar global order multiplied. Some of those visions rekindled the language of self-determination and national sovereignty that arose as the First World War struck a blow to the world of empires. Others reimagined the meaning and scope of terms such as "class struggle" and "communism" outside the European context in which they emerged. Others reinvented notions of liberalism and democracy after what appeared to be the collapse of both principles in the interwar and war years. As many across the world mobilized old and new concepts to imagine a new global order after the war, Latin Americans coalesced around the notion of a world divided between "center and periphery" and a new geography of world economic power, as proposed by Argentine economist Raúl Prebisch and *cepalinos*.

The vocabulary of "center-periphery" to characterize the world economy found a home in a new global institution. As the war came to an end, international organizations designed to safeguard postwar peace and prosperity emerged as the cornerstone of a new world order. Backed by the war victors and raising the hopes of solidarity between old and new nations, the United Nations and parallel institutions such as the International Monetary Fund (IMF) and International Bank for Reconstruction and Development (IBRD), also known as the World Bank, became the space for voicing the myriad and often conflicting visions about the future of the world's political and economic order. Invested in the remaking of the world economy, Latin Americans strove to institutionalize their concerns in both the rising IMF and the aborted International Trade Organization (ITO) until they procured an institution of their own that put the problem of global trade front and center. Sidestepping Argentina, Brazil, and Mexico, the traditional contenders for regional leadership, Chile, in the hands of Hernán Santa Cruz (who would become a highly influential human rights diplomat in the following decades), spearheaded the creation of the UN Economic Commission for Latin America (CEPAL, acronym in Spanish and Portuguese). Headquartered in Santiago, Chile, CEPAL rapidly began to move the center of gravity for worldmaking projects from the North to the South within the emerging global institutional landscape.

The worldmaking project of *cepalinos* was forged as CEPAL, the Santiago-based global institution, and the idea of center and periphery coalesced. This chapter looks at the origins of that project: the diplomatic efforts, the intellectual exchanges, and the policymaking goals that during the end of the Second World War and in the early postwar years brought together the United Nations, Prebisch, and the center-periphery manifesto. CEPAL and *cepalinos* not only put international trade front and center after it had been postponed or watered down in previous forums of global economic debate. Competing with New York and Washington, CEPAL and *cepalinos* also seized the problem of the inequality in the gains from trade that multiple international organizations were grappling with and made it the foundation of an ambitious global institution situated in the world's periphery.

Latin American Postwar Planning

The global powers' commitment to reorganize the postwar world economic order was welcomed in Latin America.[1] The Anglo-American plans that resulted in the creation of the IMF and the IBRD at the Bretton Woods meeting in 1944 had a Latin American imprint: some crucial components of the American plan had grown from US-Latin American partnerships in the previous decade.[2] Inspired by Keynesian ideas, Latin American economists and both future *cepalino* allies and opponents saw the potential in what could be a global countercyclical policy embedded in the functions of the future IMF. Unlike the old order and its rigid golden rules that forced money out of embattled countries during economic depressions, the new monetary institution provided credit to offset short-term downturns that were common for those producers of coffee, sugar, and other commodities whose prices shifted widely in the global market. Prebisch considered the "organization of an international system of credit an excellent idea" and so did Brazilian economist Octávio Gouvêa de Bulhões and Mexican economist Víctor Urquidi.[3] Similarly, the World Bank's charter gave equal consideration to development and reconstruction, and thus it represented the fulfillment of long-held aspirations to diversify export-oriented economies through industrialization.[4] Because of, not despite, their concerns with the region's specialization in the production of primary products and raw materials, Latin American economists were invested in the Bretton Woods institutions and the new order.

However, drawing from the lessons in international economic cooperation of the 1930s, the US and UK postwar planners opted to focus the discussion on financial stability and economic reconstruction, leaving the question of trade for a future moment and another institution. Although seen as a crucial mechanism for growth, international trade was the most contentious area of postwar economic reconstruction, given the nationalist and protectionist trends of the interwar years and the fear of another depression.[5] Like their Northern counterparts, Latin Americans learned many lessons from the Depression years. Despite Latin America's comparatively fast and export-driven recovery from the Great Depression, regional economists from Mexico to Argentina were struck by the detrimental effects on growth and stability of the existing pattern of international trade.[6]

Invested as they were in their principles, Latin Americans had also insisted on what was purposefully absent from the Bretton Woods institutions. They urged global attention to the particular challenges of commodity exporters and the inequality in the prevailing pattern of international trade. As "producers of primary products and raw materials," Latin American countries were "subject to more cyclical and seasonal fluctuations" than the producers of manufactures, Bulhões, a consultant for the Brazilian delegation, explained.[7] Not only were Latin American economies more prone to the fluctuations of the global economy but their effects were "deeper" and of "different character" than those experienced by the large industrialized nations, Jorge Chávez, Peruvian delegate to the Bretton Woods conference, declared in an effort to put the inequality in the pattern of international trade front and center. What countries in Latin America "needed [were] markets on which they can count, capable of absorbing sufficient amounts at reasonable prices," Chávez explained, insisting on a discussion on a reorganization of trade patterns.[8] By focusing on the monetary system, the Bretton Woods plans had "begun with [the] end," Urquidi claimed, postponing the fundamental postwar problems connected to international trade and leaving wobbly what was initially conceived as a tripartite structure.[9]

Despite these reservations of Latin Americans, the debate about the economic order advanced swiftly at Bretton Woods under the assumption of an eventual forum on trade, and of a potential international trade organization that complemented the fund and the bank.

A latecomer in the postwar institutional building process, the ITO failed to materialize. At the 1947 Havana meeting where the ITO charter was to be finalized and signed, amendments and exceptions were presented to almost every single point of the draft, demanding more discretion, fewer rules, and more autonomy for each nation. The US government, the key market on whose reduction of trade barriers the rest of the world hinged, began to lose interest in the organization. Yet, as the ITO collapsed amid world dissent and American disinterest, the rounds of negotiations for the reduction of tariffs on products that amounted to half of the world's trade led to the establishment of the General Agreement on Tariffs and Trade (GATT). Although the impact of those agreements was meager given the modest reductions, they did establish a mechanism, a legal international agreement, for the liberalization of trade, which became the privileged platform for tariff reduction in the postwar era, displacing the unborn ITO.[10] The failure of the ITO deprived the world, especially Latin Americans, who then amounted to the majority of the developing world, of a forum to discuss the inequalities and restoration of imbalances in global trade. Within a few years, another international organization headquartered in Latin America filled that vacuum.

A Space for Latin America

One month after assuming the Chilean presidency in November 1946, Gabriel González Videla appointed Hernán Santa Cruz, a lawyer he met in Rio de Janeiro in 1944 and with whom he had established a loyal friendship, as Chile's permanent delegate to the United Nations.[11] While in Rio, González Videla had learned a valuable lesson from Getúlio Vargas, the Brazilian self-declared president. When González Videla asked for Vargas's rationale behind the construction of the steel mill amid growing opposition from the financiers or the "eternal grave-diggers of the country," Vargas's response was, "What would Brazil gain by importing cheaper steel if doesn't have the dollars to buy it?"[12] The scarcity of foreign exchange, in part caused by the long-term decline in, and the short-term instability of, the prices of primary products, was a prominent concern of prominent economists and future *cepalinos*, as well as regional statesmen. Like those at Bretton Woods, González Videla insisted on the need for international

FIGURE 1.1   At the house of Hernán Santa Cruz, Salvador Allende (*left*), Eduardo Frei (*right*), and Gabriel González Videla (*center background*), future presidents of Chile, gathered in 1944. With these rising Chileans and other politicians of Peru, Venezuela, and Cuba, Santa Cruz discussed the Latin American war dilemmas and the challenges of the postwar world that led to the establishment of CEPAL. (Archivo General Histórico del Ministerio de Relaciones Exteriores de Chile.)

agreements and economic coordination to guarantee the stability of prices of raw materials, the rationalization of production, and the establishment of the capital goods industry in the region at the 1945 San Francisco conference in which the United Nations was established.[13] By appointing Santa Cruz, González Videla prompted a move at the United Nations that would have enormous consequences for the region and the world.

Soon after he arrived in New York in the winter of 1947, Santa Cruz began to envision a path for Latin America in the emerging global system. A lawyer by training with experience in criminal and administrative law, Santa Cruz felt unfit for the job at the international organization. For Santa Cruz, who had worked primarily as a jurist in military courts and university lecturer but who belonged to the circles of rising political figures such as Salvador Allende and Eduardo Frei, the position at the United Nations transformed into a lifelong and fertile career in international diplomacy[14] (figure 1.1). Chile had been elected one of the rotating members of the UN Economic and Social Council (ECOSOC) the year before, and participation in the fourth session was Santa Cruz's first task. The physical devastation and economic dislocation caused by the war were the main subjects of discussion at the UN ECOSOC and the main reason behind the creation of two regional commissions, one for Europe and one for Asia. Although Latin America had been spared from physical devastation and military occupation, it had not been sheltered from economic dislocations, Santa Cruz believed. Furthermore, the standard of living of its population was probably below that of the people in the war-torn areas, he surmised. But the urgency of reconstruction and his own unfamiliarity with ECOSOC gave Santa Cruz pause.

The Foreign Ministry had offered Santa Cruz conflicting instructions about his mission in New York. According to the minister, small states should orient their interventions based on the notion that "cooperation between great powers" was the key to world peace. The instruction implied Santa Cruz should take a back seat and leave global matters to powerholders. But the government also asked Santa Cruz to "take a leadership position" in the pursuit of "union within the Americas" without disregarding proposals that would "transcend continental cooperation." More specifically, the minister also asked Santa Cruz to "oppose any expansion in the entities, commissions, or specialized agencies already established and that could result in a rise of the [Chilean] quota."[15] For a small and distant country like Chile, the United Nations represented an enormous opportunity for global intervention, on the one hand, and an excessive burden and a reaffirmation of global power structures, on the other, making Santiago ambivalent about the emerging international system.

Given the contradicting instructions, Santa Cruz formulated a plan of action for the next meeting of the Council. "After testing the waters," Santa Cruz wrote to Santiago six months later, "I believe it's now time to submit the proposal for the creation of an economic commission for Latin America." The terms of reference for the new commission, he explained, followed verbatim those of the commissions for Europe and Asia, but they made "explicit reference to the need to adopt measures for the industrialization and economic development in order to increase the world's use of Latin America's resources." The only problem with Santa Cruz's plan was that the deadline for submitting items for the agenda was too close for him to wait for instructions and confirmation from Santiago. He opted to fly solo. Santa Cruz made his case and justified his decision based on González Videla's "statements on his tour on the Atlantic." During his visit to Buenos Aires, González Videla had reiterated his commitment to "economic independence" and internationalism distancing himself from what he deemed the "ultranationalism" of Juan Domingo Perón, his Argentine counterpart. Therefore, Santa Cruz felt confident his proposal fell in line with the agenda

FIGURE 1.2   Photograph of Hernán Santa Cruz at the United Nations Economic and Social Council (ECOSOC) discussing the proposal for an economic commission for Latin America, 1947. (Archivo General Histórico del Ministerio de Relaciones Exteriores de Chile.)

of his government.[16] Anticipating support from Santiago and with positive gestures from the Peruvian delegate and the American press, Santa Cruz confidently awaited ECOSOC's fifth session.

At ECOSOC, Santa Cruz defended his initiative (figure 1.2). With the ITO pending approval, many of the expectations voiced by Latin Americans in the Bretton Woods postwar planning moment were translated to the new organization. Larger and more diversified markets, foreign long-term aid, commodity price agreements, and short-term credits for cyclical disruptions were some of the arrangements for regulating international trade still in the minds of Latin American representatives. These countries, Santa Cruz argued, echoing the discussions at Bretton Woods, were "largely dependent on exports of agricultural products and raw materials," which made them "highly sensible to cyclical fluctuations."[17] By restoring and reforming international trade, Latin America could push forward the industrialization project that reduced its vulnerability to global markets, raise the standard of living, and foment economic development. The commission was necessary, Santa Cruz added, to address the "region's principal need of economic development, including industrialization and diversification" to reduce the overpowering role of the external sector. With the economic commission, Latin America could shape and benefit from postwar internationalism.

The initiative was received with caution at ECOSOC. While Latin American delegates gave Santa Cruz's proposed commission ample support, others vacillated. The Cuban delegate reaffirmed Latin America's particular problems as "semi-colonial" economies, exporters of raw materials and primary products, while the Venezuelan delegate reminded the audience of the "concentration in the exploitation of a single resource" that prevented the development of many countries in the region, both of which would be in the purview of the suggested global institution. Given the need for "fair export prices" and "equitable participation in the benefits of foreign aid," Latin America's function in global capitalism justified the creation of a commission to "help in the revival and normalization of international trade."[18] But other members of the Council raised arguments against the proposal, both of which questioned the extent to which the United Nations could encompass the proposed commission. Although they sympathized with Latin American goals, the delegates of New Zealand and the Soviet Union claimed the situation in Latin America was not analogous to the postwar conditions in Europe and Asia. With the announcement of the European Recovery Program, also known as the Marshall Plan, looming large over these discussions, the delegates insisted that the very existence of regional commissions undermined the commitment to global approaches and stimulated the formation of regional blocs. Coinciding in very little else at the onset of the Cold War, the Chilean initiative had, nonetheless, brought both Soviet and American opposition. The United States representative argued that, given the existence of the Pan-American Union, Latin America already had an institution devoted to economic problems, raising the possibility of duplication of functions with the proposed commission. Given the concerns raised by the delegates and the objections of the two superpowers, ECOSOC decided to create an ad-hoc commission to study the extent to which a commission for Latin America had space in the United Nations.

The proposal of the economic commission for Latin America had gained momentum by the time ECOSOC reconvened in February 1948. The idea that the problems of less developed countries required specific, regional approaches received "almost unanimous support" at the General Assembly, and a proposal for an economic commission for the Middle East started floating around.[19] In New York, Santa Cruz finally received the reluctant support of the head of the Pan-American Union, who had opposed the initiative, as had the United States delegate, based on institutional overlap with his organization, the century-long inter-American body, and the fears of creating a forum in which the United States was a not a major part. Simultaneously, in Latin America, the Chilean Foreign Ministry had championed a successful diplomatic offensive to enlist support of sixteen regional governments not present at ECOSOC, emphasizing the problem of international trade and highlighting that the proposed commission could propound for "mechanisms to expand exports of raw materials and primary products, to have competitive prices and secure markets for such products, and to make possible the recirculation of dollars coming from the rehabilitation process of Europe and Asia."[20] The ongoing tensions at the Conference on Trade and Employment at Havana, where the ITO was discussed, fed the impulse for the new organization.

The approval of the commission hinged on a formality. It was the urgency of physical devastation and the immediate reconstruction that had justified the creation of temporary regional commissions in Europe and Asia, in what many considered a departure from the UN's proclaimed multilateralism. Thus, whether the region's economic problems stemmed from the war and thus merited reconstruction and an economic commission became the object of discussion. The situation of postwar Latin America was quite different from that of Europe. The continent had been spared from physical devastation. It was also far from the Cold War theater that Europe was rapidly turning into and that gave it priority. Nonetheless, Santa Cruz proceeded to justify the creation of the commission on the specified terms, in an effort to create a space for a region that represented almost half of the United Nations at the time in the discussion of the reconstruction of the postwar economic order. Santa Cruz recalled Latin America's contribution to the war effort by "selling at export prices fixed by the buyers"—particularly significant and costly for mineral exporters such as Chile—which resulted in reduced export proceeds and, with them, fewer resources for economic development. He also insisted that the war conditions had "brought about an economic diversification to replace interrupted imports that was largely artificial and uneconomic" and had to be, like in Europe and Asia, reconstructed after the war. Insisting on the impact of the war in the region's international trade, he pointed to the restrictions and high prices of imports that hindered domestic production and generated "harmful and widespread repercussions."[21] Through the question of war dislocations and postwar reconstruction in Latin America, the function of the commission was ushered back into the realm of global trade.

The Latin American delegates at ECOSOC recast the problem of international trade as part of postwar reconstruction and successfully rallied the needed support for the commission. To do so, they mobilized the arguments provided by the small contingent of Latin American economists at the UN Secretariat in New York, one of which was Santa Cruz's brother. "Some of the most typical characteristics of the Latin American economy reveal themselves in its international economic relations," they claimed. Beyond the short-term effects initially outlined, Santa Cruz and the Latin American delegates at ECOSOC argued that the war had produced a profound change in the organization of the world economy with deep impact on Latin America. The war had changed the pattern of international trade with the loss of European markets and the increasing importance of the United States as trading partner, resulting in larger vulnerability to external fluctuations. It also halted industrialization plans that attempted to reduce such vulnerability to world economic fluctuations.[22] Despite being spared from occupation and devastation, Latin America, like the rest of the world, saw its economic fate increasingly tied to the United States as supplier of goods and capital and as market for its products. In sum, the war had exacerbated the problems created by Latin America's pattern of international trade and justified the creation of the commission.

The European support for the initiative turned the tables. To the French delegate, there was no question that the war had both "directly and indirectly affected the Latin American economies." The disruption of the international pattern of trade by which "Latin America had been able to balance its trade deficit with the United States through excess exports to Europe" was a severe dislocation intimately connected to the war and to the organization of the world economy. Therefore "his doubts were dispelled" about a regional commission.[23] With the abstention of the US and the Canadian delegates as well as the reluctant support of the Soviet representative (figure 1.3), the United Nations Economic Commission for Latin America (CEPAL) was finally approved.

With the establishment of CEPAL, Santa Cruz claimed his first diplomatic success. His goal and that of many diplomats and statesmen of this generation was to "enable Latin America to play a role in world economic reconstruction."[24] By putting the problem of international trade back in the global debates about postwar reconstruction, CEPAL was a first step in that direction. Following verbatim the terms of the other regional commissions and responding to the demands of the delegates, CEPAL's primary responsibility was to address urgent economics problems arising out of the Second World War.

Yet, in the back and forth about war effects and organizational demands, the Latin American delegates left a distinct intellectual agenda embedded in the institutional fabric of the bourgeoning organization. CEPAL was charged with the mandate to study "world economic maladjustments" and other problems connected to the world economy.[25] As the French delegate stated, "the study of regional problems in relation to world problems could only be undertaken by a Commission set up within the global United Nations."[26] CEPAL, with its focus on the changes in international trade in the emerging global order, became the site for the production of economic knowledge about global capitalism from and for Latin America.

FIGURE 1.3   The cartoon depicts Hernán Santa Cruz, the Chilean delegate to ECOSOC, accompanied by a woman labeled "United Nations," looking at a parrot who represents Andre Gromyko, the Soviet foreign minister. The parrot calls out "puppet" ("títere"), and the UN woman reassures Santa Cruz, saying, "Don't worry, Hernán, the poor animal only knows how to repeat the word that it has learned from his master as he addresses his vassals." For some, Santa Cruz and CEPAL represented an extension of US hegemony, while for others, CEPAL was a challenge to that supremacy. (*Revista Topaze*, April 2, 1948. Colección Biblioteca Nacional de Chile, available in Memoria Chilena.)

FIGURE 1.4   The first headquarters of CEPAL, shown in this 1948 photograph, were located in the borough of Providencia, near downtown Santiago, Chile. Shortly after, *cepalinos* moved to a nearby building on Av. Providencia where most of the events discussed in this book unfolded.

A Global Center in the South

By the end of ECOSOC's session in March 1948, CEPAL existed only on paper (figure 1.4). The responsibility to carry out its mandate fell on the UN Secretariat, especially on Wladek Malinowski, from the UN Department of Economic and Social Affairs in New York. With headquarters in Santiago, Chile, CEPAL needed an executive secretary to handle decisions on the ground. While UN senior staff found more suitable candidates, Eugenio Castillo, a Cuban economist residing in the United States, regarded with suspicion in Latin America for his association with US intelligence, was hastily but temporarily appointed for the job. Castillo had become friends with David Owen, the UN assistant secretary general, who was responsible for the designation.[27] Member government officials, international functionaries, and economic experts convened for CEPAL's first session shortly thereafter. Castillo and the UN staff anticipated the outcome of that gathering to be the mandate to carry out the unprecedented task of a region-wide economic survey. The task was daunting and the information about Latin America limited. Castillo and the UN staff drew on information previously compiled by the defunct League of Nations, but they also envisioned a different strategy.

While the Chilean government prepared to inaugurate the activities of CEPAL in Santiago in June that year, Castillo urged member governments to collaborate on the research enterprise. CEPAL and its secretariat—at the moment composed by Castillo and scarce clerical staff—had "insufficient resources," Castillo explained, to carry the institution's mandate.[28] So he urged the delegations to give detailed presentations of their respective economic situations to give CEPAL a foundation to start its work. Despite the short notice, the Chilean officials at the Ministry of Foreign Affairs promptly requested information from the Central Bank and the Treasury to comply with Castillo's requests.[29] As sponsors of the idea of CEPAL and as hosts of the conference, Chilean officials were committed to making the first meeting a resounding success. CEPAL's first session, a gathering of ministers of foreign affairs and treasury as well as other high-level officials, ratified the mandate of a regional economic survey, confirming the initial fears of Castillo and New York and raising the alarms of an unprepared staff.[30]

The survey became a source of tension between governments and the secretariat. Castillo had exhorted Latin American governments not only to offer detailed statements but also to carry out economic surveys themselves based on a common format to be provided by CEPAL.[31] Castillo's vision for CEPAL as an information bank was not only limited but unsuccessful. Regional governments resented the proposal. The Brazilian delegate to the United Nations criticized the secretariat for trying to divest itself from the task given. He warned against the "passive" and "unjustifiable" attitude manifest in the secretariat's proposal and suggested that, "instead of relying on the technical and statistical contribution of governments, [the commission's secretariat] should itself initiate a broad research endeavor." In fact, Latin American officials had supported the creation of CEPAL precisely because the United Nations could provide the necessary institutional and research infrastructure to remedy the lack of compiled information available in the region.[32] It was the making of broad, regional-scale surveys and the consequent advancement of policy recommendations that had justified the creation of CEPAL in the first place. By the end of the year, by which time only Uruguay had, very succinctly, responded to the questionnaire, Castillo lost hope. Running counter to one of the aims of the institution, Castillo's idea was buried.

Without a permanent executive secretary for CEPAL, Castillo struggled to keep the project of the survey afloat. Prebisch, a former professor at the university and founder of the Argentine Central Bank, initially declined the offer to lead CEPAL, although he eventually served as the longtime head of the institution. And so did Daniel Cosío Villegas, former director of the Mexican Central Bank and founder and director of *Fondo de Cultura Económica,* one of the region's prominent intellectual centers and the most important publishing house in economic and social sciences.[33] The bourgeoning organization did not yet have sufficient prestige to attract senior regional economists. The absence of a "master brain" behind the survey worried both Castillo and the senior officials in New York. In its place, Castillo relied on different international organizations such as the Food and Agricultural Organization (FAO), the International Labor Office (ILO), and the IMF either to provide information or to relocate some of their staff temporarily to Santiago. The UN Statistical Office and the European Economic Commission were also providing data. In the meantime, Castillo proceeded with the recruitment of permanent staff.[34] Despite all the shortcomings and even the deplored licenses of Castillo's approach, the making of the survey was becoming a collective and global research endeavor.

Of these partnerships in the global production of figures and ideas, the collaboration with the IMF seemed the most promising. Chilean economist Jorge del Canto, who was in charge of the southern part of IMF's Latin American Division, was committed to CEPAL's work. A former professor at *Universidad de Chile* and former adviser to his government's Central Bank, del Canto was pleased with the possibility of moving back to Santiago, even if temporarily, to aid in the production of the survey. An observer at CEPAL's first session, del Canto had noticed certain skepticism about the activities of the IMF in Latin America that perhaps the survey offered a chance to redress.[35] He agreed to submit two reports, one on the region's terms of trade and the other on inflation, therefore covering the "financial aspects of the survey."[36] The IMF was recruited to assist in what would soon become CEPAL's signature thesis: the decline of Latin America's international terms of trade.

The data on the region's international terms of trade had important political consequences for defining the postwar development strategy. In some Latin American countries, domestic industry expanded significantly after the Depression, creating expectations of overcoming the tyranny of international markets. For them, establishing the impact of international trade on the ability to sustain the growing industrial sector in the postwar era was especially crucial. In addition, the problem was central to CEPAL's mandate to understand and situate Latin America in the world economy. Since the fluctuations on the prices and the restrictions on markets were two of the main concerns justifying the creation of CEPAL, Castillo felt obliged to offer a response in the institution's first survey. Because the terms of trade and balance of payments would form an important link "in our overall analysis of foreign trade and the internal economic status of these countries," Castillo explained, "we place considerable importance on this data."[37] Later that year, del Canto reassured Castillo by saying, "I have almost everybody in my division working on the [CEPAL] projects and I am profoundly optimistic that we will meet the deadlines. . . . Despite many who—unfortunately—don't believe in [CEPAL], I am fully committed to bringing to fruition the assignments I personally accepted last June on behalf of the Fund."[38] This collaboration was the beginning of an enduring yet conflicting relationship between the two institutions that would reach a climax with the inflation debates in the late 1950s. Yet, at the moment, Castillo was hopeful that with the collaboration of the IMF staff and that of other agencies, the survey would be accomplished in time.

With less than six months before the official presentation of the survey at CEPAL's second session in Havana, senior officials in UN headquarters in New York decided to intervene. The staff in Santiago was still in the stage of data collection. They had drafted sections for certain countries on banking and industry, but the organization of the foreign trade statistics and on-the-ground collection of country-by-country agricultural data were both exhausting and lengthy jobs.[39] Imminent and substantial initiatives were necessary, given that "CEPAL's fate depended on the survey."[40] A UN statistician was sent to Santiago in January 1949 to accelerate the compilation and organizational tasks. UN-New York hired, as a second- or even third-best option, Mexican economist Gustavo Martínez Cabaña as CEPAL's executive secretary. Fernando Coire, an Argentine economist, former consultant for his country's Central Bank and disciple of Prebisch, was hired to direct the Latin American unit in New York. Assessing the status of the survey, Coire took charge of providing Santiago with timely statistics on US trade with Latin America, foreign investments in the region, and most importantly the terms of trade trends with the United States and the United Kingdom, which had just come available from H. W. Singer's study at the Department of Economic and Social Affairs.[41] The team was further strengthened as Prebisch, who had initially rejected the offer to become executive secretary of CEPAL, finally accepted a temporary consultancy in Santiago. With reinforcements, UN staff in New York were committed to make the project a success.

As New York headquarters' officials had predicted, the CEPAL-IMF partnership quickly fell apart. They had been especially skeptical about the IMF-CEPAL collaboration from the start.[42] Del Canto's studies were delayed, muddling through several clearance procedures by both senior staff and the board of directors. It was also unlikely that the IMF was going to send del Canto to Santiago in the spring, as had been agreed earlier.[43] In a meeting of Gustavo Martínez Cabañas, the recently appointed executive secretary of CEPAL, and Camille Gutt, head of the IMF, the latter outwardly rejected Martínez Cabañas's idea to circumvent the "shortage of capable economists in the region" through the "creation of a pool of Latin American economists that could work for the different organizations." Gutt argued that the IMF was "not interested in general surveys but in very specific studies which [had] to be done in Washington with participation of many other divisions."[44] Aware of the reluctance of his superior to collaborate with CEPAL, del Canto apologized and felt the need to make amends. "In order to show my willingness to do a little extra something for CEPAL, I am also attaching some preliminary data on the Balance of Payments Survey that will prove useful to you," he claimed.[45] Nonetheless, Gutt, as head of the institution, had a point: CEPAL and the IMF were organizations looking for influence and with areas of competence to protect.

In the face of impending challenges, Castillo and the rest of the staff in Santiago were forced to reappraise the survey. In the original outline drafted in July 1948, Castillo envisioned the survey to encompass three parts: "the regional economy, the national economies, and Latin America and the world economy."[46] Staff in Santiago were responsible for the first two parts, while staff in New York carried out the global portion of the survey. In this division of labor, CEPAL's portion on the national economies had already fallen through the cracks when regional government had failed to respond to numerous questionnaires and requests for information, which impeded a country-by-country coverage. The third part of the survey contemplated sections on trade, loans and investments, balance of payments, and the impact of the European recovery program. There was, however, significant overlap between the regional and the global as well as the Santiago and the New York parts of the survey. Ultimately, Alberto Santa Cruz, brother of Hernán Santa Cruz, argued that "foreign trade and balance of payments can be best studied in conjunction with development in production and public policies."[47] The internal aspects could not be divorced from the external aspects; development could not be divorced from international trade. With the elimination of the "global aspects of the survey," New York's role had become redundant while Santiago gained preeminence.

As New York and Santiago wrestled with the scope of the survey, the staff in Santiago defined the scope of CEPAL's future work. The problem of the international terms of trade was one of those prominent aspects that Santiago claimed as its own. "Since its integration to the international market in the late 19th century," staff in Santiago claimed, "Latin America's rate of development has closely depended on the external impulses" given by foreign trade and investment. Although those impulses had faded away after the Great Depression, the crucial question for Latin America's postwar development, *cepalinos* claimed, was whether they would "continue to stimulate the economy as they had in the past."[48] From the perspective of the international terms of trade, or the relation between primary products and manufactured goods, the panorama looked bleak. In the 1930s the prices of the former in relation to the latter were 64 percent of what they had been in the 1870s. In the immediate postwar years, the terms of trade had just recovered what they had lost after the Depression. There was a grueling disparity in the movement of prices for producers like Latin America and industrialized countries. With this diagnosis, the challenge for economists in Santiago was how to solve the dilemma of relying on international trade to overcome the disparity imposed by global trade. To "safeguard the economy from the adverse effects of external fluctuations," industrialization had emerged in the war years as feasible strategy. However, they claimed that, since capital goods, replacement parts, and raw materials for industry were imported to "exploit the industrial possibilities of Latin America, it is essential to have vigorous foreign trade" or to count on foreign capital.[49] Before Prebisch joined CEPAL, the *cepalino* project had begun and was already at a crossroads.

With the survey, *cepalinos* also made Santiago the privileged site for the production of ideas about the global economy from the point of view of Latin America. What began as a global enterprise in the production of ideas, facts, and figures, involving national governments, international organizations, and economists from the North and South, was gradually reduced as participants abdicated or were left out. In the vacillations about whether staff in Santiago or Washington, DC, or New York undertook overlapping and contentious aspects such as international trade and balance of payments, economists in both centers tilted the balance toward the South, initiating Santiago's position as a hotbed of ideas about Latin America and its role in global capitalism. With this perspective embedded in the institutional fabric of the commission, a space had been carved for Prebisch's notion of "center and periphery" and the birth of the *cepalino* project.

Of Center and Peripheries

Santiago economists had rushed to finish the first regional economic survey, their inaugurating endeavor, for its formal presentation to regional statesmen, diplomats, and staff of international organizations in Havana at CEPAL's second annual session. Culminating a task of that magnitude and scope in such a short time and with an institution still in the works was an accomplishment in and of itself. They had provided Latin America with the first set of consolidated and comparable quantitative figures about its economy. They had also fostered a panorama of Latin America in the world and identified the region's crucial postwar dilemma, and in so doing, had given a global institution in the South a mission and an agenda. In many ways, the survey condensed the concerns present since the initial postwar planning moment and the creation of CEPAL, and those of future *cepalinos*.

But Havana did not offer the response the economists in Santiago awaited. Whereas senior officials from the UN headquarters in New York had traveled to Santiago the year before, only Malinowski attended the meeting in Havana. Most Latin American delegates, with the conspicuous exception of Chile, sent low-level officials to CEPAL's second session. The presence of the UN Secretary General, Trygve Lie, appeared to raise the stature of the conference and the awareness of the press. Amid stupor and lack of enthusiasm, Hernán Santa Cruz and the Chilean Minister of the Economy, Alberto Baltra Cortés, went to great lengths to revitalize their own initiative. But the declaration of Argentine economist Prebisch, who had joined CEPAL in Santiago three months before, changed the mood and gave new meaning to what would have otherwise been a dull assembly.

Although he would become a cornerstone for the institution, Prebisch had come to CEPAL reluctantly. Despite narrowing career options in his native Argentina, Prebisch rejected the offer of UN Secretary General to assume the commanding role in Santiago when the Commission was established in February 1948. Prebisch feared that an institution away from New York would have no power over the postwar global order and declined the offer. As the challenges to complete the survey mounted, Castillo and UN senior officials insisted Prebisch join the team later that year. But at that time, Prebisch was negotiating a senior position at the IMF and thus agreed only to a temporary consultancy. In March 1949 the IMF position fell through. Prebisch's nomination to the IMF received the support of the United States Treasury officials but was opposed by Argentine President Juan Domingo Perón. In a fleeting moment of rapprochement in an otherwise conflictive relationship between Argentina and the United States, Perón vetoed Prebisch's appointment, and the United States supported Perón.[50] The president and many in the Argentine public distrusted Prebisch. He had begun his career working for the landed interests that Perón and his regime stood against, and he was part of the authoritarian government that Perón and the generals had ousted. Ironically, Prebisch was also considered suspicious because of his alleged connections with the US embassy.[51] Thus, when Perón came to power, he dismissed Prebisch from his position as general manager to the Central Bank in 1943. The IMF position was Prebisch's second setback caused by Perón. Prebisch's and then CEPAL's relations with Argentina were since then deeply affected. Ostracized from Argentine policy circles and having lost the opportunity to work in Washington, Prebisch hesitantly moved to Santiago. UN senior officials in New York hoped Prebisch would compile and unify the different and partial reports into a single overarching one.[52] But Prebisch isolated himself from the rush to finish the survey and devoted his time to writing a text that only became public at the Havana conference.

In Santiago, Prebisch worked on a manuscript centered on the international terms of trade that was, in many ways, the culmination of years of reflection about the ebbs and flows of the Argentine economy. Prebisch had been trained in economics at the *Universidad de Buenos Aires* in 1921 and soon thereafter became part-time professor while working for the *Sociedad Rural Argentina,* an organization that grouped together the most powerful landed and export interests in the country. But it was his experience in policymaking in the 1930s that shaped his views.[53] As economic adviser to and part of the economic team that confronted the Great Depression, Prebisch began to notice a trend. The prices of agricultural products had fallen more profoundly than those of manufactured goods, which resulted in Argentina needing to sell 73 percent more than before the Depression to acquire the necessary imported goods. At the same time, with export earnings severely restricted and compensating for the lack of imports, the manufacturing industry grew tremendously in Argentina as it did in Chile and Brazil. In his capacity as Central Bank manager in 1937, Prebisch continued to insist on the inequality in the fall of prices for primary producers compared to those of the manufactured goods, which he attributed to their inelasticity to changes in demand and to the lack of organization of producers to avoid the fall.[54] To tackle the problem, Prebisch proposed a Keynesian style of countercyclical monetary policy and state-sponsored industrialization to offset the detrimental effects of fluctuations in the international economy. Before CEPAL, Prebisch had found the economic problem and the solution that would occupy *cepalinos* in the years to come.

But it was in Santiago and with the international organizations mobilized around CEPAL that Prebisch was able first to condense and streamline ideas accumulated over the years and later to position them at the global level. In a meeting of Central Bankers in 1946, Prebisch had begun to speak of the world economy in terms of center and periphery. More specifically, he focused on a "fundamental difference in the monetary phenomena of the center and the periphery." The United States, as continental and world center, had monetary instruments at its disposal that "Latin America at the periphery of the world economy" did not have when confronted with declining prices and the detrimental effects of downward economic cycles.[55] Upon arrival in Santiago, Prebisch found himself demoralized, defeated, and perhaps even intellectually paralyzed. In April 1949 he presented a paper among the CEPAL staff and rapidly took it out of circulation. Prebisch was not satisfied, and he knew the Havana deadline was approaching. In the last month before the Havana meeting, Prebisch got a hold of a draft report from German economist Hans W. Singer, a Keynes' disciple, at the headquarters in New York. Singer's report boosted Prebisch's morale, altered his own personal trajectory and that of the Santiago-based institution, and broke Prebisch's intellectual deadlock.[56] It reaffirmed Prebisch's earlier intuitions and that of Latin American economists and policymakers who saw in CEPAL the mechanism to transform the region's position in the global economy.

Singer had joined the UN Department of Economic and Social Affairs in April 1947. A few months later, a report of the Subcommission on Economic Development prompted Singer into a consequential project. The report stated that, given the restrictions in world trade, producers of raw materials and primary products had accumulated foreign exchange but that those reserves were rapidly losing value after the war given the rise in prices of capital goods and transportation costs. The members of the subcommission pushed for an analysis of the relation between prices of primary products and manufactured goods that were hindering the economic postwar possibilities of less developed countries. Drawing on a League of Nations statistical compilation, Singer transformed the study of short-term, wartime price changes into a study of the long-term trend of international terms of trade. Singer showed that, although the terms of trade of agricultural products in relation to manufactured goods had improved during the war and early postwar years, they had "substantially declined" from the late 19th century to the eve of the Second World War. Driven by broader questions of distribution of gains of trade, Singer reached a rather radical conclusion.[57] By not receiving "in the price of their own products an equal contribution," Singer claimed, the underdeveloped countries had helped "maintain a rising standard of living in industrialized countries."[58] Crucial as it was, Singer's study was one of many devoted to the problem.

The international terms of trade, or the relation between the prices of exports and the prices of imports, encapsulated one of the fundamental problems of the postwar era. While the interwar years were marked by nationalist rhetoric and ideas of autarchy, the postwar era and the reconstruction of the global order elicited discussions about interdependence and about dependence and inequality between nation-states. Latin American delegates at Bretton Woods and UN ECOSOC had insisted that the instability of prices and the narrowing of external markets for the region as producer of primary products and raw materials justified Latin America's participation and place in the reconstruction of the global order and the international institutional system. The imminence of decolonization in Asia and Africa, mostly producers of agricultural and primary products, broadened the implications of the study on the historical terms of international trade. For the new countries, the study posed serious questions about how or even if to integrate to the global economic market with the United States at its center.

Given the United Nations's role in global governance, the institution seemed the perfect place to address the problem of terms of trade and inequality between nations. Singer's study was a direct product of that institutional milieu, as was the study carried out at the IMF on behalf of CEPAL in Santiago. For del Canto and his collaborator, Chilean economist and future *cepalino* Jorge Ahumada, the study of terms of trade served to fulfill the IMF's mission to ensure the stability of the international system. The relation of prices of exports and imports had a direct impact over the balance of payments, and one of the IMF's goals was precisely to counteract extreme global monetary fluctuations through short-term credits. Knowing of the endeavor taken on by Singer, the IMF research staff opted to limit the extent of their report. Focusing exclusively on the war and postwar years, the IMF staff study noticed an improvement in the terms of trade but suggested "the terms of trade of Latin American countries have normally moved adversely during periods of depression."[59] By the time of the meeting in Havana, the problem of the international terms of trade had mobilized the resources at the IMF in Washington, DC, the UN Department of Economic and Social Affairs in New York, and now CEPAL in Santiago.

At Havana, Prebisch introduced a new dimension to the ongoing global debate about the international terms of trade. In a grandiloquent note, Prebisch claimed that Latin American industrialization "was undermining the outdated schema of the international division of labor" of *center* and *periphery*. Under that schema, he explained, echoing the concerns that had motivated the creation of CEPAL in the first place, "the specific task that fell to Latin America as part of the *periphery* of the world-economic system, was that of producing food and raw materials for the great industrial *centers*." That division of labor was supposed to equally distribute the gains of productivity between manufacturing centers and commodity-producing peripheries, and thus there was no need for the industrialization of the periphery. But the fall in the terms of trade to the detriment of commodity-producers implied that those gains had not been equally distributed. Mobilizing the figures of the Singer study and moving away from his short-term cyclical analysis, Prebisch reiterated that the fall had been so pronounced that in the 1930s primary products could only buy 63 percent of the manufactured goods they did in the 1870s. In a masterful stroke, Prebisch folded the international terms of trade problem into a characterization of the global economic system with the provocative language of center and periphery.[60]

The denunciatory stance embedded in the concept of center and periphery was, however, a call for more, not less, international trade. First and foremost, Prebisch advocated for industrialization as a means to confront the fundamental global disparity. The industrialization of the periphery promised to reduce the dependence on exports and global markets by producing domestically and therefore reducing demand for imported goods. However, because industrialization required imports of capital goods and raw materials, and it was through exports that the region transformed savings into capital.[61] Latin America and the world's periphery needed more and better global markets.

However, access to more and better trade for the periphery was limited by a recent and fundamental change in the organization of the global economy. The rise of the United States and the fall of Great Britain dramatically transformed the relation between center and peripheries because the United States was, according to Prebisch, a less dynamic global center. With a large domestic market that was almost self-sufficient and protected with layers of tariffs, the United States imposed limits to the exports of the periphery that did not exist for the countries developing when Great Britain was the world's economic center.[62] To overcome the disparity in the global economic system "the solution does not lie in growth at the expense of foreign trade," he concluded, "but in knowing how to extract, from continuously growing trade, the elements that will promote economic development."[63] To do this, Latin America required the United States, as center of the global system, to generate demand for and open its markets to Latin American products. Both defiant and conciliatory, Prebisch used the framework of center and periphery to denounce global inequality and in the same breath to advocate for international cooperation, especially with the world's leading industrial center.

Prebisch's vocabulary was not new. German economist Werner Sombart, credited for coining the term "capitalism," used the notion of center and periphery in his classical work to refer to the unequal exchange between Great Britain and Central and Southern Europe.[64] Similar conceptualizations about the inequalities in the international division of labor had traveled to Latin America from Eastern Europe and circulated in Prebisch's circles.[65] Within Latin America, there was growing consensus among economic

policymakers about the disparities between producers of primary products and their "derivative," "reflexive," or "peripheral" character with respect to the industrial centers. Nonetheless, Prebisch captured these insights
and used the global institution to catapult them across the region and the
world.

The meeting at Havana effectively married the man to the institution and
the center-periphery text. The Latin American delegates at the conference
in Havana commended Prebisch's work. His intervention provided unity
and coordination to the work of CEPAL, the Mexican delegate asserted.[66]
Prebisch himself changed his views about CEPAL. After Havana, he became
convinced that CEPAL, not the IMF, was the vehicle to carry out the project
he had outlined in the manifesto. Thus he turned his three-month consultancy into a yearlong contract as head of the research department and
within a year became executive secretary and principal director of CEPAL,
a position he held formally for over a decade and informally for more than
three. Paradoxically, the New York headquarters' resistance to associate
the United Nations with the Prebisch manifesto further strengthened identification between the two. The denunciation of global economic inequality
at the UN forum had already found resistance when Singer presented his
study in early 1949.[67] A few months after the Havana meeting, senior UN
officials in New York argued that, contrary to UN policy, Prebisch's text
should be published under his personal name rather than under institutional
authorship. It was important for Prebisch to "take credit and (responsibility) for the report" and to "emphasize that the views expressed were
those of the author and not those of the United Nations organ," they
claimed.[68] While Singer's paper, published anonymously, faded into the
background, Prebisch's Havana text gained prominence and became the
CEPAL manifesto.

Before leaving for Havana and full of confidence on the significance of
his ideas, Prebisch had given the text to Brazilian economist Celso Furtado
for its translation into Portuguese. Outpacing the sluggish publishing procedures at the international organization, the text appeared almost simultaneously in the two most important journals in the region, the *Revista
Brasileira de Economia* of the *Fundação Getúlio Vargas* (FGV) and *El Trimestre Económico* of the Mexican *Fondo de Cultura Económica* in the
last quarter of 1949.[69] The text circulated with both the name of the author and the institution, effectively wedding the man, CEPAL, and the notion of center and periphery and the long-term decline of the terms of trade.
Prebisch was far from such political orientation, but the fears of communism
in the United States affected UN headquarters. UN New York was relieved
to see Prebisch and CEPAL take the credit for what was becoming a highly

controversial and politically relevant idea.[70] With the circulation and sway of Prebisch's framing, the denunciation of global inequality through the vocabulary of center and periphery and the evidence of the long-term decline in the terms of trade became CEPAL's and the Latin American contribution to ideas about development and global capitalism.

Although eclipsed by the manifesto, the regional economic survey had prompted a series of practices in the production of economic ideas about Latin America that Prebisch intended to carry forward. With the first regional survey, the division of labor between New York and Santiago had resolved the prevailing tension within the United Nations. The Commission in Santiago had become the privileged center for the production of ideas about Latin America, an arrangement that Prebisch proceeded to formalize, consolidating the niche for *cepalino* endeavors as well as autonomy from New York. Prebisch also envisioned the creation of a Washington, DC, CEPAL office since US sources had proved vital for the survey. Moreover, the Washington office was politically and institutionally strategic. The office could keep a close eye and establish friendly relations with international organizations like the IMF and the Organization of American States, which were competing for influence in the region.

Furthermore, the survey, a seemingly routine and plain task, inaugurated a set of practices that promised to broaden the scope of a small institution located in the southern tip of South America. Because the lack of personnel impeded the "study of conditions on the spot," Prebisch envisioned the recruitment of "local agents," a group of government functionaries to aid in the collection of data and the preparation of special reports. Making virtue out of necessity, the use of local agents gave *cepalinos* "intimate knowledge" of the national economies and "ready access to the best sources of information," while circumventing the paucity and formalities of contact with governments that had proven so hampering in the making of the first survey. In turn, the local consultants "gained a broader interest in the problem of economic development" as defined by *cepalinos* and the chance to "relate their work to that of economists in other Latin American countries,"[71] weaving a regional *cepalino* network. The path of *cepalinos* toward regional influence had just begun.

Conclusions

The worldmaking project of *cepalinos* emerged from the convergence of a global institution, an aspiring economist, and a provocative manifesto. In the war and interwar years, Latin Americans skillfully navigated across the different international organizations that came to dominate the international arena in midcentury until they secured a place in the Santiago-based CEPAL to institutionalize their concerns. With the IMF eschewing the problem of international trade and the plans for the ITO shelved, CEPAL emerged as the unfulfilled realization of the tripartite structure that was supposed to organize the postwar global order but had thus far produced only the IMF and the World Bank. From Bretton Woods to the UN CEPAL, Latin Americans pushed to square the problem of economic development with that of the restoration of international trade at a moment in which the Third World as a political force was just beginning to take shape. With CEPAL, Latin Americans began to make the United Nations the propitious forum for Third Worldism that it became in the years to come as decolonization accelerated and the countries of the global South became a majority. Rather than Prebisch making CEPAL, it was at CEPAL that Prebisch's ideas, simmering during years of policymaking experience in Argentina and exchanges with the regional economists, found a home and thrived.[72] With the convergence of Prebisch, the center-periphery manifesto, and CEPAL, the problem of the falling gains from international trade that occupied multiple international organizations and economists in the postwar era became the "Latin American" contribution to development thinking and practice.

Although the center-periphery idea was not new in the global social sciences, Prebisch's ideas acquired tremendous saliency in the context of global reorganization after the war. The growth of the world's periphery via decolonization, the faster expansion of international trade between the centers and its decline in the periphery, and the recurrent booms and busts of commodities raised the interest in these ideas. With the notion of center and peripheries, Prebisch provided a powerful and enduring concept to frame discussions about global capitalism that persists to this day. With the notion of the long-term decline in the terms of trade, he established the implications of Latin America's position in the world economy and then used CEPAL to advocate for its transformation.

Prebisch's notion of center and periphery may not have reached the peak of its influence until the mid-1960s, but it had significant intellectual and political implications for Latin America and the world since the outset. As economist Albert Fishlow argued, Prebisch "set the terms, not merely for the rich literature in Latin America that followed and would build upon the center-periphery distinction, but also for the subsequent formalization of the foreign exchange constraint in the North American literature." Global economists came to embrace the *cepalino* conceptualization of what became known as "foreign exchange gap," leading Fishlow to conclude that since Prebisch's 1948 CEPAL manifesto, "trade and development have been subsequently inextricably linked."[73] Prebisch's notion of center and periphery became the foundation of the *cepalino* worldmaking project for decades to come.

Prebisch captured the postwar dilemma in a single, timely, and easily mobile framework. His diagnosis of global inequality implied two different solutions: Latin American should either sever its ties with global markets or strengthen those ties to obtain a more advantageous position. Prebisch and CEPAL, imbued with the possibilities of internationalism and expertise, chose the latter, not without creating tensions between future *cepalinos*. In the years to come, Prebisch and *cepalinos* embarked on a long journey to put the center-periphery framework in action by formulating and spearheading a development agenda to address the "foreign exchange gap" and resolve the periphery's development paradox while resolving the fundamental ambiguity of their project.

Center and Periphery in Action

After Raúl Prebisch presented his manifesto in Havana in 1949 and took charge of the Santiago-based Economic Commission for Latin America (CEPAL), *cepalinos* strived to turn their global vision of center and periphery into action. In the early years of the institution, *cepalinos'* main task was producing annual economic surveys of the region and individual country studies. For these economists, collecting and compiling data and then turning those data into reports (e.g., *The Economic Development of Argentina, The Economic Development of Brazil*) was arduous but rewarding. The first of their kind in the region, the *cepalino* studies quickly became essential documents for academics and policymakers—"almost like a bible"—especially in Mexico and southern South America.[1] But *cepalinos* wanted to do more than produce texts that ended up on the shelves of functionaries and professors. They aspired to turn themselves and their institution into agents of economic development and thus of the transformation of Latin America's position in the world economy.

Cepalinos saw Latin American economic development as a stepwise process that began with resolving a development paradox. In the past, the world's economic powerhouses had used industrialization as the means to progress and wealth, but this same path was now harder to the latecomers on the global periphery.[2] Industrialization by import-substitution exacerbated one of the key problems it aimed to resolve by deepening countries' dependence on foreign exchange and increasing their vulnerability to the world market. For *cepalinos,* the main obstacle to Latin American economic development and the transformation in its position in the world economy was not just the lack of capital but rather the lack of hard currency. Referred to as the "foreign exchange gap," this concept became the foundation of the *cepalino* development agenda.

To move from theory to practice, *cepalinos* pursued an ambitious development agenda that ultimately captured the imagination and persuaded economists and economic policymakers across Latin America. As Chilean, Mexican, Argentinean, and Brazilian economists filled up the ranks of the Commission, *cepalinos* established both personal and institutional alliances throughout these countries. In Brazil, *cepalinos* became part of the growing development state through an approach to development planning that put the periphery's dollar shortage front and center. They disseminated their ideas and enlarged their network through training programs for civil servants. Beyond Brazil, *cepalinos* also developed an internationalist development agenda based on the cooperation between center and peripheries that rallied those frustrated with the slow pace of a global enterprise of reconstruction and development that had turned toward Europe and Asia and away from Latin America in the early postwar years. At the same time, *cepalinos* experimented with replicating the emerging experiment of European economic cooperation via a market integration project for Central America first, and for the rest of the region later. They believed both Europe and Latin America faced the limits to growth imposed by the global dollar shortage and lack of hard currency. The varied strategies and goals of this development agenda earned *cepalinos* a growing audience but also created opposition, especially among other international organizations competing for regional influence and shaping the region's economic destiny.

Capturing Brazil

In September 1951, four months after the Mexico meeting in which CEPAL was transformed from a temporary into a permanent institution, Prebisch undertook a large-scale tour in Rio de Janeiro and São Paulo, marking the beginning of a prominent and long-lasting position in Brazil. He had a full agenda, with conferences at the federation of industrialists, the economic committee of the House and the Senate, and personal interviews with the ministers of foreign relations and of finance and the head of the Bank of Brazil. In Brazil, Prebisch found that his audiences at the highest echelons of Brazilian policymaking were not only receptive to but also remarkably conversant with *cepalino* ideas. "While Prebisch's ideas are not disseminated to the extent that one would desire, they were already known by most of our experts," a reporter noted.[3] At those conferences and round-tables, attendance was five or six times greater than at previous events. "It is no exaggeration to say that all the Brazilian economists of some standing today know the basic points of the thinking of CEPAL," an observer stated. Those ideas "constitute the strongest current of thought among the younger economists," he added.[4] Within a few years, *cepalino* ideas rapidly became an obligatory point of reference for the debates about the limits and obstacles to economic development.

Celso Furtado, a young Brazilian economist who joined CEPAL shortly after its inauguration, was behind the success of the visit and, to a great extent, of the influence of *cepalinos* in Brazil. Born in the northeastern state of Paraíba and a lawyer by training, Furtado pursued doctoral studies in economics at the Sorbonne immediately after the Second World War. After a brief stop in Brazil and an unsuccessful attempt by the *Fundação Getúlio Vargas* (FGV) group to recruit him, he went to Santiago in early 1949.[5] Later that year, Furtado translated Prebisch's Havana text, discussed in the previous chapter, into Portuguese and disseminated it widely. From that moment on, the notion of the inequality in the gains of trade, framed in the vocabulary of center and periphery, captured the attention of the Brazilian academic community.

Furtado was an institution and a network builder. To gather information for *cepalino* studies in Brazil, Furtado drew on a number of mostly self-taught economists in middle-level private and public positions, creating a fertile ground for *cepalino* ideas.[6] These economists and rising bureaucrats crafted a space for *cepalinos* within the Brazilian state and within economic interest groups. The *Confederação Nacional da Indústria* (CNI), the main industrialist association, translated and republished the *cepalino* country study of 1950. Thanks to Furtado, *cepalino* ideas also found echo among the young and rising cohort at Itamaraty, the Ministry of Foreign Affairs in Brazil, some of which became the strongest advocates and disseminators of *cepalino* notions. Among Furtado's friends and allies were the close advisors to President Getúlio Vargas.[7] A couple of years later, Furtado formed a group of Brazilian economists who shared many of *cepalino* ideas and established a journal to serve as their public outlet.[8]

Among the Brazilian academic community and its international allies, Prebisch encountered more criticism. Some of the first to engage but also distance themselves from *cepalinos* were the economists at the FGV. Despite its name, the FGV held numerous Vargas's opponents that would also become *cepalino* adversaries. The FGV and its research arm, *Instituto Brasileiro de Economia*, led by economist Eugênio Gudin, hosted one of Prebisch's first talks.[9] Sympathetic to Prebisch in the early postwar years,

Gudin, who was an engineer by training, a self-taught economist, and a cornerstone of an institution that acquired enormous academic prestige, became one of Prebisch's fiercest critics. In a conference that gathered thirty of the most prominent Brazilian economists, Prebisch encountered harsh criticism of the notion of the long-term decline in terms of trade between the center and the periphery and its consequent justification for industrialization in Latin America.[10] For those economists gathered at the FGV, Prebisch was wrong in attributing the limits to economic development to the specialization in the production of primary products. Instead, the FGV's Gudin and especially Princeton University's Jacob Viner warned against the fallacious "association between agriculture and poverty." "If the export of primary products was detrimental for development, why are we not taking pity on Denmark, California, or Iowa?" Viner claimed, dismissing Prebisch's ideas of the inequality in the gains from international trade as the obstacle to development.[11] After having been invited to the FGV to discuss Prebisch and *cepalino* ideas, Harvard economist Gottfried Haberler "vehemently" criticized *cepalino* ideas in his lectures back in Cambridge.[12] Some of these criticisms continued and even intensified over the years as *cepalinos* moved from the discussion of international trade to that of inflation, as will be discussed in the next chapter.

To culminate the visit and seal the *cepalino* alliance with Brazil, Furtado accompanied Prebisch to his last and perhaps more important piece of the Brazilian tour: a meeting with President Getúlio Vargas. Furtado expected that a meeting between Prebisch and the popular yet controversial president would raise the status of the visit and increase the sway of the Santiago-based institution. With a resounding electoral victory, Vargas, the former dictator, had returned to the presidential palace earlier that year with the promise to continue the state-led industrialization project he had initiated and restore the momentum lost after the end of the war.[13] Against his critics, a group of "qualified economists and financiers" who "ruthlessly criticized" the project because it entailed paying "twice as much for steel than if imported from the United States," Vargas responded, "What would Brazil gain by importing cheaper steel if it doesn't have the dollars to buy it?"[14] Aware of the dollar scarcity and the limitations that foreign exchange imposed on development, Vargas would find in *cepalinos* crucial allies in his development project, as *cepalinos* had found an ally in Vargas.

Although he had supported CEPAL at the Mexico meeting earlier that year, Vargas knew little about the institution and, among other things, asked Prebisch about its reach and scope. During his years in government in the interwar years, Brazil had experienced severe balance of payments problems, arising from the combination of the volatility of its exports in global markets and the growing demand for imported goods for industry and basic consumption goods. The latter resulted in constraints on industry, leading Vargas to ask Prebisch if "CEPAL was concerned with monetary problems." The International Monetary Fund (IMF), Prebisch was forced to clarify, was the international organization directly concerned with those matters. But Prebisch reassured Vargas. "Since it is impossible in Latin America to separate monetary problems from those of economic development," he claimed, "CEPAL is giving increasing attention to them."[15]

For *cepalinos,* the recurrent balance of payments problems and the monetary problems that preoccupied Vargas and many policymakers in Brazil were at the crux of Latin America's development paradox. By producing for the domestic market and eventually reducing demand for imports, the industrialization by import substitution that both Vargas and Prebisch supported promised to decrease the dependence on foreign exchange and the export of a few primary products and reduce the vulnerability to changes in world market prices. Yet, in the short term, industrialization and development also triggered an increasing demand for foreign exchange to pay for imported technology and equipment. To solve the catch-22 of needing foreign exchange to propel industrialization as industrialization heightened the demand for foreign exchange, *cepalinos* put forward an ambitious development agenda with three pillars, two of which would be launched in Brazil.

In addition to Furtado's individual ventures and Prebisch's successful visit, *cepalinos* found another strategy to secure their presence in Brazil, the region's largest and perhaps most state developmentalist country.[16] After a successful experience with a training center for government functionaries and university students in Santiago, *cepalinos* began to establish training centers in Rio de Janeiro and other Latin American capitals. By working as interns at CEPAL as well as receiving lessons from *cepalinos,* the new trainees became versed in the proposed development project and broadened the *cepalino* network as they returned to their respective countries or were recruited as staff at CEPAL headquarters.[17] The first training course in Rio in 1956 brought *cepalino* instructors from Santiago but also relied on the different set of allies Furtado had begun to form: the group of Vargas's close advisors, on the one hand, and those linked to the FGV, on the other. Established in 1957, the training program in Brazil began operating in 1960 but shortly after was expanded to multiple cities of the continental-size country. The *cepalino* program was the first introduction to development economics for many economists who would become very influential in politics and academia in the decades to come, even at the turn of the twenty-first century.[18] The training courses and especially Furtado's future political endeavors would make Brazil a crucial *cepalino* stronghold.

In the early postwar years, Prebisch and *cepalinos* were confident in their ideas and were eager to put the notion of center and periphery in action. Like development experts worldwide, *cepalinos* turned to development planning.[19] The International Bank for Reconstruction and Development (IBRD), the United Nations, and the governments of recently decolonized nations in India and Indonesia were all advocating the use of investment and development plans. Unlike the IBRD project-based plans, *cepalinos* envisioned a form of overall planning that emphasized relations between the different sectors of the economy. For *cepalinos*, the incursion on the territory of development planning was their first step in the sphere of practical "inter-governmental action."[20] At the nexus of a flourishing network of development experts, *cepalinos* believed they could marshal and systematize the experience and lessons of policymakers to produce development programs more attuned with the Latin American realities. They could assist governments to plan an efficient use of their domestic resources and become intermediaries between the regional governments and the external financial institutions. By doing so, they could effectively transform themselves into agents of development and their agency into an operational, not just a research, institution.[21]

An outgrowth of the center and periphery framework, *cepalinos* elaborated what they called the "technique of programming" to solve the development paradox. The *cepalino* programming technique combined macroeconomic considerations with by-sector targets. Through the "technique," *cepalinos* aspired to devise development plans that accounted for the investment and import-substitution industrialization needs as well as the domestic savings and foreign exchange proceeds to undertake them. Because furthering the industrialization process required intensifying imports of capital goods and raw materials in a context of falling terms of trade between centers and peripheries, *cepalino* economists were invested in solving the liquidity problem upon which development hinged. Ideally, through the "technique of programming," *cepalinos* could forecast import needs and the future capacity to import to prevent external disequilibrium such as balance of payments crises that threatened the development project.[22] By adopting the *cepalino* approach to planning, Latin American economies could make careful and efficient use of scarce foreign exchange resources. An instrument to deal with monetary instability, planning was also a mechanism to move from what in the eyes of *cepalinos* had been a "spontaneous" industrialization process to a more rational one.

By specifying the sectors in which to reduce imports, this planning could help governments organize the investment and productive effort for the substitution of imports for internally produced goods.[23] The *cepalino* "technique of programming" was one of the answers to the development dilemmas imposed by a global order with the Unites States as hegemonic center.

Intrigued by their planning technique, Roberto Campos rallied the support of *cepalinos* for a bourgeoning yet pivotal development institution in Brazil. A philosophy and theology graduate, Campos began his public career at Itamaraty the Ministry of Foreign Relations, in the Brazilian embassy in Washington, DC. During his stay in the United States, Campos undertook informal studies of economics at George Washington and Columbia Universities. After his recruitment for the delegation at Bretton Woods, Campos remained within international organization diplomacy for a few years. He represented Brazil at the United Nations Conference on Trade and Employment in 1947 and supported the creation of the UN CEPAL in 1948. Furtado had found in Campos an institutional ally and a sympathizer of many of the emerging *cepalino* ideas.[24] The conviction that foreign exchange scarcity imposed limits on economic development drew Campos closer to *cepalinos*. In turn, Campos's work at the *Banco do Brasil* left Prebisch favorably impressed during his visit in 1951. Later a lecturer in the *cepalino* training course in Rio, Campos, one of the directors of the new institution, recruited *cepalinos* in 1953 for the recently established *Banco Nacional de Desenvolvimento Económico* (BNDE).

Established in mid-1952, the BNDE was the result of favorable prospects of international cooperation in the early postwar years.[25] As the IBRD was forced to reorient toward development projects after the US-sponsored Marshall Plan took over its functions of European reconstruction in 1947, the expectations of aid for other regions increased (figure 2.1). Two years later, US President Harry Truman's commitment to technical and financial assistance—in what came to be known as the Point IV program—invigorated the UN infrastructure for development. With the outbreak of the war in Korea, the support for Brazilian industrialization once again acquired strategic importance for the United States as it had in the Second World War years. Building on this cooperation momentum, the *Comissão Mista Brasil-Estados Unidos* (CMBEU) or the Joint US-Brazil Commission for economic development was established in December 1950. Vargas summoned Campos to be part of the Brazilian team that, in cooperation with US experts, would design investment projects for infrastructure and basic industries to be financed by the US Export-Import Bank and the IBRD. To provide the cruzeiro counterpart of these loans and act as an intermediary between the international credit agencies and the Brazilian private

FIGURE 2.1   The cartoon depicts Latin Americans stereotypically dressed rushing to obtain financial aid at the Organization of American States (OAS) conference in Bogotá in 1948. The Latin Americans jump back in surprise when the US sheep replies that "they will have to help Europe." The cartoon plays with a popular saying in Spanish that roughly translates, "They went for wool and got sheared." (*Revista Topaze*, April 9, 1948 Colección Biblioteca Nacional de Chile, available in Memoria Chilena.)

and public entrepreneurs, Vargas created the BNDE and rallied the Joint Commission's Brazilian team of experts to make the bank the fulcrum of the state's development project.

Having recruited international partners for their development project, Campos and Vargas turned to *cepalinos* to overcome some of the limits of the US-Brazil partnership. While the US-Brazilian technical cooperation had produced numerous individual infrastructure projects in strategic sectors for development, Campos and Vargas were not completely satisfied. Since it was necessary to frame those projects into an "overall development plan," Vargas and Campos rallied *cepalinos* to engage in a large-scale research project and to train the personnel on the ground to carry it out. Given that *cepalinos* were "elaborating development plans tailored to the realities of Latin America," Campos and the BNDE economists expected *cepalinos* to produce an overall diagnosis of the Brazilian economy and to apply the *cepalino* "structural planning technique" to Brazil. To cement the CEPAL-BNDE partnership, Prebisch and the *cepalinos* presented their "technique of programming" in Rio de Janeiro in May 1953. They insisted on the importance of planning industrialization to overcome the limits imposed by the scarcity of foreign exchange and to resolve the "development paradox" and its excruciating consequences over monetary stability.

The partnership with the Brazilian development bank was a turning point for *cepalinos*. In charge of the *cepalino* side of the partnership, Furtado and Cuban-born, Harvard-trained economist Regino Boti established themselves at the premises of the BNDE itself, setting foot inside the state apparatus and realizing the *cepalino* aspiration to turn to "concrete practical action."[26] Located in physical proximity to the main economic decision-making institutions of the country, Furtado would take the chance to circulate *cepalino* ideas into the policymaking circles and consolidate the position of *cepalinos* in Brazil. Since the *cepalino* planning technique and the partnership with the development bank generated an important controversy over planning in the country, *cepalinos* took the spotlight and became even more widely recognized.

The debate pitted *cepalinos* Furtado and Prebisch, on the one hand, Octávio Gouvêa de Bulhões and Eugênio Gudin, who had already been the protagonist of another important controversy about industrialization and planning, on the other.[27] Although *cepalinos* defended the state's role in development, their contenders criticized them for disregarding the price system as a regulator of economic activity. Whereas *cepalinos* were convinced that state intervention via planning could offset the profound disequilibria that accompanied development, Bulhões and Gudin were convinced that the state, with its layers of exchange, tariff, and price controls, was the source of monetary disequilibria. The controversy was aired in the press, transcending academic debates and delineating two projects of development for the country. Defining the terms of the debate, *cepalinos* were sidelining their opponents. With a foot on the development bank, the support of the president, and the increased resonance of their ideas among economists and policymakers, *cepalinos* had come to capture Brazil.

Although the consequences were lasting, the partnership between CEPAL-BNDE was short lived. As *cepalinos* set foot in Brazil, Vargas's government confronted an acute monetary crisis that manifested itself in severe balance of payments deficits and mounting inflation. Driven by the end of the "fleeting bonanza" and the "import rush" generated by the Korean War, the monetary crisis weakened Vargas's position.[28] The strict monetary stabilization plan formulated to confront the crisis met with increasing popular and political opposition, to which Vargas responded by closing the ranks of his administration to his most loyal friends and allies. According to Campos and Furtado, the replacement of one of their own for a career politician undermined their project.[29] As political expediencies prevailed, Campos, who imagined the bank to be a stronghold of technical expertise against party politics, resigned to the BNDE. Meanwhile, Furtado, whose work was ignored by the new BNDE president, was forced to reduce the scope of the project and finalize it without much splendor two years later.[30] Although *cepalinos* had moved from the spotlight to the background of policymaking, the CEPAL-BDNE studies would become a fundamental part of the succeeding administration of Juscelino Kubitschek and his *Plano de Metas,* while Furtado's endeavors outside the BNDE cemented the position of *cepalinos* in Brazil.

That same year, the CEPAL-BNDE partnership suffered another important blow that nonetheless paved the way for a larger *cepalino* presence in Brazil and in the rest of Latin America. When General Dwight Eisenhower replaced Truman in the American presidency, the US support for international development began to falter. Within six months, the new US administration abruptly dismantled the US-Brazil Mixed Commission and withdrew from its commitment to finance the BNDE-led economic development projects in Brazil, while deploying a "trade not aid" motto.[31] The US withdrawal led to increasing restrictions on the IBRD loans, which were contingent on sound macroeconomic stability and the absence of balance of payments deficits. The prospects of US and multilateral corporations' loans disappeared precisely at the moment when they were most needed—when the country confronted once again the consequences of volatile and dwindling export proceeds and a new balance of payments crisis (figure 2.2).

Campos, who had assumed a position in the Brazilian embassy in Washington, DC, after he left the BNDE, criticized the unfortunate turn in multilateral lending. "The International Bank seems to us at times much more concerned in determining . . . whether or not the country looks like a good credit risk, than in finding out the extent to which the Bank's investment

FIGURE 2.2   The cartoon depicts Latin America as a little girl asking for credits from Uncle Sam. She holds in her hands a box labeled "condemnation to European colonialism" that Uncle Sam refers to in dialogue that accompanies the image. The dialogue, among other things, recounts a bidding process for funds from Latin Americans asking General Marshall for funds. The absence of a "Marshall Plan" for Latin America marked the *cepalino* project and Latin American internationalism. (*Revista Topaze*, April 9, 1948. Colección Biblioteca Nacional de Chile, available in Memoria Chilena. By permission of Sebastián Ríos.)

might, by itself, change the balance of payments picture and improve the country's future ability to pay," Campos claimed.[32] Like *cepalinos,* Campos was convinced that industrialization and economic development were themselves the cause of balance of payments problems and that planning for the allocation of national and international resources to continue the process was one of the solutions to the development paradox.[33]

To protest against the negative turn of the multilateral lenders, Campos mobilized *cepalino* ideas. "In a recent United Nations report of experts on economic development," he claimed, "this type of philosophy was described as 'putting the cart of foreign exchange difficulties before the horse of economic development.'"[34] Although an opponent of *cepalinos,* Eugênio Gudin reiterated Campos's concern. He approached the president of the IBRD to advocate for greater effort to break a vicious circle of "loans not forthcoming because of the prevailing inflation and of the imbalance of international payments" while "inflation persists because foreign loans are not forthcoming."[35] As the IBRD and international donors generated frustrations in Brazil, *cepalinos* began looking for opportunities to expand their internationalist agenda and, in so doing, their influence with other Latin American governments.

Capturing Latin America

With their approach to planning and their partnership with the Brazilian state, *cepalinos* had established a toehold in Brazil, the rising regional powerhouse. They had begun to turn theory into practice. But the "technique of programming" was just the first tool with which *cepalinos* expected to resolve the periphery's development paradox and gain the confidence of the regional policymaking world. For *cepalinos*, circumventing the development paradox required not just planning and administrating but also increasing foreign resources. Latin American economists and policymakers, both *cepalinos* and their opponents alike, were frustrated with international lenders' tepid assistance, whether in the form of the IBRD's timid lending, the IMF's limited efforts to soften external blows, or the United States's retreat from the Good Neighbor policy. With Latin American policymakers eager for alternatives, *cepalinos* were ready to fill that void. To make their case, *cepalino* economists sought to mobilize and modify the existing international aid infrastructure.

The tenth Inter-American Conference, held in Caracas in March 1954, provided a chance to resurrect the old ideal of economic cooperation in the Americas. At Caracas, the Eisenhower administration attempted to rally Latin America around its international campaign against communism. US officials were alarmed at the success of Jacobo Arbenz and the Guatemalan Revolution and feared the Central American country would become the launching ground of a communist offensive in the region. Indeed, by the time of the conference, the United States had already authorized an operation to overthrow Arbenz, a plan that would ultimately succeed in late June. But in March, the United States offered numerous economic concessions to Latin American governments, even those who opposed US insinuations of intervention. One of those concessions, especially consequential for *cepalinos*, was the realization of an inter-American conference—usually dominated by security concerns—devoted exclusively to economic affairs.[36]

The resort town of Quitandinha, close to Rio de Janeiro, was the site selected for the economic forum to be organized by the Organization of American States (OAS) at the end of 1954.

Latin American economists and policymakers were unsure about what to expect from the Quitandinha meeting. In 1948, at the OAS's meeting at Bogotá, the presence of General Marshall suggested the possibility of a large-scale aid program similar to the European reconstruction package. Instead, security concerns dominated the agenda (see figures 2.1 and 2.2). Years later, Carlos Lleras Restrepo, former minister of finance and future president of Colombia, lamented that the projects of economic cooperation had then been postponed with "the same old vague statements of promotion of technical assistance and a sound commercial policy."[37] Aside from negative precedents and thwarted overtures, there were mixed messages coming from the Eisenhower administration. On the one hand, Milton Eisenhower, the president's brother and close advisor, endorsed the granting of small development loans and the Foreign Operations Office advocated for extensive development assistance and the stabilization of prices of primary products.[38] Both of these policies suggested a change toward more international cooperation for development in the region. On the other hand, Henry Holland, Deputy Secretary of State, insisted instead on the importance of private capital investments and the openness of the US markets.[39] Yet it was precisely the ability of the United States to act as an economic hegemonic power, fully opening its markets to Latin American exports and alleviating the dollar shortage that affected Europe and Latin America, that *cepalinos* were skeptical of.

Even before attendees gathered in Quitandinha, *cepalinos* eclipsed the US-dominated OAS. The two institutions, the OAS and the UN CEPAL, had been clashing for years. Ever since the announcement of the creation of CEPAL, the institution was haunted by accusations of duplication of functions with the economic arm of the Pan-American Union, the predecessor of the OAS. Up until the ratification of CEPAL as a permanent UN body in 1951, there were proposals to fuse the two organizations. However, the Pan-American Union had been particularly slow in the establishment of an institutional apparatus to tackle the economic problems of the area. It was only as a response to creation of its namesake in the United Nations that the Pan-American Union established the Inter-American Economic and Social Council in 1945.[40] It was only a Cold War context that led to the transformation of the Pan-American Union into the OAS. It was only after the establishment of CEPAL itself that the terms of reference of the OAS's Inter-American Economic and Social council were ratified.[41] While some saw CEPAL as an effort to overcome the disappointing results of the

OAS, others saw in CEPAL a duplication of functions and a redundant institution.[42]

But in 1954, recognizing their own limitations, the OAS organizers found the participation of *cepalinos* "not only possible but desirable." By calling attention to the development paradox, *cepalinos* had established a reputation and conquered a territory in the sphere of international development that was recognized by its inter-American counterpart. In May 1954 Prebisch met with the head of the Inter-American Economic and Social Council, the OAS economic arm, and swiftly assumed responsibility for the most important tasks of the agenda: the problems of international trade and the methods to finance development.[43] The meeting at Quitandinha gave *cepalinos* the chance they desired to intervene in international policy and shape the agenda to transform both centers and peripheries.

With their competitors ceding space, *cepalinos* took the lead for Quitandinha. In an effort to expand their regional reach and marshal the support of the regional leadership for their international cooperation project, Prebisch and his team summoned a group of dignitaries from different countries to Santiago. In August 1954 *cepalinos* convened a preparatory committee for the November meeting, with current and former ministers of the economy, heads of development agencies and central banks of Argentina, Brazil, Colombia, Chile, Costa Rica, and Mexico, as well as observers from international organizations such as the IMF at CEPAL's headquarters. At the gathering, they were not government representatives but simply "economists," Lleras Restrepo recalled, signaling the desire of *cepalinos* to represent a regional consensus among experts.[44] With the green light from member governments to postpone routine activities and focus on the Rio conference, *cepalinos* seized the opportunity to condense their ideas and present their platform for Latin American development.[45]

The first and most important part of the platform was a mechanism to finance development. If the Eisenhower administration stood for trade rather than aid, the *cepalino* strategy entailed aid for trade. For *cepalinos,* Latin America confronted a development paradox: industrialization promised to reduce dependence on exports, but it also increased the demand for imported machinery and equipment and hence the dependence on exports to buy imports. Therefore, financing industrialization required both more trade and more aid. Aware of the fiscal conservatism that prevailed in the US administration, *cepalinos* proposed the establishment of an inter-American fund to provide loans for industry, mining, and agriculture. Preempting conservative objections, *cepalinos* did not propose to pass the buck when it came to financing development. Instead, the *cepalino* plan envisioned shared responsibilities. The United States, as global hegemonic center, would provide half of the resources for the fund and Latin America the other half. Within the region, the fund would follow the quota distributions used by the IMF. Based in the United States and holding only US dollars, the proposed inter-American fund could raise additional resources by selling bonds in international markets.[46]

To capture the conceptual similarities to Europe while distancing themselves from the grant-based European experiment, *cepalinos* insisted that their proposal was "not a Marshall Plan for Latin America."[47] Like Europe in the early postwar years, Latin America confronted a catch-22 economic conundrum. Europe needed to revitalize its exports in order to pay for its imports, but it needed imports of raw materials and intermediary goods to export.[48] Similarly, Latin America, especially the Southern Cone area, needed increasing export proceeds to pay for the import of machinery, capital goods, and replacement parts that would in turn allow these countries to reduce the dependence on export proceeds from raw materials and primary goods. The Marshall Plan solved the European dilemma by providing the desired hard currency and by facilitating the payments of foreign goods in local currency, decreasing the pressure on hard currency.[49] The Marshall Plan caught the attention of *cepalinos* for its role in circumventing the dollar shortage and the foreign exchange gap, but they remained distrustful of its reliance on donations, subsidies, or one-sided attempts to steer a region's economy. Their vision of the inter-American fund instead represented a truly cooperative attempt that mobilized resources from both the center and the periphery to finance economic development. Since international trade was failing to provide the resources that development demanded, international aid was a privileged alternative.[50]

The second part of the *cepalino* platform contemplated significant transformations of the global center. By guaranteeing prices and markets for Latin America's exports through price stabilization agreements, *cepalinos* claimed the global economic center could reduce the risks associated with world economic fluctuations that hindered development in the periphery. If the global hegemon vouched for freer trade, *cepalinos* believed it had to lead by example. In their view, protectionism at the center—the existence of high tariff barriers for Latin American products—was one of the main limitations to the region's capacity to import and, consequently, to development. Based on the differences between center and peripheries, they argued against strict reciprocity in lowering tariff barriers and liberalizing trade. Whereas protectionism at the center actually diminished global trade, the effect of protectionism on the periphery was simply to transform the structure of trade in favor of capital goods and raw materials for industry without reducing overall trade, they claimed.

The third part of the platform contemplated changes in the periphery. First and foremost, *cepalinos* insisted on the importance of formulating and implementing economic development plans that followed the *cepalino* technique of programming. It was not merely that development plans were important for procuring foreign resources from international banks. They were also necessary to guide the import-substitution industrialization process and avoid detrimental external monetary crises. At this point, before the politics of inflation created division among them as discussed in the following chapter, *cepalinos* also recommended strong monetary and fiscal measures to halt inflation. They also insisted on implementing countercyclical policies—accumulating reserves in the upward trend of the economic cycle to be used in the downward slope—to soften the deleterious effects of the swings in international economy and maintain the rhythm of development in times of both resource-driven feast and famine.

The final part of CEPAL's platform promoted new lending criteria for international institutions such as the IBRD and the Export-Import Bank. Whereas international development organizations understood monetary stability as a prerequisite for lending, *cepalinos* insisted that lending was necessary for monetary stability. Since balance of payments crises were a product of the process of economic development itself, development aid could not only help further industrialization but also ease monetary imbalances by providing resources for capital goods and other key imports. Like *cepalinos,* who were coming to represent a regional consensus, Campos and even *cepalino* opponents like Gudin had voiced a similar demand a few years earlier when the Brazil-US commission had been unilaterally terminated. With this platform, *cepalinos* put the language of center and peripheries in action to solve the development paradox.

The *cepalino* report, which compressed their approach to development into a single policy document, circulated among the policymaking circles in the region and shaped the course of the conference. After three slow inaugural days, Jorge del Canto, a Chilean-born economist and IMF delegate to Quitandinha who would become head of the IMF's Western Hemisphere Department within a decade, reported back to headquarters that the "conference was gaining momentum," with the "emphasis falling on the financing of economic development and the basic CEPAL report."[51] CEPAL had proven to be "particularly prepared to provide the baseline documentation for the conference," the Mexican delegate claimed.[52] The relationship between CEPAL and OAS, which had been marked by years of antagonism and mutual accusations, acquired a new dimension. The tensions resolved as CEPAL gained favor. Participants contrasted the "far-from-lucid participation of the inter-American institution in economic matters" with the increased involvement of "CEPAL experts who had pertinent solutions to different problems."[53] The inter-American conference gave CEPAL a stage to define concrete proposals and reach a region-wide audience.[54] Though the conference took place under the OAS's aegis, *cepalinos* gained the upper hand as the spokesman for a regional project, dispelling doubts of those who had privileged the OAS.

Despite the final outcome at Rio, the conference represented a success for *cepalinos*. Their aim at Quitandinha was "to persuade not to innovate," Prebisch declared.[55] Latin American delegates adopted the *cepalino* tenets to advocate for the transformation of the global center and the cooperation between center and periphery. They embraced planning, supported rational protectionism in the periphery, and advocated for the use of development aid to deal with balance of payments difficulties if necessary. Echoing Prebisch's claims, the Mexican delegate argued that the low levels of trade and investment of the center in the periphery were the result of the shift in the financial leadership of the world after the First World from Great Britain to the United States, a country in itself in the process of development. The new global center therefore absorbed more than exported capital, creating immense problems for a capital and exchange-hungry periphery. This "state of affairs that our countries would have to live with for decades" justifies the "region's insistence on long-term international credits," he claimed. Following the lead of *cepalinos,* Antonio Cafiero, the Argentine representative, insisted that the instability of international prices and markets were Latin America's main economic problem. Therefore, the Argentine endorsed the *cepalino* recommendation of securing remunerative prices through international agreements and the increase of international financial and technical resources.[56] Latin American economists and policymakers were, alongside *cepalinos*, challenging the United States to act as global hegemonic center to open to trade and to transform the relationship between center and peripheries via international aid. With these tools *cepalinos* managed to set the agenda and locate themselves at the center of the discourse about economic development in Latin America.

With regard to increasing financial cooperation between center and periphery, however, Quitandinha was closer to a failure. Though some US senior officials advocated for greater development aid to Latin America, the Eisenhower administration refused to entertain the Latin American proposals. Instead, it limited its goodwill offering to a slight increase in the Export-Import Bank's lending capacity. Conference participants therefore called for a committee of experts to further study the issue to avoid the embarrassment of a failed conference. Eugene Black, president of the International Bank for Reconstruction and Development, said the institution was willing to significantly increase its disbursements, pending the improvement of Latin America's credit rating, which had been negatively affected by the balance of payments problems and "lack of capital in local currency to supplement the loans."[57] Those were, of course, precisely the reasons why *cepalinos* and the rest of the regional policymakers had advocated that the international development apparatus be overhauled. The United States's reluctance to support the Latin American initiatives discredited the United States's claims to internationalism, but it did little to erode Latin American economists' confidence in the *cepalinos* and their internationalist agenda. Claiming a delayed triumph, *cepalinos* would see their development platform reemerge as the baseline of the Alliance for Progress, as discussed in chapter 4.

Toward Latin American Integration and the "Baby Latin Fund"

The 1954 Quitandinha meeting recalibrated Latin American policymakers' expectations for international development aid. The conference barely addressed commodity price stabilization schemes or lower tariff barriers for Latin American commodities in global markets, both of which were also solutions to the development paradox. *Cepalinos* continued to insist that an economic cooperation plan was necessary, but in the face of continuous rebuffs from the United States, the IMF, and the World Bank, these economists began exploring other options. They were particularly eager to locate a solution to the region's development paradox that did not depend on cooperation between the industrial centers and the raw material–producing peripheries, although it ultimately did. In the absence of a large-scale financial scheme of cooperation between center and periphery in the mid-1950s, *cepalinos* began to float the idea of a continent-wide economic integration project.

Throughout the 1950s, Europe, which was turning the ideal of economic integration into a tangible reality, represented an important model for *cepalinos*. As early as 1948, Belgium, Netherlands, and Luxembourg came to an agreement for a customs union and signed on a common external tariff two years later. The European Recovery Program, known as the Marshall Plan, also provided a significant stimulus for economic integration since it established cooperation as a precondition for the disbursement of its large-scale aid. The Marshall Plan also provided the initial funds for the 1950 European Payments Union to facilitate intra-European trade. It also required the establishment of an institution, the Organization for European

Economic Cooperation, to produce joint economic plans for aid and recovery. That organization provided an important precedent for the establishment of the European Coal and Steel Community, a regional institution
that created a common market for coal and steel among France and Germany (wartime enemies), the Benelux countries, and Italy. That regional
institution, in turn, served as the stepping-stone for the establishment of a
further-reaching European Economic Community or the European Common
Market, in 1957. The European model, with its emphasis on aid, planning,
and payments, would influence *cepalinos'* and their contenders' views on
the possibilities and challenges of integration during that decade.

Although the European experiment was certainly in the minds of *cepalinos,* they also had direct experience with integrating markets closer to
home. In June 1951 Jorge Sol Castellanos, the minister of the economy of
El Salvador, approached Prebisch, head of CEPAL, with an offer the latter
could not refuse. As a former student of Prebisch's friend and colleague at
Harvard University, Robert Triffin, Sol Castellanos already had Prebisch's
ear.[58] After a few years in Washington, Sol Castellanos had returned to El
Salvador in 1950. In less than two years as minister, he had rallied the support of Manuel Noriega, a fellow Harvard graduate and then minister of
the economy in Guatemala, as well as of Enrique Delgado, the Nicaraguan
minister, for the project to integrate the Central American economies. The
three ministers, alongside a more reluctant Costa Rican delegate, secured
the support of the rest of the Latin American governments for the creation
of a committee for economic cooperation in Central America under the auspices of CEPAL.[59] The Central American project would become a springboard for bigger *cepalino* ambitions.

In Central America, the interests of Sol Castellanos and of *cepalinos*
aligned. For Sol Castellanos, the economic integration of the five Central
American republics offered a solution to the obstacles that El Salvador had
faced in its attempts at state-led industrialization. For Sol Castellanos, that
the United States and the Soviet Union, the world's two superpowers, were
continental-size economies confirmed the importance of "large economic
spaces" for industrialization and growth. The incipient stages of European
integration reinforced the notion that the new world order required supranational spaces "to reap the benefits of economies of scale" as well as to
"domestically produce previously imported goods."[60] El Salvador, which
had the most dynamic export economy of Central America, was also gradually establishing itself at the forefront of the state-industrialization process in the area, but it was limited by the size of the market given its small
population and a very unequal society.[61]

In the road to integration Sol Castellanos considered *cepalinos* crucial
allies, in part because of their ability to act as nonpartisan mediators in the

region's tense political landscape. The relations between these countries were, in the words of Sol Castellanos, "cool and sporadic," "dealing with each other as one power against another," which entailed that "a Central American conversation could not to be carried out by Central Americans."[62] The region, once a federation, had been torn apart by civil wars; territorial disputes were ongoing; and most importantly, deep political divisions pitted entrenched dynastic rulers in some countries and rising social democrats in others, and were further exacerbated by Arbenz and his seemingly radical transformation of Guatemala.[63]

For Prebisch and *cepalinos,* the Central American cooperation project represented the chance to move from theory to practice and to reaffirm the position of the institution in the region beyond Chile, Brazil, and the Southern Cone. In the lead-up to the agreement and to Sol Castellanos's request, *cepalino* studies had paved the ground for policymakers like Sol Castellanos by emphasizing the potential of intraregional trade. Thereafter, *cepalinos* found themselves with a seat at the table in a groundbreaking cooperation initiative that, in many ways, was their own creation.

Aside from providing *cepalinos* with critical experience in the politics of integrating markets, their involvement with the Central American market provided a base for CEPAL's expansion. In July 1951 Prebisch established in Mexico City what was going to be CEPAL's first regional office outside Santiago. Aside from providing a convenient location for conducting economic research in Central America, the office allowed Prebisch to cultivate the friendship and collegial relations he had established some years earlier with the Mexican economists at the Banco de México, the *Fondo de Cultura Económica* publishing house, and the schools of *Universidad Nacional Autónoma de México* and *El Colegio de México.* Víctor Urquidi, a young London School of Economics (LSE) graduate, member of the Mexican delegation to Bretton Woods, well connected with the national economic policymaking elite, and editor of the region-wide *El Trimestre Económico,* was Prebisch's choice for leading the Mexico office and cementing *cepalinos'* relations in northern Latin America. The son of a diplomat, Urquidi had lived in Central America during his youth. He became CEPAL's coordinator of the Central American cooperation initiative and, months later, the director of the Mexico office.

The path to integration was long and winding in Central America, but *cepalinos* were, more often than not, at the center of the project's conception. Urquidi and Prebisch paid several visits to democratic Costa Rica and revolutionary Guatemala, as well as to authoritarian Nicaragua and an uninterested Honduras, all in the name of "quiet diplomacy" to create consensus and set the agenda.[64] Given their expectation of falling international terms of trade for the periphery, *cepalinos* conceptualized the regional integration process as first and foremost an industrialization strategy to expand the size of what "were not even national but local markets."[65] The main and most controversial idea was the creation of a program of industrial integration, in which new industries would be strategically located in a specific country with the purpose of producing for the area as a whole and with the expectation of reciprocal exchange. Later on, the difficulties in the implementation of that strategy led Luis Somoza, the son and presidential heir of decades-long dictator Anastasio Somoza, to presumptuously tell Urquidi to "bring the Central American industrialists here and I will tell them where to put their factories, and problem solved."[66] Throughout the years of negotiations, *cepalinos* mediated between the push for more expedient trade solutions through bilateral or even tripartite agreements and the pull for the more arduous process toward multilateralism.[67] Delgado, the Nicaragua representative, denounced the Salvadorian attempt to "reduce the other states to the status of supplying primary products and raw materials," thus defending the *cepalino* principle of gradualism and reciprocity, which could guarantee a balanced spatial distribution of the new industries.[68] Although *cepalinos* would eventually be successful in bringing the initiative to the fore, the Central American common market bore the mark of the unresolved contradiction of the unequal trade relations between centers and peripheries within.

Even before the Central American common market took final form, *cepalinos* took the lead on a project for a continent-wide integrated market in Latin America. Like their Central American counterparts and their republic federation, southern Latin Americans had contemplated political integration since Simon Bolívar's rapidly fractured Gran Colombia and the Panama Congress of 1826, a convention designed to formulate a common position against their former empire. In the late nineteenth and early twentieth centuries, prominent intellectuals in Cuba, Argentina, Peru, and Uruguay, to a name a few, championed the idea of a unified Latin or Hispanic America, mostly in opposition to Anglo-America. In the mid-twentieth century, earlier idealism turned into concrete proposals when *cepalinos*, in the wake of the both the European and the Central American experience, took the lead once again.

For *cepalinos*, the limited scale of trade between Latin American countries served both as evidence for and a contributor to the development paradox. Driven by the impetus to industrialize, each country had developed similar industries "all struggling against the limited size of the national market." Prebisch depicted the region as a collection of "watertight compartments," with no channels of communication with one another.[69] A regional market could increase intraregional flow and break those barriers. However, the still ill-defined regional market was itself limited by the problem it was trying to resolve: the recurrent lack of dollars or convertible, hard currency resulting from the trade gap between import needs and exports proceeds and the resulting foreign exchange gap. "If intraregional trade demanded the use of hard currency," Prebisch explained, "it is evident that the initiative would face serious limitations because most countries would prefer to use convertible currencies for trade outside the region in order to obtain capital and other goods not yet produced in Latin America."[70] Thus, *cepalinos* attributed the limited size of the intraregional trade, among other factors, to the lack of a region-wide payments policy.[71] Once again, Latin America confronted the development paradox of needing dollars to eschew the need for dollars (figure 2.3).

In the early postwar years, Europeans had found a solution to a similar problem. Their approach therefore figured prominently in the minds of *cepalinos*. Established in 1951, the European Payments Union (EPU) worked as a mechanism to foment intra-European trade while circumventing the need for dollars to carry out that trade. By coordinating transactions and facilitating credits to finance temporary deficits, the EPU helped resolve a parallel problem to Latin America's development paradox. The Marshall Plan funds were the cornerstone of the EPU; in Latin America, their absence was an enormous hindrance. In its absence, the *cepalinos* proposed a "new organism," a regional clearing agent, that would allow "different countries [to] settle their accounts not against each other but to the union as a whole."[72] CEPAL proposed itself as the clearing agency, that is, the body that would act as the intermediary in paying funds and a centralized facility for settling trades. Thus, the existence of a payments union and a regional market would allow CEPAL to leave its studies behind and instead transform itself into an operational agency with leverage over monetary transactions and policies.

The *cepalino* initiative raised skepticism at the IMF. The similarities between the European and the Latin American cases that *cepalinos* capitalized on seemed exaggerated to IMF staff. First, there were no prospects of American aid—something that had been crucial for European integration (figure 2.4). Second, the Latin American intraregional trade was much more geographically concentrated and less diversified in terms of goods, compared with Europe, to justify an equally complex payments system.[73] Despite their skepticism, the IMF officials had bitter memories and compelling reasons to entertain the *cepalino* initiative. In the early postwar years, the IMF "was asked to serve as the agent of the six countries which first organized a system of monetary compensations," but, a staff member explained, the "invitation was declined by the default." In order to avoid "past mistakes"

FIGURE 2.3   *Top*, The cartoon portrays a diverse set of international characters trying to feed themselves from the "Fondo Monetario" or International Monetary Fund pot with a spoon of "cambio libre" or "free exchange rates." *Bottom*, The cartoon illustrates British Prime Minister Clement Atlee complaining to Uncle Sam about Argentina—shown here as a woman carrying bags of wheat and beef—and her withholding of food supplies. In response, Uncle Sam says, "Little Argentina if you do not give some wheat, beef, and butter, I will take away your *foreign exchange* allowance. . . ." (emphasis added). Foreign exchange and dollar scarcity were a fundamental problem for the *cepalino* project. (*Revista Topaze*, February 6, 1948. Colección Biblioteca Nacional de Chile, available in Memoria Chilena.)

FIGURE 2.4 Dwight Eisenhower and Raúl Prebisch, depicted as children, play with puzzle pieces. Prebisch's pieces are Latin American countries and Eisenhower's are European countries. Eisenhower gleefully admonishes Prebisch, saying, "Silly, you haven't finished your puzzle and I already finished mine!" Prebisch replies, "I am not surprised! Why don't you lend me some of that glue you have," referring to the "financial aid" pot of glue Eisenhower clearly has dipped his brushed in to stick the countries together. In the background appears a parental figure labeled "Fondo Monetario Internacional" or *IMF*, who sits with his back to Prebisch and Eisenhower, ignoring the efforts of both European and Latin American economic integration. (*Revista Topaze,* November 27, 1959. Colección Biblioteca Nacional de Chile, available in Memoria Chilena. By permission of Jimmy Scott.)

that would leave the IMF equally excluded from shaping policies in Latin America, the staff recommended the Board to "profess interest" in the *cepalino* initiative and "sympathy" toward a Latin American cooperation and multilateral trade project. Despite their reservations of the project being technically "ill-defined," they recognized it was driven by "strong feeling of prestige and political expediency."[74] The European precedent showed the IMF staff that they could not afford to be sidelined in Latin America.

Initially, the IMF sought a prominent role in the *cepalino* project, but this early expression of goodwill soon curdled as the initiative acquired momentum. At first, the IMF welcomed the *cepalinos'* call for technical assistance for the multilateral payments and even volunteered to "set up the machinery for better exchanges of information" between the central banks or monetary authorities who may be potentially interested in settling accounts.[75] The IMF insisted on its staff being invited to and present in all discussions with Central Banks, and it even suggested that the IMF should serve as clearing agent, even if it could not provide the financial resources that the United States had provided for the EPU.

As time went on, however, the relations between the institutions grew more tense. The IMF staff resented the idea that CEPAL might serve as an "informational clearing agent," handling and receiving reports of the balance of payments position of each country, an exchange that was usually the purview of the IMF.[76] "It makes more sense for us rather than for CEPAL to duplicate the arrangement," a staff member explained.[77] The IMF staff's hostility only increased as it became clear that CEPAL hoped to act as the actual, not just the informational, clearing agent. As tension built, criticisms became sharper.

Despite their professed sympathy with the goals of *cepalinos,* the IMF staff believed that simpler solutions were available, if the goals were to liberalize trade, establish multilateral systems, and standardize exchange practices. Rather than instituting complicated compensatory payments schemes, del Canto, the main IMF staff figure in Latin America, argued that trade could be increased by simplifying the exchange rate regimes and lowering tariff barriers. The IMF proposed working with each country individually rather than devising complicated regional arrangements to increase trade.[78] Thus, at the 1957 CEPAL plenary meeting, where *cepalinos* discussed the payments scheme under the propitious winds of the signature of the Treaty of Rome for the formation of a European Economic Community, IMF representatives "[fought] inch by inch" to "modify the language of [the] resolution."[79] Ultimately, the IMF staff believed that *cepalinos* were overly ambitious and naïve, placing "too many hopes in such machinery [for clearing balances] as the cure to more basic problems."[80] But there was more at stake in the IMF's resistance to the *cepalino* proposal than merely conceptual differences.

The IMF economists resented the *cepalinos* for their encroachment into what they considered their territory, fearing that a Latin American common market would marginalize their institution. *Cepalinos* had not limited their proposal to one that established a multilateral payments arrangement but had instead floated a plan that would affect currencies, exchange rates, and balance of payments—directly impinging on the IMF's functions and areas of competence. In offering CEPAL as the clearing agent, *cepalinos* were effectively creating mechanisms to broaden the institution's influence and power by entering into the field of monetary matters. When the idea was first raised, a member of the IMF staff countered that the "function of agent" should be open to bids. A second staff member seconded this, recognizing that multiple Latin American governments may find the "clearing agent proposal" appealing, and therefore not supporting it would alienate them from the IMF.[81]

As the proposal moved forward, the IMF's opposition grew increasingly louder and disgruntled. Their varied critiques boiled down to the idea that no new institutions were necessary to fulfill the needs of a Latin American common market like *cepalinos* proposed; any unanticipated needs that may arise could be fulfilled by the IMF. If the Latin Americans required settlement in dollars or sterling for multilateral trade for instance, they should turn to the IMF, a staff member clarified.[82] In fact, for the IMF staff, the *cepalino* proposal entailed a duplication of functions with the IMF. Del Canto reminded Prebisch that the IMF, like the *cepalino* payments union, was supposed to "utilize assets of creditor countries to give help, based on certain conditions, to debtor countries." The *cepalino* initiative, in other words, directly competed with the IMF's interests in Latin America. If there was going to be a multilateral payments scheme in Latin America, the IMF—not CEPAL—should run it.

Tensions reached an apex at the 1959 CEPAL plenary meeting in Panama, where the first complete proposal of the regional market was discussed. Building on the momentum created by Argentina, Chile, and Brazil, who agreed to create a free trade area just before the meeting, *cepalinos* recommended the creation of the regional market and urged regional governments to "implement immediately the . . . protocol leading to the establishment of a payments union with [CEPAL] as agent." Del Canto and the IMF firmly opposed.[83] "Our concern with the Latin American regional market arises from the fact that CEPAL considers a payments union an essential instrument for the regional market," del Canto explained.[84] Not only was the payments union unnecessary to foster intraregional trade when tariff reductions and exchange rate unification suffice, del Canto argued, but the *cepalino* emphasis on bilateral arrangements could also endanger multilateral trade. Prebisch countered that the IMF, fearing the loss of ground in

Latin America, would oppose any proposal that had "regional rather than global scope." Prebisch defended the proposal in a "spirited rebuttal" that argued that the European Payments Union had not just spurred European intraregional trade but also propelled world convertibility, which was in the interest of a global institution like the IMF. In response, Chilean and Argentinean representatives, whose countries were engaged in significant IMF-supported stabilization plans, defended the words and work of the IMF. With the support of major regional players, the IMF representative prevailed at Panama. The draft resolution dropped its references to a payments union as an essential component of the common market.[85] It would only take a few more months for the IMF to completely bury the *cepalino* initiative, which the Fund staff had begun to refer to derogatorily as the "baby Latin Fund."

Although the payments union initiative collapsed, and with it CEPAL's ambition for more policy leverage, the process of regional integration did commence. When the Latin American Free Trade Association (LAFTA)— undersigned by Argentina, Brazil, Chile, México, Peru, Paraguay, and Uruguay—was established in February 1960, *cepalinos* were hesitant to call it a victory. *Cepalinos* regarded the 1959 meeting as a success, but it was clear that they had begun to lose support. The Mexican and the Cuban delegations criticized *cepalinos* for endorsing the subregional proposal of Argentina, Chile, and Brazil in an effort to propel their own initiative at the cost of a truly region-wide common market. At the same time, *cepalinos'* faith in the possibility of regional cooperation dwindled as the regional discussions began to follow similar patterns as those in Central America and at the global General Agreement for Tariffs and Trade. Small countries feared the excessive power of the larger ones, agricultural-producing countries were at odds with the more industrialized ones, and there was little consensus on the goods that would be part of the common market. Chile and Argentina, initial supporters of the *cepalino* payments union and key members of the trade association, rejected the credit-awarding function that Prebisch envisioned for CEPAL. In part because LAFTA was more a declaration of good intentions than an outline for a common market, the signatories of LAFTA relegated CEPAL to an advisory body rather than the executive, operational role *cepalinos* had aspired to have.[86] By early 1960, *cepalinos* had stopped insisting on the payments union and had even called on the IMF to assume any operational role that might arise in the future.[87] Although the IMF staff would later protest that *cepalinos* were trying to revive the "Latin Fund," the payments union idea was dead. CEPAL's confrontation with the IMF, however, lived on.

Conclusions

As they transitioned from developing the center-periphery theory to implementing an approach to development based on resolving the "development paradox," *cepalinos* aspired to broaden the scope of their influence and secure the position of their institution among a competitive landscape. In the context of mushrooming international organizations, CEPAL lacked the long history of the OAS, heir to the century-long Pan-American Union, or the financial clout of the World Bank and the IMF. Despite or because of those shortcomings, *cepalinos* attempted to position their institution as the agent of large-scale development initiatives with more claws than solely recommendations. Speaking to the concerns of regional economic policymakers, *cepalinos* conceptualized the "development paradox" in ways that policymakers steering exchange-hungry economies identified with. By formulating development planning techniques, *cepalinos* inserted themselves in the bureaucracy of a fast-growing and increasingly powerful Brazil. They recruited regional policymakers into their fold and launched a bid for a "not-a-Marshall-Plan," which would have placed CEPAL in a steering role in evaluating plans and allocating resources, an ambition they would rekindle with the Alliance for Progress. They expanded to set foot in northern Latin America through their role in establishing the Central American common market project and confronted the divisions between center and peripheries at the subregional level that had haunted and would continue to haunt global discussions about trade such as those at General Agreement on Tariffs and Trade (GATT) and United Nations Conference for Trade and Development (UNCTAD). On the road to the Latin American market, they attempted to position CEPAL as the clearing agent for a regional payment union that would put their organization at the center of an economically and politically powerful instrument. They spared no effort to transform their institution into more than an advisory body.

Although these initiatives failed to bring *cepalinos* the clout they imagined, they paved the road toward the institution's regional hegemony in the field of economic ideas. The effects were long-lasting. To disseminate their ideas and facilitate the adoption of their planning techniques, *cepalinos* initiated training courses that expanded their influence not just at the top but at mid-level bureaucratic positions. These programs also helped nurture a new cohort of *cepalinos*, especially in Brazil, keeping the *cepalino* ideas alive well beyond the institution's golden years. A generation of Brazilian economists who were influential policymakers or researchers in the last decades of the century, either as opponents or defenders of *cepalino* ideas, first encountered economic development theory through the *cepalino* training programs.[88] The recruitment of economists from different nationalities, the training of civil servants and researchers in Santiago, and the mobilization of local agents throughout the region enacted the regional approach that the Commission aspired to represent. Furthermore, their internationalist agenda, at a time of perceived neglect from the world's hegemonic center toward Latin American development, gained *cepalinos* the confidence of the regional policymaking elite. By facilitating negotiations, leading discussions, and trying to craft a space for CEPAL in the institutional integration apparatus, *cepalinos* positioned themselves as the bearers of a regional project.

Beyond these important legacies, the dispute with the IMF about the payments union had important effects for both institutions. Although it didn't materialize, the *cepalino* payments union initiative created tensions that entangled the international economic community for years to come. The IMF was at the center of that dispute. First, the *cepalino* initiative forced the IMF's staff to confront its own marginalization in Europe. If they were to avoid a similar fate in Latin America, they needed to reinforce their interest in the region. Furthermore, the *cepalino* attempt to advance onto the monetary field, which the IMF considered its exclusive territory, ruffled the IMF staff's feathers. This set up a confrontation between the two institutions that would soon develop into a head-on ideological conflict when the *cepalinos* developed their "structural approach to inflation."

THREE

"Structuralism," "Monetarism," and the Politics of Inflation

After wrestling with conflicting ideas about inflation for over a decade, *cepalinos* were at the center of a controversy that was engulfing Latin America and the world beyond by 1963. From regional central bankers and ministers to leading academic researchers, *cepalino* "structuralism" became a phenomenon to come to terms with. Harvard, Oxford, and Stuttgart professors, to name a few, were compelled to respond to the ideas about the "structural" causes of inflation emerging in and rapidly spreading across Latin America. New research projects emerged in the Americas, North and South, to put *cepalino* ideas to the test. The "structural approach to inflation" inspired and fueled heated economic policy debates in Argentina, Brazil, and Chile, among other countries, breeding new *cepalino* allies as well as new adversaries. Once again, *cepalinos* were setting the intellectual and policy agenda and impelling their opponents to regroup and formulate new strategies. As a result, the confrontation between "structuralists" and "monetarists" became perhaps the most important economic policy controversy of the postwar era in Latin America.

The controversy between "structuralists" and "monetarists" was not just about ideas. Certainly, "structuralists" and "monetarists" had different diagnoses of the causes of inflation in Latin America, especially in the Southern Cone, that had hardened over the years. Whereas "structuralists" advanced a "structural approach to inflation" that identified the global inequalities in the terms of trade and the unequal land tenure structure as the causes of inflation, the International Monetary Fund (IMF) and the "monetarists" explained inflation as a result of excessive monetary expansion and fiscal and exchange mismanagement. Whereas "monetarists" privileged low inflation and monetary stability as prerequisites for economic development, "structuralists" saw monetary instability as a consequence of economic development. But the controversy also pitted two international organizations competing for influence in the region: the Economic Commission for Latin America (CEPAL) and the IMF. Amid this rivalry, it was not *cepalinos* who were losing the battle of ideas; in turn, it was the IMF staff who increasingly found themselves on the defensive.

Through the conflict between "structuralism" and "monetarism," CEPAL and the IMF came to have what economist Albert Hirschman called "institutional personalities."[1] Yet *cepalinos* were not always "structuralists" and perhaps the IMF staff were not always or not all "monetarists." As inflation came to occupy center stage in economic policy debates in the mid-1950s, *cepalinos* embarked on a search for the origins of inflation in Chile. Personal divisions, clashing political visions among *cepalinos,* and conflicting choices shaped the formulation of the "structural approach to inflation." As *cepalinos* moved between Chile and Brazil, the "structural approach to inflation" acquired new meaning. In contrast to Chile's slow growth and rapid inflation, Brazil was experiencing rapid growth and rapid inflation. Whereas concerns with income redistribution and the social costs of stabilization drove the Chilean debate and shaped the "structural approach to inflation," in Brazil "structuralism" revolved around denouncing the potential trade-offs between monetary stability and economic growth in Brazil. As the inflation debate migrated to Brazil, the "structural approach to inflation" turned *cepalinos* into "structuralists," the radical alternative to "monetarists." The ideas and "personalities" of the two institutions arose in tandem as the rise of the *cepalinos'* "structuralism" led to the denunciation and emergence of "monetarism."

Toward the *Cepalino* or "Structural" Approach to Inflation

In October 1949, breaking with a long tradition of "tolerance to inflation," the Chilean government invited the United Nations to "provide policy advice on how to harmonize economic development with monetary stability."[2] The Chilean ministers of Economy and Finance, worried that the UN mission would take too long to support an urgently needed stabilization, requested an IMF mission on credit policy as well. Given worldwide inflation in the war and early postwar years, domestic inflation did not seem a particularly significant problem for the Radical Party governments of the era. Throughout the period, inflation had been constantly increasing at an average of 20 percent, but there was no sense of threat to economic development or social peace. New industries emerged as a result of wartime shortages, and a degree of income redistribution was achieved by keeping cost-of-living increases at bay through price controls, subsidies, and wage readjustments in excess of costs for the working and middle classes, key constituencies of the Radicals. However, as inflation accelerated and highly disruptive strikes met with increased government repression, the prevailing notions of the compatibility of inflation, development, and welfarism began to falter. President Gabriel González Videla turned to the UN and the IMF for assistance.[3] In the context of the IMF and UN missions, *cepalinos* presented their initial observations about Chilean inflation.

The *cepalino* diagnosis of the Chilean inflation coincided with that of the IMF and echoed the prevailing ideas about inflation in the field. The IMF mission highlighted the wage-price spiral—the self-perpetuating cycles of wage increases leading to price increases—as the main explanation of Chile's inflationary trend.[4] For the IMF staff, the Chilean inflation was a typical case of a rise in wages transferred to consumers through higher prices and leading to further wage increases in a repetitive cycle. In turn, in his Havana speech on center and peripheries, Raúl Prebisch expressed a serious concern about the tolerance to inflation of monetary authorities in the region and questioned the alleged positive effects of inflation on economic development. Rather than stimulating investment and thus development, inflation fostered luxury consumption and speculation, a diagnosis that he and the IMF staff would reaffirm years later.[5] For *cepalinos,* the Chilean case was an uncontroversial example of a cost-driven inflation. Driven by the justifiable and commendable attempt to increase the standard of living of masses, nominal salary increases tended to go beyond rises in productivity or what could be absorbed by profits, leading to demand for credit and in turn to monetary expansion. Those members of society that, unlike white- and blue-collar workers, were not politically organized to defend their position with recurrent income readjustments bore the cost of the price increases, Raúl Prebisch explained. Within that framework, inflation became the mechanism by which one group transmitted the burden of the increase in prices to other parts of the collectivity through a long chain of wage and price increases, or a wage-price spiral[6] (figure 3.1). As a result, Chile had "not been able to escape the spiral of prices and wages that for years now has characterized its inflationary process," and thus *cepalinos* could do nothing but "confirm the widespread view that a cost-driven inflation was the best description of the phenomenon."[7] Both the IMF staff

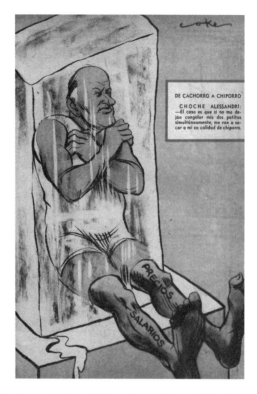

FIGURE 3.1   The image depicts Chilean Jorge Alessandri, minister of the economy in 1949, in his underwear encased in a block of ice with his legs protruding. One of his legs is labeled "prices" ("precios"), and the other is labeled "wages" ("salaries"). Reflecting prevailing ideas about how to combat inflation, the minister says, "If you don't allow me to freeze both legs at the same time, I am going to be sacrificed as a lamb." (*Revista Topaze*, August 26, 1949. Colección Biblioteca Nacional de Chile, available in Memoria Chilena.)

and *cepalinos* reaffirmed the mainstream Keynesian explanation for the Chilean war and postwar inflation.

As inflation reached unprecedented levels and social tensions in Santiago escalated, some *cepalinos* began to question their initial cost-driven approach. The workers and middle class's disenchantment with the Radicals and the political establishment more broadly brought about the triumph of General Carlos Ibáñez in 1952.[8] Running on a populist platform, the former dictator, who had been in power during the Great Depression, promised to fight corruption and inflation. His military trajectory, his appeal to workers, and his distance from the traditional political establishment reminded many of the powerful Juan Domingo Perón across the Andes.[9] Yet, instead of bringing down inflation, stimulating industrial growth, and alleviating social tensions, the Ibáñez government saw the acceleration of inflation up to 50 percent by 1955, the loss of momentum of the industrial sector, and head-on confrontation with labor. His initial support for the establishment of the *Central Unica de Trabajadores* (CUT)—an umbrella organization of white- and blue-collar workers, of Marxist and non-Marxist unions—turned into hostility with the imprisonment of its leader and the government opposition to the CUT's first general strike in February 1953.[10] In September 1954 a lengthy strike in the copper mines led to a prolonged state of siege, and the numerous demonstrations made the army a common presence in Santiago.[11] The tensions with labor and the inability to tame inflation gradually shifted Ibáñez's populist coalition to the right, leading *cepalinos* to reassess their position on the origins of inflation.

The tension between Prebisch and the younger members of the collective broke the consensus that had brought *cepalinos* together. For Brazilian economist Celso Furtado the cost-driven interpretation was not only conceptually flawed but also politically disturbing. For Furtado, the wage-price spiral was a superficial phenomenon and thus did not provide an adequate explanation of the origins of inflation. "We all know," he added, "that entrepreneurs only accept an increase in their [wage] cost if they expect demand to expand."[12] Most importantly, Furtado believed that the cost-driven approach was a deviation from *cepalino* founding tenets and therefore also conceptually flawed. The cost-inflation approach had no consideration for what *cepalinos* had repeatedly insisted on: that the position of Latin America in the periphery of global economy restricted economic development by generating the development paradox discussed in Chapter 2.[13] For Furtado, the corollary of that *cepalino* claim was that the position of Latin America in the world—and the external payments problems it generated— was at the root of the inflationary tendencies in the region as well. For Furtado, inflation was the result of the process of economic development of the periphery itself: development increased demand for imported goods such as capital and replacement parts that outpaced the growth of the dwindling export proceeds resulting from falling terms of trade, leaving the region with a big monetary gap and mismatch between supply and demand that caused inflation. Furtado insisted that inflation was not the cause but the consequence of the external disequilibrium and was therefore not a monetary phenomenon as the IMF staff and Prebisch had originally advanced.[14] With the cost-driven explanation, *cepalinos* not only had downplayed the effect of what was their most important contribution to development thinking but also had renounced to a crucial and innovative insight that Furtado hoped to rescue.

Most important for Furtado, the cost-driven approach was also politically disturbing. For him, the cost-driven perspective implied that workers
and unions were held responsible for the inflation problem. Furtado firmly
opposed Prebisch's attempt to identify labor, "the most aggressive group
in the fight for income redistribution" and "blame[d] it for inflation." That
the "phrase cost-inflation is starting to spread as a slogan of the conservative classes" should serve as a warning sign for *cepalinos*, Furtado claimed.[15]
The prevailing *cepalino* view on inflation not only disregarded some of their
most fundamental assumptions about Latin America's economic development trajectory but also appeared to threaten the bold and progressive
project they aspired to represent.

As alternatives to Prebisch's cost-driven approach, *cepalinos* entertained
other approaches that redressed some of Furtado's critiques. Even before
joining *cepalinos* in 1953, Aníbal Pinto Santa Cruz, member of one of
Chile's most traditional families and part of a political and intellectual lin-
eage of liberal ex-presidents, had insisted on conceptualizing the Chilean
inflation as a "social battle," providing a sociological approach that distanced itself from Prebisch's economic explanation. After obtaining a degree in law at the University of Chile and studying public finances at the
London School of Economics (LSE), Pinto coordinated several journalistic
enterprises, among which the most successful was perhaps the nonacademic
magazine *Panorama Económico*. The magazine was a staple within the political, economic, and intellectual elite as well as within sectors of the left,
eventually becoming a vehicle for the circulation of *cepalino* ideas.[16] From
the editorial pages of the magazine and in numerous articles, Pinto claimed
that the prevailing inflationary circumstances of strikes and repression,
wage freezes and price readjustments, were "analogous to a daily, small
war between existing social groups to avoid not losing or to win positions
in a protracted and tense battle."[17] Rather than an isolated problem of price
stability or monetary and fiscal policy, for Pinto, the problem of inflation
had a social and political character that any attempts to curb inflation had
to acknowledge.[18] Like Furtado later on, Pinto conceptualized inflationary
episodes as processes of income redistribution.

Driven by a concern with social conflict over income, Pinto and other
cepalinos began to place increasing attention on the power of labor in inflationary episodes. Unions had been a strong force in Chile's political landscape, especially in the foreign-owned mining industries such as nitrates
and copper, since the early twentieth century.[19] But with the emergence in
1953 of the CUT, labor gained a more visible role. As the struggle for redistribution unfolded, "a relatively new element in Latin America had
emerged," Pinto claimed. While entrepreneurs and the state had long used

inflation as an instrument for appropriating a larger share of national income, according to Pinto "white- and blue-collar workers organized in unions" were only recently fighting for their share. Although Pinto and other *cepalinos* defended Furtado's position, they also raised a word of caution. For the monetary and fiscal instruments to have the desired restrictive effect, the Chilean society had to come to terms with what *cepalinos* called the "unions' instrument." Without eliminating the pressure from the sector [of white- and blue-collar workers] it won't be possible to contain the [inflationary] spiral," *cepalinos* claimed. [20] If inflation was a form of social conflict, solving the problem required shared sacrifices and some form of social pact.

The prominence given to unions and labor was a double-edged sword in the spirited discussion about inflation in Chile and in Latin America. As inflation escalated, Pinto explained, it became harder to see if income was chasing prices or prices were chasing costs. The CUT "gave a significant step," Pinto explained, "by acknowledging that they could not continue to fight for mere nominal wage increments." But the CUT as well as "many leftist political platforms" failed to understand the "character of the current inflationary process," he added emphatically. Their "attempt to redistribute income without inflationary consequences was praiseworthy but illusory," Pinto claimed.[21] Wage readjustments could not simply be transferred to the foreign corporations or capitalists as some of them claimed, he added. The sheer size of the wage increases dwarfed the possibilities of squeezing them out profits. Thus, Pinto categorically questioned the beliefs of "demagogues who cannot even fool those who they are trying to favor."[22] In the face of unrelenting inflation, *cepalinos* began to fear they were also feeding agitators, opportunists, and other unwanted forces on the left.

By mid-1955, fearing to give ammunition to demagogues or to embolden conservatives, Pinto and *cepalinos* were trapped in a conundrum. With the cost approach to inflation, Prebisch put labor and the containment of wages in the crux of the struggle against inflation, aligning *cepalinos* with conservatives. By characterizing inflation as a social battle, Pinto defended labor's claims for redistribution in a response to what Furtado and others believed was the conservative cost-driven inflation approach. However, by defending labor's claims, Pinto had unintentionally downplayed the importance of the containment of the wage-price spiral, feeding the opposition to anti-inflation measures of demagogues and other forces of the left. Neither the right's strategy of containing wages nor the left's strategy of continuous above-inflation readjustments was in itself enough to stop what was considered a violent pressure of the wage-price spiral. The conundrum would be resolved after the experience of two highly controversial stabilization plans.

The first of those stabilization plans was launched in Chile in mid-1955, when a sense of chaos prevailed in the Chilean capital. Three finance ministers lost their position that year. The hostility between the government and congress increased.[23] With rising social tensions and inflation reaching an almost 100 percent annual rate, President Ibáñez, whose government coalition had turned firmly to the right, hired Klein & Saks, a Washington consulting firm with strong ties to bankers in Wall Street, to begin a definitive attack against inflation.[24] For *cepalino* economists, the decision of the Ibáñez government to consult North American advisors was almost insulting. "Not even in countries in a more incipient economic, social, or cultural evolution" than Chile, "are these missions justified," Aníbal Pinto claimed. The "national economic problems are inseparable from other social, political, and historical phenomena," and are thus, "beyond the purview of foreign experts," he explained.[25] Because Chile had "perhaps the best technical resources to deal with economic and financial problems," economists at CEPAL "were appalled" by the decision, Furtado recalled.[26]

The Klein & Saks stabilization plan laid bare a harsh reality. Even at home, *cepalinos* had little policy influence when it came to inflation and domestic monetary policy. The previous year President Ibáñez had asked Eduardo Frei, Christian Democrat senator and firm *cepalino* ally, to formulate a plan to combat inflation. In turn, Frei rallied the support of a group of economists, among which was *cepalino* Pinto himself. In Pinto's words, that plan was "put back on the shelf" shortly after being written. Instead, the Chilean government hired a foreign firm that proposed limits to credit expansion, elimination of subsidies and price controls, and a reduction in the wage readjustments, a set of policy recommendations that would become increasingly identified with "monetarism" and the IMF but some of which Pinto had himself recommended. So Pinto and *cepalinos* realized they had not been outmaneuvered by "high-caliber and responsible technical expertise."[27] In combination with more long-term fiscal and social reforms, Pinto had included in his "shelved" plan some of the short-term monetary measures proposed by the Klein & Saks mission. Rather, though *cepalinos* like Pinto and Furtado had insisted on moving beyond monetary explanations and monetary instruments, they had not presented commanding perspectives on the problem that rallied political support. That was about to change.

If *cepalinos* had been temporarily sidelined in Chile, one of them came to occupy a frontline policy position in Argentina that many at CEPAL found intolerable. A month after the arrival of the Klein & Saks mission in Chile, Prebisch accepted the invitation of General Eduardo Lonardi—who had taken over the government after the military violently ousted from

power Argentine President and General Juan Domingo Perón—to formulate and implement a stabilization plan. Despite Peronism's initial success
in terms of growth and redistribution, Argentina ended up with severe economic problems by the fall of Perón: substantial fiscal deficit, inflation,
and the loss of crucial external reserves for the exchange-hungry economies of the periphery.[28] In the words of Prebisch, Perón left Argentina in a
"crisis of production," with industries stimulated only artificially and with
a ramping inflation. Though eager to return to his native Argentina, Prebisch
was also hesitant about collaborating with a military again. After participating in the unconstitutional government of General Pedro Aramburu in the
wake of the Great Depression, he vowed not to repeat that story.[29]

But, whereas Furtado feared conservatives, Prebisch abhorred demagogues. For Prebisch, returning to Argentina and overcoming the Peronist
era was both a personal and a political necessity. With the ascent of Perón
to power in 1943, Prebisch had been ousted from the management of the
Central Bank and from his professorship at the *Universidad de Buenos
Aires* and was thus effectively sidelined from Argentine political life.[30]
General Lonardi and his *Revolución Libertadora* promised Prebisch an
opportunity to redeem himself. For Prebisch, the social gains provided by
Peronist policies were transitory and artificial and had detrimental effects
on economic growth. Not only had Peronism neglected the agricultural
sector, the main source of foreign exchange, and postponed the creation of
basic industries hindering development but it also had created conditions
that fostered inflation.[31] Increasing wages by "stretching the number of
hours it took workers to repair train engines . . . could hardly be called a
social victory" for the masses, Prebisch claimed.[32] That redistribution
was the product of artifice rather than social and economic transformation. For Prebisch, the social pact between Perón and the industrial workers,
based on subsidies for urban consumers to the detriment of rural producers and exporters, slowed both industrial and agricultural growth and
the long-term improvement of standard of living of the working classes.
The *Revolución Libertadora* also offered Prebisch the opportunity to roll
back the monetary "permissiveness" that characterized the Perón administration while rescuing Argentina from stagnation.[33] The decision would
undermine Prebisch's position.

Prebisch's plan alienated *cepalinos*. His plan for the *economic recovery
of Argentina* began "with the establishment of sound money." "No country
has escaped from inflation without sacrifices," Prebisch added.[34] Abolition
of price controls, devaluation of the peso, public deficit reduction, and controlled wage increases were among the key proposals of a plan that raised
the opposition of unions and Peronist supporters.[35] In Santiago, *cepalinos*

condemned Prebisch's analysis for the absence of the constraints imposed by Argentina's insertion in global capitalism, a fundamental *cepalino* tenet. They also bemoaned the excessive focus on monetary instruments to address the inflationary crisis. Prebisch's disregard for the notion of social conflict as an approach to inflation being cultivated in Santiago nurtured resentment.

More than his ideas, *cepalinos* condemned Prebisch's political choices. Furtado and *cepalinos* shared his condemnation of the "improvisation and amateurism" of the Peronist government but expected Prebisch to equally reprove the traditional oligarchy.[36] Unlike the "great heretic" of the initial CEPAL years, Prebisch seemed then to be more aligned with the "local orthodoxy," his peers in Santiago feared. His trip to Venezuela and the Marcos Pérez Jimenez dictatorship pushed *cepalinos* even further from his admired leader. Meanwhile, Prebisch and his plan quickly became the object of visceral attacks in Argentina. Recalling his participation in the Roca-Runciman pact that gave Britain privilege in the Argentine market in the aftermath of the Depression, critics saw his attempt to secure Argentina's membership to the IMF and get resources to contain inflation as another of his subservient strategies. Recalling his collaboration with the *Sociedad Rural Argentina,* acid critics interpreted his proposals to revitalize the agricultural sector as a defense of traditional landed elites and an attack on the working class.[37] As the political situation in Argentina deteriorated and the government became more violent and repressive, Prebisch aborted his mission and carried a failed monetary stabilization and development plan over his shoulders. Condemned as agent of imperialism and a steward of traditional landed elites in Argentina, Prebisch found himself definitively alienated from Argentina and with his moral and intellectual leadership contested in Santiago.[38]

Consolidation of the *Cepalino* Approach to Inflation

After the Argentine fiasco, Prebisch temporarily lost the intellectual and moral authority at CEPAL, and *cepalinos* took a new and unfamiliar road. Wavering between two evils, *cepalinos* had feared giving demagogues proinflation ammunition or anti-labor, pro-austerity arguments to reactionaries, both of which could have undesired effects over development. But Prebisch's proximity to military, authoritarian regimes that increasingly adopted stern monetary policies with devastating social effects more than the failure of soon-to-be "monetarist" stabilization plans gave *cepalinos* the opportunity to challenge their leader and reorient the course of their project while surpassing the conceptual and political limits of the existing approach.

After a long hiatus in the conceptual debate about the origins of inflation, in 1958 Chilean economist Osvaldo Sunkel produced a new synthesis. To do so, he recovered Mexican Juan Noyola's 1955 manuscript on inflation, buried in the stacks during the debacle of anti-inflation plans. Educated at the *Universidad de Chile* and the LSE, Sunkel took the lead in systematizing the intuitions behind Noyola's ideas that "inflation was a structural phenomenon" and that the "underlying causes of inflation" were the structural problems associated with economic development and Latin America's position in the periphery of the global economy.[39] Trained at the *Universidad Nacional Autónoma de México* (UNAM), Noyola had joined CEPAL in Santiago in 1950, after having worked at the research division of the IMF and the Ministry of the Treasury in Mexico. Before deserting *cepalinos* for a space in revolutionary Cuba a few years later as discussed in the following chapter, Noyola made a crucial contribution.

In conversation with Furtado and reacting to what they saw as Prebisch's conservative leaning and called his "monetarist" orientation, Noyola produced a new interpretation, later known as the "structuralist" approach.[40] Introduced in August 1955, just before the Klein & Saks mission arrived in Santiago, Noyola formulated a conceptual framework to understand the Chilean inflation based on the separation between "basic inflationary pressures," or the causes of inflation, and the "propagating mechanisms," or the means that reproduce and accelerate inflation.[41] Noyola identified two basic inflationary pressures or "structural" causes of inflation: the global economy, or the instability and long-term decline of the prices of the periphery's export prices, and the agricultural sector, with its low and inefficient supply of goods that increased the cost of living. Both of these "pressures" created inflation as less income (from exports) and less supply (from agriculture) met with higher development-driven demand for imported industrial goods and population growth-driven demand for food, pushing prices up.

The relation between center and periphery, what *cepalinos* had identified as the main characteristic of Latin America and the main "obstacle to development," was now conceptualized as one of the "structural determinants of inflation." Thus, Noyola reintroduced the problem of Chile's place within global capitalism into the analysis of inflation, which *cepalinos* criticized Prebisch for failing to do in Argentina.[42] In this framework, the battle over redistribution of income visible through the wage-price spiral was characterized as a "propagating mechanism" rather than a cause of inflation as in *cepalinos*' initial diagnosis. In the whirlwind of rampant inflation, stabilization plans, and the maneuvers of the generals in both Chile and Argentina, Noyola's text was initially lost and only was gradually reworked and elaborated in the coming years, culminating in Sunkel's synthesis.[43]

Noyola's approach to inflation was a radical critique on Prebisch and thus on CEPAL's increasingly conservative politics of inflation. Although "many endorse the battles against inflation," Prebisch explained, "there are few who actually recognize the severity of the problem." Some "defend anti-inflationary measures as long as their social group does not pay the cost"; others agree with "general principles but defend measures with inflationary consequences"; and there are yet others who, "despite frustrating experiences, extol the virtues of inflation" for growth.[44] Instead of finding an approach to the problem, Prebisch, concerned about the detrimental consequences of inflation, urged *cepalinos* to focus "on a policy for curbing inflation and for stabilizing economies, without injury to incentives for economic growth."[45] The insistence of Prebisch on combatting inflation and on the imposition of limits to wages, credit, and foreign reserves exasperated Noyola.

Noyola's approach was therefore a stance against what he considered Prebisch's "monetarism," a term *cepalinos* first used to describe one of their own. Moving away from money and monetary factors, Noyola declared with satisfaction, "I have shown that one can analyze inflation without mentioning 'means of payment' or 'means of circulation' and other twaddle that still circulates at CEPAL." Echoing Furtado, he reiterated that inflation was a not a monetary phenomenon but the result of disequilibria generated by the process of economic development itself. There were two "structural causes": the stagnation of agriculture driven by the push for industrialization and by the privileges of the landed elite as well as the financial vulnerability that stemmed from the position of underdeveloped countries in the global economy.[46] Prebisch reacted strongly against Noyola and "thought he could avoid [the] publication" of his seminal manuscript.[47] Although later Noyola claimed triumphantly that Prebisch had "accepted— at last!—that to analyze inflation it [was] not necessary to use monetary figures," Prebisch, as was apparent from the Argentina experiment, was not convinced. Nonetheless, after Prebisch lost moral and intellectual authority, it was Noyola's proposition that became the *cepalino* approach to inflation.

Sunkel perceived in Noyola's seminal text a masterful synthesis and made it the cornerstone of the *cepalino* approach. In the back and forth between Pinto and Prebisch, Prebisch and Furtado, Furtado and Noyola, and Noyola and Sunkel, the *cepalino*, or "structural approach to inflation," took shape.

To begin with, Noyola had been able to respond to Furtado's call for an analysis of the domestic aspects of inflation without losing the grip on the global aspects that had come to characterize *cepalino* tenets about development. Mobilizing the concept of center and periphery, *cepalinos* now insisted that the system of international trade posed limits not only to economic development but also to monetary stability. The growing demand for imports generated by development combined with the long-term deterioration of the terms of trade generated recurrent balance of payments crises in Latin American economies that in turn generated inflation. In addition, the confrontation over the need to surpass an exclusively monetary approach could be resolved through the combination of structural factors and propagating mechanisms. The *cepalino* approach to inflation did not "endorse a short-term exclusively, monetary approach," nor one based on "excess demand," Sunkel claimed. Instead, it gave monetary aspects their appropriate space and relevance.[48] However, something was lost in the synthesis. Pinto's conceptualization of inflation as a battle over income redistribution was a casualty of the synthesis. The more sociological approach was not incorporated into the *cepalino* "structuralism," although it would re-emerge in a different version in the pen of Furtado and his Brazilian-vent "structuralism." By systematizing what he called an "eclectic" approach, Sunkel had found a way to reconcile the positions of Prebisch and Noyola and with his Solomonic compromise paved the way for *cepalinos* to claim a more radical position in the battle of ideas in Latin America.

Reconfigurations into "Structuralists" and "Monetarists"

Within a few years, the "structural approach to inflation," the compromise that emerged to resolve divisions between *cepalinos* in Chile, gave rise to a more polemical and extremist "structuralism" in Brazil. In Chile the debate that gave rise to the "structural" or *cepalino* approach to inflation was driven by concerns with the social struggle over income redistribution in inflationary episodes and the social burden of stabilization. In turn, in Brazil, the region's fast-growing economy, the debate revolved around the potential trade-off between monetary stability and economic development. As it migrated to Brazil, refracted through the lens of Furtado, the "structuralist" approach to inflation began to gain the support of more radical allies and lose those on the fence such as development expert Roberto Campos, radicalizing the *cepalino* intellectual project. It was in this context that "monetarism," a term that would become pervasive in the US academic and policy milieu almost a decade later,[49] emerged to designate the alternative to progressive *cepalino* "structuralism."

The transformation of *cepalinos* into "structuralists," radical contenders of their conservative "monetarists," began with Campos's stabilization plan. In mid-1958, President Juscelino Kubitschek, JK, as the president was known, summoned one of the authors of his development plan, called *Plano de Metas,* or targets' plan, to formulate a monetary stabilization program to fight inflation. The *Plano de Metas,* the cornerstone of JK's goal of bringing "50 years of progress in five," established targets in infrastructure, transport, energy, and basic industries, relying heavily on public and foreign investment as well as on macroeconomic and development planning. Charismatic but pragmatic, JK created an atmosphere of exuberance and optimism. At the center of that atmosphere was the construction of the new capital, Brasilia, and the *Plano de Metas'* project of accelerated industrialization and development. The rapid growth of the steel, petrochemical, and especially the automobile industry was the visible symbol of that project.[50] By the end of JK's government in 1961, the development plan had resulted in an 8 percent average rate of growth, an increase from 20 to 25 percent in the participation of the industrial sector in the economy, the diversification of industry from basic consumption to include intermediary and durable goods, the expansion of the motorway network, and the meeting and even overcoming of the production goals of fertilizers, steel, aluminum, and alkalis.[51] Despite the successes of the program, financing the massive public investments via the printing press and money emissions reached its limits and threatened the fulfillment of the development targets. Gains from international trade were declining, fiscal deficits increasing, and inflation, though moderate, was accelerating, reaching 24 percent in 1958. The task that fell to Campos and his partner, Minister of the Treasury Lucas Lopes, was to maintain the development impetus while procuring monetary stability.

Although Campos had been a crucial *cepalino* ally, *cepalinos* began to represent an obstacle to achieve the goal of monetary stabilization. As a member of the Brazilian delegation to the UN in 1948, Campos had sympathized with the goals and supported the creation of CEPAL in Santiago. He had invited *cepalinos* to participate in the Brazilian state's development planning apparatus and had worked together with them in its most important institution, the *Banco Nacional de Desenvolvimento Económico* (BNDE). Like *cepalinos,* Campos was convinced that, given the periphery's shortage of foreign exchange, more aid and better trade conditions were the road to development.[52] Yet Campos was increasingly critical about *cepalinos'* ideas with regard to inflation and monetary stability. "Acknowledging the existence of structural or institutional problems," he claimed, "should not excuse the importance of proper monetary administration."[53] Unintentionally perhaps, *cepalinos* had cultivated an interpretation of the problem of inflation and development that encouraged political leaders and policymakers to underestimate the negative effects of inflation, Campos suggested.[54] For those in charge of stabilization plans, *cepalinos* turned from allies to adversaries.

Furtado's ideas shaped Campos's skepticism about *cepalinos*. Although it was Campos who had suggested Furtado as the liaison between CEPAL and BNDE a few years earlier, the two had parted ways. In his analysis of the postwar Brazilian experience, Furtado suggested that inflation redistributed income from the exporters of primary products to the importers of capital goods, which in turn generated investments in the industrial sector and overall economic development.[55] "Attributing the important magnitude of capital formation that occurred between 1948 and 1952 in Brazil to inflation," Furtado claimed, "would be a crude oversimplification." Yet, in certain cases, he claimed, "inflation cannot simply be a consequence but the cause of development."[56] The words of Furtado may have seemed inflammatory, especially for Campos, in charge of reconciling the control of inflation with the acceleration of economic development.

Whereas Furtado's ideas resonated in the environment of confidence and exuberance that characterized JK's early years, Campos's views seemed to be out of tune.[57] "Since the accelerated development of Brazil in the last fifteen years coincided with acute inflation," JK explained, many came to believe "that inflation was inherent and even necessary for development." Dispelling those myths but mostly just paying lip service to his advisors, Campos and Lopes, JK clarified that Brazilian development had occurred "despite not because of inflation."[58] Since the formulation of the *Plano de Metas,* Campos had questioned inflation's positive effects on development. "Only exceptionally and in very short periods of time, can inflation have a positive contribution to development," Campos argued. Furthermore, for inflation to translate in development, it would take rarely found altruistic and socially minded entrepreneurs that transferred prices increases "in investments of high social priority," Campos added, challenging Furtado's ideas.[59] By the end of JK's third year in government, Campos had a chance to turn the tables.

With his plan, Campos was determined to debunk the myth that "combating inflation was going to make Brazil stop."[60] Campos and Lopes, his BNDE colleague and now minister of the treasury, introduced the *Plano de Estabilização Monetaria* (PEM) in December 1958. Their plan was an expression of the classic quantity theory of money that emphasized the gap between the money supply and the national product as the source of inflation. In so doing, Campos reaffirmed a notion about the origins of inflation that *cepalinos* were categorically moving away from. Nonetheless, Campos was not just into combatting inflation. He and Lopes proposed a plan that expected to reconcile economic development with monetary stability. To do so, the plan encompassed a gradual implementation of budget cuts, credit reduction, and wage-increase deferments as well as IMF's short-term credits to minimize the negative impact over growth, external payments, and employment.[61] Campos expected the IMF approval to open the door for an Export-Import Bank loan, whose resources were destined to accelerate development, fulfilling the two prongs of the plan.

Campos and Lopes found few domestic allies for their anti-inflation and stabilization plan. Campos was skeptical about JK's own commitment to the stabilization program given his "structuralist illusions."[62] Above all, JK privileged the fulfillment of the *Planos de Metas* and especially the completion of Brasilia, both of which could be compromised by the stabilization plan if Campos did not secure additional foreign resources.[63] Furthermore, given his electoral intentions and the popular opposition to the plan, JK felt even less compelled to defend the program. Both industrialists and coffee exporters alike opposed the program.[64] Since the critiques on the stabilization plan were "based on the old argument that inflation was necessary in underdeveloped countries to increase the amount of available resources," Campos would begin to hold *cepalinos* like Furtado responsible for the imminent collapse of the plan.[65]

The plan also failed to marshal external support. Despite multiple trips of the Brazilian representatives to Washington, Campos and Lopes could not convince an inflexible IMF staff to endorse a plan designed to fulfill the requirements of the institution. Since the beginning of the decade, Edward Bernstein, director of the IMF's Research Department, had insisted that, unlike widespread beliefs, inflation in Brazil was not the product of "development at home or price changes abroad," as *cepalinos* and their allies insisted. Instead, Bernstein argued Brazilian inflation was a typical "case of policy failure." The country had lavishly granted credit without having an alternative source of revenue besides traditional export proceeds from international trade, disregarding the effects on prices.[66] Although Campos and Lopes's stabilization plan addressed head on what Bernstein had called a "policy failure" by establishing restrictions to credit, the staff in Washington did not endorse the plan because it did not touch the existing exchange rate policy (figure 3.2). The system of multiple exchange

FIGURE 3.2   Edward Bernstein, from the IMF research department, is depicted here as a doctor overseeing the treatment of a patient sick with inflation. The other two doctors are Jorge Alessandri, Chilean minister of finance, and Alberto Baltra Cortez, Chilean minister of the economy in 1949. While Alessandri and Baltra debate which anesthesia mask to use, exchange rate 1 (cambio 1) or exchange rate 2 (cambio 2), Bernstein comments, "I think it's better to anesthetize the surgeons!" Ten years later in Brazil, Bernstein was still insisting on the elimination of multiple exchange rates as one the IMF's chosen policies to combat inflation. (*Revista Topaze*, December 9, 1949. Colección Biblioteca Nacional de Chile, available in Memoria Chilena.)

rates, by giving each domestic interest group the level it desired, had been a crucial mechanism for the state to reconcile the interests of both exporters and importers, landed elites and urban industrialists, while getting fiscal revenue from the difference between the various levels. As Campos himself recognized, the multiple exchange rate system subsidized coffee exporters and importers of capital goods as well as consumers by providing cheaper wheat and gas while providing increased government revenue, and thus promoting development. However, Per Jacobsson, managing director of the IMF, insisted that dismantling the multiple exchange rate system was necessary to receive IMF support. Jacobsson and the IMF argued that the multiple rates incentivized consumption of imported goods, driving resources away from investment, and in so doing undermined development. Since the abolition of the system touched too many vested interests—including key groups like coffee exporters and industrialists—and supported the country's development, Campos and Lopes insisted on more political flexibility from the IMF to no avail.

Meanwhile, the reluctance of the IMF to support the plan was interpreted as a foreign conspiracy against national development. A rising anti-Americanism transformed the tone of the debate in the months of negotiations between Brazil and the IMF in 1959. Anti-Americanism in Latin America had deep roots in the nineteenth century, given US annexation of Mexican territory, filibusterism, and saber-rattling in the Caribbean. It reached new heights as the marines, the banks, and the spies accompanied the transformation of US policy to Latin America from gunboat to "dollar diplomacy" and then to the "Good Neighbor" and Cold War eras, culminating in the blatant subversion of Guatemalan democracy in 1954.[67] Quintessentially exemplified by the violent reaction against Vice President Richard Nixon's tour of the region in 1958, anti-Americanism reached a new peak in the region and Brazil by the time of Campos's PEM. At the time, Brazilian Vice President João Goulart condemned foreign corporations for depleting national resources and creating the economic problems that had fostered the need for a severe stabilization plan in the first place. There were student demonstrations against Campos, denouncing him as a "sellout" for advocating for the partnership of Brazilian and foreign firms in the exploitation of oil in Bolivia, leading to an animosity that transferred to his negotiation with the IMF. Being referred to as Bob Fields in an English word play of his name, Roberto Campos became the object of ridicule.[68] Government supporters and opponents publicly condemned the IMF's "unrealistic" expectations. The press and members of congress left and right, endorsed the prevailing anti-Americanist opposition against the Fund.[69] Given the deadlock in negotiations in Washington and the public reaction in Brazil, JK summoned his team back home and broke relations with the IMF.

Although Campos begrudged the dogmatism and inflexibility of the IMF staff, the episode resulted in his break with CEPAL, not the IMF. First, *cepalino* ideas had transformed into arguments against stabilization, becoming powerful political instruments in an increasingly polarized Brazil and contributing to the failure of his plan. Mobilizing some of the language and arguments contained in the "structural approach," disparate political forces had rallied together in what became "the option for growth" against the PEM and the IMF.[70] If the IMF represented imperialist attempts privileging stability over development, *cepalinos* represented the Latin American option for development, creating what for Campos was a false dilemma.

Second, *cepalinos* themselves were directly involved in the break with the IMF. *Cepalino* Furtado, among other advisers and government officials, approved JK's decision to break relations with the IMF. Like Campos,

Furtado was convinced of the importance of aid to resolve the development paradox and condemned the rigidity of the IMF and the lack of acknowledgement of national political constraints. However, for Campos, Furtado's behavior was dogmatic and inflammatory. Furtado justified his decision not just on the grounds of "political inflexibility" or "simplicity of the monetary policy." For Furtado, breaking up with the IMF was necessary to "give the institution a lesson" and show them Brazil was no "second-class" country.[71] Furtado believed the rupture to be a "denunciation of the Fund's incapacity to fulfill its statutory function to support economies undergoing external pressures."[72] In his defense of a rupture with the IMF, Furtado had taken a political stance that alienated Campos. Although both Campos and Furtado shared many misgivings with the IMF, Campos blamed *cepalinos* for the failure of his plan.[73] For Campos, Furtado had crossed the line, siding with the agitators that had condemned him as an agent of imperialism and that became an increasingly polarizing force in the following years. As Campos's stabilization plan collapsed, *cepalinos* turned from allies to rivals.

After the stabilization plan fiasco, Campos became a fervent *cepalino* critic. Against *cepalino* claims that it was Latin America's position in the periphery of the global economy that generated obstacles for monetary stability, Campos emphasized the importance of domestic policies. In most cases, the rigidities of supply that *cepalinos* adduced as "structural" were actually induced by bad policy. Even more so, "only a fertile imagination would attribute a causal role" to bottlenecks in Argentina, when it was clear that "they were the result of Peronist policies."[74] He also criticized *cepalinos* for their fixation with Chile and their generalization of its experience to the rest of the region, leading them to erroneously emphasize the stagnation of agriculture as a cause of inflation. Bottlenecks were relevant for Chile but less so for Mexico or Venezuela, he explained. Furthermore, he called into question the *cepalino* assumption that inflation differed in developed and less developed countries and thus designated the "structural approach to inflation" as an "exercise in 'unnecessary' originality."[75] Campos's rupture with *cepalinos* symbolizes the end of an amorphous consensus about economic development that *cepalinos* came to represent and the crystallization of existing differences into two opposing camps.

After the collapse of the stabilization plan and his personal break with *cepalinos*, Campos coined the categories that defined the political economy debate of the era. "In Latin American countries facing acute inflation," Campos claimed, "there is a sharp theoretical and policy clash between—for lack of better terms—the *monetarists* and the *structuralists*." Campos struggled to define the terms of the debate. The most proximate way of identification was institutional. The views of the "monetarists" were close to those imputed to the IMF, while the "'structuralists' claim to have support on the Economic Commission for Latin America (CEPAL)," he explained. In the words of Campos, the "structuralists" argue that "inflation is a natural accompaniment for growth," as the latter involves limits imposed by external trade and by rigid economic structures.[76] The "monetarists," on the other hand, emphasize the incompatibility of inflation and development while attributing those obstacles and rigidities to induced, policy distortions. The *cepalino* and the IMF approaches were now defined in relation to each other. The term "monetarism," from then on increasingly used as shorthand for a new liberal project in ascent, emerged in relation to Latin American "structuralism."

The divergence was, however, exaggerated. "The two contending views are less different than they seem," Campos quickly asserted. On the one hand, "several monetarists dissent from the IMF in many respects," he claimed, perhaps referring to more extreme versions developing around the Chicago school. Although Campos resented the IMF's decision not to support his and Lopes's gradualist approach against inflation in Brazil, he increasingly aligned himself with the IMF. On the other hand, official CEPAL statements "do not show the skepticism towards monetary and fiscal policies implied in the 'structuralist' view."[77] Recalling earlier affinities with Prebisch and other *cepalinos* who defended anti-inflation plans and warned against the dangers of demagoguery, Campos questioned the existence of an inflation-bias at CEPAL. Campos's caveats and nuances point to what is perhaps an understated convergence. Despite the caveats, the categories hardened and the rift widened.

The terms "structuralism" and "monetarism" suggest the existence of what Albert Hirschman called institutional "personalities" that in many ways defy the story of these institutions.[78] During the 1950s, *cepalinos* became "structuralists" over a serious of internal conflicts and misencounters with political allies and opponents in Chile, Argentina, and Brazil. In fact, initially *cepalinos* used the adjective "monetarist" to describe the position of one of their own. As shown in previous chapters, the relation between the staff of these two institutions was initially more fluid than the rigid labels of "structuralism" and "monetarism" indicated. During the Bretton Woods conference, Prebisch and future *cepalino* allies were compelled by the possibility of global countercyclical credit policy under the aegis of the IMF, particularly important for exchange-hungry economies in the periphery.[79] Before they were "structuralists," *cepalinos* and many of the leading economists of Latin America were attracted to the IMF as an institution. Prebisch was offered and accepted a senior position in the

IMF and initially rejected the directorship at CEPAL. Before joining the institution, founding *cepalinos* such as Jorge Ahumada and Juan Noyola both worked for the IMF and remembered their work fondly.[80] The main IMF liaison and later head of its Western Hemisphere Department was the Chilean Jorge del Canto, who gave ample support to CEPAL in its very early years. Many of the IMF staff in the early years were Latin Americans who belonged to the same circles as *cepalinos*. Some months before the arrival of the Klein & Saks mission, Pinto condemned the "anti-Yankee propaganda" surrounding an IMF mission and clarified that they were "carrying out a plan designed by the Chilean government" and not acting as "evil agents of Wall Street."[81] Yet, by the late 1950s, the institutions and the political landscape in Latin America were radically different.

With "monetarism" and "structuralism," Campos not only captured intellectual differences with regard to the relation between monetary stability and development. For many ambiguous *cepalino* allies like Campos, *cepalinos* had helped transform a fertile economic debate into an inflammatory polemic. But Campos's own categories propelled that simplification as well and gave the categories of "structuralism" and "monetarism" new meaning. He positioned CEPAL in an adversarial stance against an international organization that had increasingly come to be regarded as an instrument of US intervention and imperialism. Despite describing only one of the contending sides in the intellectual and policy disputes of the day, the term "structuralism" came to represent Latin American thought on development, while "monetarism" came to represent the foreign new liberal project in ascent. Inadvertently and perhaps even unwillingly, Campos's terms propelled the radicalization of the political economy debate as an ideological contest between local and foreign expertise and between stabilization and development.

Reverberations

The entwined categories of "structuralism" and "monetarism," emerging from bitter disputes among *cepalinos* about Chile and disencounters between *cepalinos* and their allies in Brazil, endured and catapulted *cepalinos* in the regional and global spheres. "Structuralism," a term that was increasingly used to encompass the corpus of *cepalino* ideas beyond inflation, became a force that policymakers and academics wrestled with. Those mobilizing amorphous and disjointed ideas about the trade-off between monetary stability and economic development in Brazil had found in *cepalinos* an intellectual foundation that, to the detriment of the IMF, shaped stabilization plans and economic policymaking across the region for the rest of the decade. "Structuralism" would also give rise to multiple research and intellectual projects within and beyond Latin America. It would bring the world's attention to *cepalinos* and their worldmaking project through the Inflation and Growth Conference, as their project transformed from the fulfillment of the postwar promises of internationalism into the opponent to the liberal global order.

In the academic arena, *cepalinos* gained an unprecedented presence as "structuralism" and "monetarism" defined the terms of the economic debate in the era. With a somewhat heterodox training at the University of Cambridge, British economist Dudley Seers became a staunch proponent of "structuralism" during his four-year-long work with *cepalinos* in Chile, taking their approach to Zambia, Colombia, Nigeria and thirty-five other countries in the decades to follow through consultancy jobs for multiple international organizations.[82] At the economics department of the *Universidad Católica de Chile,* the training of students abroad and the faculty exchange program with the University of Chicago were making "monetarism" the privileged orientation within the school despite the presence of *cepalino* Osvaldo Sunkel as part-time professor. Although the Chicago-Católica program was designed to counterbalance the enormous weight of *cepalino* ideas in the country and the region, the enormous influence of "structuralism" in Chilean universities secured "converts" to the *cepalino* fold. Tom Davis, "a Chicago-classical economist who believed that he could apply a few simple ideas and elucidate the problems of the Chileans," an observer noted, "has emerged quite critical of the Chicago group."[83] Inspired by *cepalino* "structuralism," Davis argued that it was impossible to "use monetary policy without considering the institutional structure of the country," siding with *cepalinos* in their insistence on the need for locally produced tools and ideas different from those produced abroad. The importance of *cepalino* ideas was such that Carlos Massad, the Chicago-trained director of the *Instituto de Economía,* and others at the *Universidad de Chile* designed an overarching, long-term quantitative research project to test "structuralism" and resolve "the conflicting hypotheses concerning the cause and cure of [inflation]" that had emerged in Chile, an endeavor that *cepalinos* were reluctant to carry forward.[84] The debate between "structuralists" and "monetarists" would reach a pinnacle at the Conference of Inflation and Growth discussed later.

In the policy arena, it was *cepalino*s, not the IMF "monetarists," who initially claimed important victories in the conflict between "structuralists" and "monetarists." It is commonly assumed that stabilization programs, such as those implemented by both right- and left-wing governments in

FIGURE 3.3   The cartoon shows Verdejo, a representation of the Chilean "masses," drowning at sea. From the shore, Chilean president Jorge Alessandri looks pleadingly at Uncle Sam asking for help. Uncle Sam has a life preserver that represents an IMF $75 million-dollar loan, while Alessandri holds his own deflated life preserver, venting air due to "bureaucracy," "deficit," "austerity," and "stabilization." Many IMF-sponsored stabilization plans were formulated and debated in the region, as *cepalinos* and IMF staff battled for positions in economic policy debates. (*Revista Topaze*, January 13, 1961. Colección Biblioteca Nacional de Chile, available in Memoria Chilena. By permission of Alejandro Crespo.)

Brazil, Argentina, and Chile in 1958 and 1959, broadened and deepened the scope of "monetarist" ideas in Latin America.[85] Yet the story of *cepalinos* suggests otherwise. In part because of the influence of *cepalino* ideas, the "monetarist" plans of Brazilian President Kubitschek, Argentine President Arturo Frondizi, and Chilean President Jorge Alessandri were also "gradualist" and unorthodox programs, departing from IMF prescriptions in some way or another.[86] In Chile, the opposition of *cepalinos* and others to the IMF and their condemnation for the institution's short-sightedness and political inflexibility in the negotiations with the Alessandri government resulted in a change of policy orientation that gave "structuralists" a larger space in a conservative government with initially "monetarist" policymaking[87] (figure 3.3). If the presence of *cepalinos* and the influence of their ideas guaranteed a partial defeat of "monetarism" in Chile, their absence was crucial for the implementation of a stabilization program in Argentina. Whether or not always directly driven by *cepalino* ideas, the rising opposition to stabilization gives credence to the IMF misgivings about the overbearing presence of *cepalinos*.

To their lament, the IMF staff and especially its regional contingent were forced to contend with the *cepalinos'* dominance and their own marginalization. Though *cepalinos* reiterated that they did not have "a leniency towards inflation," the existence of a consolidated, "structuralist" approach created enormous difficulties for the IMF economists to convince relevant authorities of the need to limit the expansion of the money supply. Since *cepalinos* "rejected the theory that inflation is caused solely by financial disorder and lack of monetary restraints" implied in the IMF's approach, del Canto was outraged. "It is a continued source of friction and embarrassment that ECLA [CEPAL] continues to provide intellectual food and ammunition to the forces opposing stabilization in Latin America,"[88] del Canto argued. The rupture of relations between the Brazilian government and the IMF was followed by catastrophic experiments of IMF-supported stabilization in Argentina and Colombia, in which anti-imperialism and the incompatibility between development and stability were the arguments deployed against the IMF. *Cepalinos* have "done well in dramatizing the need to attack the so-called structural factors," he added, but they have failed to realize that "financial stability minimizes the social strains that often make more difficult the solution of those structural problems," they continuously reiterated.[89] They failed to recognize that, given the institution's statutory area of competence, the IMF's resources "cannot be used for economic development."[90] What del Canto failed to perceive was that it was precisely the struggle over areas of competence and the overlap between economic development and monetary stability what created the contention between the two organizations. Meanwhile, through the implementation of IMF-supported stabilization plans, the notion that there were local ideas that fostered development and foreign notions that opposed it was becoming institutionally entrenched, stultifying and radicalizing the debate about development and social change while demonstrating the limits of an international institutional system that compartmentalized problems that were intrinsically connected—trade, growth, and stability—and that *cepalinos* aspired to integrate.

Far from reconciling differences, the international Conference of Inflation and Growth deepened the gap between CEPAL and the IMF. In June 1960 Richard Ruggles from Yale University convened a preparatory meeting at Bellagio, Italy, the Rockefeller Foundation's meeting center, to define and conceptualize the conference. For Ruggles, the conference was an opportunity to raise the world's awareness about Latin America's concern with inflation and growth, but most importantly to pull the world's intellectual resources to solve a conundrum that was tearing the region apart. Initially conceived with the goal of formulating policies that "promote[d] adequate growth and reasonable price stability," the conference transformed into an effort to "narrow the present gap between responsible officials in Latin American governments and international agencies such as ECLA [CEPAL] and the IMF."[91]

Even at the preparatory meeting at Bellagio, it was clear that *cepalinos* and their "structuralism" were directing the conversation. Although Roberto Campos, who had become a fierce *cepalino* critique, and Charles Schwartz from the IMF staff were part of the preparatory committee, they were outnumbered and outgunned by *cepalinos* and their allies. The "structural approach to inflation" was not the only one, but it was certainly the conceptual framework that the preparatory committee most gravitated around and that eventually became one of the theoretical frameworks orientating the actual conference. In addition, *cepalinos* produced the country case studies that guided the discussion, permeating the analysis with their approach. In fact, for the final conceptualization of the conference, Ruggles, perhaps without even realizing, adopted one of the *cepalino* tenets as one of the premises of a conference that was supposed to evenly weigh differences: "that inflation in Latin America differs from that of North America and Western Europe and thus the traditional theory produced in those countries [sic] [did] not appear to be always strictly relevant."[92] Yet, despite the overbearing dominance of *cepalinos* and their ideas, the conference organizers decided to hold the conference in Rio de Janeiro, not Santiago, as a more neutral ground.

Despite the absence of Prebisch and Per Jacobsson, the CEPAL and IMF heavy hitters, the conference was extremely well attended and had the presence of the most renowned economists in Latin America, Europe, and the United States. Albert Hirschman from Columbia, A. G. Harberger from Chicago, Gottfried Haberler from Harvard, Roy Harrod from Oxford, and Nicholas Kaldor from Cambridge were among the attendees. Of the Latin American contingent, Campos, Gudin, Pinto, Furtado, and Sunkel were the most salient representatives. The main sponsors of the conference were the Rockefeller and the Ford Foundations, but Latin American research institutions like the Brazilian *Fundação Getúlio Vargas* (FGV), the Argentine *Insitituto di Tella,* and the Chilean *Instituto de Investigación Económica* were also sponsoring the conference. Between academics, ambassadors, high-level government officials from across Latin America, and top representatives of international organizations, there were over one hundred economists gathered in Rio for a week to discuss the trade-off between economic development and monetary stability. The conference "was seldom dull and full with politics and emotion," an observer claimed. The center of the controversy was, of course, the dispute between *cepalinos* and economists at the IMF. Rather than a "lack of explanations of the relation between inflation and growth," in Latin America, there were "too many conflicting points of view."[93]

At Rio, the "debating cup," to use an expression of one participant, went to the "structuralists."[94] From the start, the IMF representatives considered themselves at a disadvantage. Although "there was an unduly heavy representation of CEPAL and its sympathizers," the IMF could not refrain from participating, as the absence would have been "more conspicuous" and would only fuel the fire.[95] The conference was therefore composed of a "vocal" majority of Latin American and US *cepalino* friends and a "silent" minority of Fund supporters and "uncommitted" economists. Criticism of the Fund came from a number of US and European economists "sympathetic to the 'structuralist' persuasion," they claimed.[96] Not only were the commentators of the papers biased, the Fund representatives explained, but the opening remarks of Dudley Seers, Oxford professor and member of CEPAL from 1957 to 1961, painted a caricature of monetarists—"as old-fashioned and reactionaries" whose "main purposes were to keep prices stable, hold money supply irrespective of growth and inflict harsh stabilization programs"—which many in the audience were willing to believe.[97] Throughout the conference, there were multiple "unpardonable," "violent," and "virulent" attacks on the organization and its policies that "went well beyond the purposes of constructive economic discussion." The IMF staff particularly accused *cepalinos* Pinto and Sunkel of being hostile and aggressive to the Fund and questioned the role of international civil servants in promoting interagency competition.[98] The IMF was clearly on the defensive in the region and seemed to have completely lost to *cepalinos* the battle of influence over defining Latin America's economic problems and solutions.

"Timely and effective," del Canto's intervention altered the mood of the conference, if only partially. Although the "Fund recognized the existence of structural problems and was in favor of development programs," its "area of responsibility was not development planning or long-term investment financing," del Canto clarified. To dispel misunderstandings and provide nuance, del Canto went to great lengths to distill the position of his institution. The IMF did not simply recommend reducing the money supply, as critics claimed, but increasing it at the pace of economic growth, he added. The IMF did not favor exclusive focus on monetary policy, as the term "monetarism" implied, but instead insisted on the importance of fiscal policy to deal with inflation and balance of payments problems. More than the clarifications, del Canto's manner and presentation won the IMF some and more vocal allies. Kaldor was an important one, after whom others followed. Despite "his structuralist leanings," Kaldor had shifted from sharply criticizing the IMF to decrying high inflation and "even defending the Fund in one occasion."[99] Concomitantly, as the interventions of *cepalinos* became more "intemperate," they also began to alienate supporters. After del Canto's declarations and some minor victories, the IMF staff remained convinced that to a large extent the bad reputation of the institution was related to misinformation. But the conference and *cepalinos* did trigger some important reflections and policy revisions within the institution.[100]

Despite the clarifications and misgivings of its staff, the conference demonstrated the IMF had been sidelined from their territory of intervention. In his concluding remarks, Ruggles outlined points of consensus that gave *cepalinos* the higher ground on the debate. He insisted that all participants saw planning for development, a point *cepalinos* had insisted on as the mechanism to reconcile development and stability. More important, he concluded, granting another important point to *cepalinos* that "monetary and fiscal policy alone were not sufficient to ensure stability and growth" and that achieving "economic development with a social orientation" was not "to be expected . . . from the spontaneous market forces alone." The emphasis on the need for "structural reforms," including areas such as land and education, were seen as victories for *cepalinos*. Even though the Alliance for Progress also championed those ideas, it was barely mentioned.[101] Furthermore, non-*cepalino* economists like Carlos Massad also defended the *cepalino* diagnosis of inflation arising from the process of economic development itself in the context of declining terms of trade. He also condemned the stabilization process for halting rather than creating a path to growth as in the case of Chile. Brazilian Mario Simonsen from the FGV, an institution that was increasingly adversarial to *cepalinos*, also granted an explicit victory to *cepalinos*, saying that "any 'human' economist would agree that development, like 'structuralists' emphasize, is unquestionably more important than stability."[102] At the end, *cepalinos* and their "structuralism" had cemented the notion of a trade-off between economic development and monetary stability that garnered them widespread support and threatened the position of what has been otherwise considered a dominant institution like the IMF.

Conclusions

In jockeying for position between the "structuralists" and the "monetarists," *cepalinos* initially gained the upper hand. The victory was especially satisfying, given the many internal debates and tensions that underpinned the emergence of the "structuralist approach" to inflation. They had traveled a long way. Almost a decade had passed since they had first argued that inflation was a problem of an expansion in the means of payment that outpaced supply and of wages catching prices. The political divisions and internal tensions among *cepalinos* led to the "structural approach to inflation" and would eventually transform *cepalinos* into "structuralists." The structural approach to inflation neither fully disregarded the monetary aspects nor completely embraced the social conflict approach, but rather represented a Solomonic compromise between visions that were tearing *cepalinos* apart.

The emergence of the "structural approach to inflation" and the transformation of *cepalinos* into "structuralists" were not just conceptual transitions. It was also a moment of realignment and radicalization. With the "structuralist approach to inflation," they affirmed a "mistrust of the Rightist sponsorship of the stabilization programs" that repositioned *cepalinos* in the regional political landscape.[103] The attacks on the IMF "were a political necessity" because these encounters also provided them a platform to attack the "reactionaries" who were the IMF's allies.[104] However, it was precisely the defiant tone and the militant position of *cepalinos*, who insisted on unbridgeable gaps between both economic stability and development and between local and foreign expertise, that put *cepalinos* in alliance with increasingly recalcitrant nationalists that were gradually taking center stage in Chile and Brazil. In the process, they alienated some of their allies who, like *cepalinos*, had supported internationalism as a means to reconcile development and stability. As a result of the confrontation between "structuralists" and "monetarists," many would come to see CEPAL as "the International Monetary Fund of the Left," as Pinto claimed years later.[105]

"Structuralism" gave rise to a "monetarism" *avant la lettre* in Latin America. In the mid-1950s, before Milton Friedman produced his major works and, along with the Chicago School, became the face of "monetarism" worldwide, *cepalinos* were using "monetarism" to contest the intellectual and moral authority of one of their own and more broadly to challenge the prevailing interpretations of the origins of inflation in the academic and policy field. By the early 1960s, *cepalinos* had become the gravitational center of the academic and policy debate, setting the contours of the conversation, providing the basic studies, inspiring projects to test their hypothesis, and inciting converts worldwide. Contrary to widespread views, it was *cepalinos* who put the IMF, the institutional embodiment of the "monetarists" in Latin America, on the defensive. "With the advent of structuralism," Hirschman argues, "those who had fancied themselves deep thinkers were suddenly told in turn that they were shallow."[106] In this juxtaposition, the IMF and the "monetarists" had left with the short end of the stick, an unusual position for an institution that traditionally dominates the international economic landscape, especially in developing countries. But as *cepalinos* were going to shortly find out in revolutionary Cuba and with their experience in the counter-revolutionary Alliance for Progress, structuralism was a double-edged sword that once again tore them apart while deepening their influence through two of the major political experiments of the era.

FOUR

Revolutions Left and Right

Shortly after the triumph of the revolutionaries in early 1959, *cepalinos,* like a myriad of writers, activists, and economists from around the world, rushed to Cuba to participate in the promising experiment. The defeat of the corrupt, dictatorial, and until recently US-supported regime of Fulgencio Batista by a small rebel army fighting for political freedom, social equality, and national autonomy created fears as well as expectations of sweeping social transformation with potential global implications. After their visits to the Cuba of Fidel Castro and Che Guevara, French writers like Jean Paul Sartre and Simone de Beauvoir as well as American sociologist C. Wright Mills proclaimed the island's revolution as an alternative to the orthodoxies of the global left.[1] While some saw in Cuba the opportunity for human socialism, others saw in it the path for national autonomy in Latin America and for decolonization in the Third World. Imbued with multiple meanings, the revolution itself transformed within less than two years. The experiment that began as an antidictatorship rebellion transformed into a Marxist-Leninist revolutionary state that, in alliance with the Soviet Union, sought socialism and the radical transformation of Cuba by late 1960. As Cuban leaders were themselves defining their own revolution, some *cepalinos,* such as Regino Boti and Juan Noyola, joined the revolution, while others observed with caution from afar.

Many of those who stayed behind rallied around the Alliance for Progress, one of the United States's anti-Cuba offensives. Launched in 1961 by President John F. Kennedy, the Alliance for Progress was imagined as the "right kind of revolution."[2] Conceived as a multiyear, multilateral, inter-

American $20 billion economic aid program for Latin America, the Alliance for Progress heralded ambitious goals of international cooperation and economic growth and equality and proclaimed sweeping land, fiscal, and urban reforms. Initially, some *cepalinos* eagerly embraced the Alliance. Though staunch critics of US policy toward the periphery, *cepalinos* saw in the Alliance a break from past trends. The program, after all, not only responded to Latin American desires for economic development, international cooperation, and social welfare but also enshrined some of the key tenets of the *cepalino* project. Raúl Prebisch and Celso Furtado, the two most prominent *cepalinos*, vigorously embraced the initiative. While Prebisch, the Economic Commission for Latin America's (CEPAL) head, saw in the Alliance the opportunity to give the organization leverage and direct influence over national policymaking, Furtado, working from an influential position in the Brazilian government, intended the Alliance to facilitate his signature project for the Brazilian Northeast. For these *cepalinos,* the Alliance for Progress became a resource for their projects, a testament to and a yardstick of their own ideas. Yet, by implementing what they thought was a revolution in Latin American development, *cepalinos* prompted a crisis of development, in general, and of their project, in particular.

Although ideologically kilometers apart, both the Cuban Revolution and the Alliance for Progress represented for *cepalinos* the culmination of their project. Both represented a path for rapid economic development and sweeping social transformations, especially in the land tenure structure. Yet, while the Alliance for Progress was premised on the cooperation between center and peripheries, one of the key tenets of the *cepalino* project, the Cuban Revolution established a direct confrontation between the two very early on. The Cuban Revolution and the Alliance for Progress not only radicalized Latin American politics but also had a profound effect over *cepalinos* and through them, over the history of economic ideas and global sciences in the region. The multiplicity of encounters and discounters between *cepalinos* and revolutionaries, between *cepalinos* and the counterrevolutionaries, deepened divisions among them and forced political realignments that shook the position of *cepalinos* and diminished their standing in the region while paving the road for *dependentistas* and other critics.

The Encounter with Cuba

Like many other Latin Americans, *cepalinos* saw the defeat of the corrupt and repressive regime of Batista in the New Year's Day of 1959 with satisfaction and optimism. Cuba had one of the highest levels of income, numbers of doctors per capita, and literacy rates in the continent. However, there were also profound inequalities between rural and urban areas and between White and Black populations. The country's economy depended almost exclusively on the production of sugar, a highly volatile commodity and a seasonal product, which, by the 1950s, had seized to spur economic growth. Notwithstanding decline, sugar represented 80 percent of all exports, while the export of sugar represented 54 percent of national income.[3] King Sugar, as it was referred to, created a profound dependence on global markets but especially on its main buyer, the United States. The seasonal sugar economy also created a highly vulnerable, illiterate, and malnourished population in the countryside, who were unemployed for most of the year. Alongside the sugar plantation owners and the seasonal rural workers, independent cane growers, small non–sugar farmers, and peasants who lived and worked in plantations all populated a conflict-ridden countryside. In many ways, Cuba represented the quintessential example of the perverse relation between center and periphery that *cepalinos* had denounced, creating economies vulnerable to global markets and societies unable to transform rigid structures like the land tenure system. Sympathizing with the revolutionary aspirations to transform an outdated model of development, many *cepalinos* would mobilize toward the Caribbean island.

In Cuba, shortly after his triumphal entry into Havana, Fidel Castro emerged as the uncontested leader of the revolution that deposed Batista. Castro was a lawyer and former member of the nationalist and reformist *Ortodoxo* party. His legislative career was thwarted when Batista called off elections in 1952; he was imprisoned for a violent attack on the Moncada barracks in 1953. He and the group of "barbudos," or bearded rebels who fought in the countryside, were perhaps the most visible group of a broad antidictatorial coalition. While the rural guerrillas, with Castro and Guevara as the most prominent figures, captured the world's attention, their triumph would have been unlikely without the support of other revolutionary groups and urban warriors, who mobilized key financial, intellectual, and public media resources for the insurrection. Students, professionals, and intellectuals, and even the Cuban bourgeoisie were part of the 26th of July Movement. While some were Marxist, other revolutionaries had liberal or social-democratic orientations.[4] The aspirations to overcome corruption, bring about economic prosperity and autonomy, and foster social justice united myriad groups and individuals in the military struggle but also obscured significant differences among them that would come to surface in the first years of government, in which the revolution would transform itself into a Marxist-Socialist revolutionary state.

The first two *cepalinos* to take part on the revolution were Regino Boti and Felipe Pazos. Trained in law at the University of Havana and in economics at Harvard, Boti returned to Cuba in 1956. After seven years at CEPAL, Boti took a leave of absence from the institution to spearhead the creation of the School of Economics at the University of Oriente, at the eastern end of Cuba, far from the country's capital. His return coincided with the inauguration of the 26th of July Movement's armed resistance against Batista, to which Boti promptly declared his support. After persecution from the embattled government and brief imprisonment, Boti returned to *cepalinos* in Santiago and Rio and would return to Cuba only after the triumph of the revolution.[5] Boti was one of the many professionals and intellectuals who supported the rebel army as it gradually became the stronghold of the anti-Batista forces.

Pazos's involvement in the revolution began even earlier. Trained in law at the University of Havana, Pazos became an economist in practice. After leading the Cuban delegation to Bretton Woods, Pazos, like other to-be *cepalinos,* joined the International Monetary Fund (IMF) in its early years. In 1949 he returned to Cuba as founder and president of the Central Bank. As IMF official and as president of the Central Bank, Pazos cultivated relations with *cepalino* economists, especially with the institution's executive director, Raúl Prebisch.[6] After Batista's coup, Pazos resigned and joined the opposition forces. At a moment in which Batista declared Castro dead to undermine the movement, Pazos facilitated an interview between the rebel leader and the *New York Times* journalist Herbert Matthews. The interview was crucial for the revolutionary forces. It began to gain him the sympathy of the American public and more importantly increased the legitimacy and visibility of the movement, catapulting Castro into the international arena.[7] But perhaps Pazos's most crucial contribution to the revolution, one that forced him into exile, was carried out in partnership with Boti.

Boti and Pazos outlined a development project for Cuba that became the economic manifesto of the movement. The manifesto circulated in Mexico, Cuba, and the rest of the Americas as the *Thesis of the July 26th Revolutionary Movement*. Against entrenched ideas in and outside of Cuba, Pazos and Boti rejected the notion that Cuba's organic function in the world economy was as a sugar-producing country and that industrialization was not feasible in the island. Instead, their plan, adhering to *cepalino* tenets, had two pillars: the transformation of the existing sugar-based economic structure and the "renegotiation of the relations between Cuba and the United States." First, since the sugar economy could no longer "spur economic growth proportional to the increase in population" nor "provide enough dollars and foreign exchange to buy machinery and consumer goods," the country had to stimulate production for the internal market, Boti and Pazos explained.[8] To make Cuba "independent of the ebbs and flows of the sugar industry" in global markets and of the size of the US sugar quota, Boti and Pazos advocated for import-substitution industrialization and for the diversification of agricultural production. As *cepalinos* had insisted again and again, the establishment of new industries would not necessarily decrease the imports of goods from the United States, as the free traders feared, but change the composition of international trade. Second, Boti and Pazos proposed a "renegotiation of the relations between Cuba and the United States" that involved limits to what had been "unrestrained foreign investment" and the reexamination of existing international agreements. The revolutionary government, though "committed to eliminating sources of social justice," had first and foremost an obligation "to make the Cuban economy growth," Boti and Pazos declared.[9] The commitment of these *cepalinos* and their allies was with economic development as well as with the transformation of the relation between center and periphery.

Key collaborators in the insurrection, Boti and Pazos earned prominent positions in the revolutionary government. After the military triumph, the rebel army, now in command of the country, purged the state of *batistanos* and filled the administration with members of the different political forces that had supported the insurrection. In particular, Pazos returned to his position as manager of the Central Bank, and Boti was appointed minister of the economy.[10] In the early days of the revolution, parallel power structures dominated by the ex-guerrilla members were also taking shape and would eventually marginalize urban allies and reformers like Boti and Pazos as the revolution itself radicalized.[11]

One of the first tests of the alliance between *cepalinos* and revolutionaries came with Castro's visit to the United States in April 1959. In their manifesto, Boti and Pazos defended not just the need for but the "feasibility" of the transformation of the bilateral trade structure in a way that "ultimately benefited both countries."[12] Rather than being "no man's land," Cuba could make "foreign capital serve the national interest," Pazos and Boti had claimed. As late as February 1959, when Castro stated that European and North American private investment were welcomed in the effort to finance industrialization, these *cepalinos* and Castro seemed to be on the same page. Even a day before the trip, Boti and Pazos believed that financial aid for the revolution was one of the main purposes of the US visit. After all, Castro publicly commanded them to initiate talks with all the institutions concerned with credit and development.[13] The results of the diplomatic engagement were, nonetheless, quite different.

As the importance of Castro rose, that of *cepalinos* receded. During the two-week-long trip, Castro met with students, mayors, and numerous members of the press, participated in television shows, and made several public appearances, including at New York's Central Park and the Bronx Zoo, in which he charmed his audiences.[14] The charisma and oratory that he had deployed at home in mass rallies and extensive radio and television coverage, inaugurating a new style of government, made him the uncontested face and leader of the revolution abroad as well.[15] Pazos and Boti shared Castro's concern to be treated as equals by the US government and saw the visit as the chance to renegotiate the rules of foreign investment and international trade, especially the deleterious sugar quota.[16] But Boti and Pazos and Castro also parted ways. Boti and Pazos wanted the cooperation of the economic centers for their development project and were willing to play by the rules of the international institutional system to get it. Therefore, they defended "financial policies as conservative as those that the [International Monetary] Fund would recommend" as well the agrarian, fiscal, and urban reforms that "appear[ed] revolutionary to the outside world."[17] The differences between Castro and his economic team had tangible consequences. Though he had endorsed Pazos and Boti consulting with US government officials, Castro granted them no authority to speak on behalf of the revolutionary government, making the meeting between Boti and Pazos and the US government officials inconsequential. As a result, the Cubans did not ask for aid, and the US representatives did not offer.[18] When Castro pubically declared that "Cuba had not come for aid," Pazos and Boti were effectively undermined, signaling a crucial change in the path of the revolution. Pazos feared that Castro's decision was a sign of new changes to come.[19] Despite, or perhaps because of their failure on the US trip, Boti and Pazos sought reinforcements.

A *cepalino* mission was their preferred option. For Boti and Pazos, state planning of industrial and agricultural production as well as of national and foreign investments was a fundamental part of their program. "A democratic state, even one with revolutionary aims, can elaborate social techniques to fulfill its goals without the recourse to violence against dissidents, discontent social classes, or interested groups," Boti and Pazos claimed. In their manifesto, they had explicitly given *cepalinos* a space in the reconstruction of Cuba after Batista in the planning effort. Since "Brazil, Chile, and Argentina had benefited from the technical expertise of CEPAL," Cuba could do the same, they argued. They believed that the *cepalino* planning techniques and their formulation of instruments proper to Latin America were important resources for outlining and implementing the revolution's development plan.[20] Although several economists, including socialists Paul Sweezy and Leo Huberman and former Oxford economist Dudley Seers, were early global witnesses of the economic revolution, *cepalinos*, upon Boti's request, were given a direct role on the revolutionary project.[21]

In Santiago, the mission to Cuba generated mixed reactions. Exhilarated by Boti's request, Juan Noyola asked Prebisch to be the leader of the advisory group. Noyola was a self-declared Marxist, one with a particular Mexican vent. Far from calling for socialist revolution, the *Universidad Nacional Autónoma de México*'s (UNAM) social economics in which Noyola was formed made Marxism a tool to conceptualize and denounce the failures of capitalism and advocate for more state intervention to redress them.[22] According to Celso Furtado, one of Noyola's closest friends at CEPAL, the Marxism of his Mexican colleague was a "mixture of agrarianism and anti-imperialism" that did not prevent him from turning to "traditional instruments of economic analysis."[23] Noyola, who like Furtado, had grown disappointed with Prebisch's political cautiousness, as discussed in Chapter 3, saw the mission as an opportunity for CEPAL's institutional renewal.[24] Shaped by his experience with Perón's populism, Prebisch was fearful of the fanaticism that surrounded the Cuban Revolution. Yet, despite his apprehensions, Prebisch could not deny Boti's request and Noyola's plead.[25] Initially, Boti expected the mission to offer advice on the modernization of the sugar industry. Gradually, the five-man mission became entrusted with the establishment of the national planning institution and the training of public bureaucrats, a crucial role given the exodus of middle-class professionals and white-collar workers from revolutionary Cuba, on the one hand, and the importance that training courses had for the expansion of the *cepalino* project, on the other. In those early years, Boti brought numerous *cepalinos*, whose fates are mostly unknown, from the headquarters in Santiago to Havana to work for the revolutionary government.[26] The advisory mission in revolutionary Cuba, the third of its kind for *cepalinos*, was the result of the attempt to renew both Cuba and the Santiago-based institution.

When *cepalinos* began operations in Havana, Castro had just enacted the Agrarian Reform Law. The highly progressive Constitution of 1940, a product of an effervescent period of reformism under an earlier Batista administration, had prohibited *latifundia* and limited foreign ownership of the land. The basic assumption that had guided the mid-century reformers as well as Boti, Pazos, and Castro himself, later on, was that the "feudal relation" between large landowners and their dependent workforce explained the inefficient use of the land.[27] "The system of exploitation, the peasant evictions, and the pervasiveness of the *latifundia* are the fundamental causes of the backwardness of the countryside and the poverty of our *guajiros*," Boti and Pazos had claimed.[28] Since the dominance of large landholdings in the fertile areas of central Cuba had forced numerous peasants to marginal lands in the hillsides, Boti and Pazos had proposed an agrarian reform project to replace the "feudal agricultural lords" and "myopic sugar growers" with a rising sector of landowning peasants. Building on the existing legal provisions, the revolutionary Agrarian Reform Law limited the size of landholdings with the exception of highly profitable ones, established government long-term bonds as compensation for the expropriation of large sugar and rice plantations, and prohibited both foreign and corporate land tenure. The new law also prohibited share-cropping, tenancy, and similar labor arrangements that dominated the countryside, especially in the provinces of Oriente, the stronghold of the rebel army and where Boti had first gone to establish the school of economics. For Boti and Pazos and their *cepalino* allies, the revolutionary process in Cuba promised to fulfill their visions of economic and social transformation.

But the revolutionary program brought a new dimension to the agrarian reform project. The Agrarian Reform Law not only provided for the redistribution of land to those landless and dependent peasants but it also propounded for the reorganization of land tenure in collective landholdings and state-owned farms.[29] A major departure from the ideas initially contemplated by Pazos, Boti, and Castro himself to those of the process of collectivization of land would acquire momentum throughout 1959, redefining the character of the revolution toward socialism. Furthermore, the National Institute of Agrarian Reform (acronym in Spanish, INRA), presided over by Castro himself, became the cornerstone of the new revolutionary state and gradually absorbed the ministers of industry and commerce, displacing those who, like Boti and Pazos, had formed the initial government.

Whereas the *cepalinos* in power were increasingly under threat, the *cepalino* mission proceeded smoothly. With the goal of "leaving in operation the machinery of programming," Noyola accompanied the creation and expansion of national statistics and planning apparatus, the result of which would be the *Junta Central de Planeación,* inaugurated in March of the following year, and of which Boti shortly after became its technical secretary. The lack of coordination of several international organizations and of personnel had created some implementation problems, Noyola told Prebisch at CEPAL's Mexico office. Nonetheless, Noyola was pleased to report "the mission was progressing satisfactorily."[30] Given the enactment of the national statistical service law and a series of training courses with over seventy students, the mission was considered a success in Santiago and in Havana, and was renewed for another year.[31] Furthermore, *cepalinos* reinforced their training program and their team with the incorporation of Chilean Jorge Ahumada, Prebisch's choice to tame the growing revolutionary spirits of Noyola. Ahumada would be in charge of teaching a course on planning for development in Cuba. While the focus of the *cepalino* mission was on development planning and training, it was the agrarian reform, the cornerstone of the revolutionary program and the quintessential expression of "structural change," that attracted the attention of *cepalinos*.

Ahumada, Noyola, and the other *cepalinos* witnessed firsthand the formative months of the revolution. The government implemented progressive tax policies that benefited Cuban over foreign interests and small over large producers, established tariffs to protect existing manufacturing industries, significantly increased wages, and reduced rural and urban rents, leading to expansion of production of domestic goods and of the population's purchasing power. But it was the agrarian reform that accelerated both the revolutionary and counterrevolutionary pace. As expected, the agrarian reform garnered the support of those sharecroppers, tenants, and peasants and raised the opposition of the large Cuban and foreign landowners. It also initially gained the support of the Cuban industrialists, who even made donations for the initiative. But it also sparked the resistance of the seasonal rural workforce, who, because of the peasant-focus of the reform, precluded them from distribution benefits.[32] Land invasions and conflicts continued while landowners fought the reform. The initial reform law was expected to affect about 10 percent of the land, but within a year of its inauguration, the government, exceeding those goals, reported to have intervened 8 million acres, delivered more than 500 land titles, formed more than 700 cooperatives or state farms, and created 1,400 *tiendas del pueblo,* or mass distribution stores.[33] Their experience in the island would lead *cepalinos* to contradictory conclusions.

Ahumada went to Cuba with another agrarian project in mind. Trained in agricultural engineering at *Universidad de Chile* and in economics at Harvard, Ahumada had joined CEPAL in 1950 after a brief period at the IMF. At the IMF, Ahumada had advised the revolutionary government in Guatemala in the establishment of the *Instituto de Fomento de la Producción.*[34] Designed to increase agricultural production, the development institution was one of the innovations of the October Revolution of 1944 that by 1953 had brought about a significant agrarian reform process in the country before being thwarted by US intervention the following year.[35] A few years later, Ahumada produced a political manifesto in Chile, in which a project of agrarian reform occupied center stage. Ahumada's manifesto became the intellectual pillar of the Christian Democrats on the rise in Chile.[36] He imagined Chileans "eager for a non-Marxist left." Ahumada defined his project as response to the stultifying rhetoric of the right, who decried state intervention in agriculture to protect interests of landowners, and of the left's exclusive focus on latifundia with its "demagogic" slogan of the "'land for those who work it.'"[37] Instead, Ahumada proposed land redistribution toward midsize properties would be accompanied by both higher agricultural prices and higher wages as well as access to credit. By doing so, the reform could check the political power of the landowners who controlled Congress while avoiding the multiplication of inefficient and impoverishing *minifundios,* the family-size plots of land that the left advocated for. Like Noyola in Mexico, Ahumada had encountered the agrarian reform in a revolutionary era in Guatemala but had proposed an alternative route for his native Chile.

After his two-month stay in Cuba, Ahumada, perhaps too disconnected from the pace of the revolution, sought for nonrevolutionary alternatives. "Many agreed with Castro about the desirability of getting rid of Batista," Ahumada claimed, but "not everyone agreed as to what to do in his stead." Castro had enormous support of the working classes, but the industrialists were on an "an attitude of wait and see." Furthermore, there was still "much basic goodwill in Cuba towards Americans," which could in turn intervene and steer in the revolution through training of workers, industrialists, and especially agrarian reformers, he suggested to a Ford Foundation official. An enemy of *latifundia* and a champion of midsize private properties with state technical and financial support, Ahumada believed that collectives or state farms, controlled and managed by INRA officials, had become the privileged form of economic organization in part because the Cubans had no other alternatives and were following the existing large-scale structure of sugar production.[38] Missing or perhaps dismissing the increasingly socialist turn of the revolution, Ahumada left, convinced that giving Cuba feasible, privately owned alternatives to collectives was an option worth pursuing and that more experts were needed to do so.

Just as Ahumada departed from Havana, Pazos found himself at odds with the revolution. The assault on the opposition that had commenced with the public trials of Batista supporters was now approaching more vexed territory. Members of the revolutionary coalition who contested Castro's rapprochement with the communist party, given its belated support for the revolution, had become the object of persecution. Other, more "liberal members" of the revolutionary coalition followed.[39] Within less than two years of its triumph, the antidictatorial, nationalist revolution turned into a full-fledged socialist and authoritarian revolution. Many factors contributed to the transformation of the revolution and the initial demise of some loyal critics including Pazos, and later Boti: the unprecedented mobilization of peasants and urban workers, women, and youth; the far-reaching economic initiatives like the Agrarian Reform Law and the nationalization of industry; the formation of a revolutionary coalition with the former communist party and the centralization of power on the figure of Castro himself; the confrontation with the United States and the consequent coop-eration with the Soviet Union. As the purge of anti-Communist 26th of July movement revolutionaries continued and the revolution assumed some of those radical traits, Pazos resigned in October 1959, and Guevara assumed the control of the Central Bank.

Within a year, Pazos transformed from a revolutionary to a counterrev-olutionary.[40] Pazos took a diplomatic position in Europe and initially refrained from publicly decrying the regime in order to ease the transition and avoid speculation about dissension and internal conflicts among the revolution-aries.[41] His conciliatory position did not last long. In the following year, Pazos not only condemned the absence of freedom of expression and partici-pation "as the worst in Cuban history" but he also challenged those who preached the economic merits of the revolution. The scarcity of food attested to the ill-conceived agrarian reform program; the reduction in the import of raw materials and equipment to the weakness of the industrialization project. Cuba was therefore an example of the "failure of socialist totalitari-anism."[42] Pazos was the first casualty of the *cepalino* and the development experts' attempt to participate in the revolution.

Noyola, in turn, found a space where Pazos had lost his. Despite CEPAL's dwindling support for the advisory mission, Noyola was relentless in his commitment. His task in the Cuban Revolution was "the most important and decisive work of his career," and he was nothing but "fortunate to participate in the most important event in Latin America since indepen-dence," Noyola declared in August 1960.[43] Noyola and the rest of the *ce-palino* mission, among which was Jacques Chonchol, a Chilean Christian Democrat who would become the architect of the agrarian reform in Chile a few years later, were fascinated by the revolution and, according to ob-servers, eager to export it to their own countries.[44] Out of the Latin Amer-ican economies, Cuba was "under the most control of imperialism," Noyola claimed.[45] Therefore, the Cuban Revolution stroke a "a severe blow to the traditional relations between imperialism and the dependent countries."[46] From the elimination of feudalism to a battle against imperialism, Noyola's diagnosis and rhetoric had transformed alongside that of the revolution.

Castro, who when initially asked to define the character of the revolu-tionary project plainly said, "Cuban and humanist," by 1961, had declared himself a "Marxist-Leninist" and so did his revolution.[47] Initially, Castro initiated a series of policies that were relatively uncontroversial. The ex-pansion of the educational system, especially in the countryside, housing programs to increase home ownership, collective organization for public works and public housing alongside more progressive forms of taxation, rent controls, and wage increases were some of these initiatives. However, the agrarian reform that had attracted the attention of *cepalinos* sparked a social revolution that acquired a momentum of its own. As the rebel army itself took control of the expropriations, INRA gave larges strides to create cooperatives while making the state a major landowner and administrator. With the redistribution-driven expansion of the internal market and the initial agrarian expansion, the demand for industrial products rose, forcing even larger state intervention in the domestic industries. When the American-owned oil refineries refused to process Soviet oil for the Cuban industry in mid-1960, Castro nationalized those companies and accelerated the expropriation of the rest of the industrial, commercial, and banking sectors, which were largely in US hands. Shortly thereafter Cuban-owned businesses followed. Sugar refineries, banks, and wholesale and retail Cuban enterprises alongside commercially owned real estate were transferred to the state-owned or social economy three months later. Within a few years, the Cuban revolution, buttressed on an unprecedented agrarian reform, had openly veered toward state-led socialism.

In response to unfair rumors and the myths that abounded, Noyola paid tribute to the political accomplishments and economic progress made by the inauguration of "a new economy based on a social revolution."[48] Against the notions of "scarcity, paralyzed industries, and disorganized agriculture," Noyola delved into the dynamism of the revolutionary economy. Both agricultural and industrial production had increased in the first two years of the revolution, he claimed. The latter grew by 17 percent and 25 percent in 1959 and 1960, respectively. Unemployment dropped by two hundred thousand people. Thus, Cuba was making important strides on import substitution industrialization. Furthermore, the prospects of commercial exchange with the Soviet bloc, unlike the trade relations with United States and the Western world, actually promised to fulfill the advantages of international trade.[49] Diversification was in the works and Cuba had found new markets for its products. According to Noyola, the revolution was nothing but a success.

The key to that success was its agrarian reform. The first and primary objective of the revolution, Noyola subsequently explained, was to transform land property relations. Since "the land tenure structure was itself the product of imperialism," the Cuban agrarian reform struck a blow to economic dependence and to the lack of productivity of the countryside. The Cuban Revolution was the only revolution, Noyola claimed, that accomplished an increase in production despite the transformation of property and social relations. The supply of meat, for instance, had increased, despite the intervention on cattle ranches. What had concerned Ahumada a

CUBANOS: —Oye, chico, mejor no entremos aquí; estos gallos están demasiado revolucionarios...

JEFE DE LA DELEGACION: —¿Periodistas de "El Diario Ilustrado"? No puedo recibirlos. Podrían traer jabón y máquinas de afeitar...

FIGURE 4.1   *Left,* The cartoon shows two bearded Cuban rebels in their military fatigues, discussing whether to attend a CEPAL meeting. Inside the building where the meeting is taking place, one delegate speaks of "proceed[ing] with a profound change in the institutional order, in the economic, social and political life of Latin America," and another is heard saying, "Replace it with a regime of social justice." In response to the comments, one Cuban says to the other, "Hey, friend, we better not go inside, these guys are too revolutionary. . . ." *Right,* The cartoon shows a Cuban in military uniform serving as a delegate to the CEPAL meeting in Santiago. He pauses smoking his cigar to speak on the phone to a well-known conservative Chilean newspaper and says, "Am I speaking to the journal *El Diario Ilustrado?* I can't meet with you, but please send some toilet paper and shaving cream . . . " The two cartoons illustrate the conflicting representations of CEPAL and *cepalinos* after the Cuban Revolution. (*Revista Topaze,* May 12, 1961, Colección Biblioteca Nacional de Chile, available in Memoria Chilena. *Left* by permission of the Sepúlveda-Salinas family. *Right* by permission of Manuel Tejeda Sotomayor.)

few months earlier was an object of pride for Noyola. The state farms, those very large land holdings, "with a high degree of mechanization and diversification," exhibited a "very rational and efficient use of resources."[50] Rather than the result of ideologies, those state farms, Noyola clarified, were the result of very pragmatic considerations. The agrarian reform had therefore accomplished a social and an economic revolution.

The involvement of Boti and Noyola with the Cuban Revolution had profound effects for CEPAL (figure 4.1). In April 1960 rumors circulated in Santiago that some *cepalinos* were behind the creation and dissemination of a prorevolutionary manifesto to be released during US President Dwight Eisenhower's visit to Chile that spring. The manifesto was a condemnation of any attempt at foreign intervention in Cuba, clearly directed at the United States, which was apparently already endorsed by Eduardo Frei and Salvador Allende, senators and future presidents of Chile. Xavier Pazos, son of Felipe Pazos and assistant to Boti, contacted former *cepalino* Celso Furtado, then one of the directors of the *Banco Nacional de Desenvolvimento Economico* (BNDE), to help him recruit the Brazilian president's support for the manifesto.[51] Confronted by the US State Department, Prebisch was forced to deny *cepalino* involvement and to reassure the US official that those accused "were not hostile to the US government." Fearing the negative impact of *cepalino* involvement in Cuba, Prebisch regretted having, hesitantly but in good faith, agreed to the institution's participation in the project. He proposed a "graceful" and gradual disengagement, which ended up finally antagonizing Noyola.[52] With deep disillusionment with his old and cherished institution, Noyola resigned from his position at CEPAL when Santiago unilaterally ended the mission in late 1960. With firm conviction on the revolution, Noyola assumed the leadership of one of the directories of the planning board that the *cepalino* mission had helped create, while instructing Guevara in economics through long private lessons for his recently assumed position in the Central Bank.[53] In turn, CEPAL lost another of its core of members, crippling the institution further after the departure of Furtado a few years earlier. By aborting the mission, CEPAL, as an institution, officially renounced Cuba at moment when many *cepalino* allies and regional governments were still defending the country's right to revolution and before the Organization of American States (OAS) adopted sanctions against Cuba. As the mission turned into a fiasco, Prebisch found himself on the defensive.

The confrontation between Noyola and CEPAL did not end with the mission. In early 1961 Noyola publicly condemned Prebisch and the institution. The *cepalino* mission to Cuba had been aborted not finished, Noyola declared.[54] It had been plagued with problems: senior experts were often absent from the island; the mission recurrently confronted staff shortages; and severe ideological disputes arose in relation to the selection of professors for the training courses. Thus, Noyola accused CEPAL of a serious attempt to undermine the mission, compromising the autonomy of *cepalinos*.

Prebisch defended his position. The termination of the *cepalino* mission, Prebisch claimed, originated in the undue involvement of Noyola. "In the past twelve years," Prebisch claimed defensively, he "had never questioned the political views of the members of his staff." Yet, with his defense of the socialist revolution, Noyola had betrayed the *cepalino* commitment to non-partisanship, Prebisch believed. This time he had been forced to do so because of the "over-enthusiasm of the head of the advisory group."[55] Those words may have further irritated Noyola and others who had seen and condemned Prebisch's direct collaboration with the military regime that deposed Argentine President Juan Domingo Perón and his official visit to Venezuelan dictator Marcos Pérez Jiménez. Furthermore, Ahumada and Prebisch both worked closely with the Christian Democrats in Chile, further undermining Prebisch's claim to the political neutrality of the institution and its members. With his public disparagement, Noyola made the encounter with Cuba a challenge to the institution.

The *cepalino* encounters with the revolution differed significantly. They ranged from the unwavering support of Noyola until his death in a plane crash in 1962 to the defection and staunch opposition of Pazos. Like other intellectuals, *cepalinos* were witnesses and agents, adherents and defectors of the Cuban Revolution.[56] Some, like Boti, were marginalized. As a form of insult, Boti was accused, among others, of being *cepalino*. It was almost a bad word in Cuba.[57] Boti, who, according to Ahumada, Furtado, and IMF officials, was "influential with Castro" at least in the first two years, became "politically suspect" and was dismissed from his position in 1964.[58] Instead of taking the European embassy Castro offered as alternative, Boti, who wanted to get his hands on organizing production in Cuba, assumed the management of the former Nestlé factory in the province of Oriente, where he received the visit of Guevara himself, and after three years, settled in Havana until his death[59] (figure 4.2). For personal reasons, Ahumada also resigned from CEPAL and continued to search for a nonrevolutionary alternative to agrarian reform, which he found in Frei's presidential candidacy.

But as an institution, CEPAL's position had been compromised. Noyola and the Cuban Revolution forced the institution's hand. Because the Caribbean nation remained formally a member, by aborting the mission, the Commission had symbolically renounced to a part of Latin America that would increasingly define the region in the following decade. *Cepalinos,* who had trumpeted this message loudly and repeatedly for a decade, could no longer claim to speak *to* and *from* Latin America. Deploying censorship and rejecting Cuba's unorthodox experiment, *cepalinos* were seeing their institution suddenly transform from an embodiment of a revolution against global inequality into a force against radical change and social justice. The lexicon of center and peripheries, unlike the notions of imperialism

FIGURE 4.2 Regino Boti and Che Guevara at the old Nestlé factory, which the Cuban state repurposed as "Fábrica de Productos Dietéticos Bayamo" in 1964. When Castro and Boti parted ways, Boti chose to become head of this plant in eastern Cuba instead of the Cuban ambassador to France. (By permission of Liliám Boti Llanés.)

and dependence, had been raised to buttress international cooperation rather than to challenge hegemonic domination. Heralds of a challenge to classic liberal orthodoxies such as the premise of comparative advantage, *cepalinos* had and continued to privilege global institutions and international cooperation as the means to transform Latin America. Their position had shifted from allies of the revolution to partners of the counterrevolutionaries, especially as they aligned with the US foreign aid program designed as a response to the Cuban Revolution.

The Allure of the Alliance

In the late 1950s, Prebisch, an unwavering advocate of foreign aid and economic cooperation between centers and peripheries, began to notice a change. The United States was increasingly acquiescing to old Latin American expectations for the organization of world economic order, especially of its hegemonic center. After the 1958 goodwill trip of Vice President Nixon confronted anti-American protesters and the revolutionary forces in Cuba gained new ground, neglect turned into enthusiasm. Within two years, the US government had set in motion three of the most important Latin American development proposals. After decades of insisting on the importance of commodity price stabilization schemes, the United States began negotiations for an international coffee agreement. The following year, the Inter-American Development Bank, whose proposal was discussed at length in the interwar years and that inspired US postwar planners for the International Bank for Reconstruction and Development (IBRD), was finally established with Felipe Herrera, Prebisch's longtime friend and partner at its head. In 1960, the United States established the Social Progress Trust Fund for education, housing, and health programs, responding to the recent demands for social development in the region sealing the commitment of the Act of Bogotá.[60] Finally, Kennedy's Alliance for Progress echoed Brazilian President Juscelino Kubitschek's *Operação Panamericana*, presented in 1958, which itself resonated with *cepalino* initiatives.[61] For Prebisch, "the new inter-American cooperation was the consequence of previous, large-scale initiatives."[62]

Despite the promissory signs of new forms of cooperation, Prebisch received the invitation to participate in the Alliance with caution. In December 1960, one of Kennedy's advisers summoned Prebisch to share his ideas with the task force in charge of preparing the Alliance. The mere fact that Latin Americans were consulted gave Prebisch confidence.[63] The task force, which itself had some academic *cepalino* allies, suggested "an

infusion of outside capital of major proportions," argued for the importance of "mitigating the instability in foreign exchange proceeds" through
commodity stabilization agreements, and insisted on the "need for US
and other nations to open their markets for Latin American exports,"
all of which had been key components of the *cepalino* agenda. However,
the task force also put the goals of the new inter-American partnership
at the service of two clear political goals: to "channel the social ferment
and demands for long-overdue reforms of which Mr. Castro is only a
symptom" and to "transform the mood of *Yanqui No* to *Yanqui*, yes" in the
region.[64] Although he was no revolutionary—in fact, he was constantly
accused in his native Argentina of being a reactionary—after his fiasco
with revolutionary Cuba earlier that year and his fervent opposition to
cepalinos' political involvement in the island, Prebisch could not afford
to get himself and *cepalinos* into the contested terrain chartered in the
proposal.

The formal announcement of the Alliance in March of 1961 began to
seal Prebisch's commitment to the Alliance (figure 4.3). In January,
after Kennedy's presidential inauguration, government officials approached
Prebisch and other Latin Americans to provide formal and detailed comments about the plan. Prebisch was surprised to see many of the points he
had raised included in Kennedy's official address, some even verbatim.[65]
The charter of the Alliance included diminishing Latin America's dependence
on exports of commodities, diversifying its economic structure through industrialization, and stabilizing commodity prices and "prevent[ing] harmful
effects of excessive fluctuations in foreign exchange earnings," all of which
struck a crucial chord among *cepalinos,* whose central concern had been
the structural disparity in international trade resulting from falling prices
of primary products. *Cepalinos* had also insisted that foreign economic
aid was the mechanism to reconcile economic development and monetary
stability and, most recently, social welfare. In the words of Furtado, former
cepalino member and Brazilian delegate at the Inter-American Conference
at Punta del Este, this overlap entailed that "the CEPAL doctrine, the most
path-breaking set of ideas emerging in Latin America, had come to orient the
United States foreign policy."[66] In that, the Alliance represented a triumph
of *cepalino* ideas.

Prebisch's enthusiastic embrace for the new inter-American partnership
came as the Alliance promised to offer Prebisch and CEPAL a prominent
role. Since CEPAL, alongside the recently endowed Organization of American States and the Inter-American Development Bank, formed the Tripartite Committee, Prebisch expected to gain influence over the implementation
of the Alliance. Though certainly influential, *cepalinos* had not been able

FIGURE 4.3   The cartoon shows Raúl Prebisch as a waiter of CEPAL offering the following menu to its disgruntled Latin American guests stereotypically dressed, who claim to be "waiting for the banquet": "appetizers sprinkled with agrarian reform," "technical assistance soup," "steak of industrial development," "ham with industrial integration," "technical assistance in every plate," "go for it" for dessert. The menu ends by stating that "Cuban cigars are forbidden" and that "Russian salad is off the menu." (*Revista Topaze,* May 5, 1961. Colección Biblioteca Nacional de Chile, available in Memoria Chilena. By permission of Alejandro Crespo.)

to secure significant and direct policy leverage with the exception of Brazil, Chile, and most recently Cuba. They outlined major economic obstacles and solutions, endowed policymakers with a powerful vocabulary, provided most of the quantitative data available, and trained regional bureaucrats. However, with the death of the payments union and the paucity of the common market, *cepalinos* had once again lost in the battle to become an "operating agency," as IMF officials once commented.[67] A few years earlier, *cepalinos* had begun to assemble advisory missions with development planning purposes with similar hopes. So, when Kennedy publicly asked for CEPAL's collaboration with the OAS in "assembling a group of economists and experts of the hemisphere to help each country develop its own development plan," Prebisch began to commit.[68] The *cepalino* advisory missions, endowed with the Alliance for Progress resources, gave Prebisch grounds to expect close work with national governments and the desired direct policy influence.

However, shortly after Kennedy's grandiose claim of inaugurating a new era for the Americas, the news of the US attempt to militarily unseat Fidel Castro shocked the region and compromised the Alliance. At the Punta del Este meeting in August in 1961, in which Kennedy's plan was to be ratified, the absence of the US President and the strong presence of Che Guevara, military commander and one of the leaders of the Cuban revolutionary government, set the tone for the meeting (figure 4.4). "A new stage in the relations of the Americas did begin," Guevara claimed, but "under the star of Cuba" not the United States. Guevara railed against the Alliance for Progress for trying to "counter the example that Cuba represents throughout Latin America."[69] Although perhaps none of them intended to follow the Cuban model, the representatives of Brazil, Argentina, Chile, and others made sure to defend Cuba's right for nonintervention. For *cepalinos,* the alignment with the United States under the Alliance for Progress began to take a toll.

At Punta del Este, it became apparent that *cepalinos* were, despite pretentions of triumphalism, in a highly precarious position. It was against the "experts" that Guevara had the fiercest critiques. While Prebisch had reveled in the Alliance's provision of expert evaluation of national development plans for foreign aid, Guevara disparaged against it. Not only was the US government steering aid according to its needs, undermining the autonomy of the "experts," but the orientation of that aid was itself flawed. Rather than propounding the industrialization of Latin America as the path to development, the Alliance for Progress's experts privileged the "construction of aqueducts, houses, sewers, and the like," fomenting what Guevara called the "planning for latrines."[70] Although Prebisch also warned against equating development aid with philanthropy and assistentialism, his endorsement of the Alliance as the mechanism through which "the revolutionary process could be achieved within the existing institutional framework," set *cepalinos* in direct confrontation with Cuba, especially after the failure of their advisory mission the previous year.[71] In a rejoinder conference to Punta del Este, Juan Noyola, former *cepalino* and head of the aborted mission, continued to critique *cepalinos* as "ideologues of reformism," supporting the United States and the Alliance for Progress and abandoning Cuba and its socialist path to development.[72] Minor partners in the Alliance for Progress and distant from revolutionary Cuba, the position of *cepalinos* had been undermined and many would begin to place them in alignment with the global orthodoxies of development.

FIGURE 4.4   The image depicts Uncle Sam asking Latin America to dance. Latin America proudly replies, "Let's dance to rhythm of che-che," alluding to Che Guevera. The latter is in the background with drums and maracas of "agrarian reform" and "alphabetization." (*Revista Topaze,* August 11, 1961, Colección Biblioteca Nacional de Chile, available in Memoria Chilena.)

Already *cepalinos* watched the Alliance unravel fast despite initial, almost continent-wide, enthusiasm. While the Latin American governments, with the few but notable exceptions of Colombia, Chile, and Venezuela, were slow in producing the mid-range development plans, the US government was slow in setting up the institutional machinery for implementation of the Alliance. The limitations of implementation in the early years were perhaps also symptoms of disengagement. While the Kennedy administration quickly fell short of securing the exuberant financial resources it initially promised, Latin American delegates were becoming increasingly skeptical about the potential of aid itself even as many Latin American governments continued to receive aid in the name of the Alliance in the following decade.[73] In 1962 a disillusioned Venezuelan diplomat captured the general mood of the regional leadership: "It is pointless to grant aid if economies are weakened by price reductions affecting Latin American exports in the markets of the countries which had granted the aid."[74] The problem of dwindling export proceeds was further amplified as the profit remittances abroad of American corporations in Latin America reached an all-time high. Brazilian economist Roberto Campos said the problem with the Alliance could be summarized in the words of Jorge Mejía Palacio, Colombian finance minister. Despite "substantial assistance," the Colombian minister claimed, "the losses suffered in the coffee market . . . are two or three times greater than the special aid received."[75] Denouncing the futility of aid given the obstacles in international trade, the Latin American government lost faith in the Alliance. By 1963 Alberto Lleras Camargo and Kubitschek, former presidents of Colombia and Brazil, respectively, and spearheads of inter-American cooperation, confidentially produced diagnoses and solutions "to save the Alliance."[76] A fundamental part of the *cepalino* project and crucial concern of Latin American governments, the commodity stabilization schemes were initially pushed aside from discussions at Punta del Este and then dismissed by the US Congress. It was becoming apparent to *cepalinos* that their commitment to the Alliance would not bear the expected fruits.

Within a year, the Alliance had left *cepalinos* discredited and empty-handed. At Punta del Este, Prebisch proposed the establishment of a panel of experts to evaluate national development plans presented to request Alliance for Progress funding. Prebisch's attempt to secure influence on the inter-American partnership was quickly cut short; the delegates, themselves noncommittal to the Alliance, turned the panel of experts, thereafter known as the Panel of Nine "wise men," into an advisory body, deprived of all decision-making power. Prebisch, who was under the impression that he would become the director of the already limited Panel of Nine, was further disappointed when he was demoted to "coordinator." The Argentine government, whose economic team despised Prebisch and *cepalinos,* opposed Prebisch's appointment to the Panel of Nine. After that, the new advisors of the Kennedy administration, unlike the initial task force, mistrusted Prebisch, and they cut him off.[77] Definitively sidelined from the Alliance, Prebisch resigned from the Panel of Nine within a year of the Punta del Este conference.

While the Alliance had brought *cepalinos* some favorable results, Prebisch was at a loss. The Alliance spurred regional demand for development experts and planning, which *cepalinos* were prompt to supply. Colombia was a case in point. With the support of a *cepalino* mission, the Colombian government formulated and presented one of the first development plans under the framework of the Alliance. With the prospect of larger advisory functions for *cepalinos* and with the support of the Inter-American Development Bank and the UN Special Fund, the *Instituto Latinoamericano de Planeación Económica y Social* (ILPES) was created in 1962 as CEPAL's sister institution. It gave additional resources to *cepalinos* and strengthened their capacity to bring CEPAL closer to national governments, especially through training courses. Despite the appeal, Prebisch found it hard to make ILPES his new home and give new life to the *cepalino* project. As his ambition to make CEPAL an operational agency with more direct influence on policymaking faltered, Prebisch was left with a bitter taste, which was especially acrid given his imminent retirement from CEPAL. After the failure of the Alliance, Prebisch engaged in a year of introspection the result of which was a policy document that rehashed some old ideas of cooperation between center and peripheries.[78]

Yet the experience with the Alliance also recalibrated Prebisch's priorities. While foreign aid and multilateral loans took a back seat in his policy recommendations, the "structural reforms," the product of the "structuralist" approach to inflation he was slow to embrace, took precedence. A few years earlier, Prebisch claimed that "there was no other alternative to avoid an economic contraction than a well-conceived plan of foreign investments that filled the gap left by credit restrictions."[79] After the Alliance, Prebisch, increasingly concerned about growing external indebtedness in the region, insisted that "international resources [were] not a solution to external disequilibrium."[80] Disillusioned with international financial cooperation, Prebisch no longer insisted on foreign aid for development and even warned against it in his farewell to CEPAL. His demotion from a leadership position in the Alliance for Progress accompanied by the paucity of the distribution of aid led Prebisch to lament the involvement of *cepalinos* with the initiative. "It was us," Prebisch insisted, "who advocated for industrialization, reaffirmed the impending necessity of agrarian reform, and called attention to the falling terms of trade, the need for change in the economic structure, and for measures to diminish [international] fluctuations," and yet there was a "tendency to present these ideas as conceived in the United States."[81] For Prebisch, *cepalino* ideas had been captured by the United States, and by association, led to the discredit of his own institution. Instead of the financial cooperation of the center with the periphery, Prebisch came to advocate more forcefully for domestic "structural reforms." A recent convert to *cepalino* "structuralism," Prebisch was perhaps coming closer to some of his more radical *cepalino* colleagues who had earlier condemned him as conservative for his "monetarist" views on inflation, as discussed in the previous chapter. His new manifesto, "Towards a Dynamic Development Policy," began with reforms to the internal structure of these countries, including the land tenure and the taxation system. Although he officially stepped down as executive director of CEPAL in 1963, Prebisch remained the uncontested leader for decades, confronting the crisis that ensued.

Allure of Revolutions

While Prebisch terminated his commitment to the Alliance, Furtado began his. After almost a decade at CEPAL, Furtado, second in leadership and prestige only to Prebisch, left the institution, disillusioned, in 1957. Prebisch's conservatism, orthodoxies, and censorship vexed Furtado.[82] While working at CEPAL in Santiago, Furtado had nonetheless solidified his presence in his native country. Since he established the *cepalino* partnership with the BNDE, the most important development institution in the country, Furtado maintained an extensive network of allies among the *tecnicos*, the politically committed technical functionaries at the BNDE, and other state economic institutions as well as among nationalist sectors of the military. The *cepalino* reports carried out under the partnership served to design President Kubitschek's *Plano de Metas*, the most important development plans in the country.[83] With the support of this network, he founded and directed the economic journal *Econômica Brasileira*, broadening his influence in both academic and policymaking circles and generating what he called a nonpartisan, "non-institutionalized political movement."[84] Well connected and influential, Furtado assumed the leadership of the development program for the Northeast, the most impoverished region in the country, upon his return to Brazil in 1958. Three years later, Furtado sought to mobilize the Alliance for Progress for his development plan and the *Superintendência do Desenvolvimento do Nordeste* (SUDENE), the federal institution he was in charge of.

Comprising nine states of the Brazilian federation and different ecological and economic zones, the Northeast, or at least, its representation in the national imagination, was dominated by the *sertão*. The first area of Portuguese colonization, the Northeast, developed a sugar-oriented, slave-based society in the narrow strip of humid areas near the Atlantic Ocean, while the rest and vast semiarid hinterland known as the *sertão* gave rise to cattle and agricultural ranches serving the sugar economy. The economic structure of the region remained basically intact—dominated by large land-owners, especially on the coastal areas, and large populations of impoverished, landless workers known as *sertanejos* in the arid ones—during the rise and fall of the empire of Brazil in the nineteenth century. The recurrent droughts in the *sertão* generated massive waves of migrants toward the coast and even to the richer Center-South and its São Paulo-Rio-Belo Horizonte industrializing axis, pushing the Northeastern elites to demand federal intervention and assistance. In turn, the Center-South elites resisted federal intervention in a region they considered a remnant of a feudal social order organized in networks of patronage and clientelism in which corruption prevailed.[85] Driven by the periodic droughts and marked by regionalist tensions, the national public discussion about the Brazilian Northeast was predominantly defined by the climatic conditions and focused on relief aid and public works until the intervention of Furtado.

In many ways, Furtado's development plan for the Brazilian Northeast captured the *cepalino* worldmaking project. Furtado first outlined an economic policy for the region when President Kubitschek summoned an emergency task force in August 1958. A severe drought affecting millions as well as electoral calculations motivated the president to call the Archbishop of Olinda and Recife, industrial leaders, and Furtado, who was then director of the BNDE, to form a task force and formulate a response.[86] Furtado, who had been thinking about the problems of the Northeast since his CEPAL years, expeditiously produced a report titled *Operação Nordeste*. Instead of focusing on natural disasters and the building of water reserves, Furtado called attention to the profound income inequality between the Northeast and the industrializing Center-South, a gap whose size was larger than the one between the Brazilian Center-South and the industrialized countries of Western Europe.

Transposing *cepalino* ideas of center and periphery from the global to the national level, Furtado explained that the Brazilian Northeast, as a producer of commodities for foreign markets and importer of manufactured goods from the Center-South, had experienced a deterioration in its terms of trade that hindered its economic development. The decline in the terms of trade combined with a system of exchange that allowed the Center-South to appropriate relatively more of the national foreign exchange earnings resulted in both the absolute and relative poverty and underdevelopment of the Brazilian Northeast. The Brazilian economy "reproduced the geographical division of labor that had corrupted the development of the global economy, with its industrialized metropoles and the primary-producing colonies," Furtado concluded.[87] Borrowing the classical *cepalino* vocabulary, Furtado recast an old problem into familiar but powerful terms.

Furtado's proposal for the development of the Northeast, along *cepalinos* lines, emphasized the state promotion of new industries, but paid special attention to the controversial question of the reorganization of the land use. Both went hand in hand. In order to create new, dynamic industrial centers of growth to displace the sugar and cotton exports, the region required stable food production for the *sertão* and therefore a revamp of agricultural production and land tenure. Initially, Furtado refrained from talking about land reform, an issue that was increasingly important for Cubans pushing for revolutions, for *cepalinos* like Ahumada and Noyola and for other social reformers across the region who attributed inefficient and impoverishing land use to existing patterns of land tenure. Instead, he proposed the irrigation of the dry lands of the *sertão*, more productive sugar plantations, the diversion of some sugar-producing areas in the coastal areas to the production of foodstuffs, and the emigration of *sertanejos* to the tropical rainforest areas toward the Amazonian frontier. Despite dismissing the agrarian reform and land tenure question as "an issue for politicians not experts," Furtado introduced the problem of land use in the Northeast, a particularly sensitive issue for the large sugar landowners and refiners of the coastal areas.[88] His attempt to be political yet not partisan, provocative but not disruptive, was embodied in SUDENE.

To carry out his long-term development plan, Furtado, an institution-builder and a firm believer in the power of the state, proposed the creation of the development agency SUDENE (figure 4.5). Reinterpreting the blueprint provided by the US Tennessee Valley Authority (TVA), regional development agencies multiplied across the world in the early post-World War II era.[89] In 1943 and 1954 Peru and Colombia, respectively, established their own regional development agencies.[90] In 1948 Brazil formed its own river valley–based autonomous agency as a solution to irrigation problems and generation of electric power but after a few years had "led a wholly undistinguished existence."[91] In 1958 Furtado proposed his own version of a regional development agency, one that purposefully had federal rather than regional authority and that went beyond public works.

FIGURE 4.5   Celso Furtado at SUDENE with the Northeast region shown in the map behind him. (By permission of Rosa Freire d'Aguiar Furtado.)

He proposed a comprehensive, regionally focused but nationally endorsed program. To avoid the piecemeal solutions and emergency responses that had characterized past state responses, SUDENE would act as the sole coordinating agency for the development of the region. To bridge the gap between federal and state interests, the state governors would have a seat in the board of the institution alongside representatives from economic ministries.

Furtado, who proved to be a skillful politician, received congressional approval for his signature project in December 1959. Because of SUDENE, Furtado confronted the opposition of some of the federal agents whose authority and financial autonomy was under threat as well as of entrenched regional economic interests. But Furtado also rallied the support of the new reformist state governors who despised the political machines created around the existing agencies; of the Catholic bishops who had supported increasing social activism among the rural poor; of the South-Center elites who trusted in the technical, nonpartisan project of Furtado and distrusted the backward, clientelist, and corrupt Northeastern elites; and of the president himself, who, as discussed in Chapter 3, received the support of Furtado and his group of *tecnicos* in the confrontation with the IMF.[92] The new federal agency, with sweeping powers and unprecedented resources, would situate him and his *tecnico* allies at the forefront of the political arena in a few years.

Having institutionalized his idea, Furtado feared for the survival of the initiative in the chaotic years that ensued. Although President Kubitschek confirmed Furtado as superintendent, that is director of the institution, he refrained from displacing Furtado's opponents in the other federal agencies of the Northeast. During the 1960 electoral year, Furtado recruited his staff, prepared the operating plan, and awaited the new president backing him and SUDENE. The new president, Jânio Quadros, whom Furtado described as grandiloquent yet irresolute, not only confirmed Furtado in his position but also raised his position to the cabinet level.[93] But the government of Quadros was short lived. The president alienated both his supporters on the right, with his sympathy for agrarian reform and nonaligned foreign policy, of which the award to Guevara became emblematic, as well as on the left with his attempt to implement a "monetarist" stabilization plan. Quadros's impetuous resignation after six months in power left the country in profound disarray as the political right and some sectors of the military blocked the ascent of labor leader and Vice President João Goulart. The Campaign for Legality, a movement led by nationalist military commanders and a labor-endorsed politician, rallied popular support and intellectuals close to Furtado, guaranteeing the ascent of Goulart. Although he endorsed the continuation of SUDENE and gave Furtado an irresolute support, Goulart's position eroded dramatically in the following years as his political allies on the recalcitrant nationalist left drove farther from a political right already opposed to Goulart.[94] Amid a complicated domestic scenario, Furtado searched for allies abroad.

For Furtado, the Northeast was the perfect scenario and SUDENE the privileged agency for the implementation of the Alliance for Progress. Mostly driven by the news of peasant leagues, social upheaval, and political mobilization, there was growing interest in the United States in this particular Brazilian region. The *New York Times* had raised awareness about the extreme poverty in the region, Furtado believed, but had also unnecessarily raised the alarms about communist agitation. In an attempt to redirect the focus away from the peasant leagues that so interested but also so intimidated the US public, Furtado engaged a reporter from the ABC TV network who visited the region and showed her not just the profound inequalities between landowners and landless peasants but, most importantly, the plans and projects of SUDENE to "overcome antiquated social structures without recourse to violence" in an effort to steer US public opinion toward financial aid for the Northeast.[95] SUDENE offered the United States and its Alliance for Progress not just a publicly appealing opportunity for intervention but an already made comprehensive and impactful program of economic development that included reform of land tenure and use, and social welfare policies. Furtado was convinced that the "clearly superior technical level" of his plan would grant SUDENE "priority over other plans in Latin America."[96] It would also give the US government the chance to break past trends and ally itself with reformist, progressive movements in Latin America. Given its technical level and alignment with its goals, Furtado was convinced that his project "would fill all the requisites of the Punta del Este charter."[97]

Enabled by foreign policy expediencies, Furtado enlisted the support of the Alliance for Progress for the Northeast. Although Furtado had submitted SUDENE's plan and budget since mid-1960, first elections and then the political disarray held up its consideration in Congress. Following up on an invitation that President Kennedy professed to President Quadros, Furtado went to Washington, DC, in July 1961 (figure 4.6). While Kennedy wanted to dissuade Quadros from his support toward Cuba and ensure Brazil's support for the Alliance for Progress, Quadros needed significant financial assistance for his stabilization plan.[98] In that context, the meetings between Furtado and Kennedy as well as between Furtado and State Department advisors cemented Kennedy's interest in the Northeast as test ground for US commitment to development and social reform. As a result of that meeting, a US State Department technical mission was scheduled to visit the Northeast later that year to evaluate the prospects of the program. A few months later, Goulart visited Washington, showing support for the Alliance for Progress and appeasing the growing US State Department concerns that his long-term ties with radical leftist politicians would give leeway to Communists in Brazil. Goulart's commitment to an independent foreign policy that included rapprochements with the Soviet bloc and support for nonintervention toward Cuba notwithstanding, the US government approved $131 million for the Northeast in an effort to bolster the Alliance for Progress in April 1962.[99] Despite financial commitments to the Northeast, the Alliance for Progress was far from a victory for Furtado.

A promoter of the Alliance for Progress, Furtado began to see the limits of the partnership very early on. Since his visit with Kennedy in Washington, Furtado perceived US attempts to take over. Although the White House officials were concerned with finding the appropriate financial multilateral

FIGURE 4.6   President John F. Kennedy and Celso Furtado in Washington, DC, in July 1961, when the former presented his plan for the Brazilian Northeast as the ideal scenario for the implementation of the Alliance for Progress. (Abbie Rowe. White House Photographs. John F. Kennedy Presidential Library and Museum, Boston.)

scheme to support Furtado's *Operação Nordeste,* the State Department delegates wanted to propose their own plan and therefore sent a technical exploratory mission. Fearing his autonomy compromised, Furtado clarified that the plans for the Northeast were already set and only financing was missing. In a compromise solution, the Inter-American Development Bank made some initial financial commitments for SUDENE, but a US technical mission to the Northeast became unavoidable.

The results of that State Department visit to the Northeast confirmed Furtado's apprehensions. Rather than an evaluation of SUDENE and Furtado's plan, the technical mission presented an alternative program for the Northeast. Instead of the industrial and agricultural development program he had proposed to address Brazil's regional inequalities and the poverty of the Northeast, the US mission program focused on what Furtado called "simple façade operations."[100] The US officials proposed the construction of fountains, health centers, employment agencies, and the provision of mobile power generators and mobile health units to address the needs for water, electricity, and social services in the Northeast.

Furtado was appalled. First, the US plan for the Northeast was almost completely focused on short-term relief solutions. Like Prebisch and Guevara in Punta del Este, Furtado feared that the Alliance for Progress's emphasis on social programs might distract from the priority of development, which entailed industrialization and growth, as well as the transformation of the relation between global centers and peripheries. The existing scholarship on the Alliance for Progress condemns the initiative for its use of aid as a tool for foreign policy and for prioritizing economic growth over deeper structural reforms.[101] Instead, Latin American leading intellectuals, including Guevara and *cepalinos* Prebisch and Furtado, who otherwise were adversaries, cast doubts over the Alliance because it veered toward assistentialism rather than overall economic transformation. Such form of "social" aid seemed to address the symptoms or the ills of the lack of development rather than promote the alleged take-off that could guarantee development in the long run. For them, the Alliance for Progress ran the risk of becoming a philanthropic initiative rather than a robust program of cooperation between global center and periphery.

For Furtado, the plan of the US technical mission was also misguided and counterproductive. To achieve high impact on public opinion, the US planners insisted on having visual connection to the Alliance for Progress by labeling the projects "Alliance for Progress health centers," "Alliance for Progress fountains," and the like. From Cubans to Americans to Soviets, it was common practice for global donors of military, financial, or ideological aid to imprint their marks and make sure the source of aid was revealed.[102] However, Furtado feared that the propaganda campaign would backfire against the project. It was not only a problem of disclosing obvious political motivations in the granting of aid. It also revealed the ignorance of the political landscape and recent history of the Northeast. Covering the Northeast with pro-American posters would enrage the progressive forces in the region and further fuel the anti-Americanism that the US officials were so eager to combat. It ignored the deep desires of Northeasterners and Latin Americans like himself who believed the orientation of development initiatives should come from within, not with "imported formulas."[103] Despite the initial rejection, Furtado persisted in his effort to enlist Alliance for Progress for his development plan.

Yet, far from collaborating, the Alliance for Progress began to compete with Furtado's SUDENE in the Northeast. Ever since his first visit with Kennedy, Furtado had struggled to make SUDENE the privileged intermediary between the Alliance for Progress's funding agencies and the Brazilian state. Furtado envisioned SUDENE to be the organization receiving and evaluating local proposals and channeling the disbursement of funds. However, the official agreement between the US and the Brazilian governments, known as the Northeast Agreement and signed in April 1962, supported not just SUDENE's but also the US State Department's plan Furtado had opposed.[104] Furthermore, the US government decided to establish its own local office of the recently created United States Agency for International Development (USAID) precisely in Recife, the capital state of Pernambuco and non-coincidentally the location of the headquarters of SUDENE. In addition, later that year, the governor of the Northeastern state of Rio Grande do Norte circumvented SUDENE and negotiated and "impact program" of primary schools and health centers directly with the US State Department.[105] To defend SUDENE without alienating US agents, Furtado convened a meeting with all the state governors and the USAID local agents to discuss the allocation of funds of the Alliance for Progress's Northeast agreement, but the authority of SUDENE was further compromised as the USAID local agency encouraged direct negotiations between the United States and the Northeastern state governors.[106] By the end of the year, not only was SUDENE undermined but it was also caught in a crossfire between the US state officials using Alliance for Progress funding to prevent the election of a popular but Communist-supported candidate for the governorship of Pernambuco and the said governor who defended SUDENE and attacked US officials and the Alliance for Progress.[107] Furtado and SUDENE's position as intermediary of Alliance for Progress was eroding.

Furtado's effort to defend the Alliance for Progress and, in doing so, strengthen SUDENE, began to take a toll on him. At the moment, Brazil was undergoing a process of extreme radicalization. While the right-wing parties, industrial entrepreneurs, and some experts rallied together in defense of economic stability and in opposition to Goulart, the labor movement and the recalcitrant nationalist left pushed the agenda of "structural reforms" further than Goulart could handle. The position vis-à-vis the United States increasingly separated the political right and left, and Furtado was caught in the middle. Although the initial activities of SUDENE privileged industry and infrastructure, leaving aside the policies related to land tenure and land use, Furtado was the target of criticism from the vested interests in the Northeast that claimed he was orchestrating communist activities, calling him a "saboteur of the Alliance."[108] The claim was echoed by a rival economist writing for the mainstream press who accused him of "preparing a totalitarian revolution from the left through his ongoing pre-revolution" and "downplaying the need to tame the inflationary process even at the cost of lowering investment for development."[109] Meanwhile, the increasingly vocal and recalcitrant nationalist left, which advocated for debt moratorium and nationalization of foreign corporations, saw his support for the Alliance as a betrayal to the cause of social transformation and called him an agent of Wall Street, especially after his formulation of the *Plano Trienal*. Furtado's partnership with the United States in the Alliance for Progress gained him numerous critics in an increasingly polarized Brazil.

Yet, despite criticisms and the Alliance for Progress's subversion of SUDENE, Furtado did not renounce the program. Instead, he repeatedly tried to save what was left of the Alliance for Progress in an effort to realize his vision of SUDENE, bolstered by the resources and leverage of the economic assistance program. He had tried to become the broker or facilitator between state governors and USAID officials and even expanded his program to align with what USAID officials imagined as Alliance for Progress goals.[110] He had unsuccessfully tried to convince the US authorities that SUDENE was their best bet. In fact, SUDENE was the mechanism that could prevent those peasant leagues and rural movements that USAID officials so feared "from being exploited by demagogues," Furtado explained.[111] Despite his efforts, the Alliance for Progress had privileged other political allies over him.

Fraught as the Alliance was, Furtado could not support what many in Brazil saw as the alternative. "Though I consider myself a man of the left," Furtado explained, "I do not believe in revolution."[112] If the US state officials lacked an understanding of the problems of the Brazilian Northeast, so did the revolutionaries who followed or were inspired by the Cuban model. Like Guevara, whom Furtado met at Punta del Este, those advocating for revolution "imagined the peasant leagues to be vigorous mass organizations, able to check an initiative of the right" and "underestimated the entrenched power structures in the Northeast."[113] Furtado believed that the militancy and mobilization of a myriad of students, peasants, and workers, whom he sympathized with, "revealed not a demand for revolution," as many interpreted, but "a demand for economic development" that could be achieved by other means. Even more so, those advocating for revolution failed to consider the cost in terms of lives and of liberties that bringing about transformation through violence entailed.[114] To speak of revolution, Furtado claimed, was also to disregard the democratic institutions, whom he considered a vital and fragile asset of Brazilian society.

By late 1962, however, Furtado joined the chorus of regional policy-makers who called for a reformulation of the Alliance. The paucity in the disbursement of funds and the delays in the implementation of programs were certainly wearing down the enthusiasm and confidence in the program. Tactful but unambiguous, Furtado began to hint what a few months later became the regional consensus: that the Alliance was not perceived as a partnership between Latin America and the United States but as an exclusive US initiative.[115] That "more emphasis was placed on 'alliance' than on 'progress'" was the main reason behind the premature failure of the Alliance, Furtado declared with a careful choice of words.[116] That the decisions of high-level officials as well as technical experts on the ground, like those in Northeast, were driven by the attempt to forestall a second Cuba was clear to Furtado, but he refrained from saying so. In an effort to "make the revolution before the people made it," Furtado argued more discreetly, the Alliance for Progress had lost track of economic development, the main goal of the program.

Critical but conciliatory, Furtado's call for more "progress" and less "Alliance" was an effort to get support for another initiative he was recently put in charge of. In late 1962, Furtado formulated a proposal for "structural reforms"—including access to land and reform of the unequal land tenure system, enfranchisement of the illiterate populations, larger access to university level education, and limits to the profits of foreign corporations, among others—to rally together what he called the "progressive forces" while giving Goulart a solid agenda for the rest of his term. Given his leadership in the "structural reforms" program, Goulart appointed Furtado as plenipotentiary minister of planning and asked him to formulate a national economic development plan to carry out those reforms while recovering monetary and financial stability amid a deepening economic crisis. What became known as *Plano Trienal* encompassed an initial stage of gradual monetary stabilization with unpopular measures such as limits to wage readjustment, fiscal cuts, and credit restrictions, and a second stage, for structural reforms and growth promotion. The *Plano* required substantial economic assistance and debt restructuring, which in turn was pending on the action of USAID officials, who had been bestowed additional powers in an effort to revamp the Alliance for Progress. Following Furtado's ideas, President Goulart therefore called for the Alliance for Progress to focus less on the symptoms of underdevelopment, such as the lack of housing, health, and education, and more on "structural" causes and reforms that development required and asked for financial support for Furtado's *Plano Trienal*.[117]

However, the *Plano Trienal* imploded, pushing Furtado toward a rupture with the Alliance. For Furtado, the US financial assistance was the mechanism to ensure the political feasibility of the stabilization reforms. It provided the means to cushion the impact of the gradual monetary stabilization and, in so doing, guarantee the popular support of the program and the political position of Goulart, whose most important base was in the labor movement. Although Furtado's appointment and his *Plano Trienal* were well received in Washington, the position of the US government toward Goulart had changed dramatically. Whereas in early 1962, US officials financially supported Goulart in an effort to allure him and bolster the Alliance for Progress, by early 1963, the Brazilian negotiators for economic assistance met with outward hostility in Washington. The resources that were made available did not correspond to the urgency and amount that Brazilian authorities required; future disbursements were conditional on implementing the policies established by the IMF. The limited financial support not only endangered the already weak financial position of the country but also bolstered the opposition of the political right already mobilized against Goulart. After popular protests against the stabilization plan, Goulart ceded to the pressure of organized labor and did not enforce the limited wage adjustment policy, effectively abandoning Furtado's *Plano Trienal*.[118] By that point, all Alliance for Progress funding for the federal government, including SUDENE, was withheld. As the Alliance for Progress went astray in Brazil, Furtado firmly and publicly denounced the United States for its "tendency to give a political character to its aid" and for trying to "take charge of Latin American development," limiting the region's autonomy.[119]

The disenchantment that began with the failure of the Alliance for Progress in the Northeast and continued with the implosion of the *Plano Trienal* deepened with the military coup that deposed President Goulart a year later. Furtado, who had been a staunch advocate of international cooperation and champion of development, became skeptical of both. Amid the severe economic crisis that led to the formulation of the *Plano Trienal*, Furtado declared in 1962 that Brazil was "not a sickened economy but a vigorous organism" that "had maintained for a long-time now one of the largest growth rates in the world."[120] Three years later, Furtado characterized the Brazilian economy as undergoing a process loosely referred to as "stagnation." Furtado called attention not just to the deceleration of economic growth but also to the collapse or at least regression of the industrialization process that underpinned the project of development he had defended.[121]

For Furtado and other *cepalinos,* Latin America was undergoing a crisis of development. In revisiting the reasons behind the failure of the *Plano Trienal,* Furtado understood that in the absence of economic assistance, Goulart was confronted with the difficult choice of having financial instability or economic recession, both of which meant losing political control given the increasing social tensions and divided political positions. Downplaying the significance of the "entrenched power structures" he had singled out in the past, Furtado tilted the balance and increasingly decried US intervention. "The region is becoming aware that the margin of self-determination in its search for ways of coping with the tendency towards economic stagnation, is being daily reduced as the imperative for US security call for a growing alienation of sovereignty on the part of national governments," he affirmed.[122] In his ideas and tone, Furtado would become increasingly militant, reinterpreting *cepalino* ideas of center and periphery as embryonic forms of anti-imperialism and denunciations of dependency, even as he and other *cepalinos* had fought long and hard for the cooperation between center and peripheries and the fulfillment of the global responsibilities of the world's hegemonic center.[123]

Conclusions

Cepalinos' successive involvement in the Cuban Revolution and the US-sponsored counterrevolutionary Alliance for Progress proved costly for their institution. As *cepalinos* and their allies flocked to Cuba to occupy high-level positions in the revolutionary government, CEPAL established a foothold in an experiment that drew the world's attention and that had important repercussions for the global Cold War and for international Third Worldism. Former *cepalino* Boti and Pazos, a *cepalino* ally, infused the economic program of the rebel 26th of July Movement with *cepalino* ideas, but the pace and parallel power structures of the revolution soon turned them into defectors. Within a few years of the revolution's triumph, their ideas had been rendered irrelevant to Cuba's future. CEPAL, as an institution, officially renounced Cuba; by doing so, it also renounced its authority to speak *for* and *from* Latin America.

Given the fiasco of CEPAL's involvement with Cuba, some *cepalinos* were attracted to the golden opportunity of working with the Alliance for Progress. Yet, rather than bolstering their position and expanding their influence, the Alliance for Progress undermined these *cepalinos.* Prebisch, who had been at the forefront of regional initiatives and had in many ways paved the way for the Alliance by generating a consensus around international cooperation, was lured into and then sidelined from its implementation. Meanwhile, Furtado, who saw in the Alliance for Progress the means to broaden and deepen the influence of his signature project in the Northeast, witnessed his federal agency be recurrently undermined by US policies. Although both men aspired to use the reins of the Alliance for their own goals, both were sidelined as the United States increasingly sought to use the economic assistance program to deter revolution in the region. Though champions of regional and national autonomy, Furtado and Prebisch's cooperation with the Alliance for Progress broadcast their antirevolutionary stance. Yet neither could convince US officials that, despite their criticism of US international trade and financial policies, they stood as trustworthy partners for the Alliance's intended goals. Their alignment with the Alliance for Progress failed to bring them the influence and sway they aspired to. It also cost them political legitimacy among the intellectual left, just as they had lost the legitimacy among the intellectual right with their "structural approach to inflation."

The successive impact of revolution and counterrevolution transformed the *cepalino* project from its vanguard position against global inequality in the early postwar years to a rearguard movement against social change in the early 1960s, initiating CEPAL's long demise. Just as they did in many other areas, the combined forces of revolutionary Cuba and the counterrevolutionary Alliance for Progress radicalized the positions of those battling the war of economic ideas. Many policymakers in Latin America applauded Prebisch's position with regard to Cuba, since they distinguished between "economic development through freedom" and "economic development through communism."[124] Less than a year after the *cepalino* mission to Cuba ended, Frei, Ahumada, and the rising Christian Democrats in Chile were declaring not only their professed and emphatic anti-Communism but also their enduring anti-Fidelism.[125]

But for many on the Latin American left, some of whom soon after became *dependentistas,* CEPAL's position as the voice of the periphery had become severely compromised by Prebisch and Furtado's relationship with the Alliance for Progress. Until 1960 Mexican sociologist Pablo González Casanova claimed, "CEPAL had represented a genuine effort to improve economic independence and development." Yet, after they embraced the US initiative, *cepalinos* had renounced their progressive "ideals of economic nationalism, González Casanova added."[126] And since the Alliance for Progress itself incorporated many of CEPAL's central tenets, the failure of its projects led *cepalinos* to question their own assumptions. It was in the early

1960s with CEPAL's position politically compromised for those on the left, not in the early 1970s with the emerging neoliberal turn, that the demise of *cepalino* influence began. Emerging from the tremendous change in the political landscape in Latin America's 1960s, CEPAL's discredit and the soul-searching process it sparked would lead to the emergence of a new worldmaking category with dependency theory.

Toward Dependency Theory

In the 1960s, as the US-led "modernization theory" was at its peak, new ideas were simmering in Latin America and putting *cepalinos* under pressure. Speaking to broader visions of development in the country, Harvard, MIT, and Chicago University experts moved into Washington agencies and New York offices to accelerate the transition of the emergent Third World from "tradition to modernity." With a sense of growing political emergency to foster the right kind of revolution, modernizers turned theory into practice. Development loans and aid for large infrastructure projects such as dams and irrigation systems aimed to catalyze economic change. Alongside philanthropic foundations, university researchers and government agencies experimented with new technologies to "feed a hungry world" and control world population.[1] While young volunteers filled the ranks of Peace Corps, attracted by the promise of helping those in need and fighting the global war on poverty, modernizers in government, foundations, and academia supported military intervention, violence, and war in the name of development and democracy. Combining reformism and force, modernization, in theory and practice, became the object of contestation worldwide. Yet, in Latin America, those ideas that coalesced into dependency theory responded more to local and regional orthodoxies of development than to "modernization theory" and Northern ones.

For a new generation of social scientists, coming of intellectual age in the apogee of the *cepalino* project, the organization's once-radical ideas had become orthodoxy. In the early 1960s the *cepalino* project became severely compromised. The disappointing economic performance in the countries with a stronger *cepalino* presence combined with the controversial position of *cepalinos* with regard to both revolutionary Cuba and the US Alliance for Progress undermined their political and intellectual legitimacy within the circles of the intellectual left and gave rise to the idea of an ongoing "development impasse." Drawing on Marxism and animated by the revolutionary fervor of the time, this new generation called into question entrenched assumptions of the *cepalino* project and its ambiguous allies across the region, including the nationalist and Communist left.

Although the backlash against *cepalinos* surfaced across the region, two of the most influential and enduring of the new intellectual projects emerged in Brazil. The site of almost incomparable *cepalino* influence and of almost unparalleled developmentalist momentum, Brazil was also considered to be in a moment of "pre-revolution" in the early 1960s. Two overlapping but distinct academic and political circles in São Paulo and Brasilia, respectively, introduced two ideas about the logics of capitalism in the global periphery that later coalesced in Chile as "dependency theory." The first of these involved sociologist Fernando Henrique Cardoso and the *paulistas,* and the second, the traveling economist Andre Gunder Frank and what would be known as Brasilia group. This chapter follows the early trajectories of Cardoso and Frank in the convoluted Brazilian landscape, examining how the interactions between them and their encounters with *cepalinos* gave rise to two conflicting meanings of dependency that, grouped together under the term "dependency theory," became globally influential as the theoretical enunciation that, from outside the world's centers of power, presented an alternative to the global North's theory and practice of modernization.

The Development Impasse

Although the enterprise of development reached an apex at the global level in the early 1960s, it ran into a profound impasse in Latin America, especially in Brazil.[2] The United Nations inaugurated a global "Decade of Development," but the project of "Fifty years of progress in five," put in place in Brazil in the previous decade, came to an end in 1960. While the US government revamped its modernization policy and foreign aid institutions with the establishment of the United States Agency for International Development (USAID), the *Banco Nacional de Desenvolvimento Económico* (BNDE) and the regional agency *Superintendência do Desenvolvimento do Nordeste* (SUDENE), two of the most prominent development institutions in Brazil, lost prestige and resources as rampant inflation and spiraling external deficits dominated the economic policy landscape. As massive infrastructure projects were completed across East Asia, the *Plano de Metas* for energy and transport infrastructure found no continuation in the ill-started government of João Goulart, mainly occupied with political survival. Whereas Egypt, India, and other countries of the decolonizing world embraced long-term planning, the 1963 *Plano Trienal,* or three-year plan formulated by *cepalino* Celso Furtado, was aborted after a few months amid vocal opposition from an increasingly radical left and dwindling support from the political right.[3] Political leaders and institutions quailed in the face of mounting economic difficulties and social tensions. The relative political consensus that had existed around state-led industrialization and development fractured as new social forces that pressed for more radical change frightened former allies of the project on the political right. The confrontation resulted in a development impasse that culminated in a military coup, deposing the president in April 1964 and inaugurating twenty years of military rule in Brazil.[4]

For both right and left, Celso Furtado represented the development project that reached an impasse in the 1960s. Since the early 1950s, Furtado had worked persistently to consolidate the *cepalino* presence in Brazil and to defend the now-embattled state-led industrial development project. Rallying together industrialists, policymakers, and academics, he inaugurated the policy and academic debate about Prebisch's notion of center and periphery and the defense of national industrialization to counteract the fall in the international terms of trade. An active public intellectual and institution builder, Furtado brought *cepalino* ideas to the forefront of the policy debate and created a wide network of *cepalino* allies among academic and policy-makers. In his many books, articles, and conferences, Furtado defended the idea that the promotion and protection of a national bourgeoisie and the expansion of the national industry producing for the domestic market was the path to national and regional autonomy from the ebbs and flows of the global economy. By establishing the *cepalino*-BNDE partnership for development planning, Furtado supported the expansion of state intervention in economic development. Spearheading the creation of SUDENE, Furtado tackled the problem of the national distribution of the benefits of development between national centers of power in São Paulo and Rio de Janeiro and the impoverished Northeast. Alongside the embattled President Goulart, Furtado defended the need for "structural reforms" in the system of land use and tenure, taxation, and enfranchisement to overcome the political obstacles to development, considered too radical for the right and not radical enough for some in the left. In the early 1960s new social forces emerged in Brazil demanding more radical change than Furtado's project had afforded.

As perhaps the most prominent development torchbearer and minister of planning of the fragile Goulart administration, Furtado unavoidably became the target of criticism, especially from the forces of the left. The peasant leagues in Furtado's native Northeast, turning to revolutionary Cuba for inspiration and financial support, initiated land invasions and rejected Furtado's development plan *Plano Trienal* as antinational and antipopular. Urban workers and unions consolidated a large and unified organization in mid-1962 that opposed the salary freezes proposed by Furtado and lambasted him as a reactionary. A new cohort of Catholic activists revitalized the national student movement and accused Furtado of failing to combat the powerful landholders and serving foreign interests. Alongside students and peasants, army junior officials began to organize in clubs and associations, demanding better working conditions, and within a few years successfully elected a congressman representing "those below." In response to the opposition and clamors of increasingly radical left, Furtado, a man who considered himself of the left, clarified with frustration that he was asked to devise a "plan for governing not for a revolution."[5] While Furtado insisted that state-led economic development could quench the thirst of those in the "pre-revolutionary stage," the mobilization of peasants, students, workers, and junior sectors of the army convinced a new generation of social scientists that Brazil was in a stage of "pre-revolution" and that the development project that Furtado defended had to be superseded.[6] Convinced of the Brazilian prerevolution, the old and the new left parted ways.

For a new cohort of social scientists coming of intellectual age after the Cuban Revolution, Furtado and *cepalinos* came to represent the orthodoxy of development.[7] Intellectuals from Mexico City to Santiago plumbed the depths of the ongoing development path. With concepts such as "arrested development," "marginality," and "internal colonialism," Latin American intellectuals began to capture the growing malaise and the unfulfilled promises of growth, inclusion, and autonomy of the *cepalino*-endorsed development project.[8] In Brazil, the challenge to the Latin American orthodoxies of development gave rise to what would be known as "dependency theory." Those to-be *dependentistas* put into question precisely what Furtado defended: that the national bourgeoisie was the bearer of economic development and autonomy. Those like Furtado, who in the previous decade were considered progressive men with transformative ambitions, became the staid figures of development orthodoxy and obstacles to revolutionary change. The project of *dependentistas* emerged in Brazil, a country beset by social tensions and confronting a political deadlock but also experiencing an unparalleled zeal and dynamism for development.

The Brazilian challenge to the orthodoxy of development, however, drove a wedge within the rising intellectual left. Two distinct but overlapping intellectual projects emerged: one in the modernist and futuristic city and University of Brasilia, the quintessential product of the development hubris, and the other in the industrial and modern city of São Paulo, the locus of the coffee economy and the country's industrial powerhouse. Each of these undertakings confronted the assumptions of the worldmaking project of *cepalinos*. In their effort to consolidate their position in Brazil, *cepalinos* built alliances with the nationalist left, and their ideas became ammunition for the Communist left. Their institution and their ideas had been the fulcrum of the political support for the bourgeoisie. Politically contentious but intellectually inspiring, the *cepalino* project was a tough bite to swallow. It was in resolving this tension that the projects of the Brasilia group and the *paulista* collective both fostered and fractured the theory of dependency.

"Development of Underdevelopment"

In January 1963, after a year and a half of travels, German-born, US-educated economist Andre Gunder Frank settled temporarily in Brasilia. Frustrated with the American academy and fed up with the comfortable yet complacent life in the North American suburbs, Frank had taken a leave of absence from his position as assistant professor at Michigan State University in 1960 to travel the world. Initially expelled from the University of Chicago's graduate program in economics, Frank returned to the institution's Center for Economic Development and Cultural Change, one of the strongholds of modernization theory. He obtained his doctorate from Chicago with a short dissertation on agriculture in the Soviet Union, which was also the first destination of his world tour. After a brief stint at the Massachusetts Institute of Technology's Center for International Studies, where Walt Rostow's theories of stages of economic growth and other classics of modernization theory were developed, Frank began a sojourn that lasted over two years and included Eastern Europe, Africa, and finally Latin America. It was his month-long stay in revolutionary Cuba that most fundamentally transformed his personal and intellectual trajectory as that of many North American intellectuals of his generation.[9]

Once at the core of the modernization theory social scientific enterprise, Frank resigned definitely to Michigan, the US academia, and the intellectual program that, in his words, "impeded more than speed up economic development."[10] Bert Hoselitz, Frank's advisor and one of the most prominent theorists of modernization, attributed his pupil's decision to Frank's relentless procurement of only "geniuses" and his "intolerance to simple-mindedness." Part of the purpose of this "voyage of discovery" was to "understand underdevelopment from the perspective of underdeveloped countries."[11] In his Latin American exploration, Frank visited Mexico, Guatemala, Peru, Venezuela, and Chile, finally settling in Brasilia.

Constructed in just four years, Brasilia was the symbol of Brazil's search for development and modernity. It was the visible representation of the "50 years of progress in 5" program designed to accelerate industrial development. Located in the interior of the country, the new capital city was an attempt to leave behind the remnants of Portuguese coastal colonization. Brasilia was conceptualized as a departure from the Atlantic-facing, imperial-era capital, Rio de Janeiro. In contrast to the European-inspired neoclassical architecture that dominated in Rio's nineteenth-century libraries, theaters, and government buildings, Brasilia, with its curved lines and wide-open spaces, was the product of Brazilian modernism. World-renowned Communist architect Oscar Niemeyer, who also designed the UN building in New York City, and urban planner Lucio Costa envisioned Brasilia as a place where the class and racial segregation that defined Rio and other cities in the country disappeared.[12] In Brasilia, the futuristic-looking and emblematic city of the Brazilian development project, ironically Frank crafted a critique of that same project.

As lecturer on sociology at the *Universidade de Brasilia* in early 1963, Frank found a space in the group led by Theotônio dos Santos, one of his students, who would become a pioneer and missionary of dependency theory in Chile years later. Established in 1962, two years after the inauguration of the city itself, the *Universidade de Brasilia* revived a defunct project of democratization of education of the Vargas era while simultaneously inaugurating a new intellectual center away from the political power of Rio and the economic power of São Paulo.[13] Despite its bare-bones existence, the university and the city engaged many important Brazilian intellectuals, including anthropologist Darcy Ribeiro and educator Anísio Teixeira, who saw in the institution an opportunity to start anew. Ribeiro and the *Universidade de Brasilia* attracted dos Santos, who after completing undergraduate studies in public administration and sociology at the federal university in his native Minas Gerais, moved to Brasilia in 1962 to begin a master's program in political science, after which he became an instructor.[14]

The political militancy of the Brasilia group captivated Frank. The Brasilia group that, aside from dos Santos, included sociologists Vânia Bambirra and Ruy Mauro Marini was also involved in Política Operaria (POLOP).

Established in 1961, the new political organization brought together university students from the states of Rio de Janeiro and Minas Gerais who were dissatisfied with the dogmatism and orthodoxy of the political left. While the Communist Party and the nationalist forces of the left defended the project of a bourgeois, democratic revolution and an alliance between workers and industrialists against the archaic landowning elite, POLOP aimed to foster a "true working-class movement" that united peasants and urban workers to bring about the socialist revolution.[15] Reunited again in Brasilia, dos Santos, Bambirra, and Marini established a reading group on the classic works of Marx, following the model of that established by the *paulistas* in their "Marx seminar." While Frank reinforced the Marxism of his mentors Paul Baran and Paul Sweezy in the Brasilia group, dos Santos and his fellow partners introduced Frank to the political effervescence of what they believed was the Brazilian "pre-revolution."[16] The intellectual and political effervescence of Brasilia shaped Frank's project.

With dos Santos and the rest of the Brasilia group, Frank began to plunge into the analysis of economic development from and for Latin America. Doing so entailed positioning the Brasilia group vis-à-vis *cepalinos*, the dominant point of reference in the region. In 1962, just before Frank arrived in Brasilia, dos Santos and Bambirra enrolled in one of the *cepalino*-BNDE training courses on economic development. In the course, they familiarized themselves with *cepalino* ideas about center and periphery and with Prebisch's thesis about the long-term decline in the international terms of trade. They were instructed in the *cepalino* project of economic development that included the industrialization of the periphery and the expansion of the domestic market to counteract the global inequality in the gains from international trade.

These *cepalino* alums began to distance themselves from their teachers. While dos Santos criticized *cepalinos* for associating themselves with the Brazilian "national bourgeoisie" and privileging a national, democratic, and bourgeois revolution as the path to development, Marini attacked *cepalinos* for giving intellectual ammunition to the Brazilian Communists in their defense of the Soviet strategy of propounding an anti-imperial and anti-feudal, bourgeois revolution in the Third World.[17] The result of the exchanges between Frank and the Brasilia group about Marxism and *cepalino* ideas was his major opus, *Capitalism and Underdevelopment in Latin America*.

Among others aims, Frank conceived *Capitalism and Underdevelopment* as a frontal attack against *cepalinos*. As Frank moved between Brasilia, Rio, Santiago, and Mexico City, the project gradually took shape. It was the result of Frank's "voyage of discovery in the region," and a collection of essays whose most relevant ones were on Chile and Brazil. According to

Frank, *cepalinos* like Chilean Aníbal Pinto had failed to understand the true origins of underdevelopment. Whereas *cepalinos* affirmed that the obstacles to development were the result of the international division of labor established in the late nineteenth century during the so-called Pax Britannica, Frank argued that "underdevelopment" began with the Iberian empires and the integration of Latin America to the world capitalist system. Frank accused *cepalinos* of defending the "inaccurate view that Chile had a closed, recluse, subsistence economy throughout the centuries before political independence" and that "subsequent underdevelopment was the result of development 'towards the outside,'" that is, the production of primary products for the global economy since the late nineteenth century.[18] For his critique of *cepalinos* on what he called the origins of "underdevelopment," Frank drew substantially from and quoted extensively from Argentine economic historians such as Sergio Bagú and Silvio Frondizi.[19] Based on their work, Frank argued that capitalism, not feudalism, characterized the Latin American economy since colonial times. "Because capitalism was already underdeveloping the country throughout the three centuries before independence," Frank claimed, *cepalinos* were wrong in assuming that "a reorientation of development from the global to the national economy could save Chile from underdevelopment."[20] While *cepalinos* identified the current unequal pattern of international trade between center and periphery as the main obstacle to development, Frank contended that capitalist development itself was the main source of underdevelopment in the periphery.

Similarly, Frank challenged *cepalinos* and their view of underdevelopment and development in Brazil. A leading *cepalino* and a noted policymaker, Furtado figured prominently in Frank's work. Frank had two critiques against Furtado: one conceptual and one political. Conceptually, Frank rejected Furtado's interpretation that there were two Brazils: one industrial and modern, centered on the São Paulo region, and another one backward and impoverished, the most emblematic example being his native Northeast. Although Furtado had spoken at length about how entwined the two Brazils were when he presented the *Operação Nordeste*, Frank condemned Furtado for failing to comprehend that Brazil was a single, capitalist economic structure since the moment of Portuguese colonization rather than a combination of a capitalist, on the one hand, and precapitalist or semifeudal Brazil, on the other.[21] Based on his assertation that capitalism, not feudalism, shaped the region since colonial times, Frank claimed that underdevelopment in Latin America, observed from the vantage point of Chile and Brazil, originated in the region's "incorporation into the world capitalist system since the 16th century."[22] This historical insertion of

Latin America as producer of primary products and raw materials for the global capitalist system was behind the stagnation of agriculture and the overall underdevelopment of the national economy.[23] This thesis became known as the "development of underdevelopment."

Politically, Frank denounced Furtado as a "leading ideologue of the bourgeoisie" for affirming that state-led, industrial development was the path to economic development and autonomy.[24] According to Frank, Furtado asserted that "that through a rising national capitalism, Brazil almost got out of the grip of the world imperialist system," failing only because of the fall in the international terms of trade after 1955.[25] Furtado believed that the *cepalino* proposals of industrialization and cooperation between center and periphery were in fact the road to development and autonomy. In other words, Furtado was convinced Brazilian development was possible. Instead, Frank argued that a metropolis like São Paulo, itself a satellite of the world's hegemonic power, simply could not achieve autonomous development. Like dos Santos and the Brasilia group and unlike Furtado and some *cepalinos,* Frank asserted that the "bourgeoisie could not carry out the national liberation process."[26] It was against *cepalinos* that Frank's "development of underdevelopment" thesis emerged in Brazil.

Yet, though he was critical of *cepalinos, cepalino* ideas had been crucial for Frank and his world system perspective. Upon his arrival to the region, Frank thought of development problems in Latin America "largely in terms of domestic factors," including "capital scarcity, feudal and traditional institutions that impede savings and investment, and concentration of power on rural and backward elites."[27] However, the prevailing ideas about economic development in the region were very different. The relation between center and periphery and their impact on development was foundational for the *cepalino* project and became foundational for Frank as well. "CEPAL [Economic Commission for Latin America] has emphasized the importance of foreign trade for the problems of domestic development" and has "suggested that recent historical trends in international trade have been prejudicial to Latin American development possibilities," he asserted. Frank proposed to expand on that intuition to "examine sources earlier in the national and even the colonial periods" to "deepen our understanding of Latin America's trade relationship with the rest of the world and its domestic structural consequences for development."[28] With the *cepalino* insight in mind, Frank had conceptualized a project on the long-run economic history of Latin America that led to his "development of underdevelopment" thesis and his challenge to *cepalino* orthodoxy.

Despite what seemed a devastating critique, Frank, like the new generation of Brazilian and Latin American intellectuals he had encountered, could not completely forego the *cepalino* project. In his course at the *Universidade de Brasilia,* Frank mapped out the global enterprise of development into the categories of myths and realities.[29] The ideas of modernization theorists and the development experts of the global North were undoubtedly categorized as myths. Walt Rostow's idea of the stages of economic growth, Ragnar Nurkse's idea of balanced growth, Ricardo's notion of comparative advantage on international trade, and the Communist Party's popular front strategies were clearly classified as myths of development. But Frank's analysis of *cepalinos* was more complicated.

For Frank, *cepalinos* and their ideas occupied a space between myth and reality. While the *cepalino,* or "structural," approach to inflation, which he considered not too different from the Keynesian or neoclassical models, was classified as a myth, Prebisch's notion of center and periphery, Pinto's idea of "arrested development," or the idea that production for the global economy hindered development, and Furtado's historical analysis of economic development, in which he incorporated Portuguese colonization, appeared in Frank's scheme as the "realities" of underdevelopment. Even though Frank's confrontation with *cepalinos* would heighten in the years to come, their ability to situate development within the historical expansion of global capitalism became the foundation for Frank's project and made it groundbreaking at the global, if not the regional, level where *cepalinos* had already filled that role. Years later, when Frank revisited what came to be known as "dependency theory," he admitted with disillusion that *cepalinos* and *dependentistas* were "perhaps less different than some of us would like to have had it."[30]

Nonetheless, at the time, Frank's "development of underdevelopment" undermined the development enterprise that many, including Goulart, *cepalinos,* and their allies in the Communist and the nationalist left, were invested in. Frank concluded that "national capitalism and the national bourgeoisie do not and could not offer any way out of underdevelopment" as *cepalinos* and their allies assumed.[31] The problem of underdevelopment was not about the size and degree of control over foreign capital as many nationalists assumed, nor the terms of international trade for the periphery of the global system as *cepalinos* insisted, nor the lack of modern entrepreneurial elites as the modernization theorists imagined. Rather the problem with development was that it was capitalist. The solution was therefore undertaking a socialist revolution, without attempting to pass through a bourgeois, democratic revolution as the Communist parties advocated. Frank was therefore on a mission to reorient the debate about development and capitalism in Latin America in order to pave the road for socialism.

Despite having recently encountered the region, Frank considered his thesis to be a product *for* and *from* Latin America. "When I got to Latin America a year ago," Frank confessed to Rodolfo Stavenhagen, Mexican anthropologist and one of Frank's intellectual partners, "I naturally thought that Latin America was feudal, or at least its agriculture and countryside." The young and old generation of intellectuals he encountered, their questions and ideas, had pushed Frank in a different direction. "I began to see the matter as you describe it and as it is seen by my Marxist friends in Brazil here at the university and many others," he confessed.[32] Unfamiliar with the classics of Marxism and thus unwilling to cast himself as a writer in the Marxist tradition, Frank instead saw his ideas as the product of the practice of revolution and his Latin American intellectual milieu.[33]

Not only was his book a Latin American product but his audience was also Latin American. Frank had come to understand his intellectual project to be about telling "people in underdeveloped countries what political economy of growth might serve them."[34] He was exasperated with the delay that the English publication was causing for the Spanish translation. So Frank clarified for his *Monthly Review* editors that the "book was written for a Spanish and Portuguese audience" and the "publication in English was only incidental."[35] Despite the misgivings of his editors in the United States, his fight was against the development orthodoxies in the region.

Frank found a space within a vibrant network of intellectuals in Brazil whose focus was capitalist development in Latin America and Latin America in global capitalism. He found these intellectuals waging a battle against *cepalinos* and their allies, one that he assumed as his own. Reclaiming one of their fundamental insights about center and periphery, Frank elaborated a long-term view of the historical evolution of the capitalist world system. Framed in the language of metropoles and satellites, Frank's "development of underdevelopment" thesis broke new ground in the global debate about development and was recognized as the founder of a new paradigm. But the group to which Frank belonged was as vibrant as it was diverse. Some of those whom Frank conceived as partners in a new intellectual project viewed Latin America, its economic development, and its place in global history very differently. They rebuked his "development of underdevelopment" thesis first, and years later, after their theses had become "dependency theory," contested his claim to speak for and from the region.

"Dependency *and* Development"

One of those intellectuals who shaped and defied Frank's view of capitalism in Latin America was Fernando Henrique Cardoso. In what was a formative year for their respective intellectual projects, Cardoso and Frank, belonging to different but overlapping circles, met several times in the tumultuous 1963. Frank spoke of Cardoso and the São Paulo, or *paulista,* group as "forward looking, relatively independent Marxists," who "largely subscribe[d] to the development of underdevelopment thesis."[36] For Frank, Cardoso and his group were partners in what he called an alternative political economy of development. Like Frank, dos Santos, and the Brasilia group, Cardoso and the *paulista* group defied the old intellectual left and its project of economic development based on a bourgeois revolution. Yet Cardoso and Frank would soon part ways. The exchanges between them and especially their interaction with *cepalinos* transformed their intellectual projects and would make "dependency theory" a battlefield. Although both became directly involved with *cepalinos,* only Cardoso captured and was captured by the *cepalino* project.

Alongside Frank, Cardoso, a young sociologist based at *Universidade de São Paulo* (USP), entered and transformed the debate about development and capitalism in Latin America. Born in Rio de Janeiro in 1931 within a family of military tradition and active in politics, Cardoso moved to São Paulo, the emerging industrial and economic center of Brazil, when he was about to start secondary school. Failing to pass all the requirements to study law, Cardoso entered the Department of Social Sciences at USP in 1949 instead. With the exception of a brief writing fellowship in Paris in 1963, Cardoso's formative academic years were in São Paulo. He was an undergraduate, master, and doctorate student, professor and researcher at USP, shaping what was becoming the influential *Paulista* School of Sociology.[37] In May 1964, escaping the military intervention, Cardoso left Brazil to join CEPAL, a decision that profoundly altered his intellectual trajectory and led to the formulation of the "dependency *and* development" thesis.

Cardoso's São Paulo was a bustling city. Founded in the mid-sixteenth century, São Paulo remained a poor and provincial town until the late eighteenth century when the sugarcane industry picked up again, but the city really flourished in the late nineteenth century when the spur of the coffee industry made Brazil the world's largest producer. With the construction of the railroad system moving coffee from the interior of the São Paulo state to the port city of Santos, the city of São Paulo became the home of the coffee barons as well as former slaves and European immigrants, sprawling into a growing metropolis that by the 1920s was also a leading manufacturing center. By the mid-twentieth century, when Cardoso and his peers sought to reorient the sociology program, São Paulo had become the symbol of progress and modernity, with its bourgeoning skyscrapers and multiplying cultural centers. USP and the *paulista* sociology group bore the imprint of their founders, São Paulo's coffee and industrial elite, who, after losing power to Vargas in the early 1930s, sought to create an intellectual counterweight to the imperial Rio.[38] Cardoso and the *paulista* social scientists strived to displace the Rio-based intellectuals that had dominated the debate about economic development in Brazil.

Unlike dos Santos and the Brasilia group to which Frank adhered, Cardoso and most members of the *paulista* school were not militants (figure 5.1). As graduate students, Cardoso and his group of friends transformed their social weekend gatherings over coffee and beer into an informal seminar about Marx's *Capital* and other Marxist theoretical texts—an idea later replicated by the Brasilia group—that profoundly shaped their academic trajectory.[39] For the *paulistas,* the rediscovery of Marxism was intellectually inspiring but not politically mobilizing. Even though Cardoso distanced himself from the Communist Party after the denunciations of Stalin's political crimes in the mid-1950s, he continued his work as editor of the journal *Fundamentos,* the academic arm of that party.[40] In a Weberian style, Florestan Fernandes, Cardoso's mentor and the architect of modern sociology in Brazil, at that time defended the academic over the political vocation. Fernandes, Cardoso, and other members of the group often published in *Revista Brasiliense,* a journal committed to adapting Marxism to the Brazilian reality. Theirs was a project of intellectual more than political transformation.

Despite defending the academic vocation, Cardoso was politically involved within the forces of the left. In the early 1950s, Cardoso collaborated with his uncle and other nationalists in the campaign for the nationalization of petroleum fields knows as "Oil is Ours" and later on, participated in his father's electoral campaign for deputy for the state of São Paulo. As representative of the alums first and then of faculty at the top-level University Council, Cardoso gained prominence in the university political landscape. Rallying the forces of the left and obtaining the respect of the right, Cardoso helped unseat a very conservative chancellor and collaborated in the creation of the São Paulo state fund for academic research.[41] Through these exchanges with the political and economic elite of São Paulo, Cardoso built the resources necessary for a new endeavor.

In the early 1960s Cardoso and the *paulista* school inaugurated a broad research program. The new cohort of *paulistas* aimed for a changing of the guard. Titled "Economy and Society in Brazil: Sociological Study of Underdevelopment," the research program marked a departure from the topics and methods that had characterized the school since Florestan Fernandes and a cohort of Brazilians took command of the social science program after the departure of the foundational French academic contingent.[42] The new program moved away from the focus on indigenous communi-

FIGURE 5.1   Fernando Henrique Cardoso (*on the left corner*) and some members of the *Paulista* school of sociology, n.d, approximately 1960 to 1962. (Acervo Presidente Fernando Henrique Cardoso.)

ties, Afro-Brazilians, and urban folklore that had characterized the *paulista* school under Fernandes. It replaced ethnographic methods with large-scale surveys and adopted structural analysis and dialectics instead of functionalism as the theoretical approach. It turned to São Paulo, the largest manufacturing region in Latin America, as the privileged site to assess the transformations industrial capitalism was bringing about in Brazil.[43] According to one of the founding members of the "Marx Seminar," they read *Capital* in order to rethink Brazil: to imagine how to foster development. Since the group expected to contribute to the most pressing political questions of the day, the program focused on the role of industrial elites, the labor movement, and the state in economic development.[44] To carry out the program, Cardoso marshaled the financial support of progressive São Paulo industrialists, the state government, and the University of Paris and founded the *Centro de Sociologia Industrial e do Trabalho* (CESIT). With the center and their project of the industrial society in Brazil, the *paulistas* encroached on what had been the nationalists' and *cepalino* territory.[45]

Cardoso's *Entrepreneurs and Economic Development* was the first result of that attempt to challenge the orthodoxies of development. Based on anecdotal use of surveys with industrialists carried out in the turmoil of the early 1960s, Cardoso challenged the idea of the national entrepreneurs as the bearers of autonomous economic development, the main assumption of both *cepalinos* and the nationalist left. According to Cardoso, the analysis of *cepalino* Celso Furtado was indifferent to what Cardoso called "the social forces [classes] that bore and oriented development." Although *cepalinos* had incorporated the global system of power—the unequal relations between developed and underdeveloped countries—in their analysis, they had also "removed the political nerve from history." Though Furtado's was a "brilliant analysis of the economic system," it reduced the process of economic development to abstract economic forces, Cardoso claimed. Furtado and *cepalinos* had failed "to even pose the question of how and why would the Brazilian entrepreneurs, in a country inserted in the global economy as producer of raw materials and primary products, would strive for national autonomy."[46] That national entrepreneurs were invested in economic development *within* the nation-state and that national industrialization entailed economic autonomy was taken for granted by *cepalinos* and their nationalist allies in a politically independent country like Brazil. Instead, Cardoso analyzed the conflicting interests and competing classes and the national politics of development.

The politics of the bourgeoisie began to transpire in the political turmoil that culminated in the 1964 military coup.[47] Amid growing inflationary pressures and declining economic activity, the government of Goulart was effectively besieged between the forces of left and right. Marginal until late 1963, some sectors of the Brazilian bourgeoisie, especially those in partnership with foreign capital, began to mobilize against Goulart, tilting the already delicate balance of political forces.[48] Highlighting the divisions within the national bourgeoisie, Cardoso showed how, as a class, the Brazilian bourgeoisie had so far wavered in its political alliances, transforming itself from the bearer of national development to the cornerstone of the development impasse. To solve its demand for larger amounts of capital, the Brazilian bourgeoisie wavered between an alliance with the state or with the foreign capitalists, both of which threatened its pretense to hegemony. Imagining itself as both part of the people and of the ruling class, the bourgeoisie, at times allied with the popular sectors out of fear of immobility, and at times allied itself with the traditional landowning, agro-exporting elites, out of fear of revolution.[49] For Cardoso, the constant swing or rather threat of a swing from revolution to counterrevolution, from coups to countercoups that had characterized the populist postwar era, was the product of a bourgeoisie that, situated in the periphery of the global economy, vacillated between an alliance with international capitalists or with the popular forces for national development. Through his direct encounter with *cepalinos,* Cardoso would transform his insight about the constraints of a national bourgeoisie in the global economic periphery into the fully-fledged notion of dependency.

While Frank's journey almost ended in Brasilia, São Paulo was the beginning of Cardoso's trajectory. With his "development of underdevelopment" thesis, Frank launched a project that he believed represented the thrust of the Latin American intellectuals he met in Brazil, including Cardoso and the *paulista* group. And to a certain extent, he was right. Those intellectuals, like many others of his generation, aimed to challenge *cepalinos* and others who represented the orthodoxy of development and who had been convinced of the emancipatory power of the national bourgeoisie. With that purpose in mind, Frank disputed the idea that underdevelopment was the result of remnant feudal structures, which could be overcome only by the triumph of the national bourgeoisie. Meanwhile Cardoso contested the notion that development was the product of a national, cross-class front against foreign interests with the bourgeoisie at the forefront.

This common aspiration notwithstanding, Frank and Cardoso thereafter parted ways. Already prescient in their initial formulations was Frank's focus on capitalism as an external social force in the region and Cardoso's interests in the internal political economy of development. Whereas Frank was briefly recruited for CEPAL but ended up in conflict with *cepalinos,* Cardoso joined, stayed, and rose through their ranks.[50] Whereas Frank's perspective of the "development of underdevelopment" was almost fully crafted by the time he left Brazil, Cardoso's interpretation came together when he moved to Santiago, where, among *cepalinos,* he wrestled with their project and advanced the notion of "dependency and development."

After the military coup in April 1964, Cardoso was on alert. The campus of the *Universidade de Brasilia* had been raided by police forces. Faculty in São Paulo, Rio de Janeiro, and Recife were imprisoned. Private and public libraries were purged of allegedly subversive materials.[51] Cardoso feared the reappraisals of a military that had embraced anticommunism and feared politicization at any level.[52] After hearing rumors that the military waited for him, Cardoso went into exile two weeks after the military coup. A year earlier, Spanish Civil War emigré José Medina Echavarría, the only sociologist among *cepalino* economists, had recruited Cardoso to produce a report on the Brazilian entrepreneurs as part of his and CEPAL's broader project on the "social aspects of development."[53] With a previous foot in the door, after a monthly sojourn in Argentina, Cardoso obtained a permanent position at CEPAL in Santiago.

FIGURE 5.2   Fernando Henrique Cardoso in his office at CEPAL in Santiago, 1965. (Acervo Presidente Fernando Henrique Cardoso.)

His departure left his colleagues in São Paulo initially perplexed. The "expected 'witch hunt' had not materialized and it might not even happen," they claimed. Many thought Cardoso had overreacted. Fernandes explained to his dearest disciple that, unlike him, he could not simply "abandon the boat" and "resign from his responsibilities."[54] Cardoso's colleagues also disproved his decision of joining CEPAL. Leaving for an international institution with a better pay and diplomatic status hardly fit the image of an engaged intellectual in exile. Instead of "a young man with deep eyes, sloppy hair, and unshaved beard writing subversive pamphlets from a cold basement" while trying to make ends meet, Cardoso wore a tie and suit and gained access to the tariff-free, imported cars that had become a cherished privilege (and business) of many CEPAL functionaries in Santiago[55] (figure 5.2). From São Paulo, the work at Santiago did not exude confidence on intellectual commitment and creativity. For Fernandes, stultifying bureaucracies, routine reports, and growing personal ambitions made the work at international organizations "uprooting" and "desensitizing."[56] But behind recriminations and bitterness lay profound anxieties about the prospect of intellectuals in Brazil and in Latin America. Going abroad was already an option for many young and talented sociologists, but with the coup, "exit could turn into a flight," Fernandes feared.[57] Content with the safe landing of a friend, Fernandes and the *paulista* group nonetheless felt the loss of a colleague.

When he arrived in Santiago in May 1964, Cardoso found *cepalinos* in disarray. They were at a loss after the twin fiascos of revolutionary Cuba and the Alliance for Progress. The political uncertainty was aggravated by an economic slowdown. The overall rate of development in the region had decelerated since 1958. Instead of shielding the region from the tyranny of global markets, economic development increased the external vulnerability of the region, shaking one of their main assumptions to the core. The routine activities of the institution—annual surveys, numerous country studies, training courses, regional forums, and in-country missions—were weighing heavily on the creative and intellectual capacity of *cepalinos* and an institution already affected by the departure of core members such as Regino Boti, Celso Furtado, Juan Noyola, and Jorge Ahumada. They were confronting what was perhaps the most important turning point in their trajectory and their legacy was at stake.

The first response of *cepalinos* to what had been gradually surfacing as a development impasse was an institutional overhaul. The idea of creating an institution parallel to CEPAL had been tentatively discussed within the UN administrative circles.[58] The Alliance for Progress renewed the enthusiasm with international cooperation for development, guaranteeing financial resources for what became the *Instituto de Planificación Económica y Social* (ILPES). Established in Santiago in mid-1962 and with the financial support of Latin American governments, the UN Special Fund, and the Inter-American Development Bank (IADB), ILPES was supposed to take over from *cepalinos* the training programs and planning missions that had come to dominate their agenda. They had devoted themselves to planning, training, and advising and had lost the space and momentum for intellectual vitality. They had been "living on an accumulated fund of theoretical interpretation which had not been progressively renewed or increased," Prebisch explained. But too much attention to practical problems turned economists into "empiricists, excessively pragmatic in their approach," while with too much research and theoretical work, got them "far removed from real-life problems in Latin America," he added.[59] The time had come to shift the balance again. The new institution gave *cepalinos* the opportunity to liberate CEPAL for more theoretical and creative endeavors. Celso Furtado, who after leaving *cepalinos* years earlier was coming back to the fold, concurred. "The legacy of the new institute, just as the legacy of CEPAL today, will be evaluated with regards to the research endeavor," he claimed.[60] It was time for a reorientation of the *cepalino* project.

As they had come to represent the orthodoxy of development, *cepalinos* opted to look back. Originally published in 1949, the text that introduced the lexicon of center and periphery and that became the symbol of the *cepalino* approach to development, by 1961, had acquired the status of a "manifesto."[61] In 1962 *cepalinos* republished that "manifesto," initiating a process of examination of their own ideas and policies.[62] In their quest for renewal, *cepalinos* also embarked in two large projects to revisit the postwar trajectory, one on the impact of foreign capital on the industrialization of the periphery and the other on the postwar development trajectory in the region.[63] María da Conceição Tavares, a Portuguese-born but Brazilian-trained economist and one of the few female economists at the institution—to whom this book returns in the Epilogue—also revisited the Brazilian case. She argued that the development project that *cepalinos* endorsed "qualitatively changed the character of the country's dependence" on the global economy.[64] Once at the forefront of development ideas, *cepalinos* were themselves taking a step back.

While Prebisch—the truly old-timer—was at the United Nations Conference on Trade and Development (UNCTAD), further discussed in Chapter 6, Celso Furtado, who had come to Santiago after the military coup in Brazil, took the lead of examination and renewal. At the core of the *cepalino* group for almost a decade, Furtado had left the institution disillusioned by rising internal frictions and the limits of international civil service. As the head of SUDENE and the former planning minister of the deposed government, Furtado fell to the initial wave of repression of the military regime.[65] With his political rights suspended and the prohibition to hold public office, Furtado found refuge among *cepalinos* before assuming his visiting professorship at Yale University and initiating a peripatetic academic life that would end in Paris. Furtado, like many other intellectuals in the coming decades including Brazilian *dependentistas*, would launch new intellectual enterprises to understand the relationship and perhaps convergence between development and dictatorship.[66]

But Furtado was himself in a moment of flux and agitation. He feared that, as economists and development experts, *cepalinos* were losing the battle of development. As discussed in Chapter 4, he had confronted the failure of his *Plano Trienal*, the crowding out of SUDENE, and the disappointment with the Alliance for Progress. Planning, international cooperation, and sound economic policymaking were unable to bring about the desired structural change that development entailed. The "instruments of the economists cannot not change the prevailing structures," Furtado claimed. The new challenge for *cepalinos* was to turn toward the "study of the conditions on which power rests, that is, the conditions that uphold those structures," transcending economics and "integrating the social and the political, in the broadest of terms." In doing so, Furtado echoed some of the critiques Cardoso and the *paulistas* had voiced against him.[67] Despite how politically involved and invested *cepalinos* were, Furtado was of the conclusion that one of the major shortcomings of the *cepalino* theories was their disregard for the national structures of power and the competing classes and interests shaping the course of development. They had blindly put their faith in an autonomous state that perhaps did not exist. They had believed that they could maneuver that state through the instruments of economic policymaking but realized their own limitations. Wavering between nostalgia and elucidation, Furtado was trying to both reassert and reassess the *cepalino* project.

Following Prebisch's cue of looking back to look forward, Furtado inaugurated an internal seminar with a discussion of the Havana "manifesto" of 1949. The seminar gathered together economists and sociologists, most of whom had joined CEPAL after the core group disintegrated. Aside from Medina Echvarría and Furtado, it included Brazilian sociologist Fernando Henrique Cardoso, the political scientist Francisco Weffort, and the Chilean economists Osvaldo Sunkel, Gonzalo Martner, Pedro Vuskovic, and Carlos Matus, and the Peruvian sociologist Aníbal Quijano, among others. They met every Wednesday afternoon for two months, starting on June 3, 1964.[68] The fundamental proposition of the "manifesto" was that the industrialization of the periphery and the trade, financial, and technical cooperation between centers and peripheries would bring about self-sustained development and economic autonomy. The corollary of that proposition was that development would in turn transform the global economy by altering the relationship between the global center and the periphery. Instead of that radical transformation of Latin America and the world that *cepalinos* expected, development prospects deteriorated amid inflation and indebtedness, social tensions and political turmoil, and stringent relations between centers and peripheries. Given that decades of import-substitution industrialization had not fulfilled the promises of increased welfare and autonomy, the key question for the seminar was why had the *cepalino* development project reached an "impasse."

For Furtado, the development impasse put into the question the soundness of their ideas, and so he impelled the group "towards a critical examination of the CEPAL model." The members of the seminar identified two potential shortcomings in the *cepalino* project. First, they had presupposed the existence of a "flexible capitalism,"—that is, an international context of cooperation between centers and peripheries through commodity price agreements, foreign aid, and state intervention—for a smooth path toward development. Second, they had also "failed to account for social and political variables."[69] This turn in their analysis was more than a shift in disciplinary orientation or interdisciplinary work. For *cepalinos*, future *dependentistas*, and new converts to dependency, their commitment to the understanding and transformation of local power structures would absorb their political energy and endeavors. In the process of reexamination of their tenets, the group pushed toward the latter, and Cardoso and Furtado took the lead.

The synergy between Cardoso and Furtado created a powerful agenda for the analysis of the politics of development in Latin America. Cardoso had positioned his project on the Brazilian entrepreneurs and the social forces of development in direct contrast to Furtado and others associated with the Brazilian nationalist left. The military intervention brought the two together in Santiago to revisit the foundational texts and key notions of the development project in Latin America. Although Furtado was only ten years older than Cardoso, theirs was an encounter between an old generation in retreat and a young one in ascent. Whereas Furtado had fallen from the high echelons of policymaking, Cardoso had an aspiring academic trajectory. Whereas Furtado was a practitioner of a discredited development project, Cardoso aspired to reinterpret development in the global periphery.

Despite pressing political concerns and lingering anxieties, their encounter restored enthusiasm and creativity in an institution already at risk of succumbing to stultifying routine and bureaucratic endeavors. "Something important is happening here," Argentine economist Benjamín Hopenhayn wrote to Prebisch. The conversation in the seminar was "animated, deep, and stimulating," he added.[70] The emergent intellectual endeavor brought *cepalinos* together again and for a time obliterated past tensions and divisions. The ruptures created by the politics of inflation as well as by the experience in revolutionary Cuba were put on hold. When Furtado left for Yale, the conversations initiated in the seminar in Santiago continued in correspondence and conferences about the politics of development.[71] The results of the exchanges with *cepalinos* redefined Cardoso's project and gave rise to the concept of dependency.

Embracing the *cepalino* effort to explain the development impasse, in November 1965, Cardoso laid the foundation for what would become his major opus two years later in a text vaguely titled *The Process of Economic Development*. It was in dealing with the questions of *cepalino* economists

that Cardoso found his voice as a sociologist. Following the global, sys-
temic approach *cepalinos* had outlined, Cardoso aspired to produce an
interpretation of capitalism from the point of view of the periphery. It
was also among *cepalinos* that Cardoso "discovered Latin America" only
to make Brazil the foundation of a new notion of the region.[72] Cardoso's
Process was the beginning of a long quest to establish the meaning and
legacy of the *cepalino* project of development, giving "dependency theory"
many lives.

In his road to the concept of dependency, Cardoso capitalized on the *cepalino* notion of center and periphery. The center-periphery idea was the
intellectual cornerstone of the *cepalino* project but most importantly
"was a fundamental asset to interpret Latin America and its development
problems," Cardoso asserted. Cardoso praised *cepalinos* because, unlike
modernization theorists, they had taken the world system as their point of
departure, and because, unlike the radical nationalists and their imperial-
colonial dyad, *cepalinos* launched a project that saw the world from the
periphery not the center. Embedded in their framework was the idea that
developed and underdeveloped economies emerged simultaneously and in
relation to each other in the historical formation of the global economy,
Cardoso affirmed.[73] By defining underdevelopment based on the position
or function of the global periphery, *cepalinos* had incorporated the global
structures of power into the analysis and had thus broken new ground.
Yet, despite their insight, *cepalinos* missed a critical component, the incorporation of the national or internal structures of power.

Rescuing the fundamental insight embedded in the *cepalino* framework,
Cardoso proposed to advance the analysis through a concept that he called
"dependency." "It is necessary to consider the 'situation of dependency'
for the analysis of the conditions of economic development in Latin America because the type of integration of the national economies to the international market creates specific and distinct forms of interrelations between
the social groups in each country and between them and the external
groups," Cardoso explained.[74] Contrary to Frank, the position of Latin
America in the global economy was the point of departure not the endpoint
of the new approach. Therefore, the concept of dependency "highlights the
structural relation between center and peripheries" but "does not reduce
the dynamic of development in the latter to the endeavors of the former,"
he insisted.[75] Along the lines of the *paulista* sociology of development, the
notion of dependency incorporated the analysis of the national social and
political forces that orient development and give it meaning.[76] But unlike
his *paulista* project, Cardoso now foregrounded the analysis of global
capitalism and adopted the worldmaking project of *cepalinos*. As such,

Cardoso's dependency was simultaneously a critique and a vindication of *cepalino* ideas.

With the concept of dependency, Cardoso also called attention to the emergence of a new international division of labor and hence a new stage in global capitalism. He called the new situation of dependency the "internationalization of the internal market," and used it to explain the fallacy of the *cepalino* project.[77] In the early postwar years, national industrialists in countries like Brazil, Mexico, and Argentina, with the support of the state, joined forces with foreign enterprises to acquire the technology and capital required for the industrialization of the periphery. As the industrial sector of these national economies became part a global system of production, the relation of dependency between center and peripheries occurred locally, Cardoso explained. A new international division of labor and hence a new stage in global capitalism emerged, binding centers and peripheries in unprecedented ways. Focusing on solving the problem of the limited capacity to import given by declining terms of international trade, *cepalinos* had disregarded the question of the ownership and control of production and accumulation in that internal market, Cardoso asserted. In their zeal for the industrialization of the periphery, *cepalinos* were at best "neutral with regards to the national or foreign control of capital," Cardoso clarified.[78] As Latin American industry grew through a partnership between foreign investors, national entrepreneurs, and a developmental state, new forms of dependence emerged that *cepalinos* had not anticipated. In the new form of dependency, "the decisions about production and consumption escaped the domestic market," the privileged site of autonomy for *cepalinos*.[79] Hence, contrary to expectations the large Latin American countries were now industrialized *and* dependent.

The effects of the new form of dependency, or the "internationalization of the internal market," were completely at odds with what *cepalinos* had anticipated. The expansion of the internal market, with the participation of foreign conglomerates, maintained rather than eased dependency. The industrialization of the periphery created "islands of prosperity" and was made "through social exclusion." Based on the connection between the public sector, the modern national capitalists, and the foreign monopolistic corporations, this development strategy required "deepening relations between producers, who then become the most important 'consumers' for economic expansion," halting the redistributive claims of the masses and the participation of other groups including the old industrialists.[80] The state became the most important source of capital for industrialization. Political consequences were disastrous as well. Given the slow process of social integration and the growing claims for change, the consolidation of power took the form of military authoritarianism not only in Brazil but in Argentina after 1966. Yet, despite the somber tone and outlook, Cardoso, now joined by Enzo Faletto gave an ambiguous interpretative key.

Having established dependency as an analytical framework, Cardoso enlisted the support of a young Chilean sociologist named Enzo Faletto to craft the historical arc of *The Process*. After culminating his graduate studies at the recently established *Escuela Latinoamericana de Sociología* in the *Facultad Latino Americana de Ciencias Sociales* (FLACSO), Faletto, a disciple of José Medina Echavarría, followed his mentor as he returned to CEPAL in 1959.[81] Cardoso, who had ascended rapidly in the *cepalino* bureaucracy to be practically in command of the Social Division, was, in the "presence of economists becoming a sociologist."[82] For almost two years, Cardoso and Faletto revisited the idea of dependency and reworked the *The Process of Economic Development* into a new manuscript, whose final version circulated in October 1967. In the new text, Cardoso and Faletto unraveled the political economy of three historical "moments," the three different "situations of dependency" enunciated in Cardoso's early draft.

For Cardoso and Faletto, the conceptual and political problem to be reckoned with in Latin America, as the title of the new manuscript encapsulated, was *Dependency and Development*. Initially assigned exclusively to the era of the "internationalization of the internal market," Cardoso and Faletto opted to extrapolate the title to the manuscript as a whole. Apparently unequivocal, dependency was, however, an ambivalent idea. A mischievously joking Faletto mentioned that "dependencia" was the product of a clerical typo for the word "decadencia."[83] The ubiquity of the term suggests otherwise, but Faletto's remark also reveals the effort to recognize its tenor and the possibility of ambiguity. On the one hand, the coexistence of dependency and development represented the impossibility of breaking free from global inequality despite the hopes of the postwar moment with its new international institutions, colonial liberations, and attempts at cooperation between both the North and South and within the South. On the other hand, *dependency and development* represented the possibility of development, of growth and even prosperity, despite dependency, which would eventually lead some to question the primacy of independence and privilege development. By calling attention to the simultaneity of development and dependency, Cardoso and Faletto reiterated the critique against *cepalinos* and other development experts for whom this coexistence was a conceptual and practical impossibility.

But Cardoso and Faletto were also taking a stand against Frank and others who believed in the "development of underdevelopment" thesis. Whereas Frank saw the same forces at play from the sixteenth century to the present, Cardoso and Faletto pushed for the recognition of difference in the new stage of the expansion of global capitalism with the "new dependency" and the "internationalization of the internal market." In opposition to the option for socialist revolution as an alternative to dependency, Cardoso and Faletto bespoke of undefined "historically viable alternatives" of "collective action that make historically feasible what is only structurally possible."[84] Each "situation of dependency" had within it social forces for both change and continuity, they claimed. Although they never really articulated what those options might look like, the subsequent trajectories of these *dependentistas* after the dependency era, discussed in the Epilogue, might give a clue. With dependency, Cardoso and Faletto aimed to create an open-ended historical trajectory beyond the dyad of domination or revolution. Embedded in the title was perhaps also the uncertainty of Cardoso and Faletto about *cepalinos* and the development project their ideas had helped cement. Both a product of and an alternative to *cepalino* ideas, Cardoso and Faletto's "dependency and development" not only nurtured a new agenda for intellectuals and activists but fostered a battle for the scope of dependency and the global legacy of Latin American intellectuals.

Conclusions

Brazil was the site of the rise but also the beginning of demise of the *cepalino* project. The two most prominent voices in what would become a wide and diverse intellectual movement against development orthodoxy emerged in what contemporaries denominated "pre-revolutionary" Brazil. It was in Brazil where *cepalinos* first built a strong presence in the state and policy circles, and it was also in this country that Fernando Henrique Cardoso, Theotônio dos Santos, and Andre Gunder Frank condemned *cepalinos* for their proximity to power and a failing project of economic development. It was in the old imperial summer town of Quitandinha where *cepalinos* launched a campaign for the financial cooperation between center and peripheries to redress global inequalities, and it was in the intellectual networks of the Brazilian Southeast where to-be *dependentistas* began to censor their neutrality or even collusion with foreign economic interests. It was in Rio's global conference that *cepalinos* became "structuralists," opponents of the "monetarist" International Monetary Fund and their local allies, and it was in Brazil where some of those *dependentistas* began to see *cepalinos* as "ideologues" of a transnational bourgeoisie. It was among Brazilian intellectuals and academics that *cepalinos* formed an influential and enduring network of allies, and it was precisely among the new cohort of academics, coming of intellectual age in what contemporaries called pre-revolutionary Brazil, that a new intellectual dissidence repositioned *cepalinos* as the orthodoxy of global development and strived to supersede them.

While critical of *cepalinos,* Frank and Cardoso could not fully dismiss their project. The *cepalinos'* concept of center and periphery placed the problem of the historical expansion of global capitalism front and center in the discussion of Latin America's development trajectory. As such, *cepalinos* provided the springboard for future *dependentistas* and their theory. Although *dependentistas* challenged *cepalinos* and aspired to usurp them out of their hegemonic position, they remained caught in their project, which partially explains why *cepalinos* and *dependentistas* are often conflated globally into one "Latin American dependency theory."

The dissident cohort that would converge and later become *dependentistas* in Santiago came from different though overlapping trajectories within Brazil. Embedded as Cardoso and Frank were in the local academic and political debates, the thrust of their critique was directed not against modernization theorists and Cold War warriors but against *cepalinos* and their allies, who made economic development the raison d'être of a globally aspiring Brazil. The *paulista*-born project of Cardoso, emerging within the country's economic powerhouse and aspiring to challenge traditional political and intellectual powerholders in Rio, resulted in the "dependency and development" thesis. In turn, the project of Frank, coalescing in modernist Brasilia and inspired by the militant trajectory of his friends and colleagues dos Santos and Bambirra, brought about the "development of underdevelopment" thesis. Whereas the "development of underdevelopment" thesis was conceptually and politically unambiguous, "dependency and development" was purposefully filled with contradictions. Despite reaching opposite conclusions, the intellectual projects of Cardoso and Frank converged in some fundamental points, which to a certain extent justifies the endurance of the umbrella term "dependency theory" to capture the intellectual movement they, at times reluctantly, spearheaded. Though either inspired or informed by Marxism, Cardoso and Frank were both reluctant to declare themselves as such. Both Cardoso and Frank rejected the mainstream North American development paradigm known as "modernization theory" because that theory did not incorporate the global economic system and its asymmetries of power and wealth. These local trajectories would have long-lasting effects as pioneer and new *dependentistas* translated their ideas into politics in Chile and the rest of the world.

SIX

The Many Lives of
Dependency Theory

As the world erupted in protest and dissent in the global 1960s, *dependentistas* transformed their ideas into a theory and a movement in Latin America. From Paris to Mexico City, students pushed the limits of the world they inherited. The struggles for desegregation and racial equality across the United States reinforced the global support for national liberation struggles in Africa. Hippies took to the streets, searching for communion and peace in a world in which superpower competition fueled militarism and a global arms' race threatened the very existence of humanity. While protesters across the world supported the anti-Vietnam War movement in the United States, US and European activists mobilized in solidarity with the victims of military dictatorships in Brazil and the Southern Cone. The denunciations of military intervention and authoritarianism were part of larger campaigns and a broader outrage against American capitalism and European colonialism. Evocative of the term *imperialism* and speaking in terms of a world system, dependency theory resonated globally, especially after *dependentistas* had set their wheels in motion in Latin America.

In Latin America, the *dependentista* movement began in Chile. Once exiled from Brazil, the pioneering *dependentistas* converged in Santiago in the late 1960s. The ideas that emerged in Brazil gave rise to "dependency theory" in Chile. Friends and collaborators first, and competitors later, the Brazilian *dependentistas* occupied universities and academic centers in Santiago, capturing the attention of an increasingly vocal and activist youth and inspiring colleagues across the disciplines. Circulating in mimeographs, journals, and books, the ideas of Andre Gunder Frank, Fernando Henrique Cardoso, Theotônio dos Santos, and others reached audiences across the region, making the notion of dependency a paradigm for the social sciences in and, shortly after, about Latin America. However, the notion of dependency was as elusive as it was provocative, and *dependentistas* and their new allies mobilized dependency ideas in multiple and sometimes contradictory directions.

Crossing the academic boundaries, the pioneer *dependentistas* as well as the new converts mobilized dependency toward political action. For those pioneer *dependentistas* escaping military repression in the mid-1960s, Santiago was an open political arena in which they quickly found a force to align with. As the country transitioned from the Christian Democratic "Revolution in Liberty" to the "Chilean Way to Socialism" and then to the Neoliberal counterrevolution, dependency theory reached its peak and its apogee in Chile, in a process whose effects reverberated throughout the rest of the region and the world. As Santiago and Chile experienced the most dramatic period in their history, the political projects of *dependentistas*—from revolutionary Third Worldism to nonaligned internationalism, from socialism in democracy to antiauthoritarian democratic socialism—flourished and shaped the course of events. Often politically at odds with each other, *dependentistas* also battled over the origins, meaning, and scope of dependency theory, in an effort to position themselves as the "Latin American" voice in a world of competing global ideologies as well as a world increasingly interested in Latin America. The parsing out of difference between *dependentistas* fed but also absorbed a substantial part of the debate within the intellectual left, giving dependency theory many lives.

Echoes

Between 1966 and 1968, a contingent of Brazilians, who like Cardoso also became *dependentistas* in Chile, arrived in Santiago. Theotônio dos Santos, his wife and colleague, Vânia Bambirra, and Ruy Mauro Marini had first come together in the student movement in the Brazilian state of Minas Gerais. After finishing undergraduate studies in economics and politics, the three reunited in São Paulo as founding members of the militant organization called Política Operaria (POLOP). Challenging the populist practices of the *Partido Trabalhista Brasileiro,* the Brazilian labor party, and the conciliatory strategies of the Communists, the organization sought to radicalize workers and peasants and bring about socialism in Brazil.[1] The three found themselves together again as lecturers at the *Universidade de Brasília*, only to find their bourgeoning careers thwarted by the military coup in Brazil in 1964. Despite POLOP's lack of political traction except among university students, dos Santos, Bambirra, and Marini were dismissed from the university, persecuted by the military, and declared subversives subject to imprisonment when the military took over. After two years in hiding, dos Santos reached out to his colleague Cardoso, by then well established at the Economic Commission for Latin America (CEPAL), to help him find employment at the institution.[2] Through the collaboration of Florestan Fernandes, Cardoso's mentor and then visiting professor in Chile, dos Santos obtained a research and teaching position at *Universidad de Chile's Centro de Estudios Socio-Económicos* (CESO) in 1967. Bambirra arrived at CESO a year later and with the support of dos Santos and the intercession of Senator Allende, Marini, who had been in exile in Mexico since 1964, joined them in 1969. Numerous Brazilian and Latin American social scientists arrived in Chile and circulated through the classrooms, living rooms, and conventions of the Brasília group (figure 6.1). For these Brazilian exiles, Chile became more than a refuge from military persecution.

As militants of the radical left, Chile captivated dos Santos and his colleagues of the Brasília group. While the military had taken over in Brazil, Bolivia, Argentina, Peru, and others, Chile remained a democratic bastion with an almost unrivaled tradition of political pluralism. Although in Brazil the Communist Party was marginal and the nationalist and populist traditions dominated the left, the Communist Party and the Socialist Party, forming a common front, had been close to winning the two previous presidential elections in Chile. Moreover, the Christian Democrats, then in power, had accelerated the pace toward deep-seated transformations in the country with their Revolution in Liberty. The ongoing agrarian reform that aimed at land redistribution for the landless and the Chileanization of the foreign-owned copper mines opened the space for a more radical left that demanded deeper and faster transformations and the complete severance of what they came to call the ties of dependency. Given the grassroots work of the Communists and the Socialists, on one hand, and the Christian Democrats, on the other, many peasants and *inquilinos* in the countryside, miners in the North, factory workers in the capital, and the residents of the sprawling slums in Santiago were socially organized and politically active. Beyond what in comparison to Brazil was an open space for socialism, Chile also offered the promises of a fruitful career and political engagement.

FIGURE 6.1   Here at Viña del Mar in 1965, Francisco Weffort (*left*) and Fernando Henrique Cardoso (*center*) were two of the numerous Brazilian exiles that found refuge in Chile after the 1964 military coup. These Brazilians along with other Latin Americans in Chile turned dependency into a movement. (Acervo Presidente Fernando Henrique Cardoso.)

Dos Santos and the rest of the Brasilia group joined a distinct social scientific community in Chile. Like in the rest of Latin America, Chilean economics and sociology, expanding rapidly since the late 1950s, had become increasingly professionalized and institutionalized through the training of faculty abroad, consolidation of the curriculum, and regularization of its faculty.[3] Perhaps unlike anywhere else the region, the Chilean social sciences had become increasingly Latin Americanized. Since the birth of CEPAL in 1948, other international organizations had established their regional headquarters in the city, fostering the circulation of Latin American and international economists and other social scientists in Santiago.[4] CEPAL's training programs for government officials, the undergraduate training programs in sociology at the UNESCO-sponsored *Facultad Latinoamericana de Ciencias Sociales* (FLACSO), and *the Escuela de Estudios Económicos Latinoamericanos* (ESCOLATINA), the graduate training program in economics at the *Universidad de Chile* reinforced that trend by attracting students and faculty from all over the region.[5] The Chilean social sciences were theoretically and ideologically diverse. They encompassed the Chicago Boys' Economic School at *Universidad Católica* as well the combined *cepalino* and neoclassical orientation at *Universidad de Chile,* for instance.[6] Meanwhile, the intellectual left had enormous prestige and freedom of expression.[7] Increasingly politicized, the Chilean social scientific departments gradually became party strongholds, especially for the left, as their faculty and students increased their political militancy and activism, a trend that the Brasilia contingent reinforced.

As dos Santos and his colleagues of the Brasilia group joined Cardoso in Santiago, "dependency theory" flourished. Since 1963 Cardoso had laid out a research agenda on the Brazilian and the Southern Cone industrial elites that he carried over to Santiago as he joined CEPAL–*Instituto Latinoamericano de Planeación Económica y Social* (ILPES). Concurrently, dos Santos took part of an ongoing research project on the Chilean entrepreneurs while deepening his analysis of the Brazilian entrepreneurs he had commenced in Brasilia. With overlapping interests, dos Santos and Cardoso began working collaboratively, teaching jointly at CESO, organizing seminars that rallied students and the core of group of *cepalinos,* some of which became *dependentistas* in the process, such as Osvaldo Sunkel and Aníbal Quijano.[8] While Cardoso, alongside Faletto, transformed the 1965 first draft into the full-blown version of *Dependency and Development* that they presented at CESO in February 1967, dos Santos wrote the first draft of his *New Character of Dependency* and published the first part in *Cuadernos del CESO* in August 1967.[9] Cardoso and Faletto had put the term "dependency" in the conversation, but both texts emphasized that, against the assumption of *cepalinos* and the nationalist and political forces in the region, industrialization was not the road to autonomy from the global forces of capital.[10] Through the lens of Brazil and Chile, dos Santos and Cardoso saw Latin America as industrializing and developing rather than "feudalist" and backward. Industrialization in Brazil, expanding through the partnership with foreign capital, brought about what Cardoso and Faletto called the new "situation of dependency" characterized by the "internationalization of the internal market," discussed in Chapter 5, and dos Santos called "the new character of dependency." Thus, it stood in stark contrast to the old dependency of commodity producers for the global economy. Converging in the new "dependency theory," Cardoso and dos Santos and the Brasilia group soon began to part ways.

In late 1967, shortly after finishing *Dependency and Development,* Cardoso went to Paris for a visiting professorship at the University of Paris X–Nanterre. Friendly and collegial, dos Santos kept Cardoso updated on the unfolding of the "dependency" project. He encouraged Cardoso and Frank to publish alongside him and in so doing, reinforced the collective project. While dos Santos, who had barely settled in Santiago, wanted to go to Europe and "breathe the air of the metropole," Cardoso, who found himself at one of the main centers of the 1968 global student protest, was initially estranged from the protesting students and desired to return.[11] For a Brazilian escaping military rule and with more "structural" problems in mind, the narrow focus of the students, advocating for "sexual freedom in the dormitories" and against the policy that "approved of girls visiting boys" but prohibited visits in the other direction, seemed an issue of "outer space."[12] His focus was on the Brazilian regime and the political economy of authoritarianism, so he pursued a way to return to Brazil.

After Cardoso left, Andre Gunder Frank, another of the pioneers, returned to Santiago and built, albeit reluctantly, the dependency momentum alongside dos Santos. Latin America was not Frank's first choice. After teaching in Mexico, Brazil, and Canada, Frank wanted to return to US academia, among other factors, because "the kind of historical-theoretical research on underdevelopment that I want to do is difficult in underdeveloped countries themselves" given the lack of bibliographical materials and other institutional infrastructure.[13] However, he struggled to find a position and finally settled for a technical job at the International Labor Organization (ILO) in Santiago, Chile. When he arrived in Santiago in October 1968, he was "detained in the airport by the Chilean government," who had also rebuffed his appointment in the international organization. With multiple friends in Santiago, Frank managed to pull some strings against an arbitrary detention. Socialist Senator and future president Salvador "Allende intervened on his behalf."[14] Instead of ILO, Frank rejoined dos Santos, his friend and colleague from the Brasilia days, at the *Universidad de Chile*. Although he confessed being tired of giving "the same lecture on the development of underdevelopment," Frank found himself pushing in the same direction in Chile.[15] Right after Frank relocated to Santiago, the Spanish translation of his *Capitalism and Underdevelopment in Latin America* finally came through. It followed the reprints in Colombia, Chile, and Argentina of "The Development of Underdevelopment," the 1966 article-size version of the book.[16] The confluence of the Brazilian pioneers in Santiago and the attraction of the new perspective prompted a broad and sprawling research agenda of "dependency."

With Cardoso absent from Santiago, dos Santos took the lead in advancing what had by then become "dependency theory." Within a few years, dos Santos became director of CESO and prominently oriented the institution and sociology toward dependency theory. Dos Santos organized a research group and seminar under the label of "dependency relations in Latin America." He recruited young and militant social scientists, and the research group produced several individual projects that launched dependency theory as framework for research in education, finance, and international relations, among other topics.[17] Dos Santos established large-scale research projects on the impact of the expansion of multinational corporations and a center of documentation of the university with archival material collected by dos Santos himself in the United States. Beyond academia, dos Santos, alongside other young Chilean intellectuals, created the periodical *Chile Hoy* to examine the Chilean situation and instruct a larger audience of students and activists in the Marxist interpretation of reality.[18] Meanwhile, Bambirra, following Cardoso's framework, launched a project "with the pretentious title of dependent structures."[19] She studied the different national "types of dependency." She confessed that Cardoso's work, establishing the distinction between enclave and nationally-owned integration to the global market, was "very useful to define the general framework" of the project. Concurrently, Rui Mauro Marini, who was perhaps the most versed on Marxist theory of the members of the Brasilia group and the most interested in providing Marxian foundations to dependency theory, settled initially at the *Universidad de Concepción*, the cradle of the Chilean Communist Party and more recently of the *Movimiento de Izquierda Revolucionaria* (MIR) as well as the site of intense labor and student movements. Absorbed by teaching within and outside the classrooms, labor organizing, and militancy at the MIR, Marini finalized his theoretical work several years later. After he joined his friends in Santiago's CESO in 1970, he finished and published his book, *Dialectics of Dependency* in 1973.[20] While in Chile, Frank, always prolific and vocal, maintained a broad and global epistolary network that extended the reach of the dependency ideas. Although the Brasilia group rejected Frank's idea of the impossibility of development in the periphery, the confluence of the four and the simultaneous publication of Marini's *Underdevelopment and Revolution,* Frank's *Underdevelopment or Revolution,* and dos Santos's *Socialism or Fascism,* began to position "dependency theory" in a more radical direction.[21]

Increasingly radicalized, *dependentistas* created institutional strongholds for dependency across the social scientific field, itself partitioned along the lines of the Chilean polity. Three schools of sociology, emerging almost simultaneously in the late 1950s, shared the goals of more empirical analysis of the "social" and of more political relevance of the discipline, all animated by the sense that "sociologists were not expected to publish but to change the world."[22] The *Universidad Católica* program, training students through social work in neighborhood organizations and mother centers, carried out the principles of "popular promotion" and communitarianism that underpinned the Christian Democratic Party as an alternative to both capitalism and socialism. After 1966 the *Universidad de Chile* school of sociology, under the directorship of Clodomiro Almeyda, a long-time member of the Socialist Party, became the party's bastion, and Marxism became the privileged theoretical orientation.[23] As Chilean sociologists later recalled, Frank and dos Santos increasingly attracted the attention of university students, who had become key political actors as access to education expanded in those years. The *Universidad de Chile*'s CESO, with dos Santos and Frank as commanding figures, became the primary pole of dependency and the bastion of the intellectual radical left.[24] Meanwhile, with Cardoso absent and Frank and dos Santos entrenched at the *Universidad de Chile*, a marginalized Faletto eventually moved to the FLACSO, as institution in which Cardoso and Faletto's *Dependency and Development* became the cornerstone of the critical sociology in the making but that, given its UNESCO sponsorship, attempted to withdraw from politics.[25] In this landscape, dos Santos and Frank's CESO was gradually emerging as the center of dependency theory in Latin America.

As *dependentistas* aligned themselves in the Chilean political landscape, dependency theory began to leave the confines of academia, broadening its reach. According to Faletto, Cardoso, as some of the Brazilian politicians in exile, professed his support for what he called the "progressive" government of Eduardo Frei.[26] Frei and the Christian Democrats' Revolution in Liberty significantly expanded land redistribution programs, fomented rural unionization, "Chileanized" copper (the traditional cornerstone of the Chilean economy), and sponsored literacy campaigns and the organization of the popular sectors.[27] The Revolution in Liberty brought about significant social transformations and encouraged wide political participation but lagged behind the expectations of many, including some of the pioneer *dependentistas*. Some adhered to alternative options that in a few years would draw regional and global attention, fomenting political radicalization in Chile.[28] Seizing the revolutionary momentum, dos Santos, a radical militant in his early years, supported and became advisor to the Socialist Party, precisely at a turning point in the party's history. Deviating from previous trends, the Socialist Party opened the door to revolution as a political strategy and affirmed its Marxist-Leninist orientation. His alignment, dos Santos believed, would take dependency ideas of "struggle against the national and international monopolies of dependent capitalism" to Salvador Allende's Chilean Way to Socialism, precisely as the world's eyes turned to Chile.[29] Meanwhile, Marini joined and contributed extensively to the MIR, a small organization founded by dissenters of the Socialist Party in 1965 that endorsed revolutionary armed struggle, and Frank publicly supported the same organization.[30] For its pioneers, dependency theory animated different and increasingly conflictive political projects.

Despite rifts opening between them, *dependentistas* as a collective were an intellectual success. Republished from Caracas to Calcutta, from Paris to Tokyo, Frank's "Development of Underdevelopment" article, to the lament of other *dependentistas*, quickly became the classical reference of the movement.[31] At first circulating in mimeograph form—like many *cepalino* documents—and becoming mandatory reading for the schools in sociology in Santiago, Lima, Bogotá, and Mexico City, *Dependency and Development in Latin America* became a best seller of *Siglo XXI* after its final publication in 1969, with fourteen editions in the following decade and translations into French, Italian, Portuguese, and later English.[32] Also published by *Siglo XXI*, dos Santos's collective volume *The Political-Economic Dependency of Latin America* and Vania Bambirra's *Latin American Dependent Capitalism* had similar editorial success across the region. Although their work was far less often translated than that of Frank or Cardoso, dos Santos and Bambirra also fostered the international circulation of dependency theory. Dos Santos introduced his ideas to the International Sociology Congress and the American Economic Association and organized seminars that brought world-renowned Marxist economists such as Paul Sweezy to Chile's CESO, disseminating dependency theory and consolidating Chile as the center of the movement. In economics and sociology, others texts inspired by dependency continued the trend, many published through the same press.[33] Speaking a similar language and representing the voice of the global South, these social scientists were all invited to a comparative Latin America-Africa forum on strategies of development at Samir Amin's African Institute of Economic Development and Planning in 1972, which only Marini could attend.[34] Despite the success, the dependency movement would eventually leave most *dependentistas* dissatisfied.

The IX Latin American Congress of Sociology, held in Mexico City in November 1969, bore witness to the momentum the notion of dependency catalyzed. The meeting brought together figures from disciplines in all social sciences, established and rising scholars, and filled the auditoriums with numerous students eager to participate in what was seen as a turning point in the discipline. The sociology of development panel, chaired by Peruvian sociologist, *cepalino*, and future postcolonial theorist Aníbal Quijano, was by far the largest. "The sociological analysis of dependency represented the leitmotiv of topics and discussion in the Congress," an observer claimed. There is a "clear thematic and perspective preference" for the analysis of "dependent character of power structure in Latin American societies," for the study of the "historical formation of dependency," and concerns for the "modification of the current pattern of dependency," the same observer summarized, in an attempt to capture the multiple variations on a privileged topic.[35] Ranging from urbanization to education and culture, from exchange policy to labor force participation, dependency had begun to shape the regional theoretical and practical research agenda and would continue to do so for years to come.[36] Through the gravitational pull of Santiago, dependency had become the main focus of the regional social sciences and due to its political experiments was also attracting global attention.

Within a few years, *dependentistas* transformed dependency theory into an intellectual movement that spread across the region and the world. With numerous monographs across disciplines and a generation trained (or retrained) as *dependentistas*, dependency theory became the lens for studies from urbanization to literary criticism, from international relations to education.[37] For those involved, there was a sense of a momentous paradigm shift in the social sciences of the 1970s and 1980s. Like in other Latin American countries, the "Peruvian social sciences were consistent with Latin American dependency theory," Peruvian anthropologist José Matos Mar claimed.[38] From Sergio Ramos's *Chile: A Dependent Country* to Edelberto Torres Rivas's *Central America: Processes and Structures of Dependent Societies* the economic histories of the region were written following the dependency theory approach.[39] While Tulio Halperín-Donghi's *Contemporary History of Latin America* was the most widely read and influential general history for a generation, other general histories of Latin America, such as Colombian economist Antonio García's *Atraso y Dependencia en América Latina*, were also crafted in the era. They all started from the basic assumption that it was Latin America's integration, or better forms of integration, to the world economy that shaped or determined the region's history. Gone were the stories of caudillos, presidents, and generals; in came the histories of economic structures, exploitation, and means of production, periodized as "colonial or neocolonial order" or "from outward looking to inward looking development." Stanley and Barbara Stein's *Colonial Heritage in Latin America*, a self-declared synthetic essay on economic dependence situating the Spanish metropole itself as dependency of Northern Europe, broke new ground for dependency theory in English. All of these works and more had been influenced by the world that created dependency in Chile and were the product of world that dependency created.

Dependency theory left academic discussion and texts and acquired a force of its own. From diplomats to armed militants, from theologians to artists, "dependency theory" became the inspiration and intellectual foundation of a renewed struggle against imperialism and oppression. Insisting on old *cepalino* proposals but with a more belligerent tone, Latin American diplomats of all the twenty-one countries of the region united in a common front to demand lower tariffs in Latin American goods and a transformation of US policy in 1969, an initiative that Frank would later decry as an indicator of the cooptation of his ideas.[40] The Chilean MIR, the Uruguayan Tupamaros, and many of the armed revolutionary movements that had university students at their core, found in the "dependency theory" an interpretation of history that justified their struggle.[41] The vehicle for that shared understanding of history was a popular pocketbook whose first praises were received outside Latin America and thereafter became the principal companion of students, artists, and revolutionaries. Inspired mainly by Frank, Eduardo Galeano's *Open Veins of Latin America* reached sixty editions in less than a decade after its publication in 1971 and shaped the widespread understanding of dependency in the region and of Latin America in the world.[42] Simultaneously, Brazilian and Peruvian Catholic priests and activists made dependency their own, informing their "theology of liberation" from poverty and oppression.[43] In Latin America, dependency theory fostered distinct struggles that nonetheless appeared to be speaking the same language.

Although *dependentistas* could point to their theory's many victories, some of them deplored the turn it had taken. At the Latin American Sociology Congress, where dos Santos and Frank were present and Cardoso and Faletto were absent, the conversation was dominated by Cardoso and Faletto's work. "Most papers elaborated on the ideas proposed by Cardoso and Faletto," an observer claimed. The contributions of Florestan Fernandes on external dependence, Vilmar Faria, and Frank himself were seen as "advancements of ideas originally proposed by Cardoso and Faletto."[44] Yet some *dependentistas* close to Cardoso were increasingly on the defensive. Shortly after Cardoso's departure and the convergence of dos Santos, Bambirra, and Frank in Santiago, Faletto denounced the overbearing weight of Frank and the Brasilia group in Chile. "I am taking up the stage as the charmer of the dependency snake" in a scenario where "too many competitors have emerged," Faletto confessed to Cardoso.[45] Overwhelmed by the thrust of the work of Frank, dos Santos, and other *dependentistas* in Chile and the radicalization of sociology, Faletto temporarily withdrew from the political debate and immersed himself in the study of literature and the nineteenth-century novel while finding refuge in the more politically neutral FLACSO.[46]

Faletto was not alone. Aníbal Quijano, who had participated in the discussions among *cepalinos* that gave rise to *Dependency and Development*, rejected the use of the term "dependency" and "its jargon" as "a deus ex

machina," as the endpoint rather than the beginning of the analysis in contrast to the emphasis on concrete historical situations that characterized
Cardoso and Faletto's work. Echoing Quijano, *cepalino* and Chilean economist Aníbal Pinto criticized Frank for using dependency as a narrative of
"original sin" that doomed Latin America to underdevelopment ever since
"Christopher Columbus departed from Palos de Moguer."[47] With these interventions, these *dependentistas* joined others in their mounting critiques
against Frank for oversimplifying the economic history of Latin America
and for placing an excessive emphasis on the "forces outside of Latin
America's control."[48] As dependency became shorthand for imperialism
and justification for revolution, Quijano, Faletto, Pinto, and others who
considered themselves part of the intellectual left also wanted to set themselves apart from those of "different ideological and theoretical affilia-
tion" who used dependency "on behalf of very different interests."[49]

There was a growing sense that "dependency" was a Pandora's box,
a concept whose meaning and implications had been let loose and had
become more radical, more simplistic, and more deterministic than they aspired it to be. In a few years, the tables would turn for these *dependentistas*,
who in the peak of revolutionary spirits were alarmed, agitated, and feared
to have lost the battle over the legacy of dependency to Frank and his regional and global followers.

Battles

Rather than a threat to the movement, the disputes among *dependentistas*
raised the stakes of the theory and gave their ideas an unprecedent political
leverage. The quarrels about the *dependentistas'* Marxist credentials, their
political affiliations and vocations, and the scope and stature of their ideas
propelled the interest in what was increasingly understood as dependency
theory. But the intellectual movement dependency theory created went
beyond the reinvention of the social sciences in and of Latin America.
Beginning with *dependentistas* and *cepalinos* themselves, many in Latin
America and later around the world mobilized dependency ideas as the
foundation for political projects that attracted regional and global followers.
Some adhering to the Socialist Party and others to the revolutionary MIR,
the members of the Brasilia group very early on found in Chile not just an
intellectual but a political vocation.

Other *dependentistas* followed. Andre Gunder Frank proposed to make
dependency theory the intellectual basis for revolutionary Cuba's Third
Worldism. Meanwhile, Raúl Prebisch, the uncontested *cepalino* leader,

dismissed the dependency theory turn and established the United Nations Conference for Trade and Development (UNCTAD) as an alternative form of non-Western internationalism. In doing so, Prebisch brought Latin American voices—which despite the rifts explored in this chapter, would later be grouped together under the umbrella term "dependency theory"—including his own, to the world stage. While Chilean economist and *cepalino* Pedro Vuskovic, retrained as *dependentista,* took the theory to the world's first experiment with a democratic way to socialism in Chile, Cardoso, a key figure in the antiauthoritarian movement in Brazil, brought dependency from the revolutionary world in which it was born to the democratic era that followed. In what follows, these individual vignettes should serve to manifest the panoply of political alternatives that dependency theory opened in the late 1960s and early 1970s and that attest to the impact of the movement.

As he prepared his return to Santiago, Frank turned once again to Cuba when the project of global revolutionary socialism was at its peak on the island. Committed to supporting the armed revolution in Latin America, Castro had sponsored filibuster operations in the Caribbean since the Sierra Maestra days and established training camps for regional fighters to "stretch thin the forces of imperialism" after the triumph of the revolution in 1959. Battling with both bullets and ideas, Castro and Che Guevara established *Prensa Latina,* a news service with offices in many Latin American capital cities, designed to disseminate favorable ideas about the revolution and inspire anti-American sentiments. Beginning in 1964, just as Prebisch began his own experiment in Third Worldism with UNCTAD, Castro inaugurated a "series of international conferences intended to unify revolutionary forces worldwide."[50] The 1966 Tricontinental Congress, bringing representatives from eighty countries of Africa, Asia, and Latin America to Havana, including then Senator and future Chilean president Salvador Allende, represented the culmination of Cuba's efforts to become the leader of the Third World. The following year, Cuba hosted the first meeting of the Organization of Latin American Solidarity in an effort to consolidate the hemispheric forces as well. As Castro reasserted the commitment to armed revolution in the Third World, the global North's New Left, frustrated with pacifist methods, saw in Havana, not in Moscow and not in China, the center of revolutionary Third Worldism.[51] Like others in the New Left, Frank saw in Cuban internationalism the opportunity he had been waiting for.

Frank was ready to offer Cuba a truly revolutionary theory as it exported the revolution to the Third World. Since the "Latin American bourgeois nationalist interest" established several institutions with the purpose of disseminating its ideology of which the "first and foremost was CEPAL," Frank proposed the creation of a similar "research and training center" with dependency theory as its intellectual foundation.[52] "If only a handful of bourgeois nationalists working together at CEPAL could gain such an enormous influence in important political and popular sectors in Latin America and the world," Frank asked Fidel, what much more could revolutionary Cuba do?[53] Thus, "inspired by your words about the ideological struggle and the need for collective scientific work at the Tricontinental," Frank wrote to Castro in early 1968, "I have decided to speak to you frankly and clearly about a project that I hope Cuba can sponsor." Just like Cuba had made *Casa de las Américas*, the country's emblematic cultural, artistic, and literary institution, a pillar for the revolution, it could do the same for economics and the social sciences, Frank affirmed.[54]

His dependency theory was the starting point. "My book *Capitalism and Underdevelopment*," he told Castro, "is the contribution to the great task of building the Latin American theory of revolution."[55] By inviting Asian and African comrades to join the Latin Americans under Cuban leadership, Frank's proposed center, "at small cost to Cuba," he added, could make a significant step in fomenting the revolution in Latin America and the rest of the world. Frank aspired to make his "development of underdevelopment" thesis, now framed under the rubric of dependency theory, the foundation for a global counter paradigm centered in Havana.

Conflicts notwithstanding, Frank succeeded at positioning dependency theory within the Cuban revolutionary world at the apogee of the influence of intellectuals in the island. In the wake of the Tricontinental Congress, a new intellectual collective project was born around the journal *Pensamiento Crítico*. The purpose of the journal, one that Frank immediately identified with, was the development of revolutionary theory from the point of view of the Third World. Frank became a regular contributor to *Pensamiento Crítico* while his "development of underdevelopment" thesis circulated as a quintessential representation of the endeavor to write from and for the Third World. Supported by the political leadership of the revolution, the journal guaranteed Frank and dependency theory a prominent role in Cuba's attempt to export the revolution, even if Frank's original proposal of a revolutionary social science center never materialized. In the Cultural Congress of 1968, the last of the initiatives in that direction, Frank cemented his role as one of the drafters of the final resolution calling for a meeting that gathered artists and social scientists from across Asia, Africa, and Latin America.[56]

However, Frank's involvement with the revolution ended shortly after as a result of a conflict with *Casa de las Américas*. After being invited to participate in a review panel for one of *Casa de las Américas'* awards, Frank sent a spirited letter questioning the deliberating and deciding procedure and challenging the decision itself. Roberto Fernández Retamar, prominent writer and literary critic, condemned Frank's letter as "unfriendly and divisive" and an additional proof of Frank's "hostile attitude" and "lack of contributions" during his visit. To deepen the wound, Frank, who had a way of alienating friends with his acerbic words, also insisted on the publication of a short essay that, in his words, "could be interpreted as a critique to the revolution" and could and should not be published outside of Cuba. In response, Fernández Retamar reminded Frank that not only "did he know very little about artistic and literary matters [to question the decision] as he himself had acknowledged," but most importantly, that by doing so, he had questioned Haydée Santamaría, head of the institution and member of the central committee of the Party, and in so doing, had questioned the revolution itself.[57] After the incident, Frank was completely cut off from Cuba just as Cuba confronted a crisis of its own that jeopardized its global leadership. With the failure of the guerrilla strategy outside of Cuba and a deep economic crisis after 1970, Havana cemented its economic and political ties with Moscow, becoming itself a dependency of another superpower and losing its appeal as the cornerstone of the revolutionary Third Worldism that attracted Frank and others of the intellectual New Left. Eventually, Frank turned his gaze from Latin America to Asia in his pursuit of the analysis of the world economic system.

While watching the dependency whirlwind from afar, Prebisch cultivated what he saw as an alternative to the revolutionary Third Worldism that dependency inspired. Filled with skepticism, Prebisch attended the 1962 Cairo conference that brought together leaders of thirty-six African, Asian, and, for the first time, Latin American nations, raising the prospects of the developing world working together as a bloc. "Impressively attended and organized" and "without inflamed North-South rhetoric," Prebisch's first meeting in Africa, nonetheless made a large impression on him.[58] So when the Cairo meeting called for an international conference under the auspices of the United Nations to address the economic relations between the developed and the developing world, Prebisch accepted the nomination to lead the new endeavor without hesitancy. From 1964 to 1968, Prebisch, who had introduced the notion of center and periphery to economic international relations, led UNCTAD, into what was in many ways his response to the bourgeoning dependency theory.

During and after UNCTAD, Prebisch distanced himself from the *dependentistas*. They represented the voice of a new generation that contested some of the principles that Prebisch and the old generation of *cepalinos* held dear, including the possibility of cooperation between center and peripheries for fairer global trade and finance.[59] Confident about his own leadership, Prebisch positioned himself as the wiser and senior "voice of the periphery" and explained the rise of dependency ideas as the product of "a new generation of men that for the first-time prod into economics and the social sciences." Although he sympathized with these ingenuous but eager "men that won't tolerate old or new forms of dependency in the intellectual and the economic field," Prebisch off-handedly dismissed the dependency movement that had come to prevail in Chile and his own intellectual circles.[60] He shut down Cardoso's project on the multinational corporations to avoid antagonizing the Brazilian government.[61] After asking for corrections, which Faletto sardonically summarized as "avoiding statements such as 'Avila Camacho is a lackey of imperialism,'" Prebisch vetoed the in-house publication of Cardoso and Faletto's *Dependency and Development in Latin America*.[62] Despite his initial rejection of the *dependentista* turn, Prebisch would later be recognized as the founder of Latin American "dependency theory" writ-large.

Precisely at the moment in which *dependentistas* such as Frank were calling the *cepalino* project into question, Prebisch defended the project by making it the foundation of UNCTAD, a new global enterprise. With a similar combative tone, deploying the same rhetoric, and rekindling the rationale of his 1949 manifesto, Prebisch's *Towards a New International Trade Policy for Development* inaugurated UNCTAD. He attributed the obstacles to development to the "persistent tendency towards disequilibrium in peripheral economies."[63] "While the export of primary products grows at a slow pace, the [developing countries'] demand for import of manufactured goods was tending to grow rapidly, at a pace that increased with the rate of development," Prebisch explained.[64] As the periphery's share of global trade declined during the postwar era, the disequilibrium increased, leading to a massive "trade gap," or deficit between export proceeds and import needs, which Prebisch estimated to reach $20 billion dollars by the end of the decade. What *cepalinos* had captured in the early 1950s with the capacity to import index and the development paradox, Prebisch catapulted to the global level as the foreign exchange gap. To solve the "trade gap," Prebisch returned to many of the cooperation strategies of the *cepalino* arsenal, such as the elimination of protectionism in the center, quotas for goods produced by the periphery, commodity price stabilization schemes, and compensatory finance for export-driven balance of payments problems. Through Prebisch's leadership, UNCTAD, like CEPAL a decade earlier, was built upon the premise of the fundamental disequilibrium between industrial centers and primary producing peripheries and the cooperation between them. Thus, Prebisch succeeded at catapulting *cepalino* ideas to the global stage precisely when they were increasingly contested in Latin America. In his articulation of the global trade gap, Prebisch was "joined by spokesman from almost all developing countries in the world," resulting in "ample support for his concepts" and raising his stature as global leader of the Third World.[65]

UNCTAD raised the enthusiasm of those who aspired for new Third World internationalism but the initiative failed to bring the results Prebisch expected. Although the Afro-Asian conference at Bandung in 1955 and the establishment of the Non-Aligned Movement in 1961 were important precedents, their membership had been limited and their focus more political than economic.[66] More propitiously, just the prospect of UNCTAD had already brought together a tricontinental group of seventy-five developing nations since the initial vote at the UN General Assembly. UNCTAD, unlike other UN forums, had no superpower veto privileges and was conceived to work in the principle of one country, one vote, which would effectively redress the existing balance of power. Through Prebisch's leadership, UNCTAD gave the G-77, as the group of developing countries was referred to, a concrete economic agenda and a common program to restructure the world economy.[67] What *The Economist* perceived as the "developing world's new rationale and phraseology," distinct from "the same [old] cry for help" incorporated in UNCTAD, had been the cornerstone of the *cepalino* global project for over a decade.[68] Yet, almost from the start, UNCTAD became a "forum of confrontation" between East and West, North and South that within a few years lost momentum plagued by lack of concrete policy successes.[69] While the commodity-by-commodity negotiations ran into difficulties and garnered Prebisch the criticism of the African group, Prebisch lost the support of the World Bank and the IMF in his attempt to bring price stabilization through buffer stocks, disappointing the G-77.[70] While the industrial nations accused Prebisch of partiality in defending the interests of the developing nations in what was supposed to be a neutral global forum, the developing countries demanded more support from Prebisch and the UNCTAD secretariat.[71] After the second UNCTAD at New Delhi was publicly declared a failure in 1968 (figure 6.2), Prebisch resigned from the endeavor and his leadership of an alternative to revolutionary Third Worldism.

While Prebisch raised to prominence as leader of Third World internationalism, Chilean and *cepalino* economist Pedro Vuskovic was retrained as a *dependentista*. With an undergraduate degree in commercial engineering, Vuskovic joined CEPAL shortly after its establishment as a statistics

FIGURE 6.2   Raúl Prebisch shakes hands with the Indian Minister of the Economy at UNCTAD-II in New Delhi in 1968. After the meeting, Prebisch stepped down from his position as head of UNCTAD and from his leadership role in negotiating a new international economic order. (UN Photo/PR.)

assistant in 1950. Participating in the core activities of the institution, Vuskovic trained regional economists, led the economic development country studies of Colombia and Peru, and contributed to the formulation of Bolivia's development plan. Simultaneously, Vuskovic taught at *Universidad de Chile*, where he cemented *cepalino* influence over the economics profession through his courses on national planning for economic development.[72] Vuskovic, alongside other Chileans who became part of the Unidad Popular government of Allende, were all active participants in the seminal discussions at CEPAL back in 1964 that resulted in the production of *Dependency and Development*. Following Cardoso and Faletto's typology—which designated different forms of dependency based on whether export sectors were national or foreign-owned—Vuskovic formulated a diagnosis of the Chilean development. He argued that the "relations of dependency" established when Chile integrated to the global economy as a mining enclave in the late nineteenth century, prompted the expansion of a modern industrial sector at the service of the export economy, whose limited spillover effects

FIGURE 6.3   Minister of the Economy Pedro Vuskovic alongside Chilean president Salvador Allende. Vuskovic, a long-time *cepalino,* was present at the seminal meetings between an old and a new guard that gave rise to the concept of dependency. Retrained as a *dependendista,* he brought dependency theory to the Chilean Way to Socialism. (Biblioteca del Congresso Nacional de Chile/Wikipedia Commons.)

over the economy as a whole resulted in contemporary sluggish growth and concentration of income.[73] But Vuskovic was not only influenced by *dependentistas* at CEPAL. Shaped by the increasingly radical vent of *dependentistas* at the *Universidad de Chile,* Vuskovic assumed the directorship of the university's *Instituto de Economía* after resigning from CEPAL in 1968 and "gave the program a Marxist cast." It was "designed along the lines of the campaign economic program of President Allende" and ended up "polariz[ing] faculty and students" even further.[74] A friend and collaborator of Senator Allende since his 1958 presidential campaign, Vuskovic became minister of the economy when his Unidad Popular coalition triumphed in 1970 (figure 6.3).

　With the political ascent of Vuskovic and other social scientists of the left, dependency theory became part of the Chilean experiment of democratic transition toward socialism. Allende, who had always "held Capital on one hand and *cepalino* studies on the other," engaged in a quite aggressive talent search to find personnel that, among others, left the *Universidad de Chile's Instituto de Economía* where Vuskovic worked highly understaffed.[75] Many economists from the same university's *Centro de Estudios Socio-Económicos* led by dos Santos and the Brasilia group also joined the new administration.

In a matter of weeks after the election, Vuskovic outlined the program of the Unidad Popular. In a terminology closer to *cepalinos,* Vuskovic had defined the Socialist Party program for the previous election back in 1964 as an effort to "combat the structural distortions that limit economic development."[76] Dependency ideas had shattered the long-held conviction in the revolutionary power of the national industrial bourgeoisie and the expansion of internal markets as the source of economic autonomy. The ownership and control of the means of production, both of which, in the emerging socialist project, belonged to the state and the organized popular forces known as "poder popular," were placed in its stead. More confident and radical, Vuskovic characterized the economic policy of the Unidad Popular as the means to "transform not reform" the system and to broaden and consolidate "popular power."[77] To do so, the primary goal was the redistribution of income through the agrarian reform, the nationalization of the copper industry, the socialization of key industrial enterprises, and the state-control of the banking sector. For social scientists and intellectuals turned *dependentistas,* the dependency turn fueled the Chilean Way to Socialism.[78]

As the transition to socialism accelerated, Vuskovic and the economics of the left became increasingly under attack. Committed to mass politics and the mobilization of the popular forces, Vuskovic became a controversial figure in a coalition government fractured among conflicting views of socialism and under acute political opposition and external pressure. On the one hand, dos Santos and others on the left applauded Vuskovic's determination to move Chile's experiment beyond "a very radical national liberation movement." By requisitioning key monopoly corporations and inaugurating the "social economic area," as the state-owned sector of the economy was called, Vuskovic had "provoked the ire and desperation of the bourgeoisie" and firmly began to organize the economy "under a clear socialist principle."[79] On the other hand, the Communist Party members increasingly criticized Vuskovic for his lack of attention to the soaring inflation, shortages, and balance of payments restrictions that plagued the economy after the second year of the administration.[80] As the political parties coalesced cornering Allende and the strikes of merchants, transporters, and other capitalists almost paralyzed the economy, Vuskovic advocated for larger popular mobilization and the deepening and accelerating of the socialist program. Allende, who advocated for gradualism and who by 1972 was desperate to appease some of his opponents, sided with the Communist Party in the need for a "less extremist" economic direction.[81] As a result, Allende asked for Vuskovic's resignation in mid-1972. As the financial and economic crisis persisted after Vuskovic's departure, some younger economists found themselves disillusioned with the left's "theoretical poverty and simplicity of economic analysis" and its inability to "move beyond dogmas and toward technical financial analysis."[82] Discredited and even at times also scapegoated, the economics of the left became the object of stringent debates about political and intellectual responsibility of the profession after the tragic end of Allende and of the socialist experiment in Chile.

While many *dependentistas* were forced out or on retreat in Chile, Cardoso and his allies were on the rise in Brazil. Upon his return from Paris in 1968, Cardoso obtained a professorship at his alma mater in São Paulo that was shortly after annulled by the military still in power. After mass protests and mounting dissent that same year, the military regime adopted a harder line that began with shutting down Congress, eliminating habeas corpus, and expanding the list of crimes subject to imprisonment, all of which curtailed expression and facilitated repression. The universities, many of which had remained relatively untouched, became the object of severe repression. While still in Santiago, Cardoso and other younger colleagues, anticipating the situation, had begun to discuss the possibility of establishing an independent research center to overcome the restraints imposed on academic life in Brazil.[83] As more professors like Cardoso were banned from universities and the spaces for academic work narrowed, the initiative acquired urgency. Familiar with the institution since his CEPAL years, Cardoso approached the Ford Foundation, which, in turn, was looking to concentrate its efforts in Latin America in a few promising institutions.[84] By rallying the financial and political support of *paulista* industrialists, journalists, artists, and politicians, Cardoso not only convinced the Ford Foundation that they could "work and assist some leftists" but he also created and broadened the social network of the future institution.[85] Although the alliance with the Ford Foundation alienated some intellectuals who feared meddling and abhorred imperialism, especially with the precedent of Project Camelot, Cardoso and his colleagues moved forward with the project, giving rise to *Centro Brasileiro de Análise e Planejamento* (CEBRAP). Spearheading an alternative institutional model for the social sciences as the military regimes across Latin America foreclosed the traditional spaces, CEBRAP also became the site where Cardoso recast dependency ideas into a new political project.[86]

In a moment of intense political repression and at the apex of the "Brazilian economic miracle," Cardoso emerged as the "military regime's most cogent intellectual critic."[87] The 1968 peak of protests and dissent and the repression that followed led to the reemergence of the armed insurrection and the intensification of policing and torturing in the hands of the state. Despite the despairing political situation, CEBRAP appeared as "one of the oases of freedom" in the country.[88] Cardoso and the senior members of

CEBRAP organized *mesões*, or roundtables, that brought together social scientists from universities in and outside of São Paulo, stimulating the country's intellectual debate on the ongoing political situation and consolidating the center as the leading institution in the country. Although the bulk of the work at CEBRAP in those years revolved around what were considered "technical" and thus politically "safe" topics such as demography and urban planning, its members produced texts on "hot" areas such as Cardoso's "Brazilian Political Model" and Paul Singer's "Contradictions of the Brazilian Miracle," among many others that helped framed the debate for the intellectual left and envision alternatives for the opposition to the regime.[89] Some of these ideas were translated to broader audiences through the regular contribution of Cardoso and Singer to the oppositionist journal *Opinião* and of them and other members to the weekly magazine *Movimento*.

From CEBRAP, Cardoso and others challenged the prevailing ideas held by the Brazilian opposition about the character and scope of the military regime. The military coup that deposed a populist and nationalist president in 1964 had transformed into an enduring military regime that maintained some trappings of democracy with alternating presidents, indirect elections, and an opposition party by the end of the decade. For Cardoso, the existing military regime was not the product of imperialist penetration that the nationalists claimed, and therefore he found the "nationalist" opposition strategy of the intellectual left ill-conceived and unproductive.[90] The regime was neither a conservative reaction of the landed interests against industrialization and development in defense of the "agrarization" of the economy, as oppositionist intellectuals like Furtado claimed. Rather, the military's economic model was the product of what Cardoso called an "associated dependent development," an alliance between foreign and local bourgeoisie, public and private enterprises, bureaucrats and middle classes, in which the dominant partner was the developmental state.[91] Therefore, instead of the stagnation that many oppositionists anticipated, the "Brazilian political model" created by the military brought economic dynamism. Instead of "pastorization" of the economy, it fostered the rapid expansion of the industrial sector. Instead of the dominance of private capital and a passive state that those who attributed the coup to capitalists imagined, the military regime had strengthened the state through the expansion of a modern and entrepreneurial public sector and a growing bureaucracy. Instead of social stagnation, the regime enabled and encouraged social mobility in an effort to create the "complacent apathy of the middle classes," as they seized education and employment opportunities and consumed the manufactured goods of a growing industry.[92]

By recasting the character of the regime, Cardoso hoped to present a strategy for the opposition to the dictatorship that was not armed revolution nor old-school nationalism. Despite his structural explanation for the rise of the military regime in Brazil, Cardoso was emphatic in declaring, "I do not think that 1964 was written in the economic logic of history."[93] Cardoso encouraged the opposition to take the aspirations for social mobility seriously and instead of rejecting the prevailing consumerism, condemn the growing inequality. Instead of deploying its "phraseology of imperialism," Cardoso urged the opposition to concentrate its efforts on the respect for civil and political liberties and in opening forms of political participation.[94] While buttressed on the analytical framework of dependency, Cardoso transitioned toward his preoccupation with authoritarianism and democracy.

As intellectual leader of the opposition, Cardoso became increasingly politically involved. Building on the concept of "associated dependent development," Cardoso envisioned an oppositionist strategy of what he called "strengthening civil society" that gradually came into being as the Catholic Church; professional associations; middle-class and favela neighborhood organizations; black, indigenous, and women movements; and especially labor unions mobilized against the military state in the late 1970s and early 1980s.[95] Simultaneously, as the *Movimento Democrático Brasileiro* (MDB), the official opposition party, seized the moment to turn direct congressional elections of November 1974 into a plebiscite against the military, the *paulista* MDB leader rallied CEBRAP's support in a congressional inquiry into the multinational corporations and, most importantly, to outline the party platform.[96] After that initial overture, the collaboration between CEBRAP and the MDB increased over the years, culminating in Cardoso's formal integration to the party and his election as deputy senator in 1978. For Cardoso, the prestige and intuitions of his *Dependency and Development* unleashed a long and controversial trajectory, further discussed in the Epilogue, that consolidated his intellectual but also his political leadership in the following decades.

Closures and Reopenings

With the one notable exception of Cardoso and his allies, the advent of authoritarian regimes shattered the projects that dependency theory and *dependentistas* had unleashed. Starting with the Brazilian military coup in 1964 that forced the pioneer *dependentistas* into exile in Chile, the military regimes shaped the dependency turn in different and sometimes unexpected ways. In the right-wing regimes of Argentina and Uruguay, the young and radical armed militants inspired by Marxism and dependency were persecuted and decimated. The social scientists, who through the 1960s made militancy and revolution the essence of academic life, were, in the following decade, the object of repression and censorship as "armless subversives." Academic and intellectual life were also narrowed in left-wing authoritarian regimes. While leading social scientists denounced cooptation in Peru, the repression against "dissident" intellectuals soared in Cuba in the early 1970s, reducing the space of dependency ideas.[97] The authoritarian turn in Chile, in which freedom of expression and pluralism prevailed like nowhere else, was perhaps the worst blow to dependency.

The military coup against Allende was a coup against the social sciences and dependency ideas. Interrogation, imprisonment, and executions of Unidad Popular members and supporters began immediately after the installation of the military junta in September 1973. *Cepalino* Carlos Matus, former minister of the economy, Central Bank manager, and head of the development corporation, was taken to the concentration camp in Isla Dawson, where he remained for two years. Torture quickly ensued. Within the first two months, over thirteen thousand people were detained, more than one thousand were killed, and seven thousand fled the country. Like many other economists, sociologists, and intellectuals, Vuskovic went into exile in Mexico, where he rallied the support of the government and spearheaded the creation of *Casa de Chile*. While Frank found a research position at the Max Planck Institute, dos Santos became professor at the *Universidad Nacional Autónoma de México* after having spent six months in the Panama embassy, taking refuge from military persecution. Hundreds of thousands left Chile during the course of the regime aided by solidarity movements in Latin America, the United States, and Europe.[98] The exodus of Chilean and foreign intellectuals and social scientists was devastating for what was a vibrant intellectual milieu.

Santiago, the hub of social sciences in Latin America in the postwar era, was shattered right at the peak of the universalization of the paradigm of dependency. Centers and institutes were dismantled, students and faculty expelled, and severe censorship from the military junta broke havoc on the institutional apparatus of dependency theory and the social sciences more broadly. The departments and institutes of sociology and political economy were the most affected, with the *Universidad de Chile* losing 90 percent of its faculty. CESO, the institution that had hosted Cardoso but had become the springboard for Frank and dos Santos, was closed permanently. Financial cuts and self-censorship deprived the remaining faculty of the possibility of engaging in creative and research work.[99] Some attempts were made by the Ford Foundation and the Social Science Research Council (SSRC) to maintain intellectual activity in Chile. Yet the panorama was bleak. Chile had become isolated. Nobody spoke. The work of Faletto, one of the few prominent intellectuals who remained in Chile, was "virtually empty."[100] As survival took precedence, work on dependency receded.

The military curtailment of intellectual endeavor notwithstanding, many Latin American intellectuals also wanted to lay dependency to rest. As revolutions were halted and revolutionaries crushed, they began to examine the shortcomings and failures of the left. Chilean sociologists began to remember the *Universidad de Chile,* traditionally associated with the Socialist Party, as the hotbed of "a vulgar form of Marxism." The Chilean intellectual community seemed increasingly baffled that dos Santos and Frank had dominated the field with a "juvenile, "student-like" language. In Frank's hands, dependency transformed into "brilliant politics without sociology and economics," a sociologist recalled.[101] Many social scientists were disoriented. Others, like FLACSO economist and future president of Chile Ricardo Lagos, had a more definitive diagnosis. "Social scientists must accept much of the responsibility for the current situation," he claimed. As so many social scientific institutions became partisan, as intellectual debate was restricted to political strategy, and as research was narrowed to whether "the Left could win the next election," the social scientists "looked almost like pamphleteers," Lagos claimed. They made the social sciences vulnerable and reduced the prestige that could have protected them from authoritarianism, Lagos added.[102] At a certain point during the military regime, the Chilean social scientists, including some *dependendistas,* began to question their assumption of the political commitment of the intellectual and the preeminence of revolutionary transformations over formal democracy. As a result, many were demoralized or even discredited.[103] The theory of dependency had been crushed from without and would be gradually undermined from within.

Although, or perhaps because, most *dependentistas* were in retreat in Latin America, dependency theory was drawing increasing attention in the rest of the world, as discussed in the Epilogue. The Cuban Revolution and the Chilean Road to Socialism had brought intellectuals from North America and Europe who wanted to participate in or at least observe these unique experiments of social and economic transformation. Simultaneously, European and especially North American institutions provided scholarships and research fellowships in an effort to understand and perhaps also contain the growing radicalism in the region.[104] In their stays, students and faculty, literary critics, and social scientists came in contact with the prevailing intellectual debates in the region, discovering dependency theory and other ideas taking shape in the increasingly radical 1960s.[105] With the advent of military regimes, foreigners and Latin Americans went into exile, taking dependency ideas with them.[106] The wave of exiles of *dependentistas* as well as their allies and their enemies complemented the efforts of Frank, Cardoso, and dos Santos, with different degrees of success, to make their ideas circulate in international academic and nonacademic circles. As a result, a radical cohort of Latin Americanists emerged in the United States in the 1960s and in Germany and others later on, who adopted dependency theory and Marxism as the privileged paradigm of research as well as the mechanism to liberate the social sciences and academia from their imperialist trappings. In spite of the success of dependency theory around the world, the pioneer *dependentistas* resented the reception of their ideas.

As the main object of condemnation, Frank became the face of the dependency movement in the global social sciences. The first of the pioneer *dependentistas* to be published and to do so in English, Frank had a comparative advantage over the others.[107] Although Frank and Cardoso were equally translated into German, for instance, the references to Frank in social scientific journals in English and Spanish of the time doubled those of Cardoso.[108] Founded by a group of radical social scientists in California, the journal *Latin American Perspectives,* to give another example, aspired to provide space to Latin American voices and instead "Frank had appeared in almost every issue, even if most often as the target of an attack."[109] Pleased to be recognized as the "point of departure" of the new dependency theory, Frank, was nonetheless, recurrently fending off criticisms for what he thought were more attacks on his "ultra-leftist" persona than on his ideas, with two exceptions. Frank took seriously the challenge of Marxist thinkers on his focus on circulation more than production as the definition of capitalist accumulation. He also appreciated the criticisms of *dependentistas* like Marini and dos Santos, who contested his emphasis on the external more than the internal structures of dependency. Both of these critiques gave Frank intellectual stimulus.[110] While cultivating enemies worldwide, Frank believed his rejoinder would come in the analysis of the world's cycles of capitalist accumulation in Asia, Africa, Middle East, and Latin America since 1500s to the present that he was devoted to. If Frank reveled in the attention, Cardoso contested it.

At the peak of influence of both dependency theory and Third World socialism, Cardoso was adamant to dispute the dominance of Frank over the meaning and scope of dependency theory. In an attempt to signal deception and reassert his position, Cardoso described the reception of dependency theory as the "propagation of a myth," an almost ritualistic repetition of archetypes of "dependency and development, exploitation and wealth, backwardness and progress," in which the "imagination is bound to preestablished models." As a result of this "ritualistic consumption" in global circles, the contribution of dependency theory was assimilated to be the "external conditioning of Latin American economies, which was taken for granted [within Latin America]" rather than the interest to "grasp the political alliances, the ideologies, and the movement of structures within dependent societies."[111] To challenge the originality and groundbreaking character of Frank's work, Cardoso situated the intellectual genealogy of "dependency" first, as product of the "critique of critics of 'orthodoxy'" that, like him, "took the CEPAL problematique and defined it radically," and second, as part of a "long tradition of Latin American thought," that periodically "resurrects Marxism to understand economic structures and structures of domination" but "does not suffocate the historical process by removing the struggle between groups and classes"[112] (figure 6.4). Like Prebisch and cepalinos had done with classical liberalism in the past, Cardoso denounced Frank and his "vulgar Marxism" as alien to an imagined "Latin American tradition." Not only was Frank's dependency not new but it was also not "Latin American." Not fully secure at the time, Cardoso would see the tables turn shortly after.

Latin American intellectuals in the United States, many of them exiles of the military regimes, quickly followed Cardoso's lead. They felt that, despite not having coined the term "dependency," Frank had become the most famous interpreter of Latin America and the spokesperson for those who claimed to speak from and for the periphery of the global economy. "Dependency analysis in the US became known not through the writing of Latin Americans but through interpreters," political scientists Samuel and Arturo Valenzuela claimed. Those interpreters pointed to Frank as the origins of the new paradigm, who in turn, had presented "oversimplified and distorted views of the Latin American contribution," they added.[113] Tulio Halperín-Donghi, Argentine historian and recent émigré to Berkeley, wrote a few years later that Frank "purported to offer a radically new view of the region" yet "based on a violent rejection of all Latin American intellectual and ideological traditions." Halperín-Donghi, author of a best-selling and enduring textbook on the history of Latin America based precisely on that 'regional intellectual tradition,' concluded that Frank's vision was instead "the child of the North American political awakening."[114] Frank was certainly one of the many outsiders who through the centuries have claimed to "discover" Latin America. But to dismiss Frank's "dependency" as foreign to Latin America, these intellectuals, despite their valid critiques emphasizing Frank's oversimplifications and generalizations, also turned a blind eye to Frank's

FIGURE 6.4 *Left to right*, Fernando Henrique Cardoso, Raúl Prebisch, José Serra, and Aníbal Pinto, old guard *cepalinos* and vanguard *dependentistas*, reunited in Santiago in the late 1970s, mending old rifts. (Acervo Presidente Fernando Henrique Cardoso.)

proximity to dos Santos and the rest of the Brasilia group since his early days and therefore to some of the voices in the regional debate.

The rejection of Frank's framing of dependency represented a broader shift within the region's political landscape. As Latin American discourse moved away from underdevelopment and revolution to the rhetoric of democracy and equality, dependency theory à la Frank fell out of fashion. By the 1970s, more than its controversial Marxist credentials, the stature of the theory's contribution had become intertwined with its locus of enunciation, so when it became associated with "North American" Frank, it lost credibility to many in the Southern Hemisphere at the very moment it was facing extreme political pressure and internal criticism.

Frank's fate among Latin Americans was similar to that of dos Santos, Bambirra, and Marini upon their return to Brazil in 1979. After almost a decade and a half of exile, dos Santos and the Brasilia group, where Frank had originally found a community in the 1960s, found themselves not only forgotten but actively sidelined. Whereas Cardoso and many of the social scientists of the *paulista* group had created an institutional space through CEBRAP, dos Santos, Bambirra, and Marini could not obtain a permanent academic position until the early 1990s. Whereas Cardoso began a political career in the 1970s and was two-times senator in the following decade, dos Santos lost the election for the governorship of his native state, Minas Gerais, in 1982 and for senator in 1986. In the words of dos Santos, he and his group found "extreme restrictions to reinsert [themselves] into the Brazilian reality." Dos Santos believed that Cardoso and others had actively tried to silence them because their views on the transition to democracy differed from those of leading intellectuals like Cardoso. Dos Santos recalled that Cardoso and José Serra's article entitled "Desventuras de la dialéctica de la dependencia," "ended with a strong statement that it was necessary to lock up [Dos Santos and the Brasilia group's] ideas in order to avoid them influencing the Brazilian youth."[115] Albeit the absence of the passage in the publication, dos Santos's claim articulated a denunciation of an active effort to undermine his and the Brasilia group's ideas in Brazil, which he attributed to "a reaction against the influence that [their] thought had achieved at the international level."[116] Dos Santos and the Brasilia group were perhaps confronting that they had become relics of the past as Cardoso's dependency became hegemonic in Brazil. By the early 1980s, as the revolutionary left lost the intellectual legitimacy it had in the previous decade, it was dos Santos and the Brasilia group who contested the predominance of Cardoso, just as Cardoso had challenged Frank's dominance in Chile, Latin America, and then the United States in the early 1970s when revolutionary fervors were at its peak.

Behind dos Santos's outcry lay social and political transformations as well as individual choices. For once, a doctoral degree, which neither dos Santos nor Marini had obtained, became a requirement in a growing university-system that aspired to compete in a global scale. In addition, the military regime had banned some of dos Santos's work, and his classic books, originally written in Spanish, had been translated into multiple languages, but they did not exist in Portuguese.[117] Dos Santos had devoted his work to the study of the international political economy and Brazil had lost preponderance. Most important perhaps were the transformations in the Brazilian political landscape and the position that dos Santos and the Brasilia group decided to occupy within it. They had been absent from Brazil in the crucial decade in which Cardoso's coalition and Luiz Inácio Lula da Silva's Workers Party, the two political forces that would shape the future of democratic Brazil, emerged and they joined neither of them. For these *dependentistas,* their project had been defeated, not coincidentally at the onset of Cardoso's political trajectory, as we shall see next.

Conclusions

Before it went global in the 1970s, "dependency theory" was intellectually and politically influential in Latin America. As Brazilian pioneer *dependentistas* converged in Santiago, ideas about dependency developed into "dependency theory," and in so doing, prompted a sprawling social scientific agenda, nurtured enduring histories of the region and its place in the world, and gave rise to a paradigm shift in which structures and classes, world systems, and market forces came to occupy center stage. Feeding and being fed by successive and radically different political experiments in Chile and the developmentalist but authoritarian regime in Brazil, "dependency theory" transformed into a movement. Many of the pioneer *dependentistas* mobilized their intellectual and political capital toward national or regionally grounded projects. They imagined Latin America at a crossroads of regional and global processes and therefore privileged the region as the site where dependency theory transformed into political praxis. As the world began to look toward Latin America and these *dependentistas* inserted themselves in more global conversations, they continued to fight their battles in Cuba, Chile, Brazil, and the rest of the region.

Far from promoting an intellectual and political consensus, the consolidation of "dependency theory" gave rise to lively debates and contending projects. In academic circles, *dependentistas* and converts discussed the genealogy and ideological underpinnings of the concept as well as the scope and political implications of the theory. Beyond academia, dependency theory galvanized political movements such as the Cuba-led revolutionary Third Worldism and the UN-sponsored economic internationalism that were at odds with each other. It inspired and promoted socialism in democracy in Chile as well as anti-authoritarian social-democracy in Brazil, just to name a few. The rapid and wide circulation of their ideas combined with the efforts of *dependentistas* themselves to translate dependency into political action raised the stakes for *dependentistas* to administer the meaning and scope of a concept embedded in some of the most salient projects of their times.

Rather than succumbing with internecine theoretical disputes and contending political ambitions, "dependency theory" gained momentum and thrived in the multiple meanings of dependency and with the frictions among *dependentistas* and their allies. Gradually, dependency theory would transform into a battle of intellectuals for position and for command over what was becoming a globally renowned category. At stake in the dispute was the ability of competing groups of intellectuals to represent Latin America in the global sphere and to interpret global capitalism from the perspective of Latin America. In the process, the stature of the concept shifted from its contested Marxist credentials to the locus of enunciation in the global South. Dependency theory became "Latin America's contribution to the debate about development and capitalism.

In this search for Latin American origins, *dependentistas* returned to *cepalinos,* giving rise to the umbrella term "dependency theory." The *cepalino* notion of center and periphery that was part of the early postwar discussion was both a very specific reference to the long-term decline international terms of trade and a broad statement about the global international division of labor. That concept both attracted and repelled *dependentistas* and their followers, who then resignified and deployed the term with dependency theory in very different contexts and in very different projects. Writ large, dependency theory became therefore associated with both the establishment, with institutions like the United Nations, and the antiestablishment with the Cuban Tricontinental Congress. It became associated with antiauthoritarianism in Brazil and Chile as well as with developmentalist military regime in Peru. In Latin America and beyond, the multiplicity of meanings and the diversity of projects that came to be associated with "dependency theory" attracted many followers and detractors and continue to do so, giving dependency theory global reach and an enduring attraction, which would soon be recognized as the world that Latin America created.

Epilogue

Dependency Theory in the World
and Back in Latin America

With dependency theory, a new generation of Latin American social scientists became the cornerstone of a forceful and far-ranging intellectual movement that captured the region and the world in the 1960s and 1970s. Dependency theory became not just a fertile intellectual paradigm for the regional social scientific community but also a politically inspiring force for *dependentistas,* new converts, and for numerous cohorts of dissenters, radicals, and revolutionaries for whom it became synonymous with anti-imperialism, anti-capitalism, and the struggle against oppression and poverty. Intellectually and politically diverse, *dependentistas* as well as their followers and allies were nonetheless left in profound disarray with the rise of military regimes across the region. The resulting repression, exile, and fear dispersed *dependentistas* and threatened to put an end to the movement. Yet those same forces that limited *dependentistas'* ability to effect change in Latin America propelled dependency theory in the world, gaining traction among the intellectual and political movements seeking to understand the postcolonial development in the global South.

By the time democracy returned at the turn of the twenty-first century in Latin America, *cepalinos* and *dependentistas* had undergone an intellectual and political realignment. They had created new institutions, formed new networks, and brokered new political alliances to oppose military regimes that opened a space for them in the new neoliberal democracies. While dependency theory traveled and conquered the world, some leading *cepalinos* and *dependentistas* directed their intellectual gaze and political capital toward national struggles. In doing so, they took the legacy of dependency in paradoxical and unforeseen ways that nonetheless kept the ideas alive even in an era that was radically different from the one in which they emerged.

Dependency theory emerged just as the world's social scientists were turning their attention to Latin America as a vital region to study and understand. The Cuban Revolution and the diverse political experiments that followed, including the Chilean Way to Socialism as well as the authoritarian turn in Peru and the Southern Cone, captivated both academics and the wider public. Important public intellectuals such as Eric Hobsbawm and Robin Blackburn in Britain, Jean-Paul Sartre and Simone de Beauvoir in France, and C. Wright Mills and Paul Sweezy in the United States contributed to putting Latin America in the spotlight of a wider discussion about underdevelopment and global inequality.[1] The rise of writers like Julio Cortázar, Gabriel García Márquez, and Mario Vargas Llosa, or what became known as the Latin American literary boom, cemented global intellectuals' interest in the region. National governments, philanthropic foundations, and private organizations channeled resources toward academic and policy research in the region. The desire to thwart subversion and communism moved those in the United States; the British were interested in rekindling commercial relations; the German and the Dutch desired to expand their international development cooperation territory. By doing so, all gradually gave rise to the field of Latin American studies worldwide.

Through the course of the 1960s, that global interest in Latin America found an academic institutional expression, creating a space for dependency theory to take hold. Western countries saw the rise of multidisciplinary Latin American studies programs, institutes, courses, as well as a growing number of faculty and students. Through these academic programs and through development cooperation initiatives in Western Europe, scholars from the global North traveled to Latin America and Latin American scholars visited these programs, fomenting an intellectual exchange precisely at the time when dependency theory was on the rise in the region. The *Latin American Research Review* (LARR) in the United States and *Journal of Latin American Studies* in Britain were established in the mid-decade to serve as rallying points and outlets of a growing community of scholars. As they found refuge in Western academic centers after being forced into exile by repressive military regimes, Latin American scholars circulated dependency theory and other ideas simmering in the region in the previous decade. Those ideas found a receptive and growing audience in North American and European universities, home to student movements against militarism, oppression, and economic and cultural imperialism. The moment was ripe to propel the dependency movement across time and space.

Emerging almost concomitantly, dependency theory transformed or in some cases shaped the Latin American studies field across the world. In the United States, dependency theory and other Marxist-inspired approaches became the dominant paradigm of a field that almost doubled its size in terms of students, faculty, and publications from the second half of the 1960s to the second half of the 1970s.[2] In the United States, the field was quickly polarized and institutionally partitioned as new "anti-establishment" institutions and journals emerged as alternatives to the Latin American Studies Association (LASA) and LARR, its journal. *Latin American Perspectives,* one of those new outlets, gave dependency theory center stage on its first edition, a position the theory would occupy in numerous others in the years to come.[3] In the United Kingdom and in West Germany, dependency theory, among other intellectual currents, fomented a shift from history and geography toward the social sciences and contemporary politics as well as a shift toward a more radical political orientation.[4] The sociologists at the Institute of Latin American Studies at the Frei University of Berlin "embraced dependency theory as the main analytical approach," particularly the "ahistorical and undialectical variant of Andre Gunder Frank," attracting numerous students to the field in the process[5] (figures E.1 and E.2). In the Netherlands, dependency theory was almost foundational for the Latin American studies field, which emerged later than its European counterparts and in close association with politically active organizations, solidarity groups, and civic institutions that embraced Chilean exiles.[6] These communities began to translate Latin American ideas to a wider European public.[7]

The dependency agenda rapidly crossed to other fields. While some British Africanists inspired by dependency ideas shifted their gaze toward Latin America, Africanist scholars discovered "Latin American" dependency theory at a time when the field was trying to shed its colonial underpinnings and incorporate more African and Third World voices.[8] Groundbreaking in this regard was perhaps the work of Walter Rodney, an Afro-Guyanese Africanist trained in the University of West Indies and in London's School of Oriental and African Studies. While influenced by radical Caribbean scholars, Rodney's *How Europe Underdeveloped Africa* was a "statement of what came to be known as dependency theory" that, according to American political activist Angela Davis, altered the field of African studies since its publication in 1972.[9] Inspired by Frank's "development of underdevelopment thesis," which Rodney identified as "reflecting the thinking of progressive intellectuals in Latin America . . .

FIGURE E.1   Fernando Henrique Cardoso (*far right*) and Andre Gunder Frank (*to Cardoso's right*) in a conference organized by FLACSO-Santiago in Berlin in 1974 at the apogee of dependency theory worldwide, 1974. (Acervo Presidente Fernando Henrique Cardoso.)

now entrenched in the metropole," Rodney introduced the problem of racial categories and identities to the evolution of the world capitalist system explored in dependency theory.[10] Within a few years, Frank's dependency theory was fostering a new agenda in African studies.[11] While Rodney's book was an important mechanism for the global diffusion of dependency ideas, other Africanists soon moved the theory beyond the area studies and into social science theory.

The network built by Egyptian economist Samir Amin spread Latin American dependency theory's influence even further. Amin—who had been trained in the University of Paris in the 1950s under the same professor of *cepalino* Celso Furtado and who was then director of the ILPES-like UN African Institute for Development and Planning located in Dakar—traveled to Santiago in 1971.[12] Andre Gunder Frank invited Amin, whom he had met in Paris a few years earlier, and introduced him to Theotônio dos Santos and other *dependentistas*. Arriving at Santiago in the successful first year of Allende's Unidad Popular government and at the apex of the dependency

FIGURE E.2   All the participants of the FLACSO conference in Berlin. Among the
attendees were *cepalinos* Celso Furtado (*fourth from the right on the second line*)
and Oswaldo Sunkel (*third row, third from the left*), retrained *dependentistas* such
as Edelberto Torres Rivas (*third row, third from the right*) as well as pioneer dependendistas Fernando Henrique Cardoso (*in the center and back*) and Andre
Gunder Frank (*last row, fifth from the right*). (Acervo Pres. Fernando Henrique Cardoso.)

movement, Amin was immediately captivated by Latin America and its intellectual revolution. The following year Amin invited Fernando Henrique
Cardoso, dos Santos, Frank, and Ruy Mauro Marini, the only one who
could attend, to Dakar for a conference on "Strategies of Economic Development" in order to "present dependency theory to Africanists."[13]
Devouring the work of Latin American *dependentistas* and their network
of dependency pioneers, disciples, and allies, Amin confidently declared,
"the center of gravity of the reflection about our contemporary society has
in the last 20 years transferred to Latin America." "Since the contribution
of Latin America to the analysis not just of underdevelopment but on the
perspective of the world-system is considerable," Amin urged European
and North American scholars to turn their gaze to the region.[14] The bridges
created by Amin would bring together Latin Americanists, such as Frank
and to a lesser extent dos Santos and Peruvian sociologist Aníbal Quijano
with Africanist scholars, such as sociologist Immanuel Wallerstein and

economist Giovanni Arrighi, who had been working on the analysis of the capitalist world system in parallel with *dependentistas.*

The world-system theory was the result of the convergence of *dependentistas* and those were observing the world economy from Africa. Like Latin America was for Frank, Africa was the road to the analysis of the world economy for Wallerstein. "It was Africa that changed the more stultifying parts of my education," he claimed, reflecting on his many years traveling the continent, observing decolonization projects.[15] It was to Frank's notion of the "development of underdevelopment" that Wallerstein attributed inspiration for his thesis in his major opus, *The Modern World-System.*[16] For Frank, Wallerstein's world-system theory was "a more erudite and detailed version" of his dependency ideas about the "world economy without a hyphen."[17] For Amin, while Frank and others described the integration of Latin America to the world economy, he and Arrighi were, "in the same wavelength," doing the same for Asia and Africa.[18] Frank and Wallerstein, Arrighi, and Amin all came together in the 1970s and 1980s and, despite differences among them, became recognized as the "gang of four" of the world-system theory. Popularizing the center and periphery (and semiperiphery) model, world-system theory once again relocated the *cepalino* concept from development theory and practice to the wider and academically far-reaching scale of social science theory as well as involvement in Third Worldism.

Both on its own and through world-system theory, dependency theory created sprawling research agendas in the social sciences, especially in the United States. In anthropology, the emergent world perspective of the 1960s became a central concern in the 1970s, leading practitioners to "situate ethnographic studies in the world-system" by analyzing the impact of industrialization, multinational corporations, or cash-crop production in different societies. Yet, whereas the world-system theory assumed or implied the unity and almost stability of the capitalist global system, anthropological critiques emphasized the nonclass, noneconomic mechanisms that subverted apparent "predictable outcomes" in which "counterforces were doomed to failure." It emphasized the coexistence of different modes of production within the periphery such as in Sidney Mintz's early work.[19] In political science, dependency theory drew attention to external forces and the impact of the international political economy on national political development, often neglected in analysis of domestic politics, especially within hegemonic powers.[20] In economics, dependency theory, although stimulating some applied research, never became part of the mainstream academic community most likely because the discipline was undergoing an important transformation away from historical and institutional approaches.[21] In history, dependency theory rekindled debates about coexisting and competing modes of production in colonial Latin America and prompted research projects on foreign investment and trade in the nineteenth century. All of this made social and economic history the foundation of the social sciences and the "queen of Latin American studies" through the 1970s and into the 1980s.[22] In sociology, dependency theory inspired a wide range of topics from the effects of economic dependence on mortality rates and internal inequality to structural dependence on peripheral urbanization and rural social change, touching almost every subfield.[23] Perhaps the largest and more long-lasting legacy of dependency theory was for sociology of development and comparative politics, especially as it helped recast the meaning of dependency and the trajectory of some of the *dependentistas* and their allies. In political sociology and comparative politics, dependency theory fostered new projects and new classics. Cardoso and Faletto's work led to the study of "industrialized yet peripheral economies" or what Wallerstein called the "semi-peripheries," of the impact of multinational corporations, and of "dependent development" in Taiwan, Korea, Singapore, as well as of Ireland and Portugal.[24] Among the new classics inspired by dependency theory were Peter Evans' *Dependent Development* and his later contributions to "bringing the state back in," and Guillermo O'Donnell's *Bureaucratic Authoritarianism*, read alongside Barrington Moore's *Social Origins of Dictatorship*.[25] Friends and collaborators Cardoso and O'Donnell would transform the legacy of dependency while cementing its intellectual and political influence in the world and in Latin America.

Renewed by dependency theory, the sociology of development worldwide elaborated on and began to challenge some of its premises. In the United States, dependency theory gave rise to a bargaining model, emphasizing the choices and opportunities available for dependent societies and states to withstand global economic forces.[26] In Germany and in the United States, there was a significant effort of both critics and supporters of dependency theory to test its hypothesis empirically, especially Frank's "development of underdevelopment thesis."[27] Especially important in cementing the influence of dependency theory was the Max Planck Institute, to which Frank relocated until 1978 and to which he tried to bring many Latin Americans to recreate the Chilean "*Centro de Estudios Socioeconomicos* (CESO) in exile"[28] (see figures E.1 and E.2). In the United Kingdom, the sociologists of development saw their work as an attempt to "modify some of the oversimplifications that certain of the new theorists of dependence have introduced with their sweeping vision," referring to Frank's work, which they nonetheless saw as a "monumental, necessary, and overdue change of emphasis." After Frank had "stormed onto the scene in the guise of an academic Che Guevara and captured the attention of undergraduates with his center-periphery model," the British sociologists innovated in new topics such as cultural and technological dependence and forced reconsideration of concepts other than class and dependence to analyze the social phenomena in developing societies.[29] In the process of empirically testing or elaborating the theory, social scientists began to gradually disassociate dependency theory from Frank and discover other *dependentistas,* ones that were more pertinent to what was increasingly perceived as a new era.

Perhaps the greatest legacy of *cepalinos* and *dependentistas,* beyond their impact on academic fields or intellectual activism, was on Third Worldism and international economic governance. They were influential in transforming the definition of the politically inspired and inspiring concept of the "Third World." Although the Third World, as a category and a movement, preceded them, the *dependentistas,* ushered in by their world-system allies, became important assets to the cause. The network-builder Amin convened Latin American *dependentistas,* Asian experts, and their African counterparts in Santiago and Dakar in the early 1970s to establish the *Third World Forum* and bring together "thinkers" not "development officials" to conceptualize the Third World from a world system perspective.[30] The Latin American contingent of the first informal group was composed of Fernando Henrique Cardoso, Celso Furtado, and Pablo González Casanova. The *Third World Forum* bore its first fruits in the following decade when Cardoso and Furtado had undertaken other political projects back in their native Brazil, but *cepalinos* and *dependentistas* were a fundamental part of Samir Amin's plan to deploy the world-system theory for Third World internationalism.

As a result of the endeavors of Amin, *dependentistas,* and many others, the "Third World" transformed from a geopolitical to an economic category. Whereas originally it designated those who did not belong to the Cold War East and West or the First and Second Worlds, by the 1970s, the Third World entailed an economic-based concept, designating the producers of raw materials and primary products in the periphery within the international division of labor.[31] Attesting to the transformation was the call for an "economic Bandung conference," pivoting away from the political and geopolitical aspirations of sovereignty and self-determination of the 1955 Asian-African summit toward the future context of the New International Economic Order (NIEO).[32]

Cepalinos and *dependentistas* were also influential in the diagnosis of global economic inequality and the "call to arms" for a transformation in international governance in the early 1970s. In the context of the economic crisis of the Western world, Cold War détente, and OPEC activism and greater economic leverage of the raw-material producers of the global South, African and Asian postcolonial leaders and Latin American statesmen joined forces to demand global economic reform and a new system of international governance that culminated in the 1974 UN Charter for a New International Economic Order. Although the political leadership of Latin America in the NIEO may have been underemphasized, the wide-casting but vague net of "dependency theory" as an intellectual precedent has been often noted in old and new literature.[33]

At the core of the NIEO was the aspiration that gave rise to the *cepalino* project in the early postwar years. Like *cepalinos*, the NIEO attempted to transform the international system of trade and, more specifically, the unequal and detrimental division of labor between the raw material–producing peripheries in the South and the industrialized nations of the North. With the creation of the UN CEPAL, Latin Americans had established an important precedent for global economic activism of the Third World *avant la letre* that the NIEO promoters followed: the use of the United Nations as the vehicle for South-led global economic reform. The *cepalino*-led 1964 UNCTAD not only provided the institutional stepping-stone for the NIEO but also provided the vocabulary and rationale. From Tanzania to Senegal, from Algeria to Mexico, the leadership of the global South embraced the diagnosis and terminology of the periphery's falling terms of trade that *cepalinos* had made their own in the early postwar years as the rationale to advocate for the NIEO. This particular legacy of *cepalinos* and *dependendistas* acquires a larger dimension considering the interest of recent scholarship on twentieth century internationalism in the NIEO.

This scholarship has placed significant weight on the NIEO as the peak of global South-led internationalism. Because the NEIO represented an auspicious but "contingent moment of political possibility," some scholars consider the NEIO as the "high mark of developing countries' efforts to influence the commanding heights of the world economy" or the "most ambitious program of anticolonial worldmaking."[34] Certainly, the NIEO encompassed and expressed wide-ranging demands that reflect what were and still are some of the most pressing and important problems affecting the world economy. It placed the system of trade, aid, and finance at the center of the global debate about poverty, economic inequality, and racial prejudice. It also embodied a moment of South-South solidarity that has allowed historians to reverse the trends in global history writing in which the South is often portrayed as a follower of the North.[35] Furthermore, through the studies of the NIEO and other initiatives, scholars have been pushing against the universalism of the North and the implicit parochialism and inward-gazing of the South. Like this book, the recent scholarship portrays midcentury state-builders and development experts like *cepalinos* as world-makers, as ambitious intellectual and political leaders aiming to transform the world economy. Seeking alternative origins to the "Wilsonian moment" that placed enduring anticolonial or counterhegemonic struggles in the White, North Atlantic, scholars have nonetheless converged in portraying the NIEO as the culmination of those struggles.

Instead, this book, like some of its main protagonists and unlike the thrust of the aforementioned scholarship, does not see the NIEO as the culmination of the midcentury worldmaking project. The cusp of the *cepalino* and *dependentista* intellectual projects, in conflicting ways, surpassed the 1970s internationalism as will be shown next. Furthermore, for *cepalinos* and *dependentistas*, Latin America, not the global arena, was the main theater of their ventures. To begin with, Latin American *dependentistas* did not see themselves represented, paradoxically, in a movement whose origins are partially attributed to them. Many of the pioneers of "dependency theory," a term often used to group and conflate the projects of *cepalinos*, *dependentistas*, and their world-system allies, had moved away from the Third World struggles or were never fully committed to them. Raúl Prebisch, for instance, who had since the postwar years advocated for internationalism and cooperation between center and periphery as the road to autonomy, resigned from the Third World struggle after the second UNCTAD meeting in 1968. Although the Santiago UNCTAD-III meeting of 1972 reignited his globalist project and would lead him to *Peripheral Capitalism*—what was perhaps his most radical work and thus, his path to rapprochement with *dependentistas*—Prebisch was at end of his career and on retreat at the moment of the NIEO.[36] For hard-core *dependentistas* like Andre Gunder Frank, the project of UNCTAD from which the NIEO most proximately emerged represented the "sloganizing of [his thesis of the] 'development of underdevelopment'" and a form of bourgeois corruption of "dependency theory."[37] Other pioneer *dependentistas* and *cepalinos*, whose trajectories will be discussed in the following section, gave "dependency theory" new and perhaps unpredictable afterlives beyond the seeming NIEO climax. They made Latin America once again the stage of *dependentista* political projects after the historical and historiographical turn that places internationalism as the main dimension of the "global" and global history. While this book shows the *dependentista* project thriving globally in the 1970s, it also imagines Latin America as important on its own right—as the site of interplay of internal and external economic and political forces—as part of global history.

The lives of some *dependentistas* and *cepalinos* after the golden years of the *cepalino* project force us to reconsider the timeline of the worldmaking development era. Instead of ending in the mid-1970s, the *cepalino* project lived on and transformed, resulting in an even more politically ambiguous legacy. As Brazil, the cradle of dependency ideas, and Chile, where *dependentistas* coalesced and their ideas flourished, succumbed to military regimes that made a devastating assault on the lives of intellectuals and intellectual life, many Latin American intellectuals, including some *cepalinos, dependentistas,* and their allies, reorganized themselves, their networks, and their ideas during the dictatorship and upon the return of democracy at the end of the twentieth century. The intellectual trajectories of Enzo Faletto and Fernando Henrique Cardoso, the authors of *Dependency and Development in Latin America,* and of Maria Conceição Tavares, perhaps the only female *cepalina* and one of the few female economists of the development era, illustrate the conflicting ways through which *cepalino* and *dependentista* ideas were reconfigured in paradoxical and unforeseen ways and ushered in a world radically distinct from which they emerged.

Faletto exemplifies one of the multiple afterlives of dependency theory after the end of its golden years. In the late 1960s, when *dependentistas* converged in Santiago, giving rise to the dependency movement that would soon after sweep the world, Faletto had already abandoned dependency theory. Referring to the *dependentistas* as "competitors" and "charmers of the dependency snake," Faletto disengaged from the acrimonious academic debates about the Marxist character of the theory and the heated controversies about the political options appropriate to *dependentistas.* Very early on, the dependency movement had illustrated for Faletto the perils of radicalization, a lesson that would be further consolidated as he and many other intellectuals searched for ways out of authoritarianism and into democracy. In the late 1970s and early 1980s, Faletto and others joined or created research centers that gradually became spaces for political debate, headquarters of banned and persecuted political parties, and strongholds for the opposition against the military regime. Later, these centers and their leaders would facilitate the transition to democracy.[38]

Faletto belonged to the *Centro de Estudios Económicos y Sociales Vector,* a research center that brought together intellectuals previously associated with Allende's Socialist Party and whose leader was Ricardo Lagos, a Duke University-trained economist, longtime faculty member of the *Universidad de Chile,* colleague and friend of Cardoso, and future president of the country. For Lagos, president of Chile from 1998 to 2004, Faletto's ideas were fundamental. Inspired by Faletto, Lagos defended a definition of socialism that was less utopian and more pragmatic, less class and more social movement based, and more consensual and less sectarian.[39] Through the process of renovation in ideology and praxis under authoritarianism, the intellectual and the political left, many of which were *dependentistas* or their allies, carved a space for themselves in the postauthoritarian era and transformed the meaning of socialism from the nationalization of the means of production to the easing of the social burden of the neoliberal model.

In the 1990s, when Faletto's political engagement had come to an end, Cardoso's was at its peak. For Cardoso, Brazil was the locus of dependency theory and its transformation into a *dependent and developed* nation in the global economy, the object of his intellectual interest and political project. This preoccupation with Brazil led Cardoso to formulate an intellectual arsenal to understand the military regime's "associated dependent development."[40] An institution and network builder, Cardoso established a research center, *Centro Brasileiro de Análise e Planejamento* (CEBRAP), that not only became the rallying point for the intellectual left but also the intellectual arm of the *Movimento Democrático Brasileiro* (MDB), the party of the opposition against the dictatorship by the mid-1970s.[41] Cardoso's intellectual prestige as a *dependentista,* his personal and family connections with progressive industrialists, publishers, and politicians, and his leading role in the opposition to the military regime facilitated his political ascent from alternate senator in the late 1970s to two-term president of the country in the mid-1990s.

Cardoso's ascent to power and his government, however, did not represent the triumph of dependency theory that many *dependentistas* and their allies in the intellectual left would have expected. He won the presidency based on the success of a monetary stabilization plan, not a development project, and in coalition with some forces of the right and against the radical forces of the left. As president, he championed Brazil's deeper and broader integration into the world economy through what he called "sovereign globalization," and implemented so-called market-oriented reforms— elimination of state monopolies, privatization of state-owned companies, liberalization of trade and finance, and equal treatment for national and foreign-owned firms—to "dismantle the Era Vargas," the symbol of mid-century state-led developmentalism in the search of economic autonomy.[42] Once a *dependentista* and prestigious leader of the Brazilian and the Latin American intellectual left, President Cardoso became the face of neoliberalism and the political right.

For Tavares, like many *cepalinos* and *dependentistas,* Cardoso's plan represented the dismantlement of the world that *cepalinos* had created. "Considering that confronting globalization is impossible, Cardoso, like other statesmen of the left, has opted to kneel before it, hoping Brazil occupies a place with the victors rather than the vanquished," Tavares, *cepalina,* House representative, and member of the left-wing Workers' Party, declared when he took office.[43] In the 1990s, Tavares found herself confronting a former

FIGURE E.3   Fernando Henrique Cardoso and Maria Conceição Tavares (*left and right in the background, respectively*) in Belo Horizonte, 1961. Friends and colleagues in the early 1960s and 1970s, they became political adversaries in the mid-1990s. (Acervo Presidente Fernando Henrique Cardoso.)

colleague, a fellow early critic of the *cepalino* project and of midcentury developmentalism, and a former partner in the struggle against both the military regime's boasted "economic miracle" and the opposition's myth of "stagnationism"[44] (figure E.3).

A Portuguese-immigrant and a mathematician, Tavares was retrained as an economist and *cepalina* in Brazil in the late 1950s and early 1960s and has since then helped cement the influence of *cepalinos* in the country. Not only did she deploy *cepalino* ideas to contest authoritarianism but she transformed old academic institutions and created new ones that bear the *cepalino* imprint to this day, including the *Universidade Estadual de Campinas* and the *Universidade do Estado do Rio de Janeiro*. She trained cohorts and cohorts of Brazilian and Latin American students on *cepalino* developmentalism from the late 1960s until her retirement from academia in 1993.[45] In the 1980s Tavares transformed from what she called a "militant academic" into a political militant. Tavares was catapulted to the public stage when she passionately defended on national television a *cepalino*-inspired, nonorthodox monetary stabilization plan as a "political vindication for the economic profession that had been reviled by technocratic abuse."[46] In the 1990s Tavares was elected to Congress in representation of the left-wing Workers' Party. As Congresswoman, Tavares, in the name of *cepalino*-inspired developmentalism, condemned the "denationalization" of the economy and the "destructuring of the productive forces" of the Cardoso reforms. Perhaps unwillingly, Tavares perpetuated the narrative that *cepalino* detractors had begun by narrowing the *cepalino* legacy to statism and industrialization. In strawman representations created by their opponents, *cepalinos* were represented as nationalists and inward-looking, especially in opposition to neoliberal cosmopolitans and globalizers. They were also seen as supporting macroeconomic populists in opposition to fiscally conscientious, neoliberal state managers.[47] Nonetheless, her own presence in Congress and her long and influential career represented a response to those forces who considered *cepalinos* old-fashioned and passé. In important ways, she has kept their project alive to this day.

In the "neoliberal" democracies that emerged after decades of authoritarianism, Faletto, Tavares, and especially Cardoso became more politically influential than perhaps ever before. As advisors and policymakers, presidents or senators, these *cepalinos* and *dependentistas,* like many intellectuals of their generation, crafted contemporary Chilean and Brazilian economies and polities. Some became advocates of a twenty-first–century approach to state-led developmentalism, while others became its fierce critics. Some became champions of a "New Left," while others became its fierce opponents. Despite their conflicting trajectories, they all drew their intellectual authority and political leadership from a shared experience as pioneer critics of the midcentury development project in the 1960s and as sharp and vocal critics of authoritarian regimes and their "economic miracles" in the 1970s. Repression and exile as well as their academic militancy made them more influential abroad, which, in turn, gave them additional protection and respect at home. It was their pedigree and legitimacy as *cepalinos* and *dependentistas* that gave these intellectuals the institutional, intellectual, and personal tools to bring about a new era in Latin America. Or in the words of Jorge Castañeda, "their ability to get to power stem[med] from the fact of their own power," which in turn emerged from the enduring legacy of the midcentury project.[48]

The conflicting trajectories of Faletto, Cardoso, and Tavares, in the aftermath of dependency theory, reaffirm the arguments this book has made and at the same time raise new questions. First, they reveal the diversity of the political projects coexisting under the often-misleading rubric of "dependency theory." For these intellectuals as well as for many *cepalinos* and *dependentistas,* the concept and vocabulary of center and periphery and many other terms encompassed in the term "dependency theory" offered a point of departure that could be taken in many and at times contradictory directions. The terms could refer to very concrete phenomena such as the long-term decline in the international terms of trade or to broader historical process like colonialism and imperialism, leading its champions to different conclusions and political choices. This book recovers that diversity and points to the malleability of the terms as one of the major explanations for the widespread influence of dependency theory as well as for its deficiencies and failures.[48] It is often forgotten that *dependentistas* themselves drew different lessons regarding the political implications of dependency theory, both then as well as at the turn of the twenty-first century.

Second, through the afterlives of these *dependentistas* and *cepalinos,* the book returns to Chile and Brazil, the sites of the rise and fall of the *cepalino* project, as a means to demystify or, better defetishize, the global turn in the recent scholarship.[49] Commendably, recent scholarship on international and global history has gone to great lengths to center those who were previously at the margins of global history and to situate seemingly national processes into global contexts. Following that impulse, this book has situated the birth of the *cepalino* project within the context of the construction of postwar global economic order. It has shown the influence of *cepalinos* on the institutions of international governance but has done so through very local and national debates, in an effort to show the world Latin America created. And yet, despite the undeniable global influence of *cepalinos* and *dependentistas,* many of the figures in this book deployed their political capital primarily within Latin America. As this book shows, it was through the transformation of the region that they aspired to transform the world. It was through their pens, speeches, and rallies that Latin America created a world that in turn became a global patrimony, hence the twofold meaning of the title.

But the "global"—the transformation of the world economy and the shaping of international governance—was not the end-all and be-all for *cepalinos* and *dependentistas,* nor the justification for this book. Neither Faletto, Cardoso, nor Tavares was drawn to the internationalism that gave rise to the *cepalino* project in the first place and that attracted many of the Third World advocates inspired by dependency theory in the late 1970s. Instead, they shifted their intellectual gaze and political energy to the national level. It was then, arguably, that *dependentistas* and *cepalinos* obtained their greatest influence. Together and in conflict with each other, Cardoso, Tavares, and other Brazilian intellectuals who came of political age under authoritarianism, contributed to keeping "dependency theory," again writ large, alive in Latin America in the era of neoliberal democracies, in which the last opportunity to tame the global forces of capitalism through South-South cooperation had passed and grand narratives were doomed to be relics of the past after the so-called "end of history." It was in observing and contrasting, interpreting, and intervening in national and regional projects, especially those of Chile and Brazil, that Latin America shaped the project of *cepalinos* and *cepalinos* shaped midcentury Latin America. They were and remained critical of those "catastrophists" who saw the destiny of Latin America as the "product of forces outside its control."[50] For the *cepalino* collective and a generation of intellectuals who spoke in terms of dependency, world system, and center and periphery, they were remarkably committed to local and national struggles.

Third, Cardoso's political trajectory after the golden years of dependency theory opens up a research agenda to explain the neoliberal turn in Brazil and Latin America more broadly. Such an agenda must move beyond the narratives of betrayal of principles, political opportunism, or the "original sin" of a less radical version of dependency theory that has characterized the story of Cardoso and others who lived and later embodied the transformation of the left after the disenchantment with Cuba first, and the end of real socialism, later.[51] The first step of that agenda was to revisit the origins, meaning, and scope of dependency theory, a task undertaken in this book. However, that agenda also entails a reconsideration of neoliberalism as well as of the role of the intellectual left in making or facilitating the project of the political right. Since, as Amy Offner has argued, the new era was carved with the tools of the old, the story of Cardoso and others may help explain the rise of neoliberalism beyond narratives that emphasize the power of the Washington consensus and the US-based institutions. We need space for accounts of agents who, like Cardoso, traveled between and bridged two seemingly contrasting eras, bridging a "Latin American" consensus for neoliberalism and envisioning a role for Latin American agents beyond either duplicity or complicity.[52]

The end of the midcentury development projects is usually attributed to the triumph of unfettered capitalism epitomized in the Washington consensus and the neoliberal turn of the late twentieth century.[53] In Latin America, the infamous Chicago Boys and their military sponsors are the main example of that narrative. They justified their project as an effort to redress "half a century of economic errors" of a developmentalism that *cepalinos* had become the primary reference of.[54] However, as this book shows, the public offensive against the *cepalino* project began with *dependentistas* and their denunciation that *cepalino*-endorsed state-led development perpetuated, rather than abolished, the periphery's dependence on global markets and forces. A private or in-house offensive against the *ce-palino* project arose in parallel to those of *dependentistas* penned by no other than Tavares herself.[55] Although at times it thrived on dissent, the *cepalino* project also eroded through the conflicts and internal divisions among the core group as its members clashed ideologically and opted for different political paths for the transformation of Latin America. Not only did the fall of the *cepalino* project involve more than the neoliberal back-lash but, as the stories of Tavares, Cardoso, and Faletto showed, it was not completely wiped out with the neoliberal turn.

The strength and endurance of the backlash against *cepalinos* from the left and the right attest to the power of the incumbents and reinforce one of the main arguments of the book. When it comes to the global under-standing of the power of economic ideas in Latin America, the Chicago Boys take center stage as the intellectual tour de force that took over the region. Yet, the raison d'être of the Chicago Boys was to knock the *cepal-inos* out of what had become an almost hegemonic position in Latin Amer-ica, especially in Chile and southern South America. It is therefore no coincidence that Chile was the cradle of the dependency movement and of neoliberal offensive.[56] These two projects that usually dominate our view of Latin American economics emerged as a reaction to a form of *cepalino* hegemony in Latin America.

The *cepalino* hegemony grew gradually over the years but had become notorious by the 1960s. The two projects that usually dominate our view of Latin American economics, Chicago Boys' neoliberalism and dependency theory, emerged as a reaction to a form of *cepalino* hegemony in Latin America. *Cepalino* regional surveys and in-country studies had become a crucial reference for policymakers and academics. The problem of the falling terms of international trade between centers and peripheries defined the scope and limits of development in Latin America and the policy response to the trifecta of trade, aid, and finance. Ideologically opposed projects such as the Cuban Revolution and the US-led Alliance for Progress adopted, al-beit temporarily, the development diagnosis and vocabulary of *cepalinos*. It was in the early 1960s that research projects in the North and South emerged to "test" some of the *cepalino* ideas about the trade-off between inflation and development. It was also in the early 1960s that world-class experts from the main universities of the North Atlantic gathered to un-derstand the debate between "structuralists" and "monetarists" that was shaping economic policymaking in Chile and Brazil. It was in that context that the staff of the International Monetary Fund (IMF), often portrayed as the dominant institution, was forced to recognize that they were losing the battle of ideas to *cepalinos*. And it was at the peak of *cepalino* influence, that *dependentistas* and the Chicago Boys enlisted the weapons against what they saw as the established orthodoxy. Within a decade, *cepalinos* had become an obligatory point of passage for a myriad of actors across the region, creating a world for and from Latin America.

But hegemony certainly did not mean consensus. Even among the *cepalinos,* there were major fractures that at times moved the project forward and others tore it apart. In fact, what is commonly referred to as "dependency theory" often conflates the projects of many, including those *cepalinos* and *dependentistas,* who were often at odds with each other, separated by an intellectual generational gap, and engaged in opposing political projects. While for *cepalinos* development was not only desirable but possible, for some *dependentistas* development was altogether impossible in a world capitalist system. Some *cepalinos* regarded international cooperation between center and peripheries as, alongside planning and state-led industrialization, the path to autonomy; for some *dependentistas,* dependency was embedded in a system that nonetheless did not preclude development. While some *cepalinos* and some *dependentistas* privileged internationalism as a strategy for development and autonomy, other *cepalinos* and *dependentistas* concentrated their cultural, social, and political capital at the national level. In both Chile and Brazil, *cepalinos* fostered allies and opponents that nonetheless reinforced their privileged position in the regional landscape. However, since the influence of *cepalinos* also varied across the continental-size Latin America, more research is needed in particular countries beyond the core ones studied in this book to understand the weight of *cepalinos* in the scale of contending political forces and the particular ways in which their ideas were received, deployed, and reimagined.

Dependency theory, the professed counterpart to the global North's modernization theory, is a less homogenous project than has often been portrayed. Our understanding of twentieth-century internationalism and development has moved away from the overbearing worldwide dominance of modernization theory foregrounded by the first wave of scholarship.[57] A much more diverse and contentious world has emerged in its stead. This book has opened up "dependency theory," a crucial worldmaking project of the global South, and in so doing, inaugurates new avenues to understand not just where the South converges—in initiatives like the NIEO, for instance—but also where it diverges. Part of that answer may lay in what *cepalinos* found as they undertook the creation of the regional market: the relentless gap between center and peripheries *within* Latin America and the global South itself. As dependency theory, a term that often encompasses world system theorists, *cepalinos, dependentistas,* and potentially many others, went global, the meanings and interpretations varied locally. Those different local or regional meanings and interpretations constitute a great avenue for further research on not just parallels but also conflicts between Asia, Africa, and Latin America.

The world that *cepalinos* and *dependentistas* created emerged from a particular global conjuncture that "Latin Americanized," for lack of a better word, wider debates. Like others around the postcolonial world, the development project of *cepalinos* was not "derivative" of Northern projects nor "imposed from outside."[58] In the early postwar years, different international organizations and economists were wrestling with the international terms of trade. When Latin Americans institutionalized their long-term concern with the "trade and development" question through the creation of the UN CEPAL and Prebisch's ideas about center and periphery found a home in the institution, the international terms of trade thesis came to represent the "Latin American" vision of development. In so doing, they inaugurated the United Nations as a site of the global South's economic agenda. Similarly, as "dependency theory" became "consumed" in the United States and the rest of the world and "mesmerized" observers of Latin America and other world regions, Cardoso and other Latin American intellectuals reclaimed theirs and thus the region's "authorship" against foreign interpreters and intruders, who they claimed deviated from the local tradition.[59] Thus, the two globally bound projects of *cepalinos* and *dependentistas* were, as this book shows, produced and refabricated as homegrown, Latin American products.

The coordinates of the world that *cepalinos* created in Latin America were global and therefore found worldwide resonance even as *cepalinos* themselves crafted and brought their project into action locally. *Cepalinos* defined their understanding of development in terms of the transformation of the global economy and the structural and functional relation between center and periphery. From the early postwar years, when development economics crafted the notion of the "national economy" as a tool of nation-state building, *cepalinos* were deploying their tools to conceptualize a "global economy" whose transformation began with the development of Latin America.[60] Instead of the "savings gap" that permeated the rhetoric of World Bankers as well as postcolonial state-builders, *cepalinos* spoke of a "foreign exchange gap" that bound the national, regional, and global economies together and generated trade-offs between economic development and monetary stability. Like some anticolonial worldmakers but unlike some of the *dependentistas* that inspired them, *cepalinos* believed in the power of internationalism in trade and aid cooperation to foster national autonomy when accompanied by state-led national industrialization.[61] It was the language of "falling international terms of trade," "foreign exchange gap" and "trade gap" that years later became foundational for the economic definition of Third Worldism as well as to the justification for the transformation of the rules of international governance, a world that *cepalinos* and Latin America also inaugurated. It was the *cepalino* project and terminology of center and periphery that gave rise to the counter-project of *dependentistas* and its enduring intellectual legacies. But perhaps the powerful *cepalino* coordinates—those that generated academic research agendas worldwide, gave rise to Marxist and liberal internationalist Third World projects, guided and inspired Latin American and policymakers from Kubitschek to Allende, and politically mobilized *cepalinos* and *dependentistas* in mid-twentieth century Latin America and beyond—transformed the world but not as *cepalinos* imagined.

The transformation of Chile and Brazil in the last thirty years, the two countries that *cepalinos* and *dependentistas* were most deeply involved with and whose trajectories most shaped their collective intellectual project, might surprise *cepalinos*. For mid-twentieth–century development economists concerned with Latin America's ancillary position in the global economy, the leap of Brazil to become the seventh largest world economy and the entrance of Brazil and Chile into the global rich men's clubs like the G-20 or the OECD would have perhaps been unimaginable. Initially concerned with growth and development more than equity, for *cepalinos,* the recent demands for better education and better health of a precarious middle class in Chile may seem as "First-World problems" compared to the midcentury battle to raise levels of income and increase access to education and health for the population.[62] It would not have crossed their minds that Brazil's BNDE, the national development bank with which *cepalinos* partnered in the 1950s and with which they trained myriad of civil servants and economists, would expand to surpass the World Bank and become second only to China's. Chile's enduring combination of growth and low inflation would have shocked *cepalinos* concerned with the country's long-term combination of sluggish growth and accelerated inflation and the negative consequences for development of aggressively arresting inflation. The *cepalino* effort to transform Brazil's, Chile's, and Latin America's position in the global economy and, by so doing, transform the global economy appeared to materialize.

Yet, Brazil and Chile were also far from making the world that *cepalinos* imagined. While the Brazilian path to development carried *cepalino* ideas to some extremes with both its high levels of protectionism and openness to foreign investment, Chile's growth path was a complete reversal of the *cepalino* development project. Although Brazil and Chile reduced their long-term dependency on US markets and capital and increased intraregional trade, they increased dependence on China. Instead of the industrial powerhouses that *cepalinos* envisioned, Brazil and Chile became top agricultural producers, whose twenty-first–century growth was driven by the export of agricultural commodities and the expansion of gigantic agrobusinesses, on whose behalf Brazil deployed North-South rhetoric and took leadership roles in international governance.[63] The Brazilian development bank, the foremost symbol of the midcentury development project and the source of the expansion of national industrial bourgeoisie, ended up benefiting large multinational corporations later involved in regionwide scandals of corruption and misappropriation of public funds. In Brazil, the social provisions and benefits designed to reduce poverty and inequality promoted the expansion of the financial system to the benefit of the private banking system. In Chile, the Socialists' efforts to redress the military regime's social debt have not met expectations.[64] The twenty-first-century transformation of Brazil, Chile, and some parts of Latin America has yet to be reckoned with as more than a defeat of the midcentury development project, especially in light of the world *cepalinos* envisioned.

There's some form of nostalgia in our current search for different world orders, for different paths to development, and for different strategies to fight the economic, political, racial, and so many other inequalities that continue to define our world. That nostalgia stands in stark contrast to the optimism, the sense of urgency, and almost zealousness that characterized the midcentury *cepalinos, dependentistas,* and many other world makers. Some might say that we should return to that midcentury world of utopias of the "impossible" in an effort to reject the pragmatism and the "economies of the possible" that we seem to be living in.[65] Although *cepalinos* and *dependentistas* put the problem of global inequality front and center and that problem still is shaping the destiny of millions around the world, the world *cepalinos* envisioned was also in some ways limited. They did not foresee something that *dependentistas* captured. Through a historical process that preceded and outlived *cepalinos* and *dependentistas,* dependency theory captured an incipient transformation in the global economy in which the relation between centers and peripheries was effectively transformed as the global periphery in Asia and Latin America industrialized and developed. The transformation of global power balances, however, did not result in the welfare and equality *within* the periphery and has left Latin America and the rest of the periphery with the greater challenge to address the internal structures of power and the economic inequalities within.

Archives

Acervo Presidente Fernando Henrique Cardoso (FHC), Instituto Fernando Henrique Cardoso, São Paulo, Brazil

Archivo Central, Universidad de Chile, Santiago, Chile

Archivo de la Administración, Santiago, Chile

Archivo de Trabajo Dr. Raúl Prebisch, CEPAL, Santiago, Chile

Archivo General Histórico, Ministerio de Relaciones Exteriores, Santiago, Chile

Archivo Histórico de El Colegio de México, Ciudad de México, México

Archivo Instituto the Planeación Económica y Social (ILPES), CEPAL, Santiago, Chile

Arquivo Itamaraty, Rio de Janeiro and Brasilia, Brazil

Arquivo Nacional, Rio de Janeiro, Brazil

Archivo Secretaría de Relaciones Exteriores, Ciudad de México, México

Biblioteca Celso Furtado, Instituto Celso Furtado de Políticas para o Desenvolvimento, Rio de Janeiro, Brazil

Biblioteca Hernán Santa Cruz, CEPAL, Santiago, Chile

Biblioteca Luis Angel Arango, Colecciones Especiales, Bogotá, Colombia

Biblioteca Nacional, Rio de Janeiro, Brazil

Biblioteca Nacional, Santiago, Chile

Centro de Pesquisa e Documentação de História Contemporânea do Brasil (CPDOC), Fundação Getúlio Vargas (FGV), Rio de Janeiro, Brazil

Departmento da Ordem Política e Social (DOPS), Rio de Janeiro and São Paulo, Brazil

Harvard University, Houghton Library, Cambridge, MA

International Institute of Social History (IISH), Amsterdam, Netherlands

International Monetary Fund (IMF) Archive, Washington, DC

Repositorio Digital Comisión Económica para América Latina (CEPAL)

Rockefeller Archive Center (RAC), Sleepy Hollow, NY

United Nations Archive, Geneva, Switzerland

United Nations Educational, Scientific, and Cultural Organization (UNESCO) Archive, Paris, France

University of California, Berkeley (UC-B), University Archives, Bancroft Library, Berkeley, CA

University of California, Riverside (UC-R), Special Collections and University Archives, Riverside, CA

University of North Carolina, Southern Historical Collection (SHC), Wilson Special Collections Library, Chapel Hill, NC

World Bank Archives, Washington, DC

York University, Clara Thomas Special Collections and Archive, Toronto, Canada

Abbreviations

BNDE	*Banco Nacional de Desenvolvimento Económico*
CEBRAP	*Centro Brasileiro de Análise e Planejamento*
CEPAL	*Comisión Económica para América Latina*
CESIT	*Centro de Sociologia Industrial e do Trabalho*
CESO	*Centro de Estudios Socio Económicos, Universidad de Chile*
CMBEU	*Comissão Mista Brasil-Estados Unidos*
CUT	*Central Única de Trabajadores de Chile*
ECOSOC	United Nations Economic and Social Council
EPU	European Payments Union
FGV	*Fundação Getúlio Vargas*
FLACSO	*Facultad Latinoamericana de Ciencias Sociales*
IADB	Inter-American Development Bank
IBRD	International Bank for Reconstruction and Development
ILPES	*Instituto Latinoamericano de Planeación Económica y Social*
IMF	International Monetary Fund
INRA	Cuban National Institute of Agrarian Reform
ITO	International Trade Organization
LAFTA	Latin American Free Trade Association
LSE	London School of Economics
MDB	*Movimento Democrático Brasileiro*
MIR	*Movimiento de Izquierda Revolucionaria*
OAS	Organization of American States
PEM	*Plano de Estabilização Monetaria*
POLOP	*Política Operaria*
SUDENE	*Superintendência do Desenvolvimento do Nordeste*
TVA	Tennessee Valley Authority
UNAM	*Universidad Nacional Autónoma de México*
UNCTAD	United Nations Commission for Trade and Development
USP	*Universidade de São Paulo*

Notes

Introduction

1. The term Caribbean was added to the title of the organization in 1984. For the period under consideration, it was the Economic Commission for Latin America.

2. On Prebisch and the world: Christopher Dietrich, *Oil Revolution: Sovereign Rights and the Economic Culture of Decolonization, 1945 to 1979* (Cambridge: Cambridge University Press, 2017); Johanna Bockman, "Socialist Globalization against Capitalist Neocolonialism: The Economic Ideas behind the New International Economic Order," *Humanity* 6, no. 1 (2015): 109–28; Giuliano Garavini, *After Empires: European Integration, Decolonization, and the Challenge from the Global South, 1957–1986* (Oxford: Oxford University Press, 2012).

3. Mark Mazower, *Governing the World: The History of an Idea, 1815 to the Present* (New York: The Penguin Press, 2012), 280.

4. Nils Gilman, *Mandarins of the Future: Modernization Theory in Cold War America* (Baltimore: John Hopkins University Press, 2004); Akira Iriya, *Global Community: The Role of International Organizations in the Making of the Contemporary World* (Los Angeles and Berkeley: University of California Press, 2002), 81–82; Michael Latham, *Modernization as Ideology: American Social Science and Nation-Building in the Kennedy Era* (Chapel Hill and London: University of North Carolina Press, 2000).

5. Joseph Hodge, "Writing the History of Development: Part 2 (Longer, Deeper, Wider)," *Humanity* 7, no. 1 (2016): 148, 157.

6. Patricia Clavin and Glenda Sluga, eds., *Internationalisms: A Twentieth-Century History* (Cambridge: Cambridge University Press, 2017); Ann Sayward, *The United Nations in International History* (London: Bloomsbury, 2014); Marc Frey, Sönke Kunkel, and Corinna R. Unger, eds. *International*

Organizations and Development, 1945–1990 (London: Palgrave MacMillan, 2015).

7. Alan McPherson and Yannick Wehrli, eds., *Beyond Geopolitics: New Histories of Latin America at the League of Nations* (Albuquerque: University of New Mexico Press, 2015), 4.

8. Eric Helleiner, *Forgotten Foundations of Bretton Woods: International Development and the Making of the Postwar Order* (Ithaca and London: Cornell University Press, 2014), Ch. 2.

9. John Toye and Richard Toye, *The UN and Global Political Economy* (Bloomington: Indiana University Press, 2004), 38–42.

10. On UN as a North-Atlantic products, see Mark Mazower, *Governing the World: The History of an Idea, 1815 to the Present* (New York: The Penguin Press, 2012).

11. On global categories: Samuel Moyn and Andrew Sartori, *Global Intellectual History* (New York: Columbia University Press, 2013), 17–18. For other world-making projects, see Adom Getachew, *Worldmaking after Empire: The Rise and Fall of Self-Determination* (Princeton: Princeton University Press, 2019).

12. Edgar Dosman, *The Life and Times of Raúl Prebisch* (Montreal: McGill-Queen's University Press, 2008).

13. Aníbal Pinto, "Si la CEPAL pudiera hablar," *Ahora*, no. 4, May 11, 1971, 63.

14. Joseph Love, *Crafting the Third World: Theorizing Underdevelopment in Rumania and Brazil* (Stanford: Stanford University Press, 1996), 175.

15. Love, *Crafting the Third World*, 126–27, 129.

16. For this categorization, see Albert Hirschman. "The Political Economy of Import-Substituting Industrialization in Latin America," *Quarterly Journal of Economics* 75, no. 1 (1968).

17. Original *cepalino* interpretations, see Aníbal Pinto, *Chile, un caso de desarrollo frustrado* (Santiago: Editorial Universitaria, 1959) and Celso Furtado, *The Economic Growth of Brazil: A Survey from Colonial to Modern Times* (Berkeley: University of California Press, 1963), 1959. New narratives inspired by *cepalinos* and *dependentistas,* see Steven Topik, Carlos Marichal, and Frank Zephyr, *From Silver to Cocaine: Latin American Commodity Chains and the Building of World Economy, 1500–2000* (Durham: Duke University Press, 2006).

18. On early industrialization, see Stephen Haber, *Industry and Underdevelopment: The Industrialization of Mexico, 1890–1940* (Stanford: Stanford University Press, 1989) and Warren Dean, *Industrialization in São Paulo, 1880–1945* (Austin: University of Texas, 1973).

19. Joseph Love, "Economic Ideas and Ideologies in Latin America since 1930," in *The Cambridge History of Latin America,* ed. Leslie Bethell (Cambridge: Cambridge University Press, 1995), 395.

20. See Enrique Cárdenas, José Antonio Ocampo, and Rosemary Thorp, eds., *An Economic History of Twentieth Century Latin America: Industrialization and the State in Latin America: The Postwar Years* (Houndmills, Basingstoke, England: Palgrave Macmillan, 2000), 12; Luis Bértola and José Antonio Ocampo, *The Economic Development of Latin America since Independence* (Oxford: Oxford University Press, 2012).

21. Garavini, *After Empires,* 12.

22. Jeffrey Taffet, *Foreign Aid as Foreign Policy: The Alliance for Progress in Latin America* (Routledge: New York and London, 2007); Burton Kaufman, *Trade and Aid: Eisenhower's Foreign Economic Policy, 1953–1961* (Baltimore: John Hopkins University Press, 1982).

23. Arturo Escobar, *Encountering Development: The Making and Unmaking of the Third World* (Princeton: Princeton University Press, 1995).

24. David Engerman, *The Price of Aid: The Economic Cold War in India* (Cambridge: Harvard University Press, 2018).

25. On IMF in Latin America: Claudia Kedar, *The International Monetary Fund and Latin America: The Argentine Puzzle in Context* (Philadelphia: Temple University Press, 2013). Sarah Babb, "Embeddedness, Inflation, and International Regimes: The IMF in the Early Postwar Period," *American Journal of Sociology* 113, no. 1 (2007): 128–64; Jon Kofas, *Sword of Damocles: The IMF, the World Bank and US Foreign Policy in Colombia and Chile, 1950–70* (Westport and London: Praeger, 2002); Manuel Pastor, *The International Monetary Fund and Latin America: Economic Stabilization and Class Conflict* (Boulder, CO: Westview Press, 1987).

26. Inderjeet Parmar, *Foundations of the American Century: The Ford, Carnegie, and Rockefeller Foundations in the Rise of American Power* (New York: Columbia University Press, 2015).

27. For a review of the literature, see David Engerman and Corinna Unger, "Toward a Global History of Modernization," *Diplomatic History* 33, no. 3 (2009): 375–38 and Joseph Hodge, "Writing the History of Development: The First Wave," *Humanity* 6, no. 3 (2016): 429–63; Joseph Hodge, "Writing the History of Development: Part 2 (Longer, Deeper, Wider)," *Humanity* 7, no. 1 (2016): 125–73. On the effort to create a global history of development, see Stephen Macekura and Erez Manela, eds., *The Development Century: A Global History* (Cambridge: Cambridge University Press, 2018).

28. See David Eckbladh, *The Great American Mission: Modernization and the Construction of the American World Order* (Princeton: Princeton University Press, 2010); Nick Cullather, *The Hungry World: America's Cold War Battle against Poverty in Asia* (Cambridge: Harvard University Press, 2010); David Engerman et al., *Staging Growth: Modernization, Development, and the Global Cold War* (Amherst and Boston: University of Massachusetts Press, 2003); Daniel Immerwahr, *Thinking Small: The United States and Community Development* (Cambridge: Harvard University Press, 2014).

29. Robert Packenham, *The Dependency Movement: Scholarship and Politics in Development Studies* (Cambridge: Harvard University Press, 1992).

30. Celso Furtado, *La fantasía organizada* (Bogotá: Tercer Mundo Editores, 1989), 90.

31. Thomas Miller Klubock, *Contested Communities: Class, Gender and Politics in Chile's El Teniente Copper Mine, 1904–1951* (Durham and London: Duke University Press, 1998).

32. Joel Wolfe, *Autos and Progress: The Brazilian Search for Modernity* (Oxford: Oxford University Press, 2010); Rafael Ioris, *Transforming Brazil: A History of National Development in the Postwar Era* (New York: Routledge, 2014);

Robert Kaufman, *The Politics of Land Reform in Chile, 1950–1970: Public Policy, Political Institutions, and Social Change* (Cambridge: Harvard University Press, 1972); Joaquín Fermandois, Jimena Bustos, and María José Schneuer, *Historia política del cobre en Chile* (Santiago: Centro de Estudios Bicentenario, 2009).

33. On transnational Latin American history, especially on Chile and Brazil, see Tanya Harmer, *Allende's Chile and the Inter-American Cold War* (Chapel Hill: University of North Carolina Press, 2011).

34. Lautaro, "Diagnóstico y catastrofismo en el continente." *Panorama Económico*, no. 252 (February–March 1970): 15–19.

35. On nineteenth century ideas of Latin America as a region, see Walter Mignolo, *The Idea of Latin America* (Willston, GB: Wiley-Blackwell, 2009); Michael Gobat, "The Invention of Latin America: A Transnational History of Anti-Imperialism, Democracy, and Race," *American Historical Review* 118, no. 5 (2013): 1345–75; Mauricio Tenorio, *Latin America: The Allure and Power of an Idea* (Chicago: Chicago University Press, 2017). On twentieth century, see Leslie Bethell, "Brazil and 'Latin America,'" *Journal of Latin American Studies* 42, no. 3 (2010): 457–85.

36. Timothy Mitchell, *The Rule of Experts: Egypt, Techno-Politics, Modernity* (Berkeley and Los Angeles: University of California Press, 2002); James Scott, *Seeing Like a State: How Certain Schemes to Improve the Human Condition Have Failed* (New Haven: Yale University Press, 1998).

37. Paul W. Drake, *Money Doctors, Foreign Debts, and Economic Reforms in Latin America, from the 1890s to the Present* (Wilmington, DE: Scholarly Resources, 1994); Emily Rosenberg, *Financial Missionaries to the World: The Politics and Culture of Dollar Diplomacy, 1900–1930* (Durham and London: Duke University Press, 2003).

38. Verónica Montecinos and John Markoff, *Economists in the Americas* (Northampton, MA: Edward Elgar, 2009); Juan Carlos Villamizar, *Pensamiento económico en Colombia: Construcción de un saber, 1948–1970* (Bogotá: Editorial Universidad El Rosario, 2013); Kathryn Sikkink, *Ideas and Institutions: Developmentalism in Brazil and Argentina* (Ithaca: Cornell University Press, 1991); Lourdes Sola, *Idéias econômicas, decisões políticas* (São Paulo Editora USP, 1998); Verónica Montecinos, *Economists, Politics and the State: Chile, 1958–94* (Amsterdam: CEDLA, 1998).

39. See, for instance, Immanuel Wallerstein, "The Unintended Consequences of Cold War Area Studies," in Noam Chomsky et al., eds., *Cold War and the University: Towards an Intellectual History of the Postwar Years* (New York: New Press, 1997). On regionalization: Zachary Lockman, *Field Notes: The Making of Middle Eastern Studies in the United States* (Stanford: Stanford University Press, 2016); Fernanda Beigel, "La Flacso chilena y la regionalización de las ciencias sociales en América Latina," *Revista Mexicana de Sociología* 71, no. 2 (2009): 319–49; A.W. Coats, ed., *The Post-1945 Internationalisation of Economics* (Durham: Duke University Press, 1995).

40. On intellectuals or technocrats, see Nicola Miller, *In the Shadow of the State: Intellectuals and the Quest for National Identity in Twentieth-Century Spanish America* (London: Verso, 1999), 6, 26–27; Claudia Gilman, *Entre la pluma*

y el fusil: Debates y dilemas del escritor revolucionario en América Latina (Buenos Aires: Siglo XXI, 2003); Miguel Centeno and Patricio Silva, eds., *The Politics of Expertise in Latin America* (New York: St. Martin's Press, 1998).

41. See, for instance, Celso Furtado, *La fantasia organizada*, 49; Joseph Kahl, *Modernization, Exploitation, and Dependency in Latin America* (New Brunswick: Transaction Books, 1976), 136.

42. First studies of *cepalinos* are those of followers and disciples who systematized and consolidated concepts spread in regional surveys and institutional reports, as well as in conference proceedings, minutes of meetings, and numerous journal articles. For traditional syntheses: Octavio Rodríguez, *La Teoria del Subdesarrollo de la CEPAL* (México, D.F.: Siglo Veintiuno, 1980); Cristobal Kay, *Latin American Theories of Development and Underdevelopment* (London: Routledge, 1989); CEPAL, *Cincuenta años del Pensamiento de la CEPAL* (Santiago: Fondo de Cultura Económica, 1998). An important exception that this book builds on is Montecinos, *Economists, Politics and the State: Chile, 1958–94* (Amsterdam: CEDLA, 1998). Given the absence of a CEPAL institutional archive, this book recovers the story of *cepalinos* through the use of the archives of other institutions and individuals. For more on the sources for a history of *cepalinos,* see Margarita Fajardo, "The UN Economic Commission for Latin America (CEPAL) and the Region's Postwar Development Project," *Oxford Research Encyclopedia of Latin American History,* June 28, 2021, https://doi.org/10.1093/acrefore/9780199366439.013.976.

1. Latin America and the Postwar Global Order

1. On the Anglo-American plans for postwar economic order, see Benn Steil, *The Battle of Bretton Woods: John Maynard Keynes, Harry Dexter White, and the Making of a New World Order* (Princeton: Princeton University Press, 2013); G. John Ikenberry, *After Victory: Institutions, Strategic Restraint, and the Rebuilding of an Order after Major Wars* (Princeton: Princeton University Press, 2001); Barry Eichengreen, *Globalizing Capital: A History of the International Monetary System* (Princeton: Princeton University Press, 1993); Alfred Eckes, *A Search for Solvency: Bretton Woods and the International Monetary System, 1941-1971* (Austin and London: University of Texas Press, 1975).

2. Eric Helleiner, *Forgotten Foundations of Bretton Woods: International Development and the Making of the Postwar Order* (Ithaca and London: Cornell University Press, 2014), 168–70.

3. Raúl Prebisch, "Observaciones sobre los Planes Monetarios Internacionales." *El Trimestre Económico,* 11, no. 42(2) (1944): 186; Relatorio Octavio Bulhões sobre os Planos Keynes e White e seus debates, 1943, EUG pi BULHÕES, G. 0000.00.00/2, Arquivo Eugênio Gudin, Centro de Pesquisa e Documentação de História Contemporânea do Brasil (CPDOC)—Fundação Getulio Vargas (FGV), Rio de Janeiro, Brazil; Víctor Urquidi, "Los proyectos monetarios de la posguerra." *El Trimestre Económico,* 10, no. 39(3) (1943): 548.

4. Helleiner, *Forgotten Foundations,* 161–63.

5. Harold James, *International Cooperation Since Bretton Woods* (Washington, DC: International Monetary Fund, Oxford University Press, 1996), 27–29,

53–54; Jeffry R. Frieden, *Global Capitalism: Its Fall and Rise in the Twentieth Century* (New York: W.W. Norton, 2006), 256–57; Susan Aaronson, *Trade and the American Dream: A Social History of Postwar Trade Policy* (Lexington: University of Kentucky), 38; G. John Ikenberry, "A World Economy Restored: Expert Consensus and the Anglo-American postwar settlement," *International Organization*, 46, no. 1 (1992): 281–321.

6. Alan Knight, "The Great Depression in Latin America: An overview," in *The Great Depression in Latin America*, ed. Paul Drinot and Alan Knight (Durham: Duke University Press, 2014), 279; Rosemary Thorp, "A Reappraisal of the Origin of Import-Substituting Industrialization, 1930-50," *Journal of Latin American Studies*, 24, (1992): 184. For a classical approach, Carlos Díaz-Alejandro, "Latin America in the 1930s," in *Latin America in the 1930s: The Role of the Periphery in World Crisis*, ed. Rosemary Thorp (Oxford: MacMillan, 1984).

7. Relatorio Octavio Bulhões sobre os Planos Keynes e White e seus debates, 1943, EUG pi BULHÕES, G. 0000.00.00/2, Arquivo Eugênio Gudin, CPDOC, FGV, Rio de Janeiro, Brazil.

8. *Proceedings and Documents of the United Nations Monetary and Financial Conference: Bretton Woods, New Hampshire, July 1-22, 1944*, 743. See also: Javier Márquez, "El Comercio de America en la Guerra," *El Trimestre Económico*, 11, no. 42(2) (1944): 230–55.

9. Urquidi, "Los proyectos monetarios," 541–42.

10. Douglas Irwin, Petros Mavroidis, and Alan Sykes, *The Genesis of the GATT* (Cambridge: Cambridge University Press, 2008), 94.

11. On González Videla and the Popular Front, see David Collier and Ruth Collier, *Shaping the Political Arena: Critical Junctures, the Labor Movement, and Regime Dynamics in Latin America* (Princeton: Princeton University Press, 1991); Paul Drake, *Socialism and Populism in Chile, 1932–1952* (Urbana: University of Illinois Press, 1978); Timothy Scully, *Rethinking the Center: Party-Politics in Twentieth Century Chile* (Stanford: Stanford University Press, 1992).

12. The original is in Spanish. Translations from Spanish and Portuguese are my own, here and thereafter. Gabriel González Videla, *Memorias* (Santiago: Gabriela Mistral, 1975): 409–10.

13. Quoted in Christian Garay, Angel Soto, and Valeska Troncoso, "Política internacional y política doméstica en González Videla, 1946–1952: La sombra de la Guerra Fría," *Cuadernos de Historia*, no. 44 (2016): 92.

14. Hernán Santa Cruz, *Cooperar o perecer: El dilema de la comunidad mundial,* in vol. 1: Los años de creación, 1941–60 (Buenos Aires: Grupo Editor Latinoamericano, 1984): 37–42.

15. Memorandum, January 25, 1947, v. 16, Fondo Organismos Internacionales, Archivo General Histórico, Ministerio de Relaciones Exteriores, Santiago, Chile.

16. Santa Cruz to Minister of Foreign Relations, July 15, 1947, v. 16, Fondo Organismos Internacionales, Archivo General Histórico, Ministerio de Relaciones Exteriores, Santiago, Chile.

17. "Proposed Economic Commission for Latin America," UN ECOSOC Official Records, Fifth Session: July-August 1947, Lake Success: United Nations.

18. "Proposed Economic Commission for Latin America," August 1, 1947, UN ECOSOC Official Records, Fifth Session: July–August 1947, Lake Success: United Nations, 131–38.

19. Informe Asamblea General, November 10, 1947, v. 16, Fondo Organismos Internacionales, Archivo Histórico del Ministerio de Relaciones Exteriores, Santiago, Chile.

20. Jorge Rosselot to Minister of Foreign Affairs, Quito, January 15, 1948, v. 2699, Fondo Histórico, Archivo General Histórico, Ministerio de Relaciones Exteriores, Santiago, Chile.

21. "Proposed Economic Commission for Latin America," 131–32.

22. "Review of Economic Conditions in Latin America," UN ECOSOC Official Records, Sixth Session: February-March 1948, suppl. no. 7. Lake Success: United Nations: 46, 48.

23. ECOSOC Official Records, Sixth Session: February-March 1948, Lake Success: United Nations: 84–85.

24. Report of the ad-hoc committee on the establishment of an economic commission for Latin America, February 9, 1948, E/630.

25. Resolution for the establishment of an economic commission for Latin America, February 25, 1948, E/712/Rev. 1.

26. ECOSOC Official Records, Sixth Session: February-March 1948, Lake Success: United Nations: 85.

27. "Víctor Urquidi," in *The Complete Oral History Transcripts from UN Voices* (New York, NY: United Nations Intellectual History Project, 2007), CD-ROM, 71–72.

28. CEPAL, "Proposals on the Need for an Economic Survey and Report: Note by the Secretariat on Item 6 of the Provisional Agenda," April 28, 1948, E/CN.12/4, https://repositorio.cepal.org/handle/11362/14160.

29. Germán Truco, May 8, 1948, v. 5475, Fondo Ministerio Relaciones Exteriores, Archivo General de la Administración, Santiago, Chile.

30. Albornoz to Barnes, June 18, 1948, and Harold Caustin to David Owen and David Weintraub, June 22, 1948, in "ECLA's First Session," s-0441-0173-10, Economic Commission for Latin America (ECLA), UN Archives, New York, NY.

31. CEPAL, "Proposals on the Need for an Economic Survey and Report," 1.

32. Joao Carlos Muniz to Raul Fernandes, May 17, 1948, 78/4/9, Organismos Internacionais, Arquivo Histórico Itamarary, Rio de Janeiro, Brazil.

33. Eugenio Castillo to Harold Caustin, August 13, 1948, 441-156-09, ECLA, UN Archives, ECLA, UN Archives, New York, NY.

34. Eugenio Castillo to Harold Caustin, November 17, 1948, 0932-012-6, ECLA, UN Archives, New York, NY.

35. "Report on the Fund's observers on the first session of ECLA," Staff Memo no. 260, July 30, 1948, IMF Archive, Washington, DC.

36. Jorge del Canto to G.F. Luthringer, November 16, 1948, and Eugenio Castillo to Camille Gutt, December 21, 1948, B. 35 F. 5, I124, ECLA, Central Files, International Organizations, United Nations, IMF Archive, Washington, DC.

37. Eugenio Castillo to F. Pazos, August 17, 1948, B. 35 F. 5, I124, ECLA, Central Files, International Organizations, United Nations, IMF Archive, Washington, DC.

38. Jorge del Canto to Eugenio Castillo, November 12, 1948, B. 35 F. 5, Central Files, International Organizations, United Nations, IMF Archive, Washington, DC.

39. Eugenio Castillo to Harold Caustin, November 17, 1948, 0932-012-6, ECLA, UN Archives, New York, NY.

40. Wladek Malinowski to Harold Caustin, November 12, 1948, 0932-012-6, ECLA, UN Archives, New York, NY.

41. Fernando Coire to Eugenio Castillo, December 28, 1948, 0932-012-6, Regional Commission Files, UN Archives, New York, NY.

42. Wladek Malinowski to Harold Caustin, November 12, 1948, 0932-012-6, ECLA, UN Archives, New York, NY.

43. Eugenio Castillo to Camille Gutt, December 21, 1948, B. 35 F. 5, Central Files, International Organizations, United Nations, IMF Archive, Washington, DC.

44. Fernando Coire to Harold Caustin. March 14, 1949, 0932-012-6, ECLA, UN Archives, UN Archives, New York, NY.

45. Jorge del Canto to Eugenio Castillo, March 16, 1949, B. 35 F. 7, Central Files, International Organizations, United Nations, IMF Archive, Washington, DC.

46. Fernando Coire to Eugenio Castillo, December 28, 1948, 0932-012-6, Regional Commission Files, UN Archives, New York, NY.

47. Alberto Santa Cruz to Harold Caustin, December 9, 1948, "Note on Latin American Survey," December 15, 1948, 0932-012-6, Regional Commission Files, UN Archives, New York, NY.

48. CEPAL, "Estudio Económico de América Latina, 1948" (Nueva York: Naciones Unidas, 1949), xi, 62, 217. On the 1948 survey, see E. V. K. Fitzgerald, "ECLA and the Formation of Latin American Economic Doctrine," in *Latin America in the 1940s*, ed. David Rock (Berkeley and Los Angeles: University of California Press, 1994), 96–99.

49. CEPAL, "Estudio Económico de América Latina, 1948," x.

50. Edgar Dosman, *The Life and Times of Raúl Prebisch* (Montreal: McGill-Queen's University Press, 2008), 233.

51. Dosman, *Life and Times,* 173–74.

52. Fernando Coire to Raúl Prebisch, April 8, 1949, f. 69, Archivo de Trabajo de Raúl Prebisch, CEPAL, Santiago, Chile.

53. Joseph Love, "Raúl Prebisch and the Origins of the Doctrine of Unequal Exchange," *Latin American Research Review* 15, no. 3 (1980): 46.

54. Love, "Raúl Prebisch and the Origins," 52.

55. "Palabras del Dr. Raúl Prebisch," (1946) Primera Reunión de Técnicos sobre Problemas de Banca Central en el Continente Americano, F. 43, Archivo de Trabajo del Dr. Raúl Prebisch, Archivo de Trabajo de Raúl Prebisch, CEPAL, Santiago, Chile.

56. Dosman, *Life and Times,* 242–43.

57. John Toye and Richard Toye, *The UN and Global Political Economy* (Bloomington: Indiana University Press, 2004), 116–20.

58. United Nations, *Relative Prices of Exports and Imports of Under-Developed Countries* (Lake Success, NY: UN Department of Economic Affairs, 1949), 126.

59. Jacques Polak to Hans W. Singer, August 30, 1948; "Terms of Trade in Latin American Countries," Statistical and Research Division, February 8, 1949, B. 35, F. 8, Central Files, International Organizations, United Nations, IMF Archive, Washington, DC.

60. Raúl Prebisch, *The Economic Development of Latin America and its Principal Problems* (New York: United Nations, 1950), 2.

61. CEPAL, *Economic Survey of Latin America, 1949* (New York: United Nations, 1950), Ch. 2, 6.

62. CEPAL, *Economic Survey of Latin America, 1949* (New York: United Nations, 1950), Ch. 3, 33–40.

63. Prebisch, *Economic Development of Latin America*, 2.

64. Fitzgerald, "ECLA and the Formation of Latin American," 94.

65. Love, "Raul Prebisch and the Origins," 61.

66. CEPAL, Summary Record of the Fourth Meeting, June 4, 1949, E/CN.12/AC.3/SR.4, https://repositorio.cepal.org/handle/11362/13512.

67. Toye and Toye, *UN and Global*, 124–25.

68. Harold Caustin to David Owen, October 12, 1949, 0932-012-7, Regional Commission Files, UN Archive, New York, NY.

69. Raúl Prebisch, "El desarrollo económico de América Latina y sus principales problemas," *El Trimestre Económico* 16, no. 63(3) (1949): 347–431; "O desenvolvimento econômico da América Latina e seus principais problemas," *Revista Brasileira de Economia*, 3, no. 3 (1949): 47–111.

70. Interview of Singer, quoted in Dosman, *Life and Times*, 520.

71. Martínez Cabañas to Harold Caustin, February 7, 1950, s-0441-156-9, ECLA, United Nations Archive, New York, NY.

72. Participants and observers have cultivated the notion that without Prebisch, "CEPAL was not yet CEPAL." Joseph Love, "Economic Ideas and Ideologies in Latin America since 1930," in *The Cambridge History of Latin America*, ed. Leslie Bethell (Cambridge: Cambridge University Press, 1995), 414; Edgar Dosman, "Markets and the State in the Evolution of the Prebisch Manifesto," *CEPAL Review* 75 (2001): 99; Octavio Rodríguez, *El estructuralismo latinoamericano* (México: Siglo XXI, 2006), 43. A nuanced version in Joseph Hodara, "Orígenes de la CEPAL," *Comercio Exterior* 37, no. 5 (1987): 383–91.

73. Albert Fishlow, "Comment," in *Pioneers in Development*, ed. Gerald M. Meier and Dudley Seers (New York: Oxford University Press, 1984), 194.

2. Center and Periphery in Action

1. Ricardo Lagos, *Mi vida: De la infancia a la lucha contra la dictadura* (Santiago: Debate/Penguin Random House, 2014), loc. 1663 of 10791, Kindle.

2. On the "advantages" not the "disadvantages "of "latecomers," see Paul Gootenberg, "Hijos de Dr. Gersehnkron: 'Latecomer' Conceptions in Latin American Economic History," in *The Other Mirror: Grand Theory through the Lens*

of Latin America, ed. Miguel Centeno and Fernando López-Alves (Princeton and Oxford: Princeton University Press, 2001).

3. "Prebisch no Rio," JSP. PI. Diario Caríoca, [1951] 00.00/005, Arquivo Jesus Soares Pereira, Centro de Pesquisa e Documentação de História Contemporânea do Brasil (CPDOC), Fundação Getúlio Vargas (FGV), Rio de Janeiro, Brazil.

4. The Visit of Dr. Raúl Prebisch, Executive Secretary of ECLA to Brazil, August 27, 1951, B. 83, F. II/4/1, Gunnar Myrdal Papers, United Nations Archive, Geneva, Switzerland.

5. Celso Furtado, *La fantasía organizada* (Bogotá: Tercer Mundo Editores, 1989), 44.

6. Furtado, *La fantasía organizada,* 64.

7. Elisa Kluger, "Meritocracia de laços: Gênese e reconfigurações do espaço dos economistas no Brasil," PhD dissertation, Universidade de São Paulo, 2015, 113, 139.

8. Lourdes Sola, *Idéias econômicas, decisões políticas* (São Paulo Editora USP, 1998), 96, 143–58.

9. Kluger, "Meritocracia de laços," 113.

10. Visit of Dr. Raúl Prebisch, Executive Secretary of ECLA to Brazil, August 27, 1951, B. 83, F. II/4/1, Gunnar Myrdal Papers, United Nations Archive, Geneva, Switzerland.

11. See Furtado, *La fantasía organizada,* 121; Jacob Viner, "A Economia do Desenvolvimento," *Revista Brasileira de Econômia* 5, no. 2 (1951); "Raul Prebisch no Rio," JSP pi dc Pereira, J.S. 1951.00.00/103, Arquivo Jesus Soares Pereira, CPDOC, FGV, Rio de Janeiro, Brazil.

12. Werner Baer, "Explorando o mundo real," *Economia Aplicada* 2, no. 4 (1998): 768.

13. On Brazilian industrialization see Celso Furtado, *Formação Econômica do Brasil* (Rio de Janeiro: Editora Fundo de Cultura, 1959); Warren Dean, *Industrialization in São Paulo, 1880–1945* (Austin: University of Texas, 1973); Oliver Dinius, *Brazil's Steel City: Developmentalism, Strategic Power, and Industrial Relations* (Stanford: Stanford University Press, 2011). On Vargas and his legacy, see Angela de C. Gomes, *A invenção do trabalhismo* (Rio de Janeiro: INPRJ, 1988); John French, *The Brazilian Workers' ABC: Class Conflict and Alliances in Modern São Paulo* (Chapel Hill: University of North Carolina Press, 1992); Barbara Weinstein, *For Social Peace in Brazil: Industrialists and the Remaking of the Working Class in São Paulo, 1920–64* (Chapel Hill and London: University of North Carolina Press, 1996); Robert Levine, *Father of the Poor?: Vargas and his Era* (Cambridge: Cambridge University Press, 1998); Antonio Negro, *Linhas de montagem: O industrialismo nacional-desenvolvimentista e a sindicalização dos trabalhadores, 1945–1978* (São Paulo: FABESP-Boitempo Editorial, 2004). On the state and economic policymaking of industrialization, see Octavio Ianni, "Estado y desarrollo económico en el Brasil," *Desarrollo Económico* 3, no. 4 (1964): 551–72; Nathaniel Leff, *Economic Policy-Making and Development in Brazil, 1947–1964* (New York: John Wiley and Sons, 1968); John D. Wirth, *The*

Politics of Brazilian Development, 1930–54 (Stanford: Stanford University Press, 1970); Luciana Leão, "A Double-Edged Sword: the Institutional Foundations of the Brazilian Developmental State, 1930–1985," in *State and Nation-Making in Latin America and Spain: The Rise and Fall of the Developmental State,* ed. Agustín Ferraro and Miguel Centeno (Cambridge and New York: Cambridge University Press, 2019).

14. The original is in Spanish. Gabriel González Videla, *Memorias* (Santiago: Gabriela Mistral, 1975), 409–10.

15. Visit of Dr. Raúl Prebisch, Executive Secretary of ECLA to Brazil, August 27,1951, B. 83, F. II/4/1, Gunnar Myrdal Papers, United Nations Archive, Geneva, Switzerland. See also Furtado, *La fantasía organizada,* 105–106.

16. On the developmental state in Brazil, see Rafael Ioris, *Transforming Brazil: A History of National Development in the Postwar Era* (New York: Routledge, 2014); Kathryn Sikkink, *Ideas and Institutions: Developmentalism in Brazil and Argentina* (Ithaca: Cornell University Press, 1991); Agustín Ferraro and Miguel Centeno, *State and Nation Making in Latin America and Spain: the Rise and Fall of the Developmental State* (Cambridge and New York: Cambridge University Press, 2019).

17. CEPAL, *Annual Report to ECOSOC,* June 15, 1951, E/CN.12/266, https://repositorio.cepal.org/handle/11362/15286; "Plans for Technical Assistance in ECLA," US Delegation to the ECLA conference in Mexico, June 1, 1951, B. 34, F. 8, Edgar Dosman Papers, Clara Thomas Archive and Special Collections, University of York, Toronto, Canada.

18. Kluger, "Meritocracia de laços," 66–68.

19. On development planning in Asia, see David Eckbladh, *The Great American Mission: Modernization and the Construction of the American World Order* (Princeton: Princeton University Press, 2010); David Engerman, "Learning from the East Soviet Experts and India in the Era of Competitive Coexistence," *Comparative Studies of South Asia, Africa and the Middle East* 33, no. 2 (2013): 227–38; Nick Cullather, *The Hungry World: America's Cold War Battle Against Poverty in Asia* (Cambridge: Harvard University Press, 2010). On development and planning in Africa, see Timothy Mitchell, *The Rule of Experts: Egypt, Techno-Politics, Modernity* (Berkeley and Los Angeles: University of California Press, 2002), Priya Lal, *African Socialism in Postcolonial Tanzania : Between the Village and the World* (New York: Cambridge University Press, 2015), and Alden Young, *Transforming Sudan: Decolonization, Economic Development, and State Formation* (Cambridge: Cambridge University Press, 2018) and

20. CEPAL, *Annual Report to ECOSOC,* June 15, 1951, E/CN.12/266, 2–3, https://repositorio.cepal.org/handle/11362/15286.

21. CEPAL, *Problemas teóricos y prácticos del desarrollo económico* (México: Naciones Unidas, 1951), E/CN.12/22, 8.

22. CEPAL, *Problemas teóricos y prácticos del desarrollo económico,* 8.

23. CEPAL, *Resumen del Estudio Preliminar de la Técnica de Programación"* (Santiago: CEPAL, 1953), E/CN.12/292.

24. As part of the Brazilian delegation, Campos writes a report about CEPAL, see also Furtado, *La fantasía organizada*, 97.

25. Maria Conceição Tavares, Hildete Melo, and Ana Caputo, "As origens do Banco Nacional Econômico (BNDE) 1952–1955," *Memórias do Desenvolvimento* 4, no. 4 (2010): 13–44; Anne Hanley et al., "Critiquing the Bank: 60 Years of BNDES in the Academy," *Journal of Latin American Studies*, no. 48 (2016): 823–50.

26. Raúl Prebisch, "Discurso ante el quinto período de sesiones de la CEPAL (10 de Abril de 1953)," *El Trimestre Económico* 20, no. 78(2) (1953): 352.

27. See Raúl Prebisch, "Mística do equlíbrio espontâneo na economia," *Diario de Noticias*, November 15, 1953; Eugênio Gudin, "Mística do Planejamento," *Diario de Noticias*, May 29 and June 2, 6, 9, and 11, 1953; Octavio Gouvea de Bulhões, "Estudos sobre a programação do desenvolvimento econômico," *Jornal de Comercio*, May 24, 1953; Celso Furtado, "A programação do desenvolvimento econômico," *Revista do Conselho Nacional de Economia* 2, no. 19–20 (1953). See also, Alexandre Andrada, Mauro Boianovosky, and Andrea Cabello, "O Clube de Economistas e a Revista Econômica Brasileira: Um Episódio na História do Desenvolvimentismo Nacionalista no Brasil. *Estudios Economicos* 48, no. 4 (2018): 72–56.

28. On the early 1950s balance of payments crisis, see Thomas Skidmore, *Politics in Brazil, 1930–64: An Experiment in Democracy* (Oxford: Oxford University Press, 1967); CEPAL, *Estudio Económico de América Latina 1951–1952*, (Santiago: CEPAL, 1953), 91–92; Pedro Bastos, "Ascencão e crise do projeto nacional-desenvolvimentista de Getúlio Vargas," in *A Era Vargas: Desenvolvimentismo, economia e sociedade*, ed. Pedro Bastos and Paulo Fonseca (São Paulo: Editora UNESP, 2011); Sergio Besserman Vianna, "Duas tentativas de estabilização: 1951–1954, in *A ordem do progresso: Cem anos de política econômica republicana, 1889–1989*, ed. Marcelo de Paiva Abreu (Rio de Janeiro: Ed. Campus, 1989), 114–15.

29. Celso Furtado, *La fantasía organizada*, 147–49; Roberto Campos, *A lanterna na popa: Memórias* (Rio de Janeiro: Top Books, 2004), 42, 194.

30. Lourdes Sola, *Idéias econômicas, decisões políticas* (São Paulo Editora USP, 1998), 118; Campos, *A lanterna na popa*, 192–93, 206–07. See also Furtado, *La fantasía organizada*, 148.

31. Campos, *A lanterna na popa*, 173; Stephen Rabe, *Eisenhower and Latin America: The Foreign Policy of Anticommunism* (Chapel Hill: University of North Carolina Press, 1988).

32. Stenographic notes on the speech of Dr. Roberto de Oliveira Campos at a meeting of the Joint Commission on July 27, 1953, RC d md 1953.07.27, Arquivo Roberto Campos, CPDOC, FGV, Rio de Janeiro, Brazil.

33. Roberto Campos, "A Crise Econômica Brasileira," *Digesto Econômico* (November 1953): 28–44.

34. "Stenographic notes on the speech of Dr. Roberto de Oliveira Campos at a meeting of the Joint Commission."

35. Eugênio Gudin to Eugene R. Black, New York, September 29, 1953, Arquivo Oswaldo Aranha, OA cp 1953.09.28, rolo 26 fot. 842, CPDOC, FGV, Rio de Janeiro, Brazil.

36. Max Paul Friedman, "Fracas in Caracas: Latin American Diplomatic Resistance to United States Intervention in Guatemala," *Diplomacy and Statecraft* 21, no. 4 (2010): 669–89.

37. Carlos Lleras Restrepo, "La Vista del Sr. Holland," *El Tiempo*, October 1, 1954; Carlos Lleras Restrepo, "Conferencia en Río," *El Tiempo*, October 8, 1954.

38. Rabe, *Eisenhower and Latin America*, 70–71.

39. "Holland señala aspectos de política económica de EE.UU. en América Latina," *El Mercurio*, October 7, 1954; Lleras Restrepo, "La Vista del Sr. Holland," *El Tiempo*, October 1, 1954.

40. Declaración hecha por el Dr. Alberto Lleras Camargo, January 22, 1948, ECOSOC, Official Records, Lake Success, NY, UN, Third year: Sixth session.

41. CEPAL, Communication of the Inter-American Economic Social Council, June 10, 1948, E/CN.12/23, https://repositorio.cepal.org/handle/11362/14181.

42. Discussion on the proposed economic commission for Latin America, 19 July–16 August 1947, ECOSOC, Official Records, Lake Success, NY, UN, Second year: Fifth session.

43. Informe Comisión Ad-Hoc Preparación Documentación Reunión Ministros de Hacienda en sesión extraordinaria del CIES, 1954, XII-1089-2, Fondo Organismos Internacionales, Archivo Secretaría de Relaciones Exteriores, México, DF, Mexico.

44. Carlos Lleras Restrepo, "El desarrollo económico continental," *El Tiempo*, August 4, 1954.

45. Armando Amador to Minister of Foreign Relations, July 20, 1954, Colaboración CEPAL Reunión Ministros de Hacienda y Economía, XII-1089-2, Fondo Organismos Internacionales, Archivo Secretaría de Relaciones Exteriores, México, DF, Mexico.

46. "Notas sobre a Conferência Econômica Interamericana no Rio de Janeiro" (Pessoal e Confidencial), 1954 RC d md 1954.11.22, Arquivo Roberto Campos, CPDOC, FGV, Rio de Janeiro, Brazil.

47. CEPAL, "La cooperación internacional en la política de desarrollo latinoamericana" (Nueva York: Naciones Unidas, 1954), E/CN.12/359, 24.

48. Barry Eichengreen, *The European Economy Since 1945* (Princeton: Princeton University Press, 2007), 65.

49. Benn Steil, *The Marshall Plan: Dawn of the Cold War* (New York: Simon and Schuster, 2018), 347–48.

50. "Discurso de Raúl Prebisch en la Conferencia de Ministros de Hacienda y Economía," *Noticias de la CEPAL*, no. 2 (January 7, 1955), 2.

51. Jorge del Canto to Merle Cochran, November 26, 1954, B. 36, F. 5, I124 Economic Commission for Latin America (ECLA), Central Files, International Organizations, IMF Archive, Washington, DC.

52. "Colaboración CEPAL Reunión Ministros de Hacienda y Economía," XII-1089-2, Fondo Organismos Internacionales, Archivo Secretaría de Relaciones Exteriores, México, DF, Mexico

53. Discurso do Ministro da Fazenda do Brasil, 1954, Arquivo Eugênio Gudin, EUG pi GUDIN, E. 1954.11.00, CPDOC, FGV, Rio de Janeiro, Brazil.

54. Invitación Ministro del Ecuador, 1954, III-2169-3, Fondo Diplomático, Archivo Secretaría de Relaciones Exteriores, México, DF, Mexico.

55. "Discurso de Raúl Prebisch en la Conferencia de Ministros de Hacienda y Economía," January 7, 1955, 2.

56. Actas IV Sesión Extradordinaria CIES, 1954, XII-1091-1, Fondo Organismos Internacionales, Archivo Secretaría de Relaciones Exteriores, México, DF, Mexico.

57. Sam Brewers, "Rio Talks Define Areas of Discord," New York Times, November 25, 1954, 11.

58. For Prebisch and Triffin, see Edgar Dosman, The Life and Times of Raúl Prebisch (Montreal: McGill-Queen's University Press, 2008), 195–202; Eric Helleiner, Forgotten Foundations of Bretton Woods: International Development and the Making of the Postwar Order (Ithaca and London: Cornell University Press, 2014), 150–53.

59. CEPAL, "Resolución 9 (IV): Desarollo Económico en Centramérica, Mexico, Cuarto Periódo de Sesiones de la CEPAL," E/CN.12/266, https://repositorio.cepal.org/handle/11362/15964.

60. Jorge Sol Castellanos, "Proceso de la integración económica centroamericana." Revista de Integración Centroamericana, no. 4 (1972): 48–51.

61. Edelberto Torres Rivas, History and Society in Central America (Austin: University of Texas Press, 1993), orig. pub. 1969, 105; Rafael Sánchez, The Politics of Central American Integration (New York: Routledge, 2009), 63–64; Victor Bulmer-Thomas, The Political Economy of Central America (Cambridge: Cambridge University Press, 1987), 118.

62. Castellanos, "Proceso de la integración económica centroamericana," 78.

63. James Cochrane, The Politics of Regional Integration: The Central American Case (New Orleans: Tulane University, 1969), 53.

64. Cochrane, Politics of Regional Integration, 51; Víctor Urquidi, "Incidentes de integración en Centroamerica y Panamá, 1952–1958," Revista de la CEPAL, no. 10 (1998): 259–67.

65. CEPAL and Comité de Cooperación Económica de los Ministros del Istmo Centroamericano, "Informe del relator," August 23, 1952, E/CN.12/AC.17/I/DR.48, https://repositorio.cepal.org//handle/11362/23373; Alberto Fuentes Mohr, La creación de un mercado común: apuntes históricos de la experiencia centroamericana (Buenos Aires: BID, 1973), 64–65.

66. Referenced in Urquidi, "Incidentes de integración en Centroamerica y Panamá," 266.

67. Sánchez, Politics of Central American Integration, 75–77; Bulmer-Thomas, Political Economy of Central America, 174.

68. Enrique Delgado, "Institutional Evolution of the Central American Common Market and the Principle of Balanced Development," in Economic Integration in Central America, ed. William Cline and Enrique Delgado (Washington, DC: Brookings Institution, 1978), 27.

69. "Exposición del Dr. Prebisch ante el Comité de Comercio," November 19, 1956, 12, 17, https://repositorio.cepal.org/handle/11362/21941.

70. "Exposición del Dr. Prebisch," November 19, 1956.

71. "Comité Comercio Internacional: Acta Resumida Primera Sesión," September 2, 1955, Sexto Periodo de Sesiones de la CEPAL, Bogotá, Colombia, E/CN.12/AC.29/SR.1.

72. "Informe de la Secretaría sobre el estado de los trabajos del Comité de Comercio," May 15, 1957, E/CN.12/439, 12–13, https://repositorio.cepal.org/handle/11362/14448.

73. Frank Southhard to Merle Cochran, November 9, 1956, B. 36, F. 6, I124 ECLA, Central Files, International Organizations, IMF Archive, Washington, DC; Irving Friedman and Jorge del Canto to Per Jacobsson, January 18, 1957, B. 36, F. 6, Central Files, International Organizations, IMF Archive, Washington, DC.

74. F. A. Keesing to Irving Friedman, January 18, 1957, B. 36, F. 6, I124 ECLA, Central Files, International Organizations, IMF Archive, Washington, DC.

75. Irving Friedman and Jorge del Canto to Per Jacobsson, January 18, 1957.

76. "Visit of Luis Swenson," July 5, 1957, B. 36, F. 7, I124 ECLA, Central Files, International Organizations, IMF Archive, Washington DC.

77. Jorge del Canto to Per Jacobsson, January 24, 1957, B. 36, F. 7, I124 ECLA, Central Files, International Organizations, IMF Archive, Washington DC.

78. Irving Friedman and Jorge del Canto to Per Jacobsson, January 18, 1957, "Proposals for Latin American Payments Arrangements," January 23, 1957, B. 36, F. 7, I124 ECLA, Central Files, International Organizations, IMF Archive, Washington, DC.

79. Jorge del Canto to Merle Cochran, May 27, 1957, B. 36, F. 7, I124 ECLA, Central Files, International Organizations, IMF Archive, Washington, DC.

80. Jorge Del Canto to Per Jacobsson, January 24, 1957, B. 36 F. 7, I124 ECLA, Central Files, International Organizations, IMF Archive, Washington, DC.

81. F. A. Keesing to Irving Friedman, January 18, 1957 and Frank Southard to Merle Cochran, November 9, 1956, B. 36, F. 7, I124 ECLA, Central Files, International Organizations, IMF Archive, Washington, DC.

82. "Memorandum on ECLA Project," January 24, 1957, B. 36, F.7, I124 ECLA, Central Files, International Organizations, IMF Archive, Washington, DC.

83. Jorge del Canto to Per Jacobsson, May 15, 1959, B. 36, F. 7, I124 ECLA, Central Files, International Organizations, IMF Archive, Washington, DC.

84. Jorge del Canto to Per Jacobsson, May 22, 1959, B. 36 F. 7, I124 ECLA, Central Files, International Organizations, IMF Archive, Washington, DC.

85. Jorge del Canto to Per Jacobsson, May 18, 1959, B. 36, F. 7, I124 ECLA, Central Files, International Organizations, IMF Archive, Washington, DC.

86. Ikuto Yamaguchi, "The Development and Activities of the Economic Commission for Asia and the Far East," in *The Transformation of the International Order of Asia: Decolonization, the Cold War, and the Colombo Plan*, ed. Shigeru Akita, Gerold Krozweski, and Shoichi Watanabe, (London and New York: Routledge, 2015), 92.

87. "Meeting with Mr. Swenson," January 12, 1961, B. 20, F. 4, Western Hemisphere Department Fund, I124 ECLA, Central Files, International Organizations, IMF Archive, Washington, DC.

88. Kluger, "Meritocracia de laços," 69, 85–88.

3. "Structuralism," "Monetarism," and the Politics of Inflation

1. Albert Hirschman, *Journeys toward Progress: Studies of Economic Policy-Making in Latin America* (New York: Twentieth Century Fund, 1963), 190.

2. Eric Lindhal to David Owen, December 30, 1949, and David Owen to Camille Gutt, March 8, 1950, B. 12, F. 7, C/840 Chile, Central Files, International Organizations, IMF Archive, Washington, DC.

3. Albert Hirschman, *Journeys toward Progress: Studies of Economic Policy-Making in Latin America*, 183–88.

4. International Monetary Fund, "A Report on the Process of Inflation in Chile: Summary and Recommendations" (Washington, DC: IMF, 1950), i–ii.

5. Raúl Prebisch, "El desarrollo económico de América Latina y sus principales problemas," *El Trimestre Económico* 16, no. 63(3) (1949): 401–03.

6. Raúl Prebisch, "Notas sobre desarrollo económico, inflación, y la política fiscal y monetaria," *Economía: Revista de la Facultad de Ciencias Económicas de la Universidad de Chile*, no. 40 (1952): 39–40.

7. CEPAL, *Estudio económico de América Latina 1953* (New York: Naciones Unidas, 1954), 89–91.

8. Hirschman, *Journeys toward Progress*, 192–94.

9. Hirschman, *Journeys toward Progress*, 192–94.

10. Tomás Moulian, *El gobierno de Ibáñez, 1952–1958* (Santiago: FLACSO, 1986), 23, 30; David Collier and Ruth Collier, *Shaping the Political Arena: Critical Junctures, the Labor Movement, and Regime Dynamics in Latin America* (Princeton: Princeton University Press, 1991), 529–30.

11. Hirschman, *Journeys toward Progress*, 199–200.

12. Celso Furtado to Raúl Prebisch, April 10, 1954, quoted in Mauro Boianovsky, "Celso Furtado and the Structuralist-Monetarist Debate on Economic Stabilization in Latin America," *History of Political Economy* 44, no. 2 (2012): 291–92, 295.

13. Celso Furtado, "Formação de capital e desenvolvimento econômico," *Revista Brasileira de Economia*, 6, no. 3 (1952): 7–46.

14. Furtado, "Formação de capital," 35; see also Boianovsky, "Celso Furtado and the Structuralist-Monetarist Debate," 295–96.

15. Celso Furtado to Raúl Prebisch, April 10, 1954, quoted in Mauro Boianovsky, "Celso Furtado and the Structuralist-Monetarist Debate," 291–92, 295.

16. Clodomiro Almeyda, *Reencuentro con mi vida* (Santiago: Ediciones El Ornitorrinco, 1987), 158.

17. Aníbal Pinto, "Lineas generales del programa de acción gubernativa," *Panorama Económico* 6, no. 81 (1953): 409–13.

18. CEPAL, *Estudio económico de América Latina 1954* (New York: United Nations, 1955), 30.

19. For instance, see Thomas Miller Klubock, *Contested Communities: Class, Gender and Politics in Chile's El Teniente Copper Mine, 1904–1951* (Durham: Duke University Press, 1998); Joaquín Fermandois, Jimena Bustos, and María

José Schneuer, *Historia política del cobre en Chile* (Santiago: Centro de Estudios Bicentenario, 2009).

20. CEPAL, *Estudio económico de América Latina 1954*, 30.

21. "Misión sin misión," *Panorama económico* 8, no. 126 (1955): 365–66.

22. "Esquina Peligrosa," *Panorama económico* 9, no. 125 (1955): 332–33.

23. Hirschman, *Journeys toward Progress*, 194–99.

24. For more on the Klein & Saks mission, see Juan Pablo Couyoumdjian (ed.), *Reformas económicas e instituciones políticas: La experiencia de la mission Klein-Saks en Chile*, (Santiago: Universidad del Desarrollo, 2011).

25. "Misión sin misión," *Panorama Económico* 8, no. 126 (1955), 365.

26. Celso Furtado, *La fantasia organizada* (Bogota: Tercer Mundo Editores, 1989), 158.

27. Aníbal Pinto, "Paradojas de una misión," *Panorama económico* 10, no. 155 (1956): 631–32.

28. Juan Carlos Korol and Claudio Belini, *Historia económica de la Argentina en los siglox XX y XXI* (Buenos Aires: Siglo XXI, 2020), 141–46.

29. Furtado, *La fantasia organizada*, 161.

30. Kathryn Sikkink, "The Influence of Raúl Prebisch on Economic Policy-Making in Argentina, 1950–1962," *Latin American Research Review* 23, no. 2 (1988): 93.

31. For the economics and political economy ofthe Prebisch plan, see Juan Carlos Korol and Claudio Belini, *Historia económica de la Argentina en los siglox XX y XXI*, 160.

32. Raúl Prebisch, "Moneda Sana o inflación incontenible/Plan de Reestablecimiento Económico" (Buenos Aires: n.p., 1956), 24.

33. Furtado, *La fantasia organizada*, 161.

34. Prebisch, "Moneda Sana o inflación incontenible," 22–23.

35. On Plan Prebisch, see Edgar Dosman, *The Life and Times of Raúl Prebisch* (Montreal: McGill-Queen's University Press, 2008), 302–303, 308–19.

36. Furtado, *La fantasia organizada*, 161.

37. For a reception of Prebisch's policies in Argentina, see Kathryn Sikkink, "The Influence of Raúl Prebisch on Economic Policy-Making in Argentina, 1950-1962." Latin American Research Review, 23, no. 2 (1988): 91–114.

38. Dosman, *Life and Times of Raúl Prebisch*, 312–17.

39. Osvaldo Sunkel, "Un esquema general para el análisis de la inflación: El caso de Chile," *Revista de desarrollo económico,* October–December (1958), 5.

40. Of Noyola and Furtado, see Boianovsky, "Celso Furtado and the Structuralist-Monetarist Debate," 281, 288–89.

41. Juan Noyola, "Inflación y desarrollo en Chile," August 1955, mimeo, CEPAL.

42. Furtado had argued for the external constraint as the mechanism that linked inflation and development in 1952. Boianovsky, "Celso Furtado and the Structuralist-Monetarist Debate," 295.

43. Hirschman, *Journeys toward Progress*, 213 (footnote).

44. "Discurso de Don Raúl Prebisch," *Noticias de la CEPAL* 3, no. 6 (1956): 6–9.

45. Raúl Prebisch to Headquarters, April 1954, quoted in Dosman, *Life and Times*, 322.

46. Juan Noyola, "El desarrollo económico y la inflación en México y en otros países," *Investigación económica* 16, no. 4 (1956): 603–48. For an analysis of Noyola's trajectory, see Colin Danby, "Noyola's Institutional Approach to Inflation," *Journal of History of Economic Thought* 27, no. 2 (2005): 161–78.

47. Juan Noyola to Raúl Prebisch, May 4, 1955, quoted in Boianovsky, "Celso Furtado and the Structuralist-Monetarist Debate," 292.

48. Sunkel, "Un esquema general para el análisis de la inflación: El caso de Chile," 6.

49. Mauro Boianovsky, "Celso Furtado and the Structuralist-Monetarist Debate," 284.

50. Joel Wolfe, *Autos and Progress: The Brazilian Search for Modernity* (Oxford: Oxford University Press, 2010).

51. Roberto Campos, *A lanterna na popa: memórias* (Rio de Janeiro: Top Books, 2004), 269. On the Targets program, see also Kathryn Sikkink, *Ideas and Institutions: Developmentalism in Brazil and Argentina* (Ithaca: Cornell University Press, 1991), 126–34; Clovis Faro and Salomão L. Quadros Silva, "A década de 50 e o Programa de Metas," in *O Brasil de JK*, ed. Angela de Castro Gomes (Rio de Janeiro: CPDOC, 1991).

52. Stenographic notes on the speech of Dr. Roberto de Oliveira Campos at a meeting of the Joint Commission on July 27, 1953; RC d md 1953.07.27, Arquivo Roberto Campos, Centro de Pesquisa e Documentação de História Contemporânea do Brasil (CPDOC), Fundação Getúlio Vargas (FGV), Rio de Janeiro, Brazil; Furtado, *La fantasía organizada*, 97, 147.

53. Roberto Campos, "La inflacion y el crecimiento equilibrado," in *El desarrollo económico y América Latina; trabajos y comentarios presentados en la conferencia de la Asociación Económica Internacional celebrada en Río de Janeiro en agosto de 1957*, ed. Howard Ellis (México: Fondo de Cultura Económica, 1960), 117.

54. "Discurso de clausura pronunciado por Roberto Campos," Séptimo periodo de sesiones de la CEPAL, May 29, 1957, E/CN.12 /481, https://repositorio.cepal.org//handle/11362/14466.

55. Celso Furtado, *A economia brasileira: Contribuição a análise do seu desenvolvimento* (Rio de Janeiro: Editora A Noite, 1954), 176.

56. Commentary to Juan Noyola, "El desarrollo económico y la inflación en México y en otros países," 636.

57. For Skidmore's "economics of confidence" and Maram's "politics of exuberance," see Thomas Skidmore, *Politics in Brazil, 1930–64: An Experiment in Democracy* (Oxford: Oxford University Press, 1967), 164; Sheldom Maram, "Juscelino Kubitschek and the Politics of Exhuberance," *Luso-Brazilian Review* 27, no. 1 (1990): 31–45.

58. Discurso inauguração curso "Desenvolvimento econômico e técnica de programação," 1956?, LL pi Lopes, L. 1956/1958.00.00, Arquivo Lucas Lopes, CPDOC, FGV, Rio de Janeiro, Brazil.

59. Roberto Campos, *Econômia, planejamento, e nacionalismo* (Rio de Janeiro: APEC Editora, 1963), 68–70

60. Roberto Campos, "Aspectos Políticos e Técnicos da Inflação," 1956, RC e bnde 55.06.30, II. 10, Arquivo Roberto Campos, CPDOC, FGV, Rio de Janeiro, Brazil.

61. Sikkink, *Ideas and Institutions,* 145; Skidmore, *Politics in Brazil,* 176.

62. Campos, *A lanterna na popa,* 352.

63. Celso Furtado, *A fantasia desfeita* (Rio de Janeiro: Paz e Terra, 1989), 73.

64. Lourdes Sola, *Idéias econômicas, decisões políticas* (São Paulo Editora USP, 1998), 199–200; Sikkink, *Ideas and Institutions,* 176.

65. Observações as críticas ao programa de estabilização monetaria, 1958, RC e bnde 55.06.30, II doc. 32, Arquivo Roberto Campos, CPDOC, FGV, Rio de Janeiro, Brazil.

66. Edward Bernstein, "Inflation in Brazil, 1940–1950," March 24, 1952, F. 721, 15, 114, Edward M. Bernstein Papers 1927–1996 #04502, The Southern Historical Collection, Wilson Special Collections Library, University of North Carolina, Chapel Hill, North Carolina.

67. On US-LA relations Peter Smith, *Talons of the Eagle: Dynamics of U.S.-Latin American Relations* (New York: Oxford University Press, 1996); Lars Schoultz, *Beneath the United States: A History of US Policy Toward Latin America* (Cambridge and London: Harvard University Press, 1998); Emily Rosenberg, *Financial Missionaries to the World: The Politics and Culture of Dollar Diplomacy, 1900–1930* (Durham: Duke University Press, 2003); Paul Max Friedman, *Rethinking Anti-Americanism: The History of an Exceptional Concept in American Foreign Relations* (Cambridge University Press: Cambridge, 2012), Ch. 4.

68. Sikkink, *Ideas and Institutions,* 146.

69. Skidmore, *Politics in Brazil,* 179–81.

70. Sola, *Idéias econômicas, decisões políticas,* 202–03.

71. Casimiro Ribeiro, Depoimento I (1975–1979), Rio de Janeiro, CPDOC, 1981, 67.

72. Furtado, *A fantasia desfeita,* 73.

73. Campos, *A lanterna na popa,* 268.

74. Roberto Campos, "Two Views on Inflation in Latin America, in *Latin American Issues,* ed. Albert Hirschman (New York: Twentieth Century Fund, 1961), 73.

75. Campos, "Two Views on Inflation in Latin America," 71; Campos, *A lanterna na popa,* 268.

76. Campos, "Two Views on Inflation in Latin America," 69.

77. Campos, "Two Views on Inflation in Latin America," 70.

78. For "personalities," see Hirschman, *Journeys toward Progress,* 190.

79. See chapter 1 and Eric Helleiner, *Forgotten Foundations of Bretton Woods: International Development and the Making of the Postwar Order* (Ithaca and London: Cornell University Press, 2014), 109, 115, 156.

80. Carlos Bazdrech, *El pensamiento de Juan Noyola* (México: Fondo de Cultura Económica, 1984), 24.

81. Aníbal Pinto, "Papelón con el Fondo," *Panorama económico* 7, no. 116 (1955): 39.

82. Richard Jolly, "Dudley Seers: His Contributions to Development Perspectives, Policy, and Studies," *IDS Bulletin* 20, no. 3 (1989).

83. Tom Davis, interview transcript, May 12, 1961, B. 32, F. 270, SG 1.2, Series 309s, Rockefeller Foundation, Rockefeller Archive Center (RAC), Sleepy Hollow, NY.

84. Interview Carlos Massad, July 22, 1964, B. 36, F. 296, 1, 4, SG 1.2, Series 309s, Rockefeller Foundation, RAC, Sleepy Hollow, NY.

85. Claudia Kedar, *The International Monetary Fund and Latin America: The Argentine Puzzle in Context* (Philadelphia: Temple University Press, 2013); Jon Kofas, *Sword of Damocles: The IMF, the World Bank and US Foreign Policy in Colombia and Chile, 1950–70* (Westport and London: Praeger, 2002).

86. Thomas Skidmore, "The Politics of Economic Stabilization in Latin America," Woodrow Wilson Center for Scholars, Washington, DC, 1979; Sikkink, *Ideas and Institutions,* 88.

87. Hirschman, *Journeys toward Progress,* 220.

88. "Report of Third Session of Trade Committee and CEPAL's Ninth Session," May 1961, B. 20, F. 4, Western Hemisphere Department, Immediate Office Records, International Organizations, IMF Archive, Washington, DC.

89. Jorge del Canto to Per Jacobsson, August 30, 1961, and Jorge del Canto to Per Jacobsson, August 13, 1962, B. 20, F. 4, Western Hemisphere Department, Immediate Office Records, International Organizations, IMF Archive, Washington, DC.

90. Jorge del Canto to Per Jacobsson, August 30, 1961, B. 20, F. 4, Western Hemisphere Department, Immediate Office Records, International Organizations, IMF Archive, Washington, DC.

91. Leland C. DeVinney, Diary, July 13–19, 1960, Conference on Inflation and Growth in Latin America, RG 12, Rockefeller Foundation, RAC, Sleepy Hollow, NY.

92. "Proposal for a Conference on Inflation and Growth," November 1960, r. 701, Grant no. 06100340, Grant Files, Ford Foundation, RAC, Sleepy Hollow, NY.

93. Richard Ruggles, "Summary of the Conference on Inflation and Growth," in *Inflation and Growth in Latin America,* ed. Werner Baer and Isaac Kerstenetzky (Homewood, IL: Irwin, 1964), 3.

94. David Felix, "Monetarists, Structuralists, and Import-Substitution Industrialization," in *Inflation and Growth in Latin America,* 371.

95. Charles Schwartz to Acting Managing Director, January 18, 1963, B. 180, F. 3, I 632, Conference on Inflation and Growth, Central Files, International Organizations, IMF Archive, Washington, DC.

96. John Adler to Geoffrey Wilson, January 15, 1963, B. 180, F. 3, I 632 Conference on Inflation and Growth, Central Files, International Organizations, IMF Archive, Washington, DC.

97. "Some Comments by the Staff on Inflation and Growth Conference," n.d., I 632 Conference on Inflation and Growth, B. 180, F. 3, Central Files, International Organizations, IMF Archive, Washington, DC.

98. Gordon Williams to Frank Southard, January 21, 1963, John Adler to Geoffrey Wilson, January 15, 1963, Jay Reid to Per Jacobsson, February 12, 1963, I 632 Conference on Inflation and Growth, B. 180, F. 3, Central Files, International Organizations, IMF Archive, Washington, DC.

99. Charles Schwartz to Acting Managing Director, January 18, 1963, and Gordon Williams to Frank Southard, January 21, 1963, B. 180, F. 3, Central Files, International Organizations, IMF Archive, Washington, DC.

100. Margarita Fajardo, "CEPAL: The International Monetary Fund of the Left? The Tale of Two Global Institutions," *American Historical Review*, under review.

101. John Adler to Geoffrey Wilson, January 15, 1963, B. 180, F. 3, I 632 Conference on Inflation and Growth, Central Files, International Organizations, IMF Archive, Washington, DC.

102. Comments by Massad and Simonsen in *Inflation and Growth in Latin America*, 105, 108.

103. David Felix, "An Alternative View of the "Monetarist"-"Structuralist" Controversy," in *Latin American Issues*, ed. Albert Hirschman (New York: Twentieth Century Fund, 1961), 83.

104. John Adler to Geoffrey Wilson, January 15, 1963, B. 180, F. 3, Central Files, International Organizations, IMF Archive, Washington, DC.

105. Lautaro, "Diagnóstico y catastrofismo en el continente," *Panorama económico*, no. 252, (February–March 1970): 15–19.

106. Hirschman, *Journeys toward Progress*, 214.

4. Revolutions Left and Right

1. See Kepa Artaraz, *Cuba and Western Intellectuals since 1959* (New York: Palgrave Macmillan, 2009) and Rafael Rojas, *Fighting Over Fidel: The New York Intellectuals and the Cuban Revolution* (Princeton: Princeton University Press, 2016).

2. For the term and its relation to modernization theory-inspired programs, see Michael Latham, *Right Kind of Revolution: Modernization, Development, and US Foreign Policy from the Cold War to the Present* (Ithacaand London: Cornell University Press, 2011).

3. Marifeli Pérez-Stable, *The Cuban Revolution: Origins, Course and Legacy* (Oxford: Oxford University Press, 1994), 15–16.

4. On the urban side of the revolution, see Julia Sweig, *Inside the Cuban Revolution: Fidel Castro and the Urban Underground* (Cambridge: Harvard University Press, 2002).

5. Phone interview with Lilian Llanés, December 29, 2020.

6. Edgar Dosman, *The Life and Times of Raúl Prebisch* (Montreal: McGill-Queen's University Press, 2008), 215, 275.

7. Paul Lewis, "Felipe Pazos, 88, Economist, Cuban Split Early with Castro," *New York Times,* March 9, 2001; Thomas Paterson, *Contesting Castro: The United States and the Triumph of the Cuban Revolution* (New York: Oxford University Press, 1994), 74–76.

8. Regino Boti and Felipe Pazos, "Algunos aspectos del desarrollo económico de Cuba," *Revista Bimestral Cubana*, no. 75 (1957), 258.

9. Boti and Pazos, "Algunos aspectos del desarrollo económico de Cuba," 251.

10. Antoni Kapcia, *Leadership in the Cuban Revolution: The Unseen Story* (London: Zed Books, 2014), 67.

11. Kapcia, *Leadership in the Cuban Revolution*, 114.

12. Boti and Pazos, "Algunos aspectos del desarrollo económico de Cuba," 259.

13. Jorge Domínguez, *Cuba: Order and Revolution* (Cambridge: Harvard University Press, 1978), 144.

14. Alan McPherson, "The Limits of Populist Diplomacy: Fidel Castro and the April 1959 Trip to North America," *Diplomacy and Statecraft*, no. 18 (2007), 237–68.

15. For Castro's art of governing and the politics of the revolution, see Lilian Guerra, *Visions of Power in Cuba: Revolution, Redemption, and Resistance, 1959-1971* (Chapel Hill: University of North Carolina Press, 2012).

16. Boti and Pazos, "Algunos aspectos del desarrollo económico de Cuba," 249–82, 258, 265; Alan McPherson, "The Limits of Populist Diplomacy," 247–48.

17. Jorge del Canto to Per Jacobsson, May 26, 1959, B. 36, F. 7, I 124, Economic Commission for Latin America (ECLA), Central Files, International Organizations, IMF Archive, Washington, DC.

18. Pérez-Stable, *Cuban Revolution*, 79.

19. Jorge Castañeda, *Compañero: The Life and Death of Che Guevara* (New York: Vintage Books, 1997), 157.

20. Boti and Pazos, "Algunos aspectos del desarrollo económico de Cuba," 270.

21. Leo Huberman and Paul Sweezy, *Cuba: Anatomy of a Revolution* (New York: Monthly Review Press, 1960); Dudley Seers, *Cuba: The Economic and Social Revolution* (Chapel Hill: University of North Carolina Press, 1964).

22. Sarah Babb, *Managing Mexico: From Nationalism to Neoliberalism* (Princeton: Princeton University Press, 2001), 57, 60.

23. Celso Furtado, *La fantasía organizada* (Bogotá: Tercer Mundo Editores, 1989), 110.

24. Furtado, *La fantasía organizada*, 166.

25. Dosman, *Life and Times*, 351.

26. Phone interview with Lilian Llanés, December 29, 2020.

27. Huberman and Sweezy, *Cuba*, 111.

28. Boti and Pazos, "Algunos aspectos del desarrollo económico de Cuba," 255.

29. Pérez-Stable, *Cuban Revolution*, 64; Domínguez, *Cuba: Order and Revolution*, 438.

30. Juan Noyola to David Pollock, September 23, 1959, B. 18, F. 8 and Ole Danielson to Bruno Leuschner, September 17, 1959. B. 18, F. 12, Edgar Dosman Papers, Clara Thomas Archive and Special Collections, University of York, Toronto, Canada.

31. CEPAL, *Annual Report to ECOSOC*, 1960, E/CN.12/AC.45/13/Rev.1, 8, https://repositorio.cepal.org/handle/11362/15016.

32. Domínguez, *Cuba: Order and Revolution*, 438; Huberman and Sweezy, *Cuba*, 121–22; Jonathan Brown, *Cuba's Revolutionary World* (Cambridge: Harvard University Press, 2017), Ch. 5.

33. Huberman and Sweezy, *Cuba*, 119.

34. Víctor Urquidi, "Jorge Ahumada (1917–1965)," *El Trimestre Económico* 34, no. 133(1) (1967): 3–10; Embajada de Chile en Guatemala, June 28, 1949, v. 2827, Fondo Histórico, Archivo Histórico del Ministerio Relaciones Exteriores de Chile, Santiago, Chile.

35. On Guatemala's agrarian reform: Piero Gleijeses, "The Agrarian Reform of Jacabo Arbenz," *Journal of Latin American Studies* 21, no. 3 (1989), 453–80.

36. On the later Chilean agrarian reform of the Christian Democrats: Robert Kaufman, *The Politics of Land Reform in Chile, 1950–1970: Public Policy, Political Institutions, and Social Change* (Cambridge: Harvard University Press, 1972); Heidi Tinsman, *Partners in Conflict: The Politics of Gender, Sexuality, and Labor in the Chilean Agrarian Reform, 1950–73* (Durham and London: Duke University Press, 2002).

37. Jorge Ahumada, *En vez de la miseria* (Santiago: Editorial del Pacífico, 1958), 15–17, 99.

38. Robert Weldham, "Conversation with Mr. Ahumada of ECLA," November 10, 1959, R. 1357, General Correspondence, Ford Foundation, Rockefeller Archive Center (RAC), Sleepy Hollow, NY.

39. Pérez-Stable, *Cuban Revolution,* 78.

40. For revolutionaries and counterrevolutionaries within the revolution, see Guerra, *Visions of Power in Cuba* and Brown, *Cuba's Revolutionary World.*

41. Rufo López Fresquet, *My Fourteen Months with Castro* (Cleveland: World Publishing Co., 1966), 99; Brown, *Cuba's Revolutionary World*, 34.

42. Felipe Pazos, "Comentarios a dos artículos sobre la Revolución Cubana," *El Trimestre Económico* 29, no. 113 (1962): 1–18.

43. J. Noyola to D. Pollock, August 9, 1960, B. 19, F. 4, Edgar Dosman Papers, Clara Thomas Archive and Special Collections, University of York, Toronto, Canada.

44. Huberman and Sweezy, *Cuba,* 90.

45. Juan Noyola, "La Revolución Cubana y sus efectos en el desarrollo económico," *El Trimestre Económico,* 28, no. 111(3) (1961): 405.

46. "Regino Boty [sic] viaja a Estados Unidos," *Diario de las Américas*, September 22, 1960.

47. Huberman and Sweezy, *Cuba,* 145.

48. *Diario de las Américas,* September 22, 1960.

49. Juan Noyola, "Aspectos económicos de la revolución cubana," *El Trimestre Económico* 21, no. 82 (1961): 331–59.

50. Noyola, "La Revolución Cubana y sus efectos en el desarrollo económico," 422.

51. Celso Furtado and Rosa d' Aguiar Furtado, *Diarios intermitentes, 1937–2002* (São Paulo: Companhia das Letras, 2019), 190.

52. William Howe to Phillip Bonsal, Santiago, April 29, 1960, B. 33, F. 11, Edgar Dosman Papers, Clara Thomas Archive and Special Collections, University of York, Toronto, Canada.

53. Celso Furtado, *A fantasia desfeita* (Rio de Janeiro: Paz e Terra, 1989), 118–119.

54. CEPAL, "Provisional Summary Record, Second Meeting, Economic and Social Development Committee, 1961, Ninth Session," May 9, 1961, E/CN.12/AC.47/SR.2, 14, https://repositorio.cepal.org/handle/11362/14010.

55. CEPAL, "Provisional Summary Record, Second Meeting, Economic and Social Development Committee," 15.

56. On intellectuals and the revolution, see Patrick Iber, *Neither Peace nor Freedom: Cultural Cold War in Latin America* (Cambridge: Harvard University Press, 2015).

57. Phone interview with Lilian Llanés, December 29, 2020.

58. Kapcia, *Leadership in the Cuban Revolution,* 126.

59. Phone interview with Lilian Llanés, December 29, 2020.

60. Michael Latham, *Modernization as Ideology: American Social Science and Nation-Building in the Kennedy Era* (Chapel Hill and London: University of North Carolina Press, 2000), 74–77; Stephen Rabe, *The Most Dangerous Area in the World: John F. Kennedy Confronts Communists Revolution in Latin America* (Chapel Hill: University of North Carolina Press, 1999), 11–12.

61. On JK's role, see Christopher Darnton, "Asymmetry and Agenda-Setting in U.S.-Latin American Relations: Rethinking the Origins of the Alliance for Progress," *Journal of Cold War Studies* 14, no. 4 (2012): 55–92.

62. Declaración Conjunta OEA, BID, y CEPAL, July 21,1961, Santiago, CEPAL.

63. Dosman, *Life and Times,* 358.

64. "Alliance for Progress: An Inter-American Partnership," F. 98, Archivo de Trabajo del Dr. Raúl Prebisch, CEPAL, Santiago, Chile.

65. Dosman, *Life and Times,* 358.

66. Furtado, *La fantasía organizada,* 118.

67. Jorge del Canto to Per Jacobsson, May 22, 1959, B. 36, F. 7, I124 ECLA, Central Files, International Organizations, IMF Archive, Washington DC.

68. Address at a White House Reception for Members of Congress and for the Diplomatic Corps of the Latin American Republics, March 13, 1961, https://www.jfklibrary.org/archives/other-resources/john-f-kennedy-speeches/latin-american-diplomats-washington-dc-19610313.

69. Ernesto Guevara, "Economics Cannot Be Separated from Politics," in *Our America and Theirs: Che, Kennedy, and the Debated on Free Trade,* ed. Aleida March (Victoria, Australia: Ocean Press, 2005), 20–21.

70. Guevara, "Economics Cannot Be Separated," 40.

71. Raúl Prebisch, "Exposición del subsecretario a cargo de la CEPAL, Dr. Raúl Prebisch, durante la Reunión Extraordinaria del CIES," *Noticias de la CEPAL* 7, no. 2 (1961): 3–7.

72. Juan Noyola, "El papel de los organismos internacionales," in *El capital extranjero en América Latina: ciclo de conferencia,* ed. Comisión Nacional Cubana de la Unesco (Havana, 1961), 123–24.

73. Jeffrey Taffet, *Foreign Aid as Foreign Policy: The Alliance for Progress in Latin America* (New York and London: Routledge, 2007), 37–43.

74. CEPAL, "Economic and Social Development Committee: Summary Record of the Fourth Meeting, May 10, 1961," E/CN.12/AC.47/SR.4, 15, https://repositorio.cepal.org/handle/11362/14012.

75. Speech by Ambassador Roberto de Oliveira Campos at the National Conference on International Economic and Social Development at Palmer House, Chicago, July 19, 1962, RC d emb 1961.10.19, pasta II, doc. 65, Arquivo Roberto Campos, Centro de Pesquisa e Documentação de História Contemporânea do Brasil (CPDOC), Fundação Getúlio Vargas (FGV), Rio de Janeiro, Brazil.

76. Fernando Ramos to the Minister of Foreign Relations, November 7, 1963, Confidential 650.22, (00), Embaixada em Santiago, Arquivo Histórico do Itamaraty, Brasilia, Brazil.

77. Dosman, *Life and Times*, 366–67.

78. Raúl Prebisch, "Hacia una dinámica del desarrollo lationamericano" April 14, 1963, E/CN.12/680, https://repositorio.cepal.org/handle/11362/13056.

79. "Discurso del Dr. Raúl Prebisch," *Noticias de la CEPAL* 3, no. 9 (1957): 8–14.

80. Prebisch, "Hacia una dinámica del desarrollo lationamericano" April 14, 1963, E/CN.12/680, 133, https://repositorio.cepal.org/handle/11362/13056.

81. CEPAL, "Summary Record of the Second Meeting of the Committee of the Whole," February 14, 1962, E/CN.12/AC.50/SR.2, https://repositorio.cepal.org/handle/11362/15098.

82. Furtado, *La fantasía organizada,* 166.

83. Elisa Kluger, "Meritocracia de laços: gênese e reconfigurações do espaço dos economistas no Brasil," PhD diss., Universidade de São Paulo, 2015, 147.

84. Furtado, *La fantasía organizada,* 149; quoted in Lourdes Sola, *Idéias econômicas, decisões políticas* (São Paulo: Editora USP, 1998), 148.

85. For a history of expert responses to the Northeast, see Eve Buckley, *Technocrats and the Politics of Drought and Development in Brazil* (Chapel Hill: University of North Carolina Press, 2017).

86. Albert Hirschman, *Journeys toward Progress: Studies of Economic Policy-Making in Latin America* (New York: Twentieth Century Fund, 1963), 55.

87. Celso Furtado, "A operação Nordeste," in *O Nordeste e a saga da Sudene, 1958–1964,* ed. Rosa Freire (Rio de Janeiro: Contraponto, 2009), 31.

88. Furtado, "A operação Nordeste," 65–66.

89. See David Eckbladh, *The Great American Mission: Modernization and the Construction of the American World Order* (Princeton: Princeton University Press, 2010), Ch. 6; Timothy Mitchell, *The Rule of Experts: Egypt, Techno-Politics, Modernity* (Berkeley and Los Angeles: University of California Press, 2002), 45.

90. Jose Carlos Orihuela, "One Blueprint, Three Translations: Development Corporations in Chile, Colombia, and Peru," in *State and Nation Making in Latin America and Spain: The Rise and Fall of the Developmental State,* ed. Agustín Ferraro and Miguel Centeno (Cambridge and New York: Cambridge University Press, 2019); Amy Offner, *Sorting Out the Mixed Economy: The*

Rise and Fall of Welfare and Developmental States in the Americas (Princeton: Princeton University Press, 2019), Ch. 1.

91. Hirschman, *Journeys toward Progress*, 55.

92. Hirschman, *Journeys toward Progress*, 76–88.

93. Furtado, *A fantasia desfeita*, 122–23.

94. Furtado, *A fantasia desfeita*, 128–29.

95. Furtado, *A fantasia desfeita*, 108.

96. Gustavo Louis Pinto and Rafael Gumiero, "Auge y declive de la relaciones entre la SUDENE y la Alianza para el Progreso," *Revista CIDOB d'Afers Internacionals*, no. 120 (2018), 82.

97. Furtado, *A fantasia desfeita*, 129.

98. Taffet, *Foreign Aid as Foreign Policy*, 98–99.

99. Taffet, *Foreign Aid as Foreign Policy*, 100–102.

100. Furtado, *A fantasia desfeita*, 129.

101. See, for instance Taffet, *Foreign Aid as Foreign Policy;* Rabe, *Most Dangerous Area*, 1999.

102. I would like to thank Amy Offner for this remark.

103. Celso Furtado, "O Plano Trienal e o desenvolvimento," *Ultima Hora*, December 30, 1962.

104. Pinto and Gumiero, "Auge y declive de la elaciones entre la SUDENE y la Alianza para el Progreso," 88.

105. Ricardo Ribeiro, "A Aliança para o Progresso e as relações Brasil-Estados Unidos," PhD diss., Universidade Estadual de Campinas, 2006, 185.

106. Ribeiro, "A Aliança para o Progresso e as relações Brasil-Estados Unidos," 186.

107. See footnote 392 in Ribeiro, "A Aliança para o Progresso e as relações Brasil-Estados Unidos," 187.

108. Hirschman, *Journeys toward Progress*, 90.

109. Eugênio Gudin, "Econômia política e literaria," *O Globo*, November 28, 1962; "Erros de Optica," *O Globo*, January 3, 1963.

110. Pinto and Gumiero, "Auge y declive de la relaciones entre la SUDENE y la Alianza para el Progreso," 86–87.

111. Furtado, *A fantasia desfeita*, 131.

112. "Exposição Celso Furtado," May 17, 1962, B. 120, Fundo Conselho Nacional de Econômia, Arquivo Nacional, Rio de Janeiro, Brazil.

113. Furtado, *A fantasia desfeita*, 119.

114. Celso Furtado, "Reflexiones sobre la prerevolución brasileña," *El Trimestre Económico* 29, no. 115(3) (1962): 373, 379–82.

115. Ribeiro, "A Aliança para o Progresso e as relações Brasil-Estados Unidos," 207.

116. Discurso Celso Furtado, na quarta sessão plenária, October 24, 1962, B. 89078, Assuntos Econômicos-OEA, Arquivo Histórico do Itamaraty, Brasilia, Brazil.

117. Ribeiro, "A Aliança para o Progresso e as relações Brasil-Estados Unidos," 193.

118. For an excellent analysis of the politics of the *Plano Trienal*, see Lourdes Sola, *Idéias econômicas, decisões políticas* (São Paulo Editora USP, 1998), Ch. 7.

119. Furtado, *A fantasia desfeita*, 131.

120. Furtado, "O Plano Trienal e o desenvolvimento," December 30,1962.

121. Celso Furtado, "Desarrollo y estancamiento en América Latina (enfoque estructuralista)," *Desarrollo Económico* 6, no. 22/23: (1966): 191–223.

122. Celso Furtado, "US Hegemony and the Future of Latin America," *World Today* 12, no. 9 (1966): 375–86.

123. Celso Furtado, *Os ares do mundo* (Rio de Janeiro: Paz e Terra, 1991), 32.

124. CEPAL, "Provisional Summary Record, Second Meeting, Economic and Social Development Committee," 15.

125. Eduardo Frei, "Opposition Parties in Chile," *New York Times*, March 24, 1961.

126. Pablo González Casanova, "Las Ciencias Sociales en América Latina," In *Balance y perspectivas de los estudios latinoamericanos* (México: UNAM, 1984), 29.

5. Toward Dependency Theory

1. Nick Culather, *The Hungry World: America's Cold War Battle against Poverty in Asia* (Cambridge: Harvard University Press, 2010); Matthew Connelly, *Fatal Misconception: The Struggle to Control World Population* (Cambridge: Harvard University Press).

2. See David Eckbladh, *The Great American Mission: Modernization and the Construction of the American World Order* (Princeton: Princeton University Press, 2010); Culather, *The Hungry World*; Michael Latham, *Right Kind of Revolution: Modernization, Development, and US Foreign Policy from the Cold War to the Present* (Ithaca and London: Cornell University Press, 2011).

3. Angela de Castro Gomes and Jorge Ferreira, *João Goulart: Uma biografia* (Rio de Janeiro: Civilização Brasileira, 2011), 328–29.

4. The literature on politics in Brazil before the coup is extensive, see the classic: Thomas Skidmore, *Politics in Brazil, 1930–64: An Experiment in Democracy* (Oxford: Oxford University Press, 1967) and more recent interpretation: Daniel Reis Aarão, Marcelo Ridenti, and Rodrigo Patto Sá Motta, *A ditadura que mudou o Brasil: 50 anos do golpe de 1964* (Rio de Janeiro: Zahar, 2014). Structuralist explanations began with *cepalinos* and *dependentistas*, see Celso Furtado, "Obstaculos políticos del desarrollo económico en Brazil," *Desarrollo Económico* 4, no. 16 (1965): 373–89; Fernando Henrique Cardoso, *O modelo político Brasileiro e outros ensaios*, 2nd ed. (São Paulo: Difusão Europeia do Livro, 1973).

5. Gomes and Ferreira, *João Goulart*, 270–79, 328–29.

6. Celso Furtado, "Reflexiones sobre la prerevolución brasileña," *El Trimestre Económico* 29, no. 115(3) (1962): 383; Theotônio dos Santos, "A crise de Agosto," *Revista Brasiliense* 38 (1961): 27.

7. I would like to thank Matthew Ellis for helping conceptualize the notion of *cepalino* ideas as orthodoxy as here used.

8. Aníbal Pinto, *Chile, un caso de desarrollo frustrado* (Santiago: Editorial Universitaria, 1959). For the notion of "internal colonialism," see Rodolfo Stavenhagen, "Siete Tesis Equivocadas de América Latina," originally published in

El Día, México, June 25 and 26, 1965, and for the notion of "marginality," see, for instance, Aníbal Quijano, "Dependencia, Cambio Social y Urbanización en América Latina," *Revista Mexicana de Sociología* 30, no. 3 (1968): 525–70. See also Mariano Plotkin, "US Foundations, Cultural Imperialism and Transnational Misunderstanding: The Case of the Marginality Project," *Journal of Latin American Studies* no. 47 (2014): 65–92; Patrick Iber, "Social Science, Cultural Imperialism, and the Ford Foundation in Latin America in the 1960s," in *The Global 1960s: Convention, Contest, and Counterculture,* ed. Tamara Chaplin and Jadwiga Pieper Mooney (New York: Routledge, 2018).

9. See, for instance, Rafael Rojas, *Fighting over Fidel: The New York Intellectuals and the Cuban Revolution* (Princeton: Princeton University Press, 2016) or Javier Treviño, *C. Wright Mills and the Cuban Revolution* (Chapel Hill: University of North Carolina Press, 2017).

10. A. Frank, open letter, January 1, 1964, http://www.rrojasdatabank.info /agfrank/online.html#auto. On Frank's intellectual trajectory, see Cody Stephens, "An Accidental Marxist," *Modern Intellectual History* (2016). Available on *Cambridge Journals Online,* 2016 https://doi:10.1017/S1479244311 6000123.

11. Bert Hoselitz to Andre Gunder Frank, September 3, 1961, B. 1, Andre Gunder Frank (AGF) Archive, International Institute of Social History (IISH), Amsterdam, Netherlands.

12. On Brasilia as symbol of modernization: James Scott, *Seeing Like a State: How Certain Schemes to Improve the Human Condition Have Failed* (New Haven: Yale University Press, 1998), Ch. 4; James Holston, *The Modernist City: An Anthropological Critique of Brasília* (Chicago: University of Chicago Press, 1989).

13. Helena Bomeny, "Universidade de Brasília: filha da utopia de reparação." Special issue, *Sociedade e Estado* 31 (2016): 1003–28.

14. Curriculum vitae, Theotônio dos Santos, March 1968, São Paulo, Instituto FHC.

15. Daniel Aarão Reis, "Classe operária, partido de quadros e revolução socialista. O itinerário da Política Operária-Polop (1961–1986)," in *As esquerdas no Brasil: Revolução e democracia,* ed. Daniel Aarão Reis and Jorge Ferreira (Rio de Janeiro: Civilização Brasileira, 2007), 58; Maria Paula de Nascimento Araujo, *A utopia fragmentada: As novas esquerdas no Brasil e no mundo na década de 1970s* (Rio de Janeiro: FGC, 2001), 76–78.

16. Theotônio dos Santos, *Memorial,* mimeo., (2006), 20–21; Elisa Kluger, "Meritocracia de laços: Gênese e reconfigurações do espaço dos economistas no Brasil," PhD dissertation, Universidade de São Paulo, 2015, 333.

17. Entrevista com Theotônio dos Santos, CEPPES, no. 4, July 2, 2009, https:// ceppes.org.br/revista/versao-impressa/4/entrevista-com-theotonio-dos-santos; Marini quoted in Elisa Kluger, "Meritocracia de laços," 334.

18. Andre Gunder Frank, *Capitalism and Underdevelopment in Latin America: Historical Studies of Chile and Brazil* (New York: Monthly Review Press, 1967), 4, 5.

19. Stephens, "An Accidental Marxist," 20.

20. Frank, *Capitalism and Underdevelopment in Latin America,* 6.

21. Frank, *Capitalism and Underdevelopment in Latin America,* 146.

22. Research proposal, January 1965, B. 129, AGF Archive, IISH, Amsterdam, Netherlands.

23. Frank, *Capitalism and Underdevelopment in Latin America,* 239.

24. Frank, *Capitalism and Underdevelopment in Latin America,* 227.

25. Frank, *Capitalism and Underdevelopment in Latin America,* 202.

26. Frank, *Capitalism and Underdevelopment in Latin America,* 146.

27. Frank, *Capitalism and Underdevelopment in Latin America,* xvii.

28. "Research Proposal for Historical Dimension of Development and Underdevelopment," July 1, 1963, B. 129, AGF Archive, IISH, Amsterdam, Netherlands.

29. Curso de posgraduação, Relações entre Subdesenvolvimento e Desenvolvimento, UNB, July 1, 1963, B. 201, AGF Archive, IISH, Amsterdam, Netherlands.

30. Andre Gunder Frank, "Dependence is Dead, Long Live Dependence and the Class Struggle: An Answer to Its Critics," *Latin American Perspectives* 1, no. 1 (1974): 90.

31. Frank, *Capitalism and Underdevelopment in Latin America,* xv.

32. Andre G. Frank to Rodolfo Stavenhagen, June 1, 1963, AGF Archive, IISH, Amsterdam, Netherlands.

33. Stephens, "An Accidental Marxist," 22; Frank, *Capitalism and Underdevelopment in Latin America,* xviii.

34. Frank, *Capitalism and Underdevelopment in Latin America,* xviii.

35. Andre G. Frank to Harry Braverman, September 20, 1967, B. 12, AGF Archive, IISH, Amsterdam, Netherlands.

36. Andre G. Frank to Paul Sweezy, July 18, 1963, B. 5, Paul Sweezy Archive, Houghton Library, Harvard University, Cambridge, MA.

37. On the paulista school, see Maria Arminda do Nascimento Arruda, "A Sociologia no Brasil: Florestan Fernandes e a 'escola paulista,'" in *História das Ciências Sociais no Brasil,* ed. Sergio Miceli (São Paulo: Editora Sumaré; IDESP, 1995); Luiz Carlos Jackson, "Generaciones pioneras de las ciencias sociales brasileñas," in *Historia de los intelectuales en América Latina,* ed. Carlos Altamirano (Buenos Aires: Katz Editores, 2010).

38. On the founding of the *Universidade de São Paulo* and its influence on the French social sciences, see Ian Merkel, *Terms of Exchange* (Chicago: University of Chicago Press, forthcoming).

39. On the Marx seminar: Fernando Henrique Cardoso, "Memórias da Maria Antônia," in *Maria Antônia: uma rua na contramão,* ed. Maria Loschiavo (São Paulo: Nobel, 1988); Joseph Kahl, *Modernization, Exploitation, and Dependency in Latin America* (New Brunswick: Transaction Books, 1976), 133–35; Lidiane Rodrigues, "A produção social do marxismo universitário em São Paulo: Mestres, discípulos, e um seminário," PhD dissertation, Universidade de São Paulo, 2011.

40. Luiz Carlos Jackson, "A sociologia paulista nas revistas especializadas (1940–1965)," *Tempo Social* 16, no. 1 (2004): 263–83; Sergio Montalvao, "Historias

cruzadas: una proposopografia dos fundadores da Revista Brasiliense," *História* 36, no. 7 (2017): 1–28.

41. Kluger, "Meritocracia de laços," 285–86.

42. Thomas Skidmore, "Lévi-Strauss, Braudel and Brazil: A Case of Mutual Influence," *Bulletin of Latin American Research* 22, no. 3 (2003): 340–49; Ian Merkel, "Fernand Braudel, Brazil, and the Empire of French Social Science," *French Historical Studies* 40, no. 1 (2017): 129–60.

43. Warren Dean, *Industrialization in São Paulo, 1880–1945* (Austin: University of Texas, 1973).

44. "Economia e Sociedade do Brasil: analise sociológica do desenvolvimento," in *Sociologia numa era de revolução social,* ed. Florestan Fernandes (São Paulo: Companhia Editora Nacional, 1963).

45. On the nationalist left, see Daniel Aarao Reis, "As esquerdas no Brasil: Culturas, políticas e tradições," in *História e perspectivas da esquerda,* ed. Alexandre Fortes (São Paulo: Fundação Perseu Abramo, 2005); Alzira Alves de Abreu, "Instituto Superior de Estudos Brasileiros," 415; Lucilia de Almeida Neves Delgado, "Nacionalismo como Projeto de Nação: A Frente Parlamentar Nacionalista (1956–64)," in *As esquerdas no Brasil: Revolução e democracia,* ed. Daniel Aarão Reis and Jorge Ferreira (Rio de Janeiro: Civilização Brasileira, 2007): 361–67.

46. Fernando Henrique Cardoso, *Empresariado industrial e desenvolvimento no Brasil* (São Paulo: Difusão Europeia do Livro, 1964), 74–79.

47. Angela de Castro Gomes and Jorge Ferreira, *1964: O golpe que derrubou um presidente, pôs fim ao regime democrático e instituiu a ditadura no Brasil* (Rio de Janeiro: Civilização Brasileira, 2014).

48. See Rene Dreifuss, *1964: A conquista do estado: ação política, poder e golpe de classe* (Petropolis: Vozes, 2006).

49. Cardoso, *Empresariado industrial e desenvolvimento no Brasil,* 178–79.

50. Interview with Enzo Faletto: Gerónimo de Serra, "Ciencias Sociales en Chile y Uruguay," in *Las ciencias sociales en América Latina: de los inicios de la sociología a la teoría de la dependencia,* ed. Hélgio Trindade (Buenos Aires: Eudeba, 2013), 254.

51. Rodrigo Motta, *As universidades e o regime militar: Cultura política brasileira e modernização autoritaria* (Rio de Janeiro: Zahar, 2014), Ch. 1.

52. Kahl, *Modernization, Exploitation, and Dependency,* 135.

53. For more on the "social aspects of development" project, see Margarita Fajardo, "Latin America's Dependency Theory: A Counter Cold War Social Science?," in *Cold War Social Science: Transnational Connections,* ed. Mark Solovey and Christian Dayé (New York: Palgrave Macmillan, 2021).

54. Florestan Fernandes to Fernando Henrique Cardoso, June 8, 1964, Acervo Fernando Henrique Cardoso (FHC), São Paulo, Brazil. Cardoso later concluded the same. See Joseph Kahl, *Modernization, Exploitation, and Dependency in Latin America,* 135.

55. Paulo Poppovic to Fernando Henrique Cardoso, May 24, 1964, Acervo FHC, São Paulo, Brazil; Correspondence CEPAL, i.e., vols. 230, 259, etc., Organismos Internacionales, Archivo General Histórico del Ministerio de Relaciones Exteriores, Santiago, Chile.

56. Florestan Fernandes to Fernando Henrique Cardoso, July 11, 1964, Acervo FHC, São Paulo, Brazil.

57. Florestan Fernandes to Fernando Henrique Cardoso, July 11, 1964, Acervo FHC, São Paulo, Brazil.

58. For an institutional history of ILPES, see Rolando Franco, *La invención del ILPES* (Santiago: CEPAL, 2013). See also Edgar Dosman, *The Life and Times of Raúl Prebisch* (Montreal: McGill-Queen's University Press, 2008), 347–49.

59. "Annual Report to the ECOSOC, covering the period 16 May 1961 to 16 February 1962," (Nueva York: Naciones Unidas, 1962) E/CN.12/AC. 50/11/Rev. 1, https://repositorio.cepal.org/handle/11362/15017.

60. ILPES, "Actas Resumidas de la Cuarta Reunión del Consejo Directivo," Santiago, January 13–14, 1964, INST/32/Rev.1, 10, https://repositorio.cepal .org//handle/11362/17615.

61. Albert Hirschman, "Ideologies of Economic Development in Latin America," in *Latin American Issues: Essays and Comments* (New York: Twentieth Century Fund, 1961), 13.

62. Raúl Prebisch, "El desarrollo económico de la América Latina y algunos de sus principales problemas," *Boletín Económico para América Latina* 7, no. 1 (1962): 1–24.

63. CEPAL, "External Financing in the Economic Development of Latin America," tenth session, Mar del Plata, Argentina, 1963, E/CN.12/649, https:// repositorio.cepal.org/handle/11362/29257; CEPAL, "Economic Development of Latin America in the Postwar Period," tenth session, Mar del Plata, Argentina, 1963, E/CN.12/659, https://repositorio.cepal.org/handle/11362/29258.

64. María da Conceição Tavares, "Auge y declinio del proceso de sustitución de importaciones el Brasil," *Boletín Económico de América Latina* 9, no. 1 (1964): 3, 59.

65. Celso Furtado, *A fantasia desfeita* (Rio de Janeiro: Paz e Terra, 1989): 172–78, 198–200.

66. See for instance Furtado's edited volume, Celso Furtado, *Brazil Hoy* (México: Siglo XXI Editores, 1968). See also Jeremy Adelman and Margarita Fajardo, "Between Capitalism and Democracy: A Study in the Political Economy of Ideas in Latin America, 1968–1980," *Latin American Research Review* 51, no. 3 (2016): 3–22.

67. ILPES, "Actas Resumidas de la Cuarta Reunión del Consejo Directivo," 12.

68. Celso Furtado, *Os Ares do Mundo* (Rio de Janeiro: Paz e Terra, 1991), 31–32.

69. Benjamín Hopenhayn to Raúl Prebisch, June 5, 1964, Archivo del ILPES, CEPAL, Santiago, Chile.

70. Benjamín Hopenhayn to Raúl Prebisch, June 5, 1964, Archivo del ILPES, CEPAL, Santiago, Chile.

71. Furtado, "Obstáculos políticos del desarrollo económico en Brazil," 373–89; Aníbal Pinto, "Political Aspects of Economic Development," in *Obstacles to Change in Latin America*, ed. Claudio Veliz (London: Oxford University Press, 1965). See C. Furtado to F. H. Cardoso, May 6, 1965, and multiple correspondence between Furtado and Cardoso in Acervo FHC, São Paulo, Brazil.

72. Quoted in Kahl, *Modernization, Exploitation, and Dependency*, 136.

73. Fernando Henrique Cardoso, *El proceso de desarrollo en América Latina: Hipótesis para una interpretación sociológica*, mimeo, November 1965, ILPES, Acervo FHC, São Paulo, Brazil, 13.

74. Cardoso, *El proceso de desarrollo en América Latina*, 18.

75. Cardoso, *El proceso de desarrollo en América Latina*, 18.

76. Cardoso, *Empresariado industrial e desenvolvimento no Brasil*, 69.

77. Cardoso, *El proceso de desarrollo en América Latina*, 31.

78. Cardoso, *El proceso de desarrollo en América Latina*, 36.

79. Cardoso, *El proceso de desarrollo en América Latina*, 33–34.

80. Fernando Henrique Cardoso and Enzo Faletto, *Dependencia y desarrollo en América Latina*, mimeo, October 1967, ILPES, Acervo FHC, São Paulo, Brazil, 168–70.

81. José Luis Reyna, "Enzo Faletto, intelectual Latinoamericano," Recuerdos de la FLACSO, October 2007.

82. Quoted in Kahl, *Modernization, Exploitation, and Dependency*, 137.

83. Interview with E. Faletto, Gerónimo de Serra, "Ciencias Sociales en Chile y Uruguay," 245.

84. Fernando Henrique Cardoso and Enzo Faletto, *Dependencia y desarrollo en América Latina* (México: Siglo XXI, 1969), 166.

6. The Many Lives of Dependency Theory

1. Claudia Wasserman, *A teoria da dependência: do nacional-desenvolvimentismo ao neoliberalismo* (Rio de Janeiro: FGV Editora, 2017), 63–64.

2. Theotônio dos Santos to Fernando Henrique Cardoso, March 1966, Acervo Fernando Henrique Cardoso (FHC), São Paulo, Brazil.

3. Manuel Antonio Garretón, Miguel Murmis, Gerónimo de Sierra, and Hélgio Trindade, "Social Sciences in Latin America: A Comparative Perspective-Argentina, Brazil, Chile, Mexico, and Uruguay," *Social Science Information*, no. 557 (2005): 557–93.

4. Fernanda Beigel, "La Flacso chilena y la regionalización de las ciencias sociales in América Latina," *Revista Mexicana de Sociología* 71, no. 2 (2009): 319–49.

5. J. Strasma, "Personal Notes on Escolatina," January 24, 1972, Escolatina Grant No. 0160032, r. 2478; "Survey of Student Leader Opinions," 1967, Escolatina Grant No. 0160032, r. 3126, Ford Foundation, Rockefeller Archive Center (RAC), Sleepy Hollow, NY.

6. L. Jarvis to D. Bell, January 2, 1974, Escolatina Grant No. 0160032, r. 3126, Ford Foundation, RAC, Sleepy Hollow, NY.

7. Cristina Moyano and Ivette Lozoya, "'Intelectuales de izquierda en Chile': ¿de la politización a la tecnocracia? Debates sobre la función política y el ser del intelectual entre 1960 y 1990," *Signos Históricos* 21, no. 41 (2019): 206.

8. "Programa Cursos CESO and FLACSO," 1967, mimeo., Acervo Fernando Henrique Cardoso (FHC), São Paulo, Brazil.

9. A February mimeo draft of *Dependency and Development* is referenced in Theotônio dos Santos, "La crisis del desarrollo y las relaciones de dependencia," n.d., ca. 1968, mimeo, Acervo FHC, São Paulo, Brazil; Theotônio

dos Santos, "El nuevo carácter de la dependencia," *Cuadernos del Centro de Estudios Socio-Económicos,* no. 6 (1967): 7–55.

10. Wasserman, *A teoria da dependência,* 77.

11. Theotônio dos Santos to Fernando Henrique Cardoso, n.d., ca. February 1968, Acervo FHC, São Paulo, Brazil.

12. See Joseph Kahl, *Modernization, Exploitation, and Dependency in Latin America* (New Brunswick: Transaction Books, 1976), 137.

13. Andre Gunder Frank, "Open letter to friends," July 1, 1964, http://www.rrojasdatabank.info/agfrank/online.html#auto.

14. Andre Gunder Frank to Manuel Maldonado, December 9, 1968, B. 1, Andre Gunder Frank (AGF) Archive, International Institute of Social History (IISH), Amsterdam, Netherlands.

15. Andre Gunder Frank to Kathleen Aberle, September 20, 1967, B. 1; A. Frank to Robin and Perry, December 8, 1968, B. 2, AGF Archive, IISH, Amsterdam, Netherlands.

16. Andre Gunder Frank, "The Development of Underdevelopment," *Monthly Review Press,* 1966, https://www.rrojasdatabank.info/agfrank/underdev.html; Andre Gunder Frank, *Capitalism and Underdevelopment in Latin America: Historical Studies of Chile and Brazil* (New York: Monthly Review Press, 1967).

17. Curriculum vitae, Theotônio do Santos, May 1968, Acervo FHC, São Paulo, Brazil, 3.

18. Theotônio dos Santos, "Memorial," Rio de Janeiro, 1996, mimeo., 30–33, 39.

19. V. Bambirra to F. H. Cardoso, October 1968, Acervo FHC, São Paulo, Brazil.

20. Wasserman, *A teoria da dependência,* 120; Ruy Mauro Marini, *Memorias,* http://www.marini-escritos.unam.mx/002_memoria_marini_esp.html.

21. Theotônio dos Santos, *Socialismo o Fascismo: el dilema latinoamericano* (Santiago: Editorial Prensa Latinoamerican, 1969); Mauro Marini, *Subdesarrollo y revolución* (México: Siglo XXI, 1969); Andre Gunder Frank, *Latin America: Underdevelopment or Revolution?* (New York: Monthly Review Press, 1969).

22. Alicia Barrios and Jose Joaquin Brunner, *La sociología en Chile: Instituciones y practicantes* (Santiago: FLACSO, 1988), 29–31; Manuel Antonio Garretón, "Social Sciences and Society in Chile: Insititutionalization, Breakdown, and Rebirth," *Social Science Information,* no. 44 (2005): 359–409, 370–71, quoted in José Joaquín Brunner and Alicia Barrios, *Inquisición, mercado y filantropía: Ciencias sociales y autoritarismo en Argentina, Brasil, Chile y Uruguay* (Santiago: FLACSO, 1987), 81.

23. Barrios and Brunner, *La sociología en Chile,* 35.

24. On dependency and the radical left: Aldo Marchesi, *The Latin American Radical Left: Rebellion and Cold War in the Global 60s* (Cambridge: Cambridge University Press, 2017), 114; Clodomiro Almeyda, *Reencuentro con mi vida* (Santiago: Ediciones El Ornitorrinco, 1987), 152–53.

25. "Annual Report for 1970 submitted by FLACSO-ELAS to the Ford Foundation," 1970, B. 486, F. 50, Ford Foundation, RAC, Sleepy Hollow, NY; Rolando Franco, *La FLACSO clásica: visicitudes de las ciencias sociales latinoamericanas* (Santiago: FLACSO, 2007), 105.

26. Interview of Faletto in Gerónimo de Serra, "Ciencias Sociales en Chile y Uruguay," in *Las ciencias sociales en América Latina: De los inicios de la sociología a la teoría de la dependencia,* ed. Hélgio Trindade (Buenos Aires: Eudeba, 2013), 255.

27. For agrarian reform, see Heidi Tinsman, *Partners in Conflict: The Politics of Gender, Sexuality, and Labor in the Chilean Agrarian Reform, 1950–73* (Durham: Duke University Press, 2002); Robert Kaufman, *The Politics of Land Reform in Chile, 1950–1970: Public Policy, Political Institutions, and Social Change* (Cambridge: Harvard University Press, 1972). On promotion popular, see Andrew Kirkendall, *Paulo Freire and the Cold War Politics of Literacy* (Chapel Hill: University of North Carolina Press, 2010).

28. For the shift in Chilean politics and society around 1967–68, see Barbara Stallings, *Class Conflict and Economic Development in Chile, 1958–1973* (Stanford: Stanford University Press, 1978); Sofía Correa et al., *Historia del Siglo XX Chileno* (Santiago: Editorial Sudamericana, 2003), 254–57.

29. dos Santos, "Memorial," Rio de Janeiro, 1996, mimeo., 36.

30. Joaquín Fermandois, *La revolución inconclusa: la izquierda chilena y el gobierno de la Unidad Popular* (Santiago: Centro de Estudios Políticos, 2013), 153–57.

31. Andre Gunder Frank, Bibliography of Publications, https://www.rrojasdatabank.info/agfrank/gunderbib.html.

32. *Dependencia y desarrollo en América Latina* (Lima: Instituto de Estudios Peruanos, 1966); Robert Packenham, *The Dependency Movement: Scholarship and Politics in Development Studies* (Cambridge: Harvard University Press, 1992), 188–90.

33. Carlos Perzebal, *Acumulación capitalista dependiente y subordinada: el caso de México (1940–1978)* (Mexico: Siglo XXI, 1979); Juan Villareal, *El capitalismo dependiente: estudio sobre estructura de clase en Argentina* (Mexico: Siglo XXI, 1978); Alvaro Briones, *Economía y política del fascismo dependiente: estado y seguridad nacional* (México: Siglo XX, 1978); Salomón Kalmanovitz, *Ensayos sobre el desarrollo del capitalismo dependiente* (Bogotá: Editorial Pluma, 1977); Carlos Cepeda, *Crisis de una burguesía dependiente; balance económico de la "Revolución Argentina" 1966–1971* (Buenos Aires: Ediciones La Rosa Blindada, 1973).

34. Samir Amin to Fernando Henrique Cardoso, November 18, 1971; Hector Silva Michelena to Fernando Henrique Cardoso, November 18, 1971, Acervo FHC, São Paulo, Brazil.

35. *IX Latin American Congress of Sociology,* unofficial report, 1969, B. 58, F. 1498, Ford Foundation, RAC, Sleepy Hollow, NY.

36. See, for instance, Ricardo French-Davis, "Dependencia, subdesarrollo, y política cambiaria," *Trimestre Económico* 37, no. 146(2) (1970): 273–95; Pedro F. Paz, "Dependencia financiera y desnacionalización de la industria interna," *El Trimestre Económico* 37, no. 146(2) (1970): 297–329; M. Morse, "Primacía, regionalización, dependencia: enfoques sobre las ciudades latinoamericanas en el desarrollo nacional," *Desarrollo Económico* 11, no. 41 (1971): 55–85.

37. To name a few of the daunting number of works: Aldo Buntig, *Religión-enajenación en una Sociedad dependiente* (Buenos Aires: Editorial Guadalupe, 1973); Martha Schteingart, *Urbanización y Dependencia en América Latina* (Buenos Aires: Ediciones Nuevo Mundo, 1973); Juan Reyes, *Dependencia, desarrollo y educación* (Caracas: Universidad Central de Venezuela, 1972); Tomás Vasconi, *Dependencia y superestructura y otros ensayos* (Caracas: Ediciones de la Biblioteca, Universidad Central de Venezuela, 1970).

38. "The Social Sciences in Latin America," December 5, 1973, report no. 010152, Ford Foundation, RAC, Sleepy Hollow, NY.

39. Edelberto Torres Rivas, *Procesos y estructuras de una sociedad dependiente (Centroamerica)* (Santiago: Prensa Latinoamerica, 1969).

40. Hal Brands, *Latin America's Cold War* (Cambridge: Cambridge University Press, 2012), 93–94; Frank, "La dependencia ha muerto: Viva la dependencia y la lucha de clases. Una respuesta a críticos," *Desarrollo Económico* 13, no. 49 (1973): 204.

41. Marchesi, *Latin American Radical Left,* 136–37; Marian E. Schlotterbeck, *Beyond the Vanguard: Everyday Revolutionaries in Allende's Chile* (Oakland: University of California Press, 2018), 30.

42. Aldo Marchesi, "Imaginación política del antiimperialismo: Intelectuales y política en el Cono Sur a fines de los sesenta," *EIAL* 17, no. 1 (2006): 150.

43. Gustavo Gutiérez, *Hacia una teología de la liberación* (Bogotá: Indo-American Press Service, 1971).

44. *IX Latin American Congress of Sociology,* B. 58, F. 1498.

45. E. Faletto to F. H. Cardoso, September 13, 1969, Acervo FHC, São Paulo, Brazil.

46. Barrios and Brunner, *La sociología en Chile,* 47.

47. Aníbal Pinto, "Diagnósticos y catastrofismo en el contintente," *Panorama Económico,* no. 252 (1970): 15–19.

48. Some critiques include S. Barraclough to A. Frank, September 27, 1968, B. 1, AGF Archive, IISH, Amsterdam, Netherlands; possibly Roberto Cabral to A. Frank, August 27, 1969, B. 1, AGF Archive, IISH, Amsterdam, Netherlands. For a review of Frank's critiques and his responses, see André Gunder Frank, "Dependence is Dead, Long Live Dependence and the Class Struggle: An Answer to Its Critics," *Latin American Perspectives* 1, no. 1 (1974): 87–106.

49. "Conclusiones del IX Congreso Latinoamericano de Sociología," *Revista Mexicana de Sociología,* 32, no. 5 (1970): 1375.

50. Jonathan Brown, *Cuba's Revolutionary World* (Cambridge: Harvard University Press, 2017), 216.

51. Brown, *Cuba's Revolutionary World,* 218; Kepa Artaraz, *Cuba and Western Intellectuals since 1959* (New York: Palgrave Macmillan, 2009), 140–41.

52. Andre Gunder Frank, *Latin America: Underdevelopment or Revolution?,* 1969, 405–407.

53. Andre Gunder Frank to Fidel Castro, February 2, 1968, B. 21, AGF Archive, IISH, Amsterdam, Netherlands.

54. Andre Gunder Frank to Fidel Castro, February 2, 1968, B. 21, AGF Archive, IISH, Amsterdam, Netherlands.

55. Andre Gunder Frank to Fidel Castro, February 2, 1968, B. 21, AGF Archive, IISH, Amsterdam, Netherlands.

56. Artaraz, *Cuba and Western Intellectuals*, 43.

57. Andre Gunder Frank to *Casa de las Américas*, August 17, 1970; R. Fernandez Retamar to A. Frank, October 9, 1970, B. 21, AGF Archive, IISH, Amsterdam, Netherlands.

58. Edgar Dosman, *The Life and Times of Raúl Prebisch* (Montreal: McGill-Queen's University Press, 2008), 379–81.

59. Frank, "Development of Underdevelopment."

60. Raúl Prebisch, *Transformación y desarrollo: La gran tarea de América Latina*, April 17, 1970, mimeo, Biblioteca CEPAL, Santiago, Chile, 23.

61. Dosman, *Life and Times*, 448.

62. Enzo Faletto to Fernando Henrique Cardoso, August 15, 1968, Acervo FHC, São Paulo, Brazil.

63. "Las declaraciones de Prebisch," *Información Comercial Española*, n. 365, f. 112, Archivo de Trabajo de Raúl Prebisch, CEPAL, Santiago, Chile, 1625.

64. Raúl Prebisch, *Hacia una nueva política commercial en pro del desarrollo* (New York: Naciones Unidas), 1964.

65. Sydney Weintraub, "The foreign exchange gap of developing countries," *Essays in International Finance* no. 48 (1965): 1; "Discurso del presidente de la Asamble General en la reunión del grupo de los 77," October 28, 1971, B. 5, no. 134, Archivo de Trabajo Raúl Prebisch, CEPAL, Santiago, Chile.

66. Mark Berger, "After the Third World? History, Destiny and the Fate of Third Worldism," *Third World Quarterly* 25, no. 1 (2004): 11–12.

67. Jeffrey Byrne, *Mecca of Revolution: Algeria, Decolonization, and the Third World Order* (Oxford: Oxford University Press, 2016), 3.

68. "Undevelopment: The Geneva Marathon Starts," *The Economist*, March 21, 1964.

69. Dosman, *Life and Times*, Ch. 17–18.

70. John Toye, "Assessing the G77: 50 Years after UNCTAD and 40 Years after the NIEO," *Third World Quarterly* 35, no. 10 (2014): 1762–63.

71. John Toye and Richard Toye, *The UN and Global Political Economy* (Bloomington: Indiana University Press, 2004), 212.

72. J. Strasma, "A Note on Chilean Economics in 1960," 1972, Escolatina Grant No. 0160032, r. 3126, Ford Foundation, RAC, Sleepy Hollow, NY.

73. Pedro Vuskovic, "Algunas experiencias del desarrollo latinoamericano," in *Dos polémicas sobre el desarrollo de América Latina* (textos del ILPES) (Santiago: Editorial Universitaria, 1970), 140–41.

74. L. Jarvis to D. Bell, January 2, 1974, r. 3126, Escolatina Grant No. 0610032, Ford Foundation, RAC; J. Strasma, "Some Personal Notes on the History of the Graduate Program," February 3, 1972, r. 2478, Escolatina Grant No. 0610032, Ford Foundation, RAC, Sleepy Hollow, NY.

75. Quoted in Veronica Montecinos, *Economists, Politics and the State: Chile, 1958–94* (Amsterdam: CEDLA, 1998), 53; L. Jarvis to D. Bell, January 2,

1974, r. 3126, Escolatina Grant No. 0160032, Ford Foundation, RAC, Sleepy Hollow, NY.

76. "Una política económica popular, 1964," in Raúl Maldonado, *Obras Escogidas: Pedro Vuskovic* (Santiago: Centro de Estudios Simón Bolívar, 1993).

77. Pedro Vuskovic, "La política de transformación y el corto plazo," in *El pensamiento económico del gobierno de Allende,* ed. Gonzalo Martner (Santiago: Ediorial Universitaria, 1972), 97; Pedro Vuskovic, "La experiencia chilena: problemas económicos," in *Transición al socialimo y experiencia chilena,* ed. Lelio Bassto (Santiago: CESO-CEREN, 1972), 101.

78. dos Santos, "Memorial," Rio de Janeiro, 1996, mimeo., 36.

79. Theotônio dos Santos, "Dos años y el programa," *Chile Hoy,* November 10–16, 1972.

80. Montecinos, *Economists, Politics and the State,* 60.

81. "Presentación de José Cademartori," in *Chile 1972: Desde "El Arrayán hasta el paro de octubre,* ed. Pedro Milas (Santiago: Universida Alberto Hurtado, 2013), 169–70.

82. Montecinos, *Economists, Politics and the State,* 58.

83. Bernardo Sorj, *A construção intelectual do Brasil contemporâneo, da resistência à ditadura ao governo FHC* (Rio de Janeiro: Centro Edelstein de Pesquisas Sociais, 2008), 30.

84. Sergio Miceli, "A Fundação Ford e os Cientistas Sociais no Brasil, 1962–1992," in *História das Ciências Sociais no Brasil,* ed. Sergio Miceli (São Paulo: Editora Sumaré; IDESP, 1995), 369; Sorj, *A construção intelectual do Brasil contemporâneo, da resistência à ditadura ao governo FHC.*

85. "OLAC and the Social Sciences," December 5, 1973, Report No. 010152, Ford Foundation, RAC, Sleepy Hollow, NY; Sorj, *A construção intelectual do Brasil contemporâneo, da resistência à ditadura ao governo FHC,* 32–33.

86. Jeremy Adelman and Margarita Fajardo, "Between Capitalism and Democracy: The Political Economy of Social Science in Latin America, 1968–1980," *Latin American Research Review* 51, no. 3: 1–30.

87. John French, "The Professor and the Worker: Using Brazil to Better Understand Latin America's Plural Left," in *Rethinking Intellectuals in Latin America,* ed. Mabel Moraña and Bret Gustafesen (Madrid, Frankfurt, and Norwalk: Iberoamericana Vervuert Pub. Corp, 2010), 100.

88. "Social Sciences in Latin America," December 5, 1973, Report No. 010152, Ford Foundation, RAC, Sleepy Hollow, NY.

89. Sorj, *A construção intelectual do Brasil contemporâneo, da resistência à ditadura ao governo FHC,* 54–55.

90. Fernando Henrique Cardoso, "Mitos da Oposição-I" *Opinião,* no. 19, February 19–26, 1973.

91. Fernando Henrique, "El modelo político brasileño," *Desarrollo Económico* 11, no. 42/44 (1971): 221–29.

92. Fernando Henrique Cardoso, "The Brazilian Political Model," November 1971, mimeo, 8, Acervo FHC, São Paulo, Brazil.

93. F. H. Cardoso, "The Brazilian Political Model," November 1971, mimeo. Acervo FHC, São Paulo, Brazil.

94. Fernando Henrique Cardosos, "Mitos da Oposição-I" *Opinião*, no. 19, February 19–26, 1973.

95. Margaret Keck, *The Workers' Party and Democratization in Brazil* (New Haven: Yale University Press, 1992), 44; Fernando Henrique Cardoso, "El modelo político brasileño," *Desarrollo Económico, 11*, no. 42/44 (1971): 217–47; Fernando H. Cardoso, "A Questão da Democracia," (Rio de Janeiro: Instituto de Estudos Políticos e Sociais, 1973); Milton Lahuerta, "Intelectuais e resistência democrática: vida acadêmica, marxismo e política no Brasil," *Cadernos AEL, 8*, no. 14–15 (2001): 57–92; Afranio Garcia, "A dependência da política: Fernando Henrique Cardoso e sociologia no Brasil," *Tempo Social 16*, no. 1 (2004): 285–300; José Guilherme C. Magnani, "Las contradicciones del desarrollo asociado," *Desarrollo Económico 14*, no. 53 (1974): 3–32.

96. Sorj, *A construção intelectual do Brasil contemporâneo, 61*; Thomas Skidmore, *The Politics of Military Rule in Brazil, 1964–1985* (Oxford: Oxford University Press, 1990), 171.

97. "Social Sciences in Latin America," December 5, 1973, Report no. 010152, Ford Foundation, RAC, Sleepy Hollow, NY; Artaraz, *Cuba and Western Intellectuals, 43*.

98. Tanya Harmer, "The View from Havana: Chilean Exiles in Cuba and Early Resistance to Chile's Dictatorship, 1973–77," *Hispanic American Historical Review 96*, no. 1 (2016): 109–46; Claudia Fedora Rojas, "Los anfitriones del exilio chileno en México, 1973–1993," *Historia Crítica*, no. 60 (2016): 123–40; Margaret Power, "The US Movement in Solidarity with Chile in the 1970s," *Latin American Perspectives 36*, no. 6 (2009): 46–66.

99. Manuel Antonio Garretón, *Las ciencias sociales en Chile: Situación, problemas y perspectivas* (Santiago: FLACSO, 1982).

100. Notes for Social Science Meeting, Villa de Levya, August 1976, B. 48, F. 444, Ford Foundation, RAC, Sleepy Hollow, NY.

101. Barrios and Brunner, *La sociología en Chile*, 44–47.

102. "Social Sciences in Latin America," December 5, 1973, Report no. 010152, Ford Foundation, RAC, Sleepy Hollow, NY.

103. Manuel Antonio Garreton, *Las ciencias sociales en Chile: Situación, problemas y perspectivas* (Santiago: Universidad Academia de Humanismo Cristiano, 1982), 51. On the intellectual left under authoritarianism, see Jeffrey Puryear, *Thinking Politics: Intellectuals and Democracy in Chile* (Baltimore: Johns Hopkins University Press, 1994); Barrios and Brunner, *Inquisición, mercado y filantropía* (Santiago: FLACSO, 1987); Ignacio Walker, *Socialismo y Democracia: Chile y Europa en perspectiva comparada* (Santiago: CIEPLAN, 1990).

104. See Helen Delpar, *Looking South: The Evolution of Latin Americanist Scholarship in the United States, 1850–1975* (Tuscaloosa: University of Alabama Press, 2008), Ch. 8; Inderjeet Parmar, *Foundations of American Century: The Ford, Carnegie, and Rockefeller Foundations in the Rise of American Power* (New York: Columbia University Press, 2012), Ch. 7.

105. Rory Miller, "Academic Entrepreneurs, Public Policy, and the Growth of Latin American Studies in Britain during the Cold War," *Latin American Perspec-*

tives 45, no. 4 (2018), 53–55, 59; Michael Baud, "Between Academia and Civil Society: The Origins of Latin American Studies in the Netherlands," *Latin American Perspectives* 45, no. 4 (2018): 10, 4, 107–108.

106. See, for instance, Clara Ruvituso, "From the South to the North: The Circulation of Latin American Dependency Theories in the Federal Republic of Germany," *Current Sociology,* 68, no. 1 (2019): 25–26.

107. Steve Stern, "Feudalism, Capitalism, and the World-System in the Perspective of Latin America and the Caribbean," *American Historical Review* 93, no. 4 (1988): 836.

108. Ruvituso, "From the South to the North," 27; database built by the author.

109. Dale Johnson to Ronald Chilcote, January 30, 1976, B. 1, LAP Issues, Latin American Perspectives Archive, University of California-Riverside (UC-R), Riverside, CA.

110. Frank, "La dependencia ha muerto," 200, 204, 213–14.

111. Fernando H. Cardoso, "Consumption of Dependency Theory in the United States," *Latin American Research Review* 12, no. 3 (1976): 7, 9.

112. Cardoso, "Consumption of Dependency Theory," 12, 10, 17.

113. Samuel Valenzuela and Arturo Valenzuela, "Modernization and Dependency: Alternative Perspectives in the Study of Latin American Underdevelopment," *Comparative Politics* 10, no. 4 (1978): 535–57.

114. Tulio Halperín-Donghi, "'Dependency Theory' and Latin American Historiography," *Latin American Research Review* 17, no. 1 (1982): 115–30.

115. dos Santos, "Memorial," Rio de Janeiro, 1996, mimeo., 61.

116. Wasserman supports this view in her book. Wasserman, *A teoria da dependência,* 21–22, 111–15; Fernando H. Cardoso and José Serra, "Las desventuras de la dialéctica de la dependencia," *Revista Mexicana de Sociología* 40, no. 1 (1978): 9–55.

117. dos Santos, "Memorial," Rio de Janeiro, 1996, mimeo., 82.

Epilogue

1. Helen Delpar, *Looking South: The Evolution of Latin Americanist Scholarship in the United States, 1850–1975* (Tuscaloosa: University of Alabama Press, 2008), 167.

2. Delpar, *Looking South,* 168, 175.

3. On the two conflicting perspectives of the state of Latin American studies field in the United States, see Ronald Chilcote, "The Cold War and the Transformation of Latin American Studies in the United States," *Latin American Perspectives* 45, no. 4 (2018): 27–30, and Robert Packenham, *The Dependency Movement: Scholarship and Politics in Development Studies* (Cambridge: Harvard University Press, 1992), 269–71. See also, Margarita Fajardo, "Latin America's Dependency Theory: A Counter Cold War Social Science?," in *Cold War Social Science: Transnational Connections,* ed. Mark Solovey and Christian Dayé (New York: Palgrave Macmillan, 2021).

4. Rory Miller, "Academic Entrepreneurs, Public Policy, and the Growth of Latin American Studies in Britain during the Cold War," *Latin American Perspectives* 45, no. 4 (2018): 59.

5. Hans-Jürgen Puhle, "Between Academia and Politics Latin American Studies in Germany during the Cold War," *Latin American Perspectives* 45, no. 4 (2018): 81.

6. Dirk Kruijit, "Latin American Studies in the Netherlands: Economy and Sociology," *Boletín de Estudios Latinoamericanos y del Caribe,* no. 44 (1988): 41–42.

7. Michael Baud, "Between Academia and Civil Society: The Origins of Latin American Studies in the Netherlands," *Latin American Perspectives* 45, no. 4 (2018): 104; Clara Ruvituso, "From the South to the North: The Circulation of Latin American Dependency Theories in the Federal Republic of Germany," *Current Sociology* 68, no. 1 (2020): 28.

8. Miller, "Academic Entrepreneurs, Public Policy," 59; Immanuel Wallerstein, "Evolving Role of Africa Scholar in African Studies," *Canadian Journal of African Studies* 17, no. 1 (1983): 11–12.

9. James Sidaway, "Walter Rodney," in *Fifty Development Thinkers,* ed. David Simon (New York: Routledge, 2006), 208. For Davis's remark, see Walter Rodney, *How Europe Underdeveloped Africa* (1972; repr., New York: Verso, 2018), ix.

10. Rodney, *How Europe Underdeveloped Africa,* 357.

11. For a critique of that agenda, see A. G. Hopkins, "On Importing Andre Gunder Frank into Africa," *African Economic History Review* 2, no. 1 (1975): 13–21.

12. For biographical sketches of Amin, see Mohamed Salih, "Samir Amin," in *Fifty Development Thinkers,* ed. David Simon (New York: Routledge, 2006); Ingrid Harvold, "Samir Amin: A Pioneering Marxist and Third World Activist," *Development and Change* 51, no. 2 (2019): 631–49.

13. Andre Gunder Frank, "Immanuel and Me With-out Hyphen," *Journal of World-System Research* 11, no. 2 (2000): 217.

14. Translation is my own. Samir Amin, "À propos de "7 thèses erronées sur l'Amérique Latine," *L'Homme e la Société,* no. 27 (1973): 177, 187.

15. Quoted in Nicole Aschoff, "The Brilliant Immanuel Wallerstein Was Anti-Capitalist until the End," *Jacobine,* September 5, 2019, https://jacobinmag.com/2019/09/immanuel-wallerstein-world-systems-theory.

16. Wallerstein, *The Modern World-System: Capitalist Agriculture and the Origins of the European World-Economy in the Sixteenth Century* (Berkeley and Los Angeles: University of California Press, 2001), xviii; June Nash, "Ethnographic Aspects of the World Capitalist System," *Annual Review of Anthropology* no. 10 (1981): 401.

17. Frank, "Immanuel and Me," 218.

18. Samir Amin, "A Note on the Death of Andre Gunder Frank," *Monthly Review,* May 21, 2005, https://monthlyreview.org/commentary/a-note-on-the-death-of-andre-gunder-frank-1929-2005/.

19. June Nash, "Ethnographic Aspects of the World Capitalist System," *Annual Review of Anthropology* no. 10 (1981): 408.

20. Peter Gurevitch, "The Second Image Reversed: The International Sources of Domestic Politics," *International Organization* no. 32 (1978): 882–91.

21. Mary Morgan and Malcolm Rutherford, "American Economics: The Character of the Transformation," *History of Political Economy* 30, no. 5 (1998): 1–26.

22. Steve Stern, "Feudalism, Capitalism, and the World-System in the Perspective of Latin America and the Caribbean," *American Historical Review* 93, no. 4 (1988): 829–72; Paul Gootenberg, "Between a Rock and a Softer Place: Reflections on Some Recent Economic History of Latin America," *Latin American Research Review* 39, no. 2 (2004): 239.

23. Packenham, *Dependency Movement*, 243.

24. On semi-peripheries, see, for instance, Jessica Drangel and Giovanni Arrighi, "The Stratification of the World-Economy: An Exploration of the Semiperipheral Zone," *Review Fernand Braudel Center* 10, no. 1 (1986): 9–74; Nicos Mouzelis, "On the Demise of Oligarchic Parliamentarism in the Semi-Periphery: A Balkan-Latin American Comparison," *Sociology* 17, no. 1 (1983): 28–43; Sharif S. Elmusa, "Dependency and Industrialization in the Arab World," *Arab Studies Quarterly* 8, no. 2 (1986): 253–67. On dependent development, see Hyan-Chin Lin, *Dependent Development in Korea, 1963–1987* (Honolulu: Hawaii University Press, 1987) and Frederic Deyo, *Dependent Development and Industrial Order: An Asian Case Study* (New York: Praeger, 1981); Packenham, *Dependency Movement*, 244. On multinational corporations, see Richard Sklar, *Corporate Power in an African State: The Political Impact of Multinational Mining Companies in Zambia* (Los Angeles: University of California Press, 1976); Colin Kirkpatrick and Frederick Nixson, "Transnational Corporations and Economic Development," *Journal of Modern African Studies* 19, no. 3 (1981): 367–99; Volker Bornschier and Christopher Chase-Dunn, *Transnational Corporations and Underdevelopment* (New York: Praeger, 1985).

25. Peter Evans, *Dependent Development: The Alliance of Multinational, State, and Local Capital in Brazil* (Princeton: Princeton University Press, 1979) and Peter Evans, Theda Skocpol, and Dietrich Rueschmeyer, *Bringing the State Back In* (Cambridge: Cambridge University Press, 1985). Other works along similar line, Douglas C. Bennett and Kenneth E. Sharpe, "Agenda Setting and Bargaining Power: The Mexican State Versus Transnational Automobile Corporations," *World Politics* 32, no. 1 (1979): 57–89. Specially illuminating of the reconfiguration of dependency theory is the dissertation-to-book transformation of Thomas Gold, *State and Society in Taiwan Miracle* (Armonk, NY: Sharpe, 1986). On O'Donnell, see Guillermo O'Donnell, *Modernization and Bureaucratic Authoritarianism: Studies in South American Politics* (Berkeley: Institute of International Studies, University of California, 1973); Jeremy Adelman and Margarita Fajardo, "Between Capitalism and Democracy: A Study in the Political Economy of Ideas in Latin America, 1968–1980," *Latin American Research Review* 51, no. 3 (2016): 3–22.

26. See, for instance, Theodore Moran, *Multinational Corporations and the Politics of Dependence: Copper in Chile* (Princeton: Princeton University Press, 1974) and Joseph Grieco, "Between Dependency and Autonomy: India's Experience with the International Computer Industry," *International*

Organization 36, no. 3 (1981): 609–32; Packenham, *Dependency Movement,* 241.

27. See, for instance, James C. W. Ahiakpor, "The Success and Failure of Dependency Theory: The Experience of Ghana," *International Organization* 39, no. 3 (1985): 535–52; Patrick McGowan and Dale Smith, "Economic Dependency in Black Africa: An Analysis of Competing Theories," *International Organization* 32, no. 1 (1978): 179–235; Robert Kaufman, Daniel Geller, and Harry Chernotzky, "A Preliminary Test of Dependency Theory," *Comparative Politics* 7, no. 3 (1975): 303–30; Ruvituso, "From the South to the North," 32–33.

28. Multiple correspondence, 1973–1974, B. 2, Andre Gunder Frank Archive, International Institute of Social History (IISH), Amsterdam, Netherlands; Cristóbal Kay, "Andre Gunder Frank: Unity in Diversity from the Development of Underdevelopment to the World System," *New Political Economy* 16, no. 4 (2011): 523–38.

29. Emanuel de Kadt, ed., *Sociology of Development* (London: Routledge, 1974), 2–4.

30. Samir Amin, *A Life Looking Forward: Memoirs of an Independent Marxist* (London and New York: Zed Books, 2007), 204, 224.

31. Christoph Kalter, *The Discovery of the Third World: Decolonization and the Rise of the New Left in France, c. 1950–1976* (Cambridge: Cambridge University Press, 2016), 54.

32. Quoted in Daniel Whelan, " "Under the Aegis of Man': The Right to Development and the Origins of the New International Economic Order," *Humanity* 6, no. 1 (2015): 93; Victor Uchendu, "Dependency and the Development Process," *Journal of African Studies* 14, no. 1 (1979): 5; Mark Berger, "After the Third World? History, Destiny and the Fate of Third Worldism," *Third World Quarterly* 25, no. 1 (2004): 21.

33. Robert Meagher, *An International Redistribution of Wealth and Power: A Study of the Charter of Economic Rights and Duties of States* (New York: Pergamon Press, 1979), 22; Christy Thornton, "A Mexican International Economic Order? Tracing the Hidden Roots of the Charter of Economic Rights and Duties of States," *Humanity* 9, no. 3 (2018): 390; Adom Getachew, *Worldmaking after Empire: The Rise and Fall of Self-Determination* (Princeton: Princeton University Press, 2019), 152–53. See also the articles by Patrick Shama, Daniel Whelan, and Nils Gilman in *Humanity* 6, no. 1 (2015).

34. Thornton, "A Mexican International Economic Order?," 390; Getachew, *Worldmaking after Empire,* 144, Patrick Sharma, "Between North and South: The World Bank and the New International Economic Order," *Humanity* 6, no. 1 (2015): 189.

35. See Lal's useful discussion about this question with regard to "development" and Thornton's extended discussion about the global turn; Priya Lal, *African Socialism in Postcolonial Tanzania: Between the Village and the World* (New York: Cambridge University Press, 2015), 13–17; Thornton, "A Mexican International Economic Order?," 391.

36. "Declaración hecha por el señor Raúl Prebisch," Actas de la Conferencia de las Naciones Unidas sobre Comercio y Desarrollo: Tercer periodo de sesiones (Nueva York: Naciones Unidas, 1972), Vol.1, 391–95; Edgar Dosman, *The Life and Times of Raúl Prebisch* (Montreal: McGill-Queen's University Press, 2008), 476.

37. Andre Gunder Frank, "The Development of Underdevelopment," 1996, https://www.rrojasdatabank.info/agfrank/underdev.html.

38. For the politics of the research centers in Chile and the politics of transition, see José Joaquín Brunner and Alicia Barrios, *Inquisición, mercado y filan-tropía: Ciencias sociales y autoritarismo en Argentina, Brasil, Chile y Uruguay* (Santiago: FLACSO, 1987); Jeffrey Puryear, *Thinking Politics: Intellectuals and Democracy in Chile* (Baltimore: Johns Hopkins University Press, 1994), 116–19. For political transition from below, see Alison Bruey, *Bread, Justice, and Liberty: Grassroots Activism and Human Rights in Pinochet's Chile* (Madison: University of Wisconsin Press, 2018).

39. Ricardo Lagos, *Mi vida: De la infancia a la lucha contra la dictadura*, Loc. 6233; Faletto's work with Vector, Enzo Faletto, "Clases sociales y opciones política en Chile," in *Temas Socialistas*, ed. Eduardo Ortiz (Santiago: Vector, 1983).

40. Fernando Henrique Cardoso and José Guilherme C. Magnani, "Las contradicciones del desarrollo asociado," *Desarrollo Económico* 14, no. 53 (1974): 3–32.

41. On CEBRAP, see Bernardo Sorj, *A construção intelectual do Brasil contemporâneo, da resistência à ditadura ao governo FHC* (Rio de Janeiro: Centro Edelstein de Pesquisas Sociais, 2008); Ronald Chilcote, *Intellectuals and the Search for National Identity in Twentieth Century Brazil* (Cambridge: Cambridge University Press, 2014); Margaret Keck, *The Workers' Party and Democratization in Brazil* (New Haven: Yale University Press, 1992), 44.

42. Fernando Henrique Cardoso, *A arte da política: a história que vivi* (Rio de Janeiro: Civilização Brasileira, 2006), 115.

43. Antonio Martins, "É hora de resistir-entrevista com Maria Conceição Tavares," *Teoria e Debate*, no. 28, March 10, 1995, https://teoriaedebate.org.br/1995/03/10/e-hora-de-resistir-entrevista-com-maria-da-conceicao-tavares/.

44. Some of Tavares's most important works are: María da Conceição Tavares, "Auge y declinio del proceso de sustitución de importaciones en el Brasil," *Boletín Económico de América Latina* 9, no. 1 (1964): 1–62; Maria da Conceição Tavares and Justo Serra, "Mas alla del estancamiento: una discusion sobre el estilo de desarrollo reciente," *El Trimestre Económico* 38, no. 152 (1971): 905–50.

45. Elisa Kluger, "Meritocracia de laços: gênese e reconfigurações do espaço dos economistas no Brasil," PhD diss., Universidade de São Paulo, 2015, 528–42.

46. *Livre Pensar*, dir. José Mariani, Rio de Janeiro, 2019, Andaluz Produções; José Antonio Ocampo, "Una evaluación comparativa de cuatro planes anti-inflacionarios recientes." Special issue, *El Trimestre Económico* 54 (1987): 14.

47. See, for instance, Rudiger Dornbusch and Sebastian Edwards, eds., *Macro-economics of Populism in Latin America* (Chicago: University of Chicago Press, 1991).

48. Jorge Castañeda, *Utopia Unarmed: The Latin American Left after the Cold War* (New York: Vintage Books, 1994), 197.

48. I would like to thank Priya Lal for stimulating me to make this point more explicitly.

49. Jeremy Adelman, "What is global history now?," *Aeon*, March 1, 2017, https://aeon.co/essays/is-global-history-still-possible-or-has-it-had-its-moment. On the intersection of economic and global history, see Jeremy Adelman and Jonathan Levi, "The Fall and Rise of Economic History," *The Chronicle of Higher Education*, December 1, 2014, https://www.chronicle.com/article/the-fall-and-rise-of-economic-history/.

50. Lautaro, "Diagnósticos y 'catastrofismo' en el continente," *Panorama Económico*, February–March 1970, 15–19.

51. On the transformations of the intellectual left, see Cecilia Lesgart, *Usos de la transición a la democracia: Ensayo, ciencia y política en la década del '80* (Rosario: Homo Sapiens Ediciones, 2003); Jeffrey Puryear, *Thinking Politics: Intellectuals and Democracy in Chile* (Baltimore: Johns Hopkins University Press, 1994); Clodomiro Almeyda, *Reencuentro con mi vida* (Santiago: Ediciones El Ornitorrinco, 1987); Jorge Castañeda, *Utopia Unarmed: The Latin American Left after the Cold War* (New York: Vintage Books, 1994); and Gustavo Cuevas, *La renovación ideológica en Chile: Los partidos y su nueva visión estratégica* (Santiago de Chile: Universidad de Chile, Instituto de Ciencia Política, 1993). On the transition to democracy from below and its relation with the political left, Bruey, *Bread, Justice, and Liberty*.

52. Amy Offner, *Sorting out the Mixed Economy: The Rise and Fall of Welfare and Developmental States in the Americas* (Princeton: Princeton University Press, 2019), 1.

53. See, for instance, Francis Fukuyama, *The End of History and the Last Man* (New York: Simon and Schuster, 2006), 100–101.

54. Peter Winn, *Victims of the Chilean Miracle: Workers and Neoliberalism in the Pinochet era, 1973–2002* (Durham: Duke University Press, 2004), 27. On the "failure" of ISI, Sandra Kuntz, "From Structuralism to the New Institutional Economics: The Impact of Theory on the Study of Foreign Trade in Latin America," *Latin American Research Review* 40, no. 3 (2005), 151–52; Joseph Love, "The Rise and Decline of Economic Structuralism in Latin America: New Dimensions," *Latin American Research Review* 40, no. 3 (2005), 121; John Coatsworth, "Structures, Endowments, and Institutions in the Economic History of Latin America," *Latin American Research Review* 40, no. 3 (2005): 136–37.

55. Tavares, "Auge y declinio del proceso de sustitución de importaciones en el Brasil," 1–62.

56. Hirschman refers to the "unholy alliance against development economics" in Albert Hirschman, *Essays in Trespassing: Economics to Politics and Beyond* (New York: Cambridge University Press, 1981), 21.

57. Joseph Hodge, "Writing the History of Development: The First Wave," *Humanity* 6, no. 3 (2016): 429–63.

58. Lal, *African Socialism in Postcolonial Tanzania,* 232; Thornton, "A Mexican International Economic Order?," 390.

59. Gootenberg, "Between a Rock and a Softer Place," 241; Fernando Henrique Cardoso, "Consumption of Dependency Theory in the United States," *Latin American Research Review* 12, no. 3 (1976): 7–24.

60. On the construction of the "national economy," see Young, *Transforming Sudan,* 11–13, 16; Timothy Mitchell, *The Rule of Experts: Egypt, Techno-Politics, Modernity* (Berkeley and Los Angeles: University of California Press, 2002), 82–84; Tim Shenk, "Inventing the American Economy," PhD dissertation, Columbia University, 2016.

61. Getachew, *Worldmaking after Empire,* 170.

62. See two similar interpretations of the 2019 protests coming from two opposing sides of the political spectrum, Sebastián Edwards, "Social Revolt in Chile: The End of Neoliberalism?," *The Milken Institute Review: A Journal of Economic Policy,* April 2020; Ariel Dorfman, "Chile: Notes from a Revolt," *New York Review of Books,* March 13, 2020, https://www.nybooks.com/daily/2020/03/13/chile-notes-from-a-revolt/.

63. Kristen Hopewell, *Breaking the WTO: How Emerging Powers Disrupted the Neoliberal Project* (Stanford: Stanford University Press, 2018), Ch. 5.

64. Thomas Martin and Alberto Saad Filho, "Brazil and Neoliberalism," In *Crisis and Sequels: Capitalism and the New Economic Turmoil since 2007,* ed. Thomas Martin (Leiden and Boston: Brill, 2017), 272–73, 276; Kenneth Roberts, "Chile: the Left after Neoliberalism," in *The Resurgence of the Latin America Left,* ed. Steven Levitsky and Kenneth Roberts (Baltimore: Johns Hopkins University Press, 2011), 346.

65. Javier Santiso, *Latin America's Political Economy of the Possible* (Cambridge: MIT Press, 2007).

Acknowledgments

I here hope to thank and honor all colleagues and mentors, archivists and students, and family and friends who helped me with this book project and encouraged me and supported me over more than a decade. Many, many thanks!

Over the years, I received crucial financial and research support for this book project that allowed me both to travel around two hemispheres hunting for sources and to stay at home to write, rewrite, and revise. During my graduate school years, Princeton's History Department, the Program of Latin American Studies (PLAS), and the Institute for International and Regional Studies (PIIRS) provided the fundamental building blocks. As a junior scholar, I was deeply grateful to receive the support of Duke's Center for the History of Political Economy and extremely honored to be granted a National Endowment for the Humanities (NEH) fellowship. Both of these helped advance the manuscript in two crucial moments of rethinking and rewriting, and both were possible thanks to a release from teaching coursework and especially the flexibility and fluidity provided by Sarah Lawrence College (SLC), my home institution. The Cambridge Center for History and Economics, the Institute for New Economic Thinking, and the History of Economic Society gave short travel grants, for which I am also grateful.

Aside from the numerous staff members at libraries and archives who work behind the scenes, I would like to thank a few individuals who not only facilitated my source hunt but also lightened long archival days with smiles and fun chats. Some of them even gave their friendship when I was far away from home, and I will remember them always. My deepest gratitude goes to Javier Mejía from the Archivo Histórico del Ministerio de Relaciones Exteriores in Santiago, Renan de Castro and Mariana Zelesco from CPDOC in Rio, Claudia Vilches from CEPAL in Santiago, Premela Isaac from the IMF in Washington, DC, and Bethany Antos from the Rockefeller Archive Center in New York. I learned a lot from Liz Milewicz, and her team at Duke's Digital Scholarship services devoted a lot of time and energy to my citation and data mining project on dependency theory. Finally, I would like to thank Geoffrey Danisher from the Sarah Lawrence Library, who speedily got countless Inter-Library Loan requests in my hands, as well as my student assistants, Christina Kelley and Caroline Beegan, who promptly and effectively searched, scanned, and organized numerous files for me.

The photographs, cartoons, and other images that illustrate this book are also the product of the dedication of multiple archivists and the generosity of several families. I am especially grateful to Claudio Aguilera from the *Biblioteca Nacional de Chile,* who answered multiple queries and, most importantly, who helped me locate and contact the artists, or their families, whose cartoons illustrate many of the book chapters. Santiago "Jimmy" Scott and the families of Manuel "Mono" Tejeda, Luis Sepúlveda Donoso "Alhué," Luis Goyenechea Zegarra "Lugoze," and René Rios Boettiger "Pepo" generously and kindly granted permission to use cartoons that manifestly evoke an era and perhaps, more than my own words, powerfully capture key ideas of this book. Locating and identifying those cartoons were possible with the help of Camila Sanhueza, a wonderful research assistant in Chile, who also helped round up research work in the last few years of the project. Lilian Boti Llanés, whom I met only recently, opened up her and her family's memory and photographic archive and has opened new avenues of research for me, for which I am very grateful and excited about for the future. Renata Basseto from the Acervo Presidente Fernando Henrique Cardoso, Rosa Freire d'Aguiar Furtado, and the staff at CEPAL facilitated my use of numerous images and were always enthusiastic to work with me on this project.

I am grateful to the following publishers for the opportunity to publish earlier versions of ideas that are expanded and deepened in the book. Chapters 1, 2, and 3 expand on ideas briefly discussed in "The Economic Commission for Latin America (CEPAL) and the Latin America's Postwar Development Project," my contribution to the *Oxford Research Encyclopedia on Latin American History.* Chapter 5 advances work I presented in "Circumventing Imperialism: The Global Economy in Latin American Social Sciences," in *Empire and the Social Sciences,* edited by Jeremy Adelman, Bloomsbury Academic, 2019, and in "Latin America's Dependency Theory: A Counter-Cold War Social Science?" edited by Mark Solovey and Christian Dayé, *Cold War Social Science, Transnational Connections,* Palgrave Macmillan, 2021. I am also extremely grateful to Andrew Kinney and the editorial team at Harvard University Press for their patience, understanding, support, and diligence with the publishing process, especially at this special time in my personal life.

Thanks to generous, kind, and perceptive friends, colleagues, mentors, and peers, this book matured and improved enormously over the years. Early on, the support of friends and colleagues of the Princeton Latin American History Workshop, or "workshopcito," Princeton History of Capitalism group, the History of Science crowd, and the PLAS and PIIRS graduate workshops were a receptive and stimulating audience. At Sarah Lawrence, I am especially grateful to Matthew Ellis for his insightful comments, his constant mentoring, and his loyal friendship as well as to my colleagues and friends Michelle Hersch and Isabel de Sena, who have supported me and this project in multiple ways. Special thanks to my SLC colleagues Philip Nielsen, Lyde Syzer, and Una Chung for their comments, advice, and support. The feedback from the New York City History Workshop, especially Eric Zolov, the Newberry History of Capitalism Workshop, especially Gema Santamaria and Rudi Betzell, the History of Political Economy Seminar, especially Kevin Hoover, the Triangle Intellectual History Seminar, especially James Chappel, Jolie Olcott, and Steve Vincent, and the Oxford Global History Seminar was all extremely useful as I reworked and finalized the project. I am very grateful to Angus Burgin, Mila Burns, Mauro Boianovsky, Guiliana Chamedes, Marcela Echeverri, Marshall Eakin, Pedro G. Duarte, John French, Paul Gootenberg, Cristobal Kay, Claudia Kedar, Priya Lal, Aldo Marchesi, Amy Offner, Sebastián Ramírez, Karin Rosemblatt, and Clara Ruvituso for reading book proposals, chapter versions, or even the whole manuscript and providing generous and very useful feedback.

A special thanks to all my mentors. Mauricio Nieto from *Universidad de los Andes* in Bogotá is a wonderful teacher, committed mentor, and dear friend. I would also like to thank Princeton faculty and staff, all of whom went beyond the call of duty to support me and my project, especially to Vera Candiani, Miguel Centeno, Michael Gordin, Lili Schwartz, Dan Rodgers, and Stanley Stein as well as to Kristy Novak. I am also fortunate to have worked with Rob Karl. I cannot thank him enough for his commitment to helping me thrive as a scholar, teacher, and faculty member and especially for his reliable and enduring friendship. Finally, I am hugely indebted and extremely grateful to Jeremy Adelman, my advisor and mentor, who began supporting me before I even arrived at Princeton and has not stopped ever since. His constant push to focus on the big picture in this book and beyond, his insightful and perceptive comments, his holistic advice on professional opportunities and choices, and his unrelenting faith and enthusiasm with the project have made a substantial difference for me as a graduate student and junior scholar. He once told me he had my back, and he truly meant it, thank you!

I am absolutely blessed with the generous, kind, and constant support of many friends and family. They have encouraged me in low points, celebrated numerous steps in this long process, and have, from near and far, made themselves present. I would like thank Meg Leja, Ana Sabau, and Sebastián Ramírez, with whom I have shared this path for several years and whose company has made the journey easier. A very special thanks to Iwa and Josh, Diana and Sudhir, Erin (for her beautiful shots) and Pascal, Marina and Marcelo, Luis, Joel, Jess, Elisa, and Alex. I am extremely grateful to my brother Uri for supplying a couch and car for multiple research trips in California as well as a beach getaway every time I needed a break, but especially for his unrelenting faith in and love for me.

My parents, Edgar and Aura Cecilia, and especially my husband, Ollie, to all of whom this book is dedicated, have been with me every step of the way, and so this book is also theirs. *A mis papás, mil gracias por enseñarme tenacidad y perseverancia, por su paciencia con la distancia que nos separa y por disfrutar al máximo cada reencuentro; gracias por tantas palabras de aliento y por sus diarios mensajes de "buenos días" y "buenas noches" que alegran mi corazón y han hecho más ligero y certero este viaje. Este libro es por ustedes, un pequeño tributo por inspirarme a darlo todo por lo que se quiere y por quienes se quiere.* To Ollie, my deepest gratitude and love, for with this book and our numerous hikes we have learned what it means to walk a path together. Thanks for helping me carry the extra weight, for navigating through the twists and turns, for commemorating every peak no matter how small, and for lifting me up when I fell. A dedicated husband and fellow historian, you patiently waited with a gourmet dinner on the table until I got the sentence or paragraph "right," enthusiastically carried on numerous conversations to think ideas through together, and struggled with me to find the appropriate expression, all with a smile on your face. Thanks, my love! And to my little one, whose kicks and turns brightened days and nights as this book and he were getting ready to see the world, I can't wait to meet you both in person! Thanks be to God.

Index